UNDER THE
TUSCAN SUN

BELLA TUSCANY

UNDER THE TUSCAN SUN

BELLA TUSCANY

FRANCES MAYES

BANTAM
SYDNEY • AUCKLAND • TORONTO • NEW YORK • LONDON

UNDER THE TUSCAN SUN and BELLA TUSCANY
a Bantam book

This omnibus edition first published in Australia and New Zealand in 2004
by Bantam

Mayes, Frances.
    Under The Tuscan Sun and Bella Tuscany.

    ISBN 1 86325 4587.

Transworld Publishers,
a division of Random House Australia Pty Ltd
20 Alfred Street, Milsons Point, NSW 2061
http://www.randomhouse.com.au

Random House New Zealand Limited
18 Poland Road, Glenfield, Auckland

Transworld Publishers,
a division of The Random House Group Ltd
61-63 Uxbridge Road, Ealing, London W5 5SA

Random House Inc
1745 Broadway, New York, New York 10036

Cover design by Darian Causby/Highway 51
Printed and bound by Griffin Press, Netley, South Australia

10 9 8 7 6 5 4 3

UNDER THE TUSCAN SUN

AT HOME IN ITALY

FRANCES MAYES

ACKNOWLEDGMENTS

Many thanks to my agent, Peter Ginsberg, of Curtis Brown Ltd. And to Jay Schaefer, my editor at Chronicle Books. Special thanks to Kate Chynoweth, also of Chronicle Books. Jane Piorko of *The New York Times*, Elaine Greene of *House Beautiful*, and Rosellen Brown, guest editor of *Ploughshares*, published early versions of parts of this book: *mille grazie*. Friends and family members deserve at least a bottle of Chiante and a handful of Tuscan poppies: Todd Alden, Paul Bertolli, Anselmo Bettarelli, Josephine Carson, Ben Hernandez, Charlotte Painter, Donatella di Palme, Rupert Palmer, Lyndall Passerini, Tom Sterling, Alain Vidal, Marcia and Dick Wertime, and all the Willcoxons. Homage to the memory of Clare Sterling for the gift of her verve and knowledge. To Ed Kleinschmidt and Ashley King, incalculable thanks.

for ANN CORNELISEN

"WHAT ARE YOU GROWING HERE?" THE UPHOLSTERER lugs an armchair up the walkway to the house but his quick eyes are on the land.

"Olives and grapes," I answer.

"Of course, olives and grapes, but what else?"

"Herbs, flowers—we're not here in the spring to plant much else."

He puts the chair down on the damp grass and scans the carefully pruned olive trees on the terraces where we now are uncovering and restoring the former vineyard. "Grow potatoes," he advises. "They'll take care of themselves." He points to the third terrace. "There, full sun, the right place for potatoes, red potatoes, yellow, potatoes for *gnocchi di patate*."

And so, at the beginning of our fifth summer here, we now dig the potatoes for our dinner. They come up so easily; it's like finding Easter eggs. I'm surprised how clean they are. Just a rinse and they shine.

The way we have potatoes is the way most everything has come about, as we've transformed this abandoned Tuscan house and land over the past four years. We watch Francesco Falco, who has spent most of his seventy-five years attending to grapes, bury the tendril of an old vine so that it shoots out new growth. We do the same. The grapes thrive. As foreigners who have landed here by grace, we'll try anything. Much of the restoration we did ourselves; an accomplishment, as my grandfather would say, out of the fullness of our ignorance.

2

In 1990, our first summer here, I bought an oversized blank book with Florentine paper covers and blue leather binding. On the first page I wrote ITALY. The book looked as though it should have immortal poetry in it, but I began with lists of wildflowers, lists of projects, new words, sketches of tile in Pompeii. I described rooms, trees, bird calls. I added planting advice: "Plant sunflowers when the moon crosses Libra," although I had no clue myself as to when that might be. I wrote about the people we met and the food we cooked. The book became a chronicle of our first four years here. Today it is stuffed with menus, postcards of paintings, a drawing of a floor plan of an abbey, Italian poems, and diagrams of the garden. Because it is thick, I still have room in it for a few more summers. Now the blue book has become *Under the Tuscan Sun,* a natural outgrowth of my first pleasures here. Restoring, then improving, the house; transforming an overgrown jungle into its proper function as a farm for olives and grapes; exploring the layers and layers of Tuscany and Umbria; cooking in a foreign kitchen and discovering the many links between the food and the culture—these intense joys frame the deeper pleasure of learning to live another kind of life. To bury the grape tendril in such a way that it shoots out new growth I recognize easily as a metaphor for the way life must change from time to time if we are to go forward in our thinking.

During these early June days, we must clear the terraces of the wild grasses so that when the heat of July strikes and the land dries, we'll be protected from fire. Outside my window, three men with weed machines sound like giant bees. Domenico will be arriving tomorrow to disc the terraces, returning the chopped grasses to the soil. His tractor follows the looping turns established by oxen long ago. Cycles. Though the weed machines and the discer make shorter work, I still feel that I fall into this ancient ritual of summer. Italy is thousands of years deep and on the top layer I am standing on a small plot of land, delighted today with the wild orange lilies spotting the hillside. While I'm admiring them, an old man stops in the road and asks if I live here. He tells me he knows the land well. He pauses and looks along the stone wall, then in a quiet voice tells me his brother was shot here. Age seventeen, suspected of being a Partisan. He keeps nodding his head and I know the scene he looks at is not my rose garden, my hedge of sage and lavender. He has moved beyond me. He blows me a kiss. *"Bella casa, signora."* Yesterday I found a patch of blue cornflowers around an olive tree where his brother must have fallen. Where did they come from? A seed dropped by a thrush? Will they spread next year over the crest of the terrace? Old places exist on sine waves of time and space that bend in some logarithmic motion I'm beginning to ride.

I open the blue book. Writing about this place, our discoveries, wanderings, and daily life, also has been a pleasure. A Chinese poet many centuries ago noticed that to re-create something in words is like being alive twice. At the taproot, to seek change probably always is related to the desire to enlarge the psychic place one lives in. *Under the Tuscan Sun* maps such a place. My reader, I hope, is like a friend who comes to visit, learns to mound flour on the thick marble counter and work in the egg, a friend who wakes to the four calls of the cuckoo in the linden and walks down the terrace paths singing to the grapes; who picks jars of plums, drives with me to hill towns of round towers and spilling geraniums, who wants to see the olives the first day they are olives. A guest on holiday is intent on pleasure. Feel the breeze rushing around those hot marble statues? Like old peasants, we could sit by the fireplace, grilling slabs of bread and oil, pour a young Chianti. After rooms of Renaissance virgins and dusty back roads from Umbertide,

I cook a pan of small eels fried with garlic and sage. Under the fig where two cats curl, we're cool. I've counted: the dove coos sixty times per minute. The Etruscan wall above the house dates from the eighth century B.C. We can talk. We have time.

Cortona, 1995

4

BRAMARE: (ARCHAIC) TO YEARN FOR

I AM ABOUT TO BUY A HOUSE IN A FOREIGN COUNTRY. A house with the beautiful name of Bramasole. It is tall, square, and apricot-colored with faded green shutters, ancient tile roof, and an iron balcony on the second level, where ladies might have sat with their fans to watch some spectacle below. But below, overgrown briars, tangles of roses, and knee-high weeds run rampant. The balcony faces southeast, looking into a deep valley, then into the Tuscan Apennines. When it rains or when the light changes, the facade of the house turns gold, sienna, ocher; a previous scarlet paint job seeps through in rosy spots like a box of crayons left to melt in the sun. In places where the stucco has fallen away, rugged stone shows what the exterior once was. The house rises above a *strada bianca*, a road white with pebbles, on a terraced slab of hillside covered with fruit and olive trees. Bramasole: from *bramare*, to yearn for, and *sole*, sun: something that yearns for the sun, and yes, I do.

The family wisdom runs strongly against this decision. My mother has said "Ridiculous," with her certain and forceful stress on the second syllable, "RiDICulous," and my sisters, although excited, fear I am eighteen, about to run off with a sailor in the family car.

I quietly have my own doubts. The upright seats in the *notaio*'s outer office don't help. Through my thin white linen dress, spiky horsehairs pierce me every time I shift, which is often in the hundred-degree waiting room. I look over to see what Ed is writing on the back of a receipt: Parmesan, salami, coffee, bread. How can he? Finally, the signora opens her door and her torrential Italian flows over us.

The *notaio* is nothing like a notary; she's the legal person who conducts real-estate transactions in Italy. Ours, Signora Mantucci, is a small, fierce Sicilian woman with thick tinted glasses that enlarge her green eyes. She talks faster than any human I have ever heard. She reads long laws aloud. I thought all Italian was mellifluous; she makes it sound like rocks crashing down a chute. Ed looks at her raptly; I know he's in thrall to the sound of her voice. The owner, Dr. Carta, suddenly thinks he has asked too little; he *must* have, since we have agreed to buy it. We think his price is exorbitant. We *know* his price is exorbitant. The Sicilian doesn't pause; she will not be interrupted by anyone except by Giuseppe from the bar downstairs, who suddenly swings open the dark doors, tray aloft, and seems surprised to see his *Americani* customers sitting there almost cross-eyed in confusion. He brings the signora her midmorning thimble of espresso, which she downs in a gulp, hardly pausing. The owner expects to claim that the house cost one amount while it really cost much more. "That is just the way it's done," he insists. "No one is fool enough to declare the real value." He proposes we bring one check to the *notaio*'s office, then pass him ten smaller checks literally under the table.

Anselmo Martini, our agent, shrugs.

Ian, the English estate agent we hired to help with translation, shrugs also.

Dr. Carta concludes, "You Americans! You take things so seriously. And, *per favore*, date the checks at one-week intervals so the bank isn't alerted to large sums."

Was that the same bank I know, whose sloe-eyed teller languidly conducts a transaction every fifteen minutes, between smokes and telephone calls? The signora comes to an abrupt halt, scrambles the papers into a folder and stands up. We are to come back when the money and papers are ready.

✳

A window in our hotel room opens onto an expansive view over the ancient roofs of Cortona, down to the dark expanse of the Val di Chiana. A hot and wild wind—the *scirocco*—is driving normal people a little crazy. For me, it seems to reflect my state of mind. I can't sleep. In the United States, I've bought and sold a few houses before—loaded up the car with my mother's Spode, the cat, and the ficus for the five- or five-thousand-mile drive to the next doorway where a new key would fit. You *have* to churn somewhat when the roof covering your head is at stake, since to sell is to walk away from a cluster of memories and to buy is to choose where the future will take place. And the place, never neutral of course, will cast its influence. Beyond that, legal complications and contingencies must be worked out. But here, absolutely everything conspires to keep me staring into the dark.

Italy always has had a magnetic north pull on my psyche. Houses have been on my mind for four summers of renting farmhouses all over Tuscany. In the first place Ed and I rented with friends, we started calculating on the first night, trying to figure out if our four pooled savings would buy the tumbled stone farm we could see from the terrace. Ed immediately fell for farm life and roamed over our neighbors' land looking at the work in progress. The Antolinis grew tobacco, a beautiful if hated crop. We could hear workers shout *"Vipera!"* to warn the others of a poisonous snake. At evening, a violet blue haze rose from the dark leaves. The well-ordered farm looked peaceful from the vantage point of our terrace. Our friends never came back, but for the next three vacations, the circuitous search for a summer home became a quest for us—whether we ever found a place or not, we were happening on places that made pure green olive oil, discovering sweet country Romanesque churches in villages, meandering the back roads of vineyards, and stopping to taste the softest Brunello and the blackest Vino Nobile. Looking for a house gives an intense focus. We visited weekly markets not just with the purchase of picnic peaches in mind; we looked carefully at all the produce's quality and variety, mentally forecasting birthday dinners, new holidays, and breakfasts for weekend guests. We spent hours sitting in piazzas or sipping lemonade in local bars, secretly getting a sense of the place's ambiance. I soaked many a heel blister in a hotel bidet, rubbed bottles of lotion on my feet, which had covered miles of stony streets. We hauled histories and guides and wildflower books and novels in and out of rented houses and hotels. Always we asked local people where they liked to eat and headed to restaurants our many guidebooks never mentioned. We both have an insatiable curiosity about each jagged castle ruin on the hillsides. My idea of heaven still is to drive the gravel farm roads of Umbria and Tuscany, very pleasantly lost.

Cortona was the first town we ever stayed in and we always came back to it during the summers we rented near Volterra, Florence, Montisi, Rignano, Vicchio, Quercegrossa, all those fascinating, quirky houses. One had a kitchen two people could not pass in, but there was a slice of a view of the Arno. Another kitchen had no hot water and no knives, but the house was built into medieval ramparts overlooking vineyards. One had several sets of china for forty, countless glasses and silverware, but the refrigerator iced over every day and by four the door swung open, revealing a new igloo. When the weather was damp, I got a tingling shock if I touched anything in the kitchen. On the property, Cimabue, legend says, discovered the young Giotto drawing a sheep in the dirt. One house had beds with back-crunching dips in the middles. Bats flew down the chimney and buzzed us, while worms in the beams sent down a steady sifting of sawdust onto the pillows. The fireplace was so big we could sit in it while grilling our veal chops and peppers.

We drove hundreds of dusty miles looking at houses that turned out to be in the flood plain of the Tiber or overlooking strip mines. The Siena agent blithely promised that the view would be wonderful again in twenty years; replanting stripped areas was a law. A glorious medieval village house was wildly expensive. The saw-toothed peasant we met in a bar tried to sell us his childhood home, a windowless stone chicken house joined to another house, with snarling dogs lunging at us from their ropes. We fell hard for a farm outside Montisi; the *contessa* who owned it led us on for days, then decided she needed a sign from God before she could sell it. We had to leave before the sign arrived.

As I think back over those places, they suddenly seem pre-posterously alien and Cortona does, too. Ed doesn't think so. He's in the piazza every afternoon, gazing at the young couple trying to wheel their new baby down the street. They're halted every few steps. Everyone circles the carriage. They're leaning into the baby's face, mak-ing noises, praising the baby. "In my next life," Ed tells me, "I want to come back as an Italian baby." He steeps in the piazza life: the sultry and buffed man pushing up his sleeve so his muscles show when he languidly props his chin in his hand; the pure flute notes of Vivaldi drifting from an upstairs window; the flower seller's fan of bright flow-ers against the stone shop; a man with no neck at all unloading lambs from his truck. He slings them like flour sacks over his shoulder and the lambs' eyeballs bulge out. Every few minutes, Ed looks up at the big clock that has kept time for so long over this piazza. Finally, he takes a stroll, memorizing the stones in the street.

Across the hotel courtyard a visiting Arab chants his prayers toward dawn, just when I finally can fall asleep. He sounds as though he is gargling with salt water. For hours, he rings the voice's changes over a small register, over and over. I want to lean out and shout, "Shut up!" Now and then I have to laugh. I look out, see him nodding in the window, a sweet smile on his face. He reminds me so much of tobacco auctioneers I heard in hot warehouses in the South as a child. I am seven thousand miles from home, plunking down my life savings on a whim. Is it a whim? It feels very close to falling in love and that's never really whimsical but comes from some deep source. Or does it?

Each time we step out of the cool, high rooms of the hotel and into the sharp-edged sun, we walk around town and like it more and more. The outdoor tables at Bar Sport face the Piazza Signorelli. A few farmers sell produce on the steps of the nineteenth-century *teatro* every morning. As we drink espresso, we watch them holding up rusty hand scales to weigh the tomatoes. The rest of the piazza is lined with perfectly intact medieval or Renaissance *palazzi*. Easily, someone might step out any second and break into *La Traviata*. Every day we visit each keystoned medieval gate in the Etruscan walls, explore the Fiat-wide stone streets lined with Renaissance and older houses and the even narrower *vicoli*, mysterious pedestrian passageways, often steeply stepped. The bricked-up fourteenth-century "doors of the dead" are still visible. These ghosts of doors beside the main entrance were designed, some say, to take out the plague victims—bad luck for them to exit by the main entrance. I notice in the regular doors, people often leave their keys in the lock.

Guidebooks describe Cortona as "somber" and "austere." They misjudge. The hilltop position, the walls and upright, massive stone buildings give a distinctly vertical feel to the architecture. Walking across the piazza, I feel the abrupt, angular shadows fall with Euclidean purity. I want to stand up straight—the upright posture of the buildings seems to carry over to the inhabitants. They walk slowly, with very fine, I want to say, *carriage*. I keep saying, "Isn't she beautiful?" "Isn't he gorgeous?" "Look at *that* face—pure Raphael." By late afternoon, we're sitting again with our espressi, this time facing the other piazza. A woman of about sixty with her daughter and the teenage granddaughter pass by us, strolling, their arms linked, sun on their vibrant faces. We don't know why light has such a luminous quality. Perhaps the sunflower crops radiate gold from the surrounding fields. The three women look peaceful, proud, impressively pleased. There should be a gold coin with their faces on it.

11

Meanwhile, as we sip, the dollar is falling fast. We rouse ourselves from the piazza every morning to run around to all the banks, checking their posted exchange rates. When you're cashing traveler's checks for a last-minute spree at the leather market, the rate doesn't matter that much, but this is a house with five acres and every lira counts. A slight drop at those multiples makes the stomach drop also. Every hundred lire it falls, we calculate how much more expensive the house becomes. Irrationally, I also calculate how many pairs of shoes that could buy. Shoes, before, have been my major purchase in Italy, a secret sin. Sometimes I'd go home with nine new pairs: red snakeskin flats, sandals, navy suede boots, and several pairs of black pumps of varying heels.

Typically, the banks vary in how much commission they bite when they receive a large transfer from overseas. We want a break. It looks like a significant chunk of interest they'll collect, since clearing a check in Italy can take weeks.

Finally, we have a lesson in the way things work. Dr. Carta, anxious to close, calls his bank—the bank his father and his father-in-law use—in Arezzo, a half hour away. Then he calls us. "Go there," he says. "They won't take a commission for receiving the money at all, and they'll give you whatever the posted rate is when it arrives."

His savvy doesn't surprise me, though he has seemed spectacularly uninterested in money the entire time we have negotiated—just named his high price and stuck to it. He bought the property from the five old sisters of an landowning family in Perugia the year before, thinking, he said, to make it a summer place for his family. However, he and his wife inherited property on the coast and decided to use that instead. Was that the case, or had he scooped up a bargain from ladies in their nineties and now is making a bundle, possibly buying coast property with our money? Not that I begrudge him. He's smart.

Dr. Carta, perhaps fearing we might back out, calls and asks to meet us at the house. He roars up in his Alfa 164, Armani from stem to stern. "There is something more," he says, as though continuing a conversation. "If you follow me, I will show you something." A few hundred feet down the road, he leads us up a stone path through fragrant yellow broom. Odd, the stone path continues up the hill, curving along a ridge. Soon we come to a two-hundred-degree view of the valley, with the cypress-lined road below us and a mellow landscape dotted with tended vineyards and olive groves. In the distance lies a blue daub, which is Lake Trasimeno; off to the right, we see the red-roofed silhouette of Cortona cleanly outlined against the sky. Dr. Carta turns to us triumphantly. The flat paving stones widen here. "The Romans—this road was built by the Romans—it goes straight into Cortona." The sun is broiling. He goes on and on about the large church at the top of the hill. He points out where the rest of the road might have run, right through Bramasole's property.

Back at the house he turns on an outside faucet and splashes his face. "You'll enjoy the finest water, truly your own abundant *acqua minerale*, excellent for the liver. *Eccellente!*" He manages to be at once enthusiastic and a little bored, friendly and slightly condescending. I am afraid we have spoken too bluntly about money. Or maybe he has interpreted our law-abiding American expectations about the transaction as incredibly naive. He lets the faucet run, cupping his hand under the water, somehow leaning over for a drink without dislodging the well-cut linen coat tossed over his shoulders. "Enough water for a swimming pool," he insists, "which would be perfect out on the point where you can see the lake, overlooking right where Hannibal defeated the Romans."

We're dazzled by the remains of a Roman road over the hill covered with wildflowers. We will follow the stone road into town for a coffee late in the afternoons. He shows us the old cistern. Water is precious in Tuscany and was collected drop by drop. By shining a flashlight into the opening, we've already noticed that the underground cistern has a stone archway, obviously some kind of passageway. Up the hill in the Medici fortress, we saw the same arch in the cistern there and the caretaker told us that a secret underground escape route goes downhill to the valley, then to Lake Trasimeno. Italians take such remains casually. That one is allowed to own such ancient things seems impossible to me.

13

*

When I first saw Bramasole, I immediately wanted to hang my summer clothes in an *armadio* and arrange my books under one of those windows looking out over the valley. We'd spent four days with Signor Martini, who had a dark little office on Via Sacco e Vanzetti down in the lower town. Above his desk hung a photo of him as a soldier, I assumed for Mussolini. He listened to us as though we spoke perfect Italian. When we finished describing what we thought we wanted, he rose, put on his Borsolino, and said one word, *"Andiamo,"* let's go. Although he'd recently had a foot operation, he drove us over nonexistent roads and pushed through jungles of thorns to show us places only he knew about. Some were farmhouses with roofs collapsed onto the floor, miles from town and costing the earth. One had a tower built by the Crusaders, but the *contessa* who owned it cried and doubled the price on the spot when she saw that we really were interested. Another was attached to other farmhouses where chickens were truly free range—they ran in and out of the houses. The yard was full of rusted farm equipment and hogs. Several felt airless or sat hard by the road. One would have required putting in a road—it was hidden in blackberry brambles and we could only peer in one window because a coiled black snake refused to budge from the threshold.

We took Signor Martini flowers, thanked him and said good-bye. He seemed genuinely sorry to see us go.

The next morning we ran into him in the piazza after coffee. He said, "I just saw a doctor from Arezzo. He might be interested in selling a house. *Una bella villa,*" he added emphatically. The house was within walking distance of Cortona.

"How much?" we asked, although we knew by then he cringes at being asked that direct question.

"Let's just go take a look," was all he said. Out of Cortona, he took the road that climbs and winds to the other side of the hill. He turned onto the *strada bianca* and, after a couple of kilometers, pulled into a long, sloping driveway. I caught a glimpse of a shrine, then looked up at the three-story house with a curly iron fanlight above the front door and two tall, exotic palm trees on either side. On that fresh morning, the facade seemed radiant, glazed with layers of lemon, rouge, and terra-cotta. We both became silent as we got out of the car. After all the turns into unknown roads, the house seemed just to have been waiting all along.

"Perfect, we'll take it," I joked as we stepped through the weeds. Just as he had at other houses, Signor Martini made no sales pitch; he simply looked with us. We walked up to the house under a rusted pergola leaning under the weight of climbing roses. The double front door squawked like something alive when we pushed it open. The house's walls, thick as my arm is long, radiated coolness. The glass in the windows wavered. I scuffed through silty dust and saw below it smooth brick floors in perfect condition. In each room, Ed opened the inside window and pushed open the shutters to one glorious view after another of cypresses, rippling green hills, distant villas, a valley. There were even two bathrooms that functioned. They were not beautiful, but *bathrooms*, after all the houses we'd seen with no floors, much less plumbing. No one had lived there in thirty years and the grounds seemed like an enchanted garden, overgrown and tumbling with blackberries and vines. I could see Signor Martini regarding the grounds with a countryman's practiced eye. Ivy twisted into the trees and ran over fallen terrace walls. *"Molto lavoro,"* much work, was all he said.

During several years of looking, sometimes casually, sometimes to the point of exhaustion, I never heard a house say *yes* so completely. However, we were leaving the next day, and when we learned the price, we sadly said no and went home.

During the next months, I mentioned Bramasole now and then. I stuck a photo on my mirror and often wandered the grounds or rooms in my mind. The house is a metaphor for the self, of course, but it also is totally real. And a *foreign* house exaggerates all the associations houses carry. Because I had ended a long marriage that was not supposed to end and was establishing a new relationship, this house quest felt tied to whatever new identity I would manage to forge. When the flying fur from the divorce settled, I had found myself with a grown daughter, a full-time university job (after years of part-time teaching), a modest securities portfolio, and an entire future to invent. Although divorce was harder than a death, still I felt oddly returned to myself after many years in a close family. I had the urge to examine my life in another culture and move beyond what I knew. I wanted something of a *physical* dimension that would occupy the mental volume the years of my former life had. Ed shares my passion for Italy completely and also shares the boon of three-month summer breaks from university teaching. There we would have long days for exploring and for our writing and research projects. When he is at the wheel, he'll *always* take the turn down the intriguing little road. The language, history, art, places in Italy are endless—two lifetimes wouldn't be enough. And, ah, the foreign self. The new life might shape itself to the contours of the house, which already is at home in the landscape, and to the rhythms around it.

In the spring, I called a California woman who was starting a real-estate development business in Tuscany. I asked her to check on Bramasole; perhaps if it had not sold, the price had come down. A week later, she called from a bar after meeting with the owner. "Yes, it's still for sale, but with that particular brand of Italian logic, the price has been raised. The dollar," she reminded me, "has fallen. And that house needs a lot of work."

Now we've returned. By this time, with equally peculiar logic, I've become fixed on buying Bramasole. After all, the only thing wrong is the expense. We both love the setting, the town, the house and land. If only one little thing is wrong, I tell myself, go ahead.

Still, this costs a *sacco di soldi*. It will be an enormous hassle to recover the house and land from neglect. Leaks, mold, tumbling stone terraces, crumbling plaster, one funky bathroom, another with an adorable metal hip bathtub and a cracked toilet.

Why does the prospect seem fun, when I found remodeling my kitchen in San Francisco a deep shock to my equilibrium? At home, we can't even hang a picture without knocking out a fistful of plaster. When we plunge the stopped-up sink, forgetting once again that the disposal doesn't like artichoke petals, sludge seems to rise from San Francisco Bay.

On the other hand, a dignified house near a Roman road, an Etruscan (Etruscan!) wall looming at the top of the hillside, a Medici fortress in sight, a view toward Monte Amiata, a passageway underground, one hundred and seventeen olive trees, twenty plums, and still uncounted apricot, almond, apple, and pear trees. Several figs seem to thrive near the well. Beside the front steps there's a large hazelnut. Then, proximity to one of the most superb towns

I've ever seen. Wouldn't we be crazy not to buy this lovely house called Bramasole?

What if one of us is hit by a potato chip truck and can't work? I run through a litany of diseases we could get. An aunt died of a heart attack at forty-two, my grandmother went blind, all the ugly illnesses . . . What if an earthquake shakes down the universities where we teach? The Humanities Building is on a list of state structures most likely to fall in a moderately severe quake. What if the stock market spirals down?

I leap out of bed at three A.M. and step in the shower, letting my whole face take the cold water. Coming back to bed in the dark, feeling my way, I jam my toe on the iron bed frame. Pain jags all the way up my backbone. "Ed, wake up. I think I've broken my toe. How can you sleep?"

He sits up. "I was just dreaming of cutting herbs in the garden. Sage and lemon balm. Sage is *salvia* in Italian." He has never wavered from his belief that this is a brilliant idea, that this is heaven on earth. He clicks on the bedside lamp. He's smiling.

My half-on toenail is hanging half off, ugly purple spreading underneath. I can't bear to leave it or to pull it off. "I want to go home," I say.

He puts a Band-Aid around my toe. "You mean Bramasole, don't you?" he asks.

❋

This sack of money in question has been wired from California but has not arrived. How can that be, I ask at the bank, money is wired, it arrives instantaneously. More shrugs. Perhaps the main bank in Florence is holding it. Days pass. I call Steve, my broker in California, from a bar. I'm shouting over the noise of a soccer match on the TV. "You'll have to check from that end;" he shouts back, "it's long gone

17

from here and did you know the government there has changed forty-seven times since World War II? This money was well invested in tax-free bonds and the best growth funds. Those Australian bonds of yours earned seventeen percent. Oh well, *la dolce vita*."

The mosquitoes (*zanzare* they're called, just like they sound) invade the hotel with the desert wind. I spin in the sheets until my skin burns. I get up in the middle of the night and lean out the shuttered window, imagining all the sleeping guests, blisters on their feet from the stony streets, their guidebooks still in their hands. We could still back out. Just throw our bags in the rented Fiat and say *arrivederci*. Go hang out on the Amalfi coast for a month and head home, tanned and relaxed. Buy lots of sandals. I can hear my grandfather when I was twenty: "Be realistic. Come down out of the clouds." He was furious that I was studying poetry and Latin etymology, something utterly useless. Now, what am I thinking of? Buying an abandoned house in a place where I hardly can speak the language. He probably has worn out his shroud turning over in his grave. We don't have a mountain of reserves to bale us out in case that mysterious something goes wrong.

*

What is this thrall for houses? I come from a long line of women who open their handbags and take out swatches of upholstery material, colored squares of bathroom tile, seven shades of yellow paint samples, and strips of flowered wallpaper. We love the concept of four walls. "What is her house like?" my sister asks, and we both know she means what is *she* like. I pick up the free real-estate guide outside the grocery store when I go somewhere for the weekend, even if it's close to home. One June, two friends and I rented a house on Majorca; another summer I stayed in a little *casa* in San Miguel de Allende in which I developed a serious love for fountained courtyards and bedrooms with bougainvillea cascading down the balcony, the austere Sierra Madre. One summer in Santa Fe, I started looking at adobes there, imagining I would become a Southwesterner, cook with chilies, wear squash blossom turquoise jewelry—a different life, the chance to be extant in another version. At the end of a month I left and never have wanted to return.

I love the islands off the Georgia coast, where I spent summers when I was growing up. Why not a weathered gray house there, made of wood that looks as though it washed up on the beach? Cotton rugs, peach iced tea, a watermelon cooling in the creek, sleeping with waves churning and rolling outside the window. A place where my sisters, friends, and their families could visit easily. But I keep remembering that anytime I've stepped in my own footprints again, I haven't felt renewed. Though I'm susceptible to the pull to the known, I'm just slightly more susceptible to surprise. Italy seems endlessly alluring to me—why not, at this point, consider the opening of *The Divine Comedy*: What must one do in order to grow? Better to remember my father, the son of my very literal-minded, penny-pinching grandfather. "The family motto," he'd say, "is 'Packing and Unpacking.'" And also, "If you can't go first class, don't go at all."

Lying awake, I feel the familiar sense of The Answer arriving. Like answers on the bottom of the black fortune-telling eight ball that I loved when I was ten, often I can feel an idea or the solution to a dilemma floating up through murky liquid, then it is as if I see the suddenly clear white writing. I like the charged zone of waiting, a mental and physical sensation of the bends as something mysterious zigzags to the surface of consciousness.

What if you did *not* feel uncertainty, the white writing says. Are you exempt from doubt? Why not rename it excitement? I lean over the wide sill just as the first gilded mauve light of sunrise begins. The Arab is still sleeping. The undulant landscape looks serene in every direction. Honey-colored farmhouses, gently placed in hollows, rise like thick loaves of bread set out to cool. I know some Jurassic upheaval violently tossed up the hills, but they appear rounded as though by a big hand. As the sun brightens, the land spreads out a soft spectrum: the green of a dollar bill gone through the wash, old cream, blue sky like a blind person's eye. The Renaissance painters had it just right. I never thought of Perugino, Giotto, Signorelli, et al., as realists, but their background views are still here, as most tourists discover, with dark cypress trees brushed in to emphasize each composition the eye falls on. Now I see why the red boot on a gold and blond angel in the Cortona museum has such a glow, why the Madonna's cobalt dress looks intense and deep. Against this landscape and light, everything takes on a primary outline. Even a red towel drying on a line below becomes totally saturated with its own redness.

Think: What if the sky doesn't fall? What if it's glorious? What if the house is transformed in three years? There will be by then hand-printed labels for the house's olive oil, thin linen curtains pulled across the shutters for siesta, jars of plum jam on the shelves, a long table for feasts under the linden trees, baskets piled by the door for picking tomatoes, arugula, wild fennel, roses, and rosemary. And who are we in that strange new life?

❉

Finally the money arrives, the account is open. However, they have no checks. This enormous bank, the seat of dozens of branches in the gold center of Italy, has no checks to give us. "Maybe next week," Signora Raguzzi explains. "Right now, nothing." We sputter. Two days later, she calls. "I have ten checks for you." What is the big deal with checks? I get boxes of them at home. Signora Raguzzi parcels them out to us. Signora Raguzzi in tight skirt, tight T-shirt, has lips that are perpetually wet and pouting. Her skin glistens. She is astonishingly gorgeous. She wears a magnificent square gold necklace and bracelets on both wrists that jangle as she stamps our account number on each check.

"What great jewelry. I love those bracelets," I say.

"All we have here is gold," she replies glumly. She is bored with Arezzo's tombs and piazzas. California sounds good to her. She brightens every time she sees us. "Ah, California," she says as greeting. The bank begins to seem surreal. We're in the back room. A man wheels in a cart stacked with gold ingots—actual small bricks of gold. No one seems to be on guard. Another man loads two into dingy manila folders. He's plainly dressed, like a workman. He walks out into the street, taking the ingots somewhere. So much for Brinks delivery— but what a clever plainclothes disguise. We turn back to the checks. There will be no insignia of boats or palm trees or pony express riders, there will be no name, address, driver's license, Social Security number. Only these pale green checks that look as though they were printed in the twenties. We're enormously pleased. That's close to citizenship—a bank account.

Finally we are gathered in the *notaio's* office for the final reckoning. It's quick. Everyone talks at once and no one listens. The baroque legal terms leave us way behind. A jackhammer outside drills into my brain cells. There's something about two oxen and two days. Ian, who's translating, stops to explain this archaic spiral of language as an eighteenth-century legal description of the amount of land, measured by how long it would take two oxen to plow it. We have, it seems, two plowing days worth of property.

I write checks, my fingers cramping over all the times I write *milione*. I think of all the nice dependable bonds and utility stocks and blue chips from the years of my marriage magically turning into a ter-raced hillside and a big empty house. The glass house in California where I lived for a decade, surrounded by kumquat, lemon, mock orange, and guava, its bright pool and covered patio with wicker and flowered cushions—all seem to recede, as though seen through the long focus in binoculars. *Million* is such a big word in English it's hard to treat it casually. Ed carefully monitors the zeros, not wanting me to unwittingly write *miliardo*, billion, instead. He pays Signor Martini in cash. He never has mentioned a fee; we have found out the normal percentage from the owner. Signor Martini seems pleased, as though we've given him a gift. For me this is a confusing but delightful way to conduct business. Handshakes all around. Is that a little cat smile on the mouth of the owner's wife? We're expecting a parchment deed, lettered in ancient script, but no, the *notaio* is going on vacation and she'll try to get to the paperwork before she leaves. *"Normale,"* Signor Martini says. I've noticed all along that someone's word is still taken for that. Endless contracts and stipulations and contingencies simply have not come up. We walk out into the brutally hot afternoon with nothing but two heavy iron keys longer than my hand, one to a rusted iron gate, the other to the front door. They look nothing like the keys to anything I've ever owned. There is no hope for spare copies.

Giuseppe waves from the door of the bar and we tell him we have bought a house. "Where is it?" he wants to know.

"Bramasole," Ed begins, about to say where it is.

"Ah, Bramasole, *una bella villa!*" He has picked cherries there as a boy. Although it is only afternoon, he pulls us in and pours a *grappa* for us. "Mama!" he shouts. His mother and her sister come in from the back and everyone toasts us. They're all talking at once, speaking of us as the *stranieri*, foreigners. The *grappa* is blindingly strong. We drink ours as fast as Signora Mantucci nips her espresso and wander out in the sun. The car is as hot as a pizza oven. We sit there with the doors open, suddenly laughing and laughing.

*

We'd arranged for two women to clean and for a bed to be delivered while we signed the final papers. In town we picked up a bottle of cold *prosecco*, then stopped at the *rosticceria* for marinated zucchini, olives, roast chicken, and potatoes.

We arrive at the house dazed by the events and the *grappa*. Anna and Lucia have washed the windows and exorcised layers of dust, as well as many spiders' webs. The second-floor bedroom that opens onto a brick terrace gleams. They've made the bed with the new blue sheets and left the terrace door open to the sound of cuckoos and wild canaries in the linden trees. We pick the last of the pink roses on the front terrace and fill two old Chianti bottles with them. The shuttered room with its whitewashed walls, just-waxed floors, pristine bed with new sheets, and sweet roses on the windowsill, all lit with a dangling forty-watt bulb, seems as pure as a Franciscan cell. As soon as I walk in, I think it is the most perfect room in the world.

We shower and dress in fresh clothes. In the quiet twilight, we sit on the stone wall of the terrace and toast each other and the house with tumblers of the spicy *prosecco*, which seems like a liquid form of the air. We toast the cypress trees along the road and the white horse in the neighbor's field, the villa in the distance that was built for the visit of a pope. The olive pits we toss over the wall, hoping they will spring from the ground next year. Dinner is delicious. As the darkness comes, a barn owl flies over so close that we hear the whir of wings and, when it settles in the black locust, a strange cry that we take for a greeting. The Big Dipper hangs over the house, about to pour on the roof. The constellations pop out, clear as a star chart. When it finally is dark, we see that the Milky Way sweeps right over the house. I forget the stars, living in the ambient light of a city. Here they are, all along, spangling and dense, falling and pulsating. We stare up until our necks ache. The Milky Way looks like a flung bolt of lace unfurling. Ed, because he likes to whisper, leans to my ear. "Still want to go home," he asks, "or can this be home?"

A HOUSE AND THE LAND IT TAKES
TWO OXEN TWO DAYS TO PLOW

I ADMIRE THE BEAUTY OF SCORPIONS. THEY LOOK LIKE black-ink hieroglyphs of themselves. I'm fascinated, too, that they can navigate by the stars, though how they ever glimpse constellations from their usual homes in dusty corners of vacant houses, I don't know. One scurries around in the bidet every morning. Several get sucked into the new vacuum cleaner by mistake, though usually they are luckier: I trap them in a jar and take them outside. I suspect every cup and shoe. When I fluff a bed pillow, an albino one lands on my bare shoulder. We upset armies of spiders as we empty the closet under the stairs of its bottle collection. Impressive, the long threads for legs and the fly-sized bodies; I can even see their eyes. Other than these inhabitants, the inheritance from the former occupants consists of dusty wine bottles—thousands and thousands in the shed and in the stalls. We fill local recycling bins over and over, waterfalls of glass raining from boxes we've loaded and reloaded. The stalls and *limonaia* (a garage-sized room on the side of the house once used for storing pots of lemons over the winter) are piled with rusted pans, newspapers from 1958, wire, paint cans, debris. Whole ecosystems of spiders and scorpions are destroyed, though hours later they seem to have regenerated. I look for old photos or antique spoons but see nothing of interest except some handmade iron tools and a "priest," a swan-shaped wooden form with a hook for a hanging pan of hot coals, which was pushed under bed-covers in winter to warm the clammy sheets. One cunningly made tool, an elegant little sculpture, is a hand-sized crescent with a worn chestnut handle. Any Tuscan would recognize it in a second: a tool for trimming grapes.

When we first saw the house, it was filled with fanciful iron beds with painted medallions of Mary and shepherds holding lambs, wormy chests of drawers with marble tops, cribs, foxed mirrors, cradles, boxes, and lugubrious bleeding-heart religious pictures of the Crucifixion. The owner removed everything—down to the switchplate covers and lightbulbs—except a thirties kitchen cupboard and an ugly red bed that we cannot figure out how to get down the narrow back stairs from the third floor. Finally we take the bed apart and throw it piece by piece from the window. Then we stuff the mattress through the window and my stomach flips as I watch it seem to fall in slow motion to the ground.

The Cortonese, out for afternoon strolls, pause in the road and look up at all the mad activity, the car trunk full of bottles, mattress flying, me screaming as a scorpion falls down my shirt when I sweep the stone walls of the stall, Ed wielding a grim-reaper scythe through the weeds. Sometimes they stop and call up, "How much did you pay for the house?"

I'm taken aback and charmed by the bluntness. "Probably too much," I answer. One person remembered that long ago an artist from Naples lived there; for most, it has stood empty as far back as they can remember.

Every day we haul and scrub. We are becoming as parched as the hills around us. We have bought cleaning supplies, a new stove and fridge. With sawhorses and two planks we set up a kitchen counter. Although we must bring hot water from the bathroom in a plastic

laundry pan, we have a surprisingly manageable kitchen. As one who
has used Williams-Sonoma as a toy store for years, I begin to get back
to an elementary sense of the kitchen. Three wooden spoons, two for
the salad, one for stirring. A sauté pan, bread knife, cutting knife, cheese
grater, pasta pot, baking dish, and stove-top espresso pot. We brought
over some old picnic silverware and bought a few glasses and plates.
Those first pastas are divine. After long work, we eat everything in sight
then tumble like field hands into bed. Our favorite is spaghetti with
an easy sauce made from diced *pancetta*, unsmoked bacon, quickly
browned, then stirred into cream and chopped wild arugula (called
ruchetta locally), easily available in our driveway and along the stone
walls. We grate *parmigiano* on top and eat huge mounds. Besides the
best salad of all, those amazing tomatoes sliced thickly and served with
chopped basil and mozzarella, we learn to make Tuscan white beans
with sage and olive oil. I shell and simmer the beans in the morning,
then let them come to room temperature before dousing them with
the oil. We consume an astonishing number of black olives.

  Three ingredients is about all we manage most nights, but that
seems to be enough for something splendid. The idea of cooking here
inspires me—with such superb ingredients, everything seems easy. An
abandoned slab of marble from a dresser top serves as a pastry table
when I decide to make my own crust for a plum tart. As I roll it out
with one of the handblown Chianti bottles I rescued from the debris,
I think with amazement of my kitchen in San Francisco: the black and
white tile floor, mirrored wall between cabinets and counter, long
counters in gleaming white, the restaurant stove big enough to take off
from the San Francisco airport, sunlight pouring in the skylight, and,
always, Vivaldi or Robert Johnson or Villa Lobos to cook to. Here,
the determined spider in the fireplace keeps me company as she
knits her new web. The stove and fridge look starkly new against the
flaking whitewash and under the bulb hanging from what looks like
a live wire.

Late in the afternoons I take long soaks in the hip bath filled with bubbles, washing spiderwebs out of my hair, grit from my nails, necklaces of dirt from around my neck. I have not had a necklace of dirt since I used to play Kick the Can on long summer evenings as a child. Ed emerges reborn from the shower, tan in his white cotton shirt and khaki shorts.

The empty house, now scrubbed, feels spacious and pure. Most of the scorpions migrate elsewhere. Because of the thick stone walls, we feel cool even on the hottest days. A primitive farm table, left in the *limonaia*, becomes our dining table on the front terrace. We sit outside talking late about the restoration, savoring the Gorgonzola with a pear pulled off the tree, and the wine from Lake Trasimeno, just a valley away. Renovation seems simple, really. A central water heater, with a new bath and existing baths routed to it, new kitchen—but simple, soul of simplicity. How long will the permits take? Do we really need central heat? Should the kitchen stay where it is, or wouldn't it really be better where the ox stall currently is? That way, the present kitchen could be the living room, with a big fireplace in it. In the dark we can see the shadowy vestiges of a formal garden: a long, overgrown boxwood hedge with five huge, ragged topiary balls rising out of it. Should we rebuild the garden with these strange remnants? Cut them out of the hedge? Take out the ancient hedge altogether and plant something informal, such as lavender? I close my eyes and try to have a vision of the garden in three years, but the overgrown jungle is too indelibly imprinted in my brain. By the end of dinner, I could sleep standing up, like a horse.

The house must be in some good alignment, according to the Chinese theories of Feng Shui. Something is giving us an extraordinary feeling of well-being. Ed has the energy of three people. A lifelong insomniac, I sleep like one newly dead every night and dream deeply harmonious dreams of swimming along with the current in a clear green river, playing and at home in the water. On the first night,

I dreamed that the real name of the house was not Bramasole but Cento Angeli, One Hundred Angels, and that I would discover them one by one. Is it bad luck to change the name of a house, as it is to rename a boat? As a trepid foreigner, I wouldn't. But for me, the house now has a secret name as well as its own name.

*

The bottles are gone. The house is clean. The tile floors shine with a waxy patina. We hang a few hooks on the backs of doors, just to get our clothes out of suitcases. With milk crates and a few squares of marble left in the stall, we fashion a couple of bedside tables to go with our two chairs from the garden center.

We feel prepared to face the reality of restoration. We walk into town for coffee and telephone Piero Rizzatti, the *geometra*. The translations "draftsman" or "surveyor" don't quite explain what a *geometra* is, a professional without an equivalent in the United States— a liaison among owner, builders, and town planning officials. Ian has assured us that he is the best in the area, meaning also that he has the best connections and can get the permits quickly.

The next day Ian drives out with Signor Rizzatti and his tape measurer and notepad. We begin our cold-eyed tour through the empty house.

The bottom floor is basically five rooms in a row—farmer's kitchen, main kitchen, living room, horse stall, another stall—with a hall and stairs after the first two rooms. The house is bisected by its great stairwell with stone steps and handwrought iron railing. A strange floor plan: The house is designed like a dollhouse, one room deep with all the rooms about the same size. That seems to me like giving all your children the same name. On the upper two floors, there are two bedrooms on either side of the stairs; you must go through the first room to get to the other. Privacy, until recently, wasn't much of an issue for Italian families. Even Michelangelo, I recall, slept four abed with his masons when he worked on a project. In the great Florentine *palazzi,* you must go through one immense room to get to the next; corridors must have seemed a waste of space.

The west end of the house—one room on each floor—is walled off for the *contadini,* the farm family who worked the olive and grape terraces. A narrow stone stairway runs up the back of that apartment and there's no entrance from the main house, except through that kitchen's front door. With their door, the two doors going into the stalls, and the big front door, there are four French doors across the front of the house. I envision them with new shutters, all flung open to the terrace, lavender, roses, and pots of lemons between them, with lovely scents wafting into the house and a natural movement of inside/outside living. Signor Rizzatti turns the handle of the farm kitchen door and it comes off in his hand.

At the back of the apartment, a crude room with a toilet cemented to the floor—one step above a privy—is tacked onto the third floor of the house. The farmers, with no running water upstairs, must have used a bucket-flush method. The two real bathrooms also are built off the back of the house, each one at a stair landing. This ugly solution is still common for stone houses constructed before indoor plumbing. Often I see these loos jutting out, sometimes supported by flimsy wooden poles angling into the walls. The small bath, which I take to be the house's first, has a low ceiling, stone checkerboard floor, and the charming hip bath. The large bathroom must have been added in the fifties, not long before the house was abandoned. Someone had a dizzy fling with tile—floor-to-ceiling pink, blue, and white in a butterfly design. The floor is blue but not the same blue. The shower simply drains into the floor, that is to say, water spreads all over the bathroom. Someone attached the showerhead so high on the wall that the spray creates a breeze and the angled shower curtain we hung wraps around our legs.

We walk out onto the L-shaped terrace off the second-floor bedroom, leaning on the railing for the stupendous view of the valley from one direction and of fruit and olive trees from the others. We're imagining, of course, future breakfasts here with the overhanging apricot tree in bloom and the hillside covered with wild irises we see the scraggly remains of everywhere. I can see my daughter and her boyfriend, slathered in tanning oil, reading novels on chaise longues, a pitcher of iced tea between them. The terrace floor is just like the floors in the house, only the tile is beautifully weathered and mossy. Signor Rizzatti, however, regards the tiles with a frown. When we go downstairs, he points to the ceiling of the *limonaia,* just underneath the terrace, which also is caked with moss and is even crumbling in some spots. Leaks. This looks expensive. The scrawls on his notepad cover two pages.

We think the weird layout suits us. We don't need eight bedrooms anyway. Each of the four can have an adjoining study/sitting room/dressing room, although we decide to turn the room next to ours into a bathroom. Two bathrooms seem enough but we'd love the luxury of a private bath next to the bedroom. If we can chop out the farmers' crude toilet attached to that room, we'll have a closet off the bath, the only one in the house. With his metal tape, the *geometra* indicates the ghost of a door leading into the farmer's former bedroom from the bedroom we'll have. Reopening it, we think, will be a quick job.

On the bottom floor, the line of rooms is not that convenient. When we first saw the house, I'd said airily, "We can knock these walls out and have two big rooms down here." Now our *geometra* tells us we may open the walls only about six feet because of earthquake precautions. Staying here has given me an inner sense of the construction. I see how the first floor walls bow near the floor, accommodating the large stones in the foundation. The house was built in a way not unlike the stone terraces, without mortar, stones stacked and wedged. From the depths of the doorways and windowsills, I see that the walls thin as they go up. The yard-thick walls on the first floor are maybe half that on the third. What holds the house together as it goes up? Can inserting a few modern I beams of steel in those openings do the job of stones I couldn't even reach around?

When the great dome of the *duomo* was conceived in Florence, no one knew the technique for constructing so large a half sphere. Someone proposed building it over an immense mound of dirt piled in the cathedral. Money would be hidden throughout the pile and, on completion of the dome, the peasants would be invited to dig for coins and cart away the dirt. Fortunately, Brunelleschi figured out how to engineer his dome. I hope someone built this house on solid principles also but still I begin to have misgivings about taking out the fortress-thick walls on the first floor.

The *geometra* is full of opinions. He thinks the apartment's back staircase should come out. We love it, a secret escape. He thinks we should replaster the cracked and crumbling stucco facade, paint it ocher. No way. I like the colors that change as the light does and the intense glow of golds when it rains, as though the sun seeps into the walls. He thinks our first priority should be the roof. "But the roof doesn't leak—why bother it, when there are so many other pressing things?" We explain to him that we won't be able to do everything at once. The house cost the earth. The project will have to be spread out. We will do much of the work ourselves. Americans, I try to explain, sometimes are "do it yourself" people. As I say this I see a flash of panic cross Ed's face. "Do it yourself" doesn't translate. The *geometra* shakes his head as though all is hopeless if he has to explain things as basic as these.

He speaks to us kindly, as if through precise enunciation we will understand him. "Listen, the roof must be consolidated. They will preserve the tiles, number them, place them again in the same order, but you will have insulation; the roof will be strengthened."

32

At this point, it's either the roof or central heating, not both. We debate the importance of each. After all, we'll be here mostly in the summer. But we don't want to freeze at Christmas when we come over to pick the olives. If we're ever going to put heat in, it needs to go in at the same time as the water system and plumbing. The roof can be done anytime—or never. Right now, water is held in a cistern in the farmer's bedroom. When you shower or flush, a pump comes on and well water gurgles into the cistern. Individual hotwater heaters (miraculously, they work) hang above each shower. We'll need a central water heater, a large cistern connected to it so that the noisy pump isn't continuously working.

We decide on the heating. The *geometra*, feeling sure that we will come to our senses, says he will apply for a roof permit as well.

At some low point in the house's life, someone madly painted the chestnut beams in every room with a hideous vinegar varnish. This unimaginable technique once was popular in the South of Italy. You paint over real beams with a sticky goo, then comb through it to simulate wood! Sandblasting, therefore, is a top priority. An ugly job but fast, and we'll do the sealing and waxing ourselves. I once refinished a sailor's sea chest and found it fun. We'll need door and window repairs. All the window casements and interior shutters are covered with the same faux wood concoction. This genius of the beams and windows is probably responsible for the fireplace, which is covered with ceramic tiles that resemble bricks. What a strange mind, to cover the real thing with an imitation of something real. All this must go, along with the blue tiles covering the wide windowsill, the butterflies in the bathroom. Both the main kitchen and the farmers' kitchen sport ugly cement sinks. His list is now three pages long. The farmers' kitchen has floors made of crushed marble tiles, super ugly. There are a lot of ancient-looking wires coiled near the ceilings on white porcelain knobs. Sometimes sparks come flying out when I switch on a light.

The *geometra* sits on the terrace wall, mopping his face with an enormous monogrammed linen handkerchief. He looks at us with pity.

❋

Rule one in a restoration project: Be there. We will be seven thousand miles away when some of the big work is done. We brace ourselves for bids for the work.

Nando Lucignoli, sent to us by Signor Martini, drives up in his Lancia and stands at the bottom of the driveway, looking not at the house but at the view of the valley. I think he must be a deep admirer of landscape but see that he is talking on a cellular phone, waving his cigarette and gesturing to the air. He tosses the phone onto the front seat.

"*Bella posizione.*" He waves his Gauloises again as he shakes hands, almost bowing to me. His father is a stonemason and he has become a contractor, an extraordinarily good-looking one. Like many Italian men, his cologne or aftershave surrounds him with a lemony, sunny aura only slightly dispelled by the cigarette smoke. Before he says anything more, I'm sure he's the contractor for us. We take him on a tour of the house. "*Niente, niente,*" he repeats, nothing. "We'll run the heating pipes in channels on the back of the house, a week; the bathroom—three days, signora. One month, everything. You'll have a perfect house; just lock the door, leave me the key and when you come back, everything will be taken care of." He assures us he can find old bricks to match the rest of the house for the new kitchen in the stall. The wiring? He has a friend. The terrace bricks? He shrugs, oh, some mortar. Opening the walls? His father is expert in that. His slicked-back black hair, wanting to revert to curls, falls over his forehead. He looks like Caravaggio's Bacchus—only he has moss-green eyes and a slight slouch, probably from leaning into the speed of his

Lancia. He thinks my ideas are wonderful, I should have been an architect, I have excellent taste. We sit out on the stone wall and have a glass of wine. Ed goes inside to make coffee for himself. Nando draws diagrams of the water lines on the back of an envelope. My Italian is charming, he says. He understands everything I try to say. He says he will drop off his estimate tomorrow. I am sure it will be reasonable, that through the winter Nando and his father and a few trusted workers will transform Bramasole. "Enjoy yourself—leave it to me," he says as his tires spin on the driveway. As I wave good-bye, I notice that Ed has stayed on the terrace. He's noncommittal about Nando, saying only that he smelled like a *profumeria,* it's affected to smoke Gauloises, and that he didn't think the central heating could be installed that way at all.

Ian brings up Benito Cantoni, a yellow-eyed, solidly built short man who bears a strange resemblance to Mussolini. He's around sixty so he must have been a namesake. I remember that Mussolini actually was named for the Mexican Benito Juárez, who fought French oppression. Odd to think of that revolutionary name travelling through the dictator and into this quiet man whose wide, blank face and bald head shine like a polished nut. When he speaks, which is little, he uses the local Val di Chiana dialect. He cannot understand a word either of us says and we certainly can't understand him. Even Ian has trouble. Benito worked on the restoration of the chapel at Le Celle, a nearby monastery, a solid recommendation. We're even more impressed when Ian drives us out to look at a house he's restoring near Castiglione del Lago, a farmhouse with a tower supposedly built by the Knights Templar. The work looks careful. His two masons, unlike Benito, have big smiles.

Back at Bramasole, Benito walks through, not even taking a note. He radiates a calm confidence. When we ask Ian to request an estimate, Benito balks. It is impossible to know the problems he might run into. How much do we want to spend? (What a question!) He is not sure about the floor tiles, of what he will uncover when he takes the bricks off the upstairs terrace. A small beam, he notices, needs replacing on the third floor.

Estimates are foreign to builders around here. They're used to working by the day, with someone always at home to know how long they were there. This projecting is just not the way they do business, although they will sometimes say "Under three days" or *"Quindici giorni." Quindici giorni*—fifteen days—we learned is simply a convenient term meaning the speaker has no idea but imagines that the time is not entirely open ended. *"Quindici minuti,"* we'd learned by missing a train, means a few minutes, not the fifteen it indicates, even when spoken by the train conductor about a departure. I think most Italians have a longer sense of time than we do. What's the hurry? Once up, a building will stand a long, long time, perhaps a thousand years. Two weeks, two months, big deal.

Removing the walls? He doesn't advise it. He makes gestures, indicating the house collapsing around us. Somehow, Benito will come up with a number and will give it to Ian this week. As he leaves he flashes a smile at last. His square yellow teeth look strong enough to bite through brick. Ian endorses him and discounts Nando as "the playboy of the western world." Ed looks pleased.

Our *geometra* recommends the third contractor, Primo Bianchi, who arrives in an Ape, one of those miniature three-wheel trucks. He, too, is miniature, scarcely five feet tall, stout and dressed in overalls with a red kerchief around his neck. He rolls out and salutes us formally with an old word, *"Salve, signori."* He looks like one of Santa's workers, with gold-rimmed glasses, flyaway white hair, tall boots. *"Permesso?"* he asks before we go through the door. At each door he pauses and repeats, *"Permesso?"* as though he might surprise someone undressing. He holds his cap in his hand in a way I recognize from my father's mill workers in the South; he's used to being the "peasant" speaking to the *"padrone."* He has, however, a confident sense of himself, a pride I often notice in waiters, mechanics, delivery people here. He tries the window latches and swings the doors. Pokes the tip of his knife in beams to check for rot, wiggles loose bricks.

He comes to a spot in the floor, kneels and rubs two bricks that are a slightly lighter color. *"Io,"* he says, beaming, pointing to his chest, *"molti anni fa."* He replaced them many years ago. He then tells us he was the one who installed the main bath and that he used to come every December and help haul the big lemon pots that lined the terrace into the *limonaia* for the winter. The house's owner was his father's age, a widower then, whose five daughters had grown and moved away. When he died, the daughters left the house vacant. They refused to part with it but no one cared for the place for thirty years. Ah, the five sisters of Perugia I imagine in their narrow iron beds in five bedrooms, all waking at once and throwing open the shutters. I don't believe in ghosts, but from the beginning I sensed their heavy black braids twisted with ribbons, their white nightgowns embroidered with their initials, their mother with silver brushes lining them up before the mirror each night for one hundred strokes.

On the upstairs terrace, he shook his head. The bricks must come up, then an underlayer of tarpaper and insulation installed. We had a feeling he knew what he was talking about. The central heating? "Keep the fire going, dress warmly, signora, the cost is formidable." The two walls? Yes, it could be done. Decisions are irrational. We both knew Primo Bianchi was the right man for the restoration.

✳

If the gun is on the mantel in chapter one, there must be a bang by the end of the story.

The former owner had not just affirmed the bounty of water, he had waxed lyrical. It was a subject of great pride. When he showed us around the property's borders, he'd opened a garden faucet full blast, turning his hands in the cold well water. "This was a watering spot for the Etruscans! This water is known to be the purest—the whole Medici water system," he said, gesturing to the walls of the fifteenth-century fortress at the top of the hill, "runs through this land." His English was perfect. Without doubt, he knew about water. He described the watercourses of the mountains around us, the rich supply that flowed through our side of Monte Sant'Egidio.

Of course, we had the property inspected before we bought it. An impartial *geometra* from Umbertide, miles away over the hills, gave us detailed evaluations. The water, he agreed, was plentiful.

While I am taking a shower after six weeks of ownership, the water slows, then trickles, then drips, then stops. Soap in hand, I stand there without comprehension for several moments, then decide the pump must have been turned off accidentally, or, more likely, the power has gone off. But the overhead light is on. I step out and rub off the soap with a towel.

Signor Martini drives out from his office bringing a long string marked with meters and a weight on the end. We lift the stone off the well and he lowers the weight. *"Poco acqua,"* he announces loudly as the weight hits bottom. Little water. He hauls it up, black roots hanging off, and only a few inches of string are wet. The well is a measly twenty meters deep, with a pump that must have ushered in the Industrial Revolution. So much for the expertise of the impartial *geometra* from Umbertide. That Tuscany is in the third year of a serious drought doesn't help either.

"Un nuovo pozzo," he announces, still louder. Meanwhile, he says, we will buy water from a friend of his who will bring it in a truck. Fortunately, he has a "friend" for every situation.

"Lake water?" I ask, imagining little toads and slimy green weed from Trasimeno. He assures us it's pure water, even has fluoride in it. His friend simply will pump umpteen liters into the well and it will be adequate for the rest of the summer. In fall, a new *pozzo*, deep, with fine water—enough for a swimming pool.

The swimming pool had become a leitmotif while we were looking for houses. Since we are from California, everyone who showed us a house assumed that naturally we would want a pool first thing. I remembered that years ago, while visiting in the East, I was asked by the pale-faced son of a friend if I taught my classes in my bathing suit. I liked his vision. After owning a pool, I think the best way to enjoy the water is to have a friend who has a pool. Dealing with overnight neon green transformations of water is not in my vacation plans. There is trouble enough here.

And so we buy a truckload of water, feeling half foolish and half relieved. We only have two weeks left at Bramasole and paying Martini's friend certainly is cheaper than going to a hotel—and not nearly as humiliating. Why the water doesn't just seep into the dried-out water table, I don't know. We shower fast, drink nothing but bottled water, eat out frequently, and enrich the dry cleaners. All day we hear the rhythmic pounding of well-drilling equipment rising from the valley below us. Others, it seems, don't have deep wells either. I wonder if anyone else in Italy ever has had a load of water dumped into the ground. I keep confusing *pozzo*, well, with *pazzo*, crazy, which is what we must be.

By the time we start to get a grasp on what the place needs—besides water—and who we are here, it's time to go. In California, students are buying their texts, consulting their class schedules. We arrange for permit applications. The estimates are all astronomical—we'll have to do more of the work ourselves than I imagined. I remember getting a shock when I changed the switchplate on an electrical outlet in my study at home. Ed once put his foot through the ceiling when he climbed into the attic to check for a roof leak. We call Primo Bianchi and tell him we'd like for him to do the main work and will be in touch when the permits come through. Bramasole, fortunately, is in a "green zone" and a "*belle arti* zone," where nothing new can be built and houses are protected from alterations that would change their architectural integrity. Because permits require both local and national approval, the process takes months—even a year. We hope Rizzatti is as well-connected as we have heard he is. Bramasole must stand empty for another winter. Leaving a dry well leaves a dry taste as well.

When we see the former owner in the piazza just before we leave, he is congenial, his new Armani tossed over his shoulders. "How is everything at Bramasole?" he asks.

"Couldn't be better," I reply. "We love everything about it."

❋

As I closed the house, I counted. Seventeen windows, each with heavy outside shutters and elaborate inside windows with swinging wooden panels, and seven doors to lock. When I pulled in the shutters, each room was suddenly dark, except for combs of sunlight cast on the floor. The doors have iron bars to hook in place, all except the *portone*, the big front door, which closes with the iron key and, I suppose, makes the elaborate locking of the other doors and windows moot, since a determined thief easily could batter his way in, despite the solid *thumft, thumft* of the lock turning twice. But the house has stood here empty through thirty winters; what's one more? Any thief who pushed into the dark house would find a lone bed, some linens, stove, fridge, and pots and pans.

Odd, to pack a bag and drive away, just leave the house standing there in the early morning light, one of my favorite times, as though we'd never been there at all.

We head toward Nice, across Tuscany toward the Ligurian coast. The toasted hills, fields of drooping sunflowers, and the exit signs with the magical names flash by: Montevarchi, Firenze, Montecatini, Pisa, Lucca, Pietrasanta, Carrara with its river milky with marble dust. Houses are totally anthropomorphic for me. They're so *themselves*. Bramasole looked returned to itself as we left, upright and contained, facing the sun.

I keep hearing myself singing, "The cheese stands alone" as we whiz in and out of tunnels. "What *is* that you're singing?" Ed is passing cars at 140 kilometers an hour; I'm afraid he has taken rather naturally to the blood sport of Italian driving.

"Didn't you play The Farmer in the Dell in first grade?"

"I was into Capture the Flag. Girls played those singing games."

"I always liked it at the end when we boomed out, 'The cheese stands alone,' emphasizing every syllable. It's sad to leave, knowing the house will just stand there all winter and we'll be busy and won't even think about it."

"Are you crazy—we'll be thinking every day about where we want things, what we'll plant—and how much we're going to be robbed."

At Menton, we check into a hotel and spend the late afternoon swimming in the Mediterranean. Italy is now that far off arm of land in the hazy twilight. Somewhere, light years away, Bramasole is now in shadow; the afternoon sun has dipped below the crest of the hill above us. Further light years away, it's morning in California; light is spilling into the dining room where Sister the cat is warming her fur on the table under the windows. We walk the long promenade into town and have bowls of *soupe au pistou* and grilled fish. Early the next day we drive to Nice and fly away. As we speed down the runway, I glimpse a fringe of waving palms against the bright sky; then we lift off and are gone for nine months.

JUNE. WE'RE TOLD THAT WINTER WAS FIERCE AND SPRING was unusually profligate with bloom. Poppies have lingered and the fragrance of spiky yellow broom still fills the air. The house looks as if more sun soaked in during these months I've been gone. The finish that faux painters all over creation are trying to perfect, the seasons have managed admirably. Otherwise, all is the same, giving me the illusion that the months away were only a few days. A moment ago I was hacking weeds and now I'm at it again, though frequently I stop. I am watching for the man with the flowers.

A sprig of oleander, a handful of Queen Anne's and fennel bound with a stem, a full bouquet of dog roses, dandelion puffs, buttercups, and lavender bells—every day I look to see what he has propped up in the shrine at the bottom of my driveway. When I first saw the flowers, I thought the donor was a woman. I would see her soon in her neat navy print dress with a market bag hung over the handlebars of a battered bicycle.

A bent woman in a red shawl does come early some mornings. She kisses her fingertips, then touches them to the ceramic Mary. I have seen a young man stop his car, jump out for a moment, then roar off. Neither of these brings flowers. Then one day I saw a man walking down the road from Cortona. He was slow and dignified. I heard the crunch of his steps on the road stop for a moment. Later, I found a fresh clump of purple sweet peas in the shrine, and yesterday's wild asters thrown down into the pile of other wilting and dead bundles.

Now I wait for him. He examines what wildflowers the roadside and fields offer, leans to pick what he fancies. He varies his selection, bringing new blooms as they spring up. I'm up on a high terrace, hacking ivy off stone walls and chopping off dry limbs of neglected trees. The profusion of flowers stops me every few minutes. I don't know enough of the English names, much less the Italian. One plant, shaped like a little tabletop Christmas tree, is spiked all over with white flowers. I think we have wild red gladioluses. Lusty red poppies literally carpet the hillsides, their vibrancy cooled by clusters of blue irises, now withering to an ashy gray. The grass brushes my knees. When I stop just to look, the pilgrim is approaching. He pauses in the road and stares up at me. I wave but he does not wave back, just blankly stares as though I, a foreigner, am a creature unaware of being looked at, a zoo animal.

The shrine is the first thing you see when you come to the house. Cut into a curved stone wall, it's an ordinary one in these parts, a porcelain Mary on a blue background, in the Della Robbia style, centered in an arched niche. I see other shrines around the countryside, dusty and forgotten. This one is, for some reason, active.

He's an old man, this wayfarer with his coat draped over his shoulders and his slow contemplative walk down the road. Once I passed him in the town park and he gravely said, *"Buon giorno,"* but only after I spoke first. He had taken off his cap for a moment and I saw a fringe of white hair around his bald crown, which is bright as a lightbulb. His eyes are cloudy and remote, a stony blue. I also have seen him in town. He is not gregarious, does not join friends for

coffee at bars, does not stop his stroll through the main street to greet
anyone. I begin to get the idea that he is possibly an angel, since his
coat always hangs around his shoulders, and since he seems to be invisible to everyone but me. I remember the dream I had the first night
I spent here: I would discover one hundred angels one by one. This
angel, though, has a body. He wipes his forehead with his handkerchief.   *43*
Perhaps he was born in this house, or he loved someone here. Or the
pointed cypresses that line this road, each one commemorating a local
boy who died in World War I (so many from such a small town), remind
him of friends. His mother was a great beauty and stepped into carriages on this spot, or his father was tight as a whip and forbade him
to enter the house ever again. He thanks Jesus daily for saving his
daughter from the perils of surgeons in Parma. Or perhaps this is
just the far point of his daily walk, a pleasant habit, a tribute to the
Walk God. Whatever, I hesitate to wipe the road dust from Mary's face,
or shine the blue to gloss with a cloth, even to disturb the mound
of stiff bouquets piled on the ground, still intact. There's a life in old
places and we're always passing through. He makes me feel wide circles surrounding this house. I will be learning for years what I can
touch and what I can't, and how I can touch. I imagine the five sisters
of Perugia who held this family property, letting the closed stone
rooms grow coats of fluffy white mold, letting vines strangle the
trees, letting plums and pears thud to the ground summer after summer. They would not let go. As girls here, did they wake at the same
moment in the mornings, push open the shutters of five bedrooms,
and draw the same breath of new green air? Some such memory held
the house to them.

     Finally they let go and I, who simply happened by, now
hold eighteenth-century maps showing where the property ends. At
a triangular point below that, I discover cantilevered steps jutting out
of a stone wall that was put together as neatly as a crossword puzzle.
The sculptural integrity of limestone stairs extending into the air was

only some farmer's ingenious method of stepping up to the next terrace. Lacy blue and gray lichen over the years erased the evidence of a foot, but when I run my hand over the step, I feel a slight dip in the center.

From this high terrace I look down on the house. In places where the plaster is broken, the stone called *pietra serena*, square and solid, shows. In front, the two palm trees rising on either side of the front door make the house look as though it should be in Costa Rica or Tangier. I like palms, their dry rattle in the wind and their touch of the exotic. Over the double front door, with its fanlight, I see the stone and wrought-iron balcony, just large enough to step out on and admire the spilling geraniums and jasmine I will plant.

From this terrace, I can't see or hear the workers' chaos going on below. I see our olive trees, some stunted or dead from the famous freeze of 1985, others flourishing, flashing silver and green. I count three figs with their large improbable leaves, visualizing yellow lilies beneath them. I can rest here marveling over the hummocky hills, cypress-lined road, cerulean skies with big baroque clouds that look as if cherubs could peer from behind them, distant stone houses barely brushed in, neat (will ours ever look like that?) terraces of olive and grape.

That I have acquired a shrine amazes me. What amazes me more is that I have taken on the ritual of the man with the flowers. I lay the clippers down in the grass. He approaches slowly, the bouquet almost behind him. When he is at the shrine I never watch. Later, I will walk down the terrace, down the driveway to see what he left. The brilliant yellow broom called *ginestra* and red poppies? Lavender and wheat? I always touch his blade of weed tying that ties them together.

＊

Ed is two levels up, chopping rampaging ivy out of a black locust tree. At every ominous crack or snap I expect to see him careening down the terraces. I pull at tough runners in a stone wall. Ivy kills. We have miles of the stuff. It causes stone walls to fall. Some of the trunks are as big as my ankle. I think of the ivy I have in pretty jardinières on my mantle in San Francisco, imagine that in my absence they will bolt, strangle the furniture, cover the windows. As I move along this wall, my footing becomes more canted because the terrace starts to angle down. The cool scents of crushed lemon balm and *nepitella,* tiny wild mint, rise from around my feet. I lean into the wall, cut a runner of ivy, then rip it out. Dirt flies in my face and little stones crumble out, hitting my shoes. I disturb not at all a long snake taking a siesta. Its head is (how far?) in the wall, tail dangling out about two feet. Which way would he exit—back out or go farther in and U-turn? I skip ten feet on either side and begin to snip again. And then the wall disappears and I almost disappear into a hole.

I call Ed to come down. "Look—is this a well? But how could there be a well *in* the wall?" He scrambles down to the terrace just above me and leans over to look. Where he is, both ivy and blackberries are unnaturally dense.

"It looks like an opening up here." He turns on the weed machine then, but when blackberries keep choking the filaments, he resorts to the grim-reaper scythe. Slowly, he uncovers a chute lined with stones. The immense back stone curves down like a playground slide and disappears underground, opening in the wall I'm trimming. We look at the terrace above him—nothing. But two terraces up, in a line from here, we see another unnaturally large blackberry clump.

Perhaps we just have water and wells on the brain. A few days before, when we arrived for the summer, we were greeted by trucks and cars along the road and a pile of dirt in the driveway. The new well, drilled by a friend of Signor Martini, was almost finished. Giuseppe, the plumber who was installing the pump, somehow had driven his venerable *cinque cento* over a low stone edge of the driveway. He introduced himself to us politely, then turned to kick and curse the car.

"Madonna serpente! Porca Madonna!" The Madonna is a snake? A pig? He raced the engine but the three wheels remaining on the ground couldn't get enough traction to spin his axle off the stone. Ed tried to rock the car and dislodge it. Giuseppe kicked his car again. The three well drillers laughed at him, then helped Ed literally lift the toy-sized car off and over to level ground. Giuseppe hoisted the new pump out of the car and headed for the well, still muttering about the Madonna. We watched them lower it the three hundred feet down. This must be the deepest well in Christendom. They had hit water quickly but Signor Martini told them to keep going, that we never wanted to run out of water again. We found Signor Martini in the house, overseeing Giuseppe's assistant. Without our even thinking of it, they have moved the water heater from the older bathroom to the kitchen so we'll have hot water in our improvised kitchen this summer. I'm touched that he has had the house cleaned and has planted marigolds and petunias around the palm trees—a touch of civilization in the overgrown yard.

He looks tanned already and his foot is healed. "How is your business?" I ask. "Sell many houses to unsuspecting foreigners?"

"Non c'è male," not bad. He beckons for us to follow. At the old well, he pulls a weight out of his pocket and plunks it down the opening. Immediately we hear it hit water. He laughs. *"Pieno, tutto pieno."* Over the winter the old well has completely filled.

I read in a local history book that Torreone, the area of Cortona where Bramasole sits, is a watershed; on one side of us, water runs to the Val di Chiana. On the other, water runs down to the valley of the Tiber. We already are intrigued by the underground cistern near the driveway. Shining a light down the round opening, we've contemplated the stone arch tall enough to stand under and a deep pool our longest stick can't measure. I remember a Nancy Drew I liked at nine, *The Mystery in the Old Well*, though I don't recall the story. Medici escape routes seem more dramatic. Looking down into the cistern taps my first memory of historical Italy—Mrs. Bailey, my sixth-grade teacher, drawing the soaring arches of a Roman aqueduct on the board, explaining how ingenious the ancient Romans were with water. The Acqua Marcia was sixty-two miles long—that's two thirds of the way from Fitzgerald, Georgia, to Macon, she pointed out—and some of the arches still exist from the year 140. I remember trying to grasp the year 140, meanwhile overlapping the arches onto the Ben Hill County highway north.

47

The cistern opening seems to disappear into a tunnel. Though there is footing on either side of the pool, neither of us is brave enough to lower ourselves the fifteen dank feet underground to investigate. We stare into the dark, wondering how large the scorpions and vipers are, just out of sight. Above the cistern a *bocca*, a mouth, opens in the stone wall, as though water should pour into the cistern.

As we strip the ivy's thick roots and webs off the stone walls, we realize that the chute we're uncovering must be connected to the opening above the cistern. Over the next few days we discover four stone chutes running downhill from terrace to terrace and ending at a large square mouth that goes underground for about twenty-five feet, then reappears on the lowest terrace above the cistern, just as we suspected. The backs of all the chutes have the big single stone curved for the water to flow down. When the channels are cleaned out, water will cascade into the cistern after rains. I start to wonder if, with a small recirculating pump connected to the cistern, perhaps some of the water can fall all the time. After the experience of the dry well, the trickle and splash of falling water would be music indeed. Fortunately, we didn't stumble into these chutes last year as we blithely meandered the terraces admiring wildflowers and identifying fruit trees.

On the third-level terrace wall, a rusted pipe crumbles off as we hack at thorny blackberries. At the base, we discover a flat stone. As we shovel off dirt and pour on water, it grows. Something gigantic is buried here. Slowly, we uncover the roughly carved stone sink that once was used in the kitchen, before the "improved" concrete sink was installed. I'm afraid it's broken but we scrub mud away, wedge it out of its hole with a pick, and find intact the single stone, four feet long, about eighteen inches wide and eight inches thick, with a shallow indented basin for washing and with drainage ridges chipped out on either side. The corner drain is clogged with roots. We've been sorry our house didn't have this original and very characteristic object. Many old houses have similar sinks in place, draining directly out the kitchen wall and off a scallop-shaped stone shelf into the yard. I would like to wash my glasses in this prototype sink. We'll put it against the house outside under the trees, a place to keep ice and wine for parties and to wash up after gardening. It has been used to scrub enough crusty pots in its day; from now on: an honored place to fill a glass, a place for a pitcher of roses on the stone. It will be returning to good use after many years buried in dirt.

After a few more minutes of chopping, I'm about twelve feet down from the stone sink when two rusted hooks appear under the leaves. Beneath them, again we see a glimpse of flat stone. Ed shovels off a mound of dirt. In the middle, he hits a latch, around which is twisted a rusty coil of wire. We make out a circular opening. He has to angle the shovel in the crack to pry up the long-covered stone lid.

It is late afternoon, just after a thunderstorm, when the light turns that luminous gold I wish I could bottle and keep. Off comes the lid and the light that falls down strikes clear water in a wide natural cleft of white stone. We can see another undulation of the stone, too, where the water becomes aqua. We lie on our stomachs on the ground, taking turns sticking our heads and the flashlight down the hole. Fig roots seeking moisture slither down the rock wall. On the bottom, we see a big can on its side and easily read the magnified green words *Olio d'Oliva*. Not exactly like finding a Roman torso or amphora with dancing satyrs. A rusty pipe leans against the back of the white stone and we notice that it emerges just below the two hooks—someone stopped it up with a wine cork. It now seems obvious that the hooks once secured a hand pump and that this is a lost natural spring, hidden for years. How long? But wait. Just beneath the stone covering lies a remnant of another opening. What appears to be a corner of two layers of carved travertine lintel angles for a couple of feet, then disappears into rock. If the top were dug away, would this be an open pool? I read about a man nearby who went in his backyard on Christmas Eve to pick lettuce for dinner and caved into an Etruscan tomb with elaborate sarcophagi. Is this simply a fortuitous opening in rock that supplied water for farming? Why the carving? Why was the carving recovered with a plainer stone? This must have been covered when the second well nearby was dug. Now we have a third well; we're the latest layer of water seekers, our technology—the high-whining drills able to pierce any rock—long removed from that of the discoverer of this secret opening in the earth.

We call Signor Martini to come see this miraculous finding. Hands in pockets, he doesn't even lean over. *"Boh,"* he says (*boh* is an all purpose word, sort of "Well," "Oh," "Who knows?" or dismissal), then he waves a hand over it. *"Acqua."* He regards our fascination with abandoned houses and such things as ancient wells as further evidence that we are like children and must be humored in our whimsies. We show him the stone sink and explain that we will dig it out, clean it, and have it put up again. He simply shakes his head.

Giuseppe, who has come along, gets more excited. He should have been a Shakespearean actor. He punctuates every sentence with three or four gestures—his body totally participates in every word he speaks. He practically stands on his head looking down the hole. *"Molto acqua."* He points in both directions. We thought the well opened only in one, but because he is dangling upside down, he sees that the natural declivity of the rock extends in the opposite direction also. "O.K., yes!" These are his only English words, always uttered with arms wide apart, embracing an idea. He wants to install a new hand pump for garden use. We already have seen bright green pumps in the hardware store out in the Val di Chiana farm country. We buy one the next day, uncork the pipe, and place the pump right on the old hooks. Giuseppe teaches us to prime the pump by pouring water into it while pumping the handle rhythmically. Here's a motion long lost to my gene pool, but the creaky-smooth movement feels natural. After a few dry gulps, icy fresh water spills out into the bucket. We do have the presence of mind not to drink untested water. Instead, we open a bottle of wine on the terrace. Giuseppe wants to know about Miami and Las Vegas. We're looking out over the jungle growth on the hills. Giuseppe thinks the palm trees are what we really need to tend to. How will we ever trim them? They're taller than any ladder. After two glasses, Giuseppe shimmies up to the top of the taller one. He has the biggest grin I've ever seen. The tree leans and he slides down fast, too fast, lands in a heap on the ground. Ed quickly opens another bottle.

✳

As it turns out, the former owner was right about the water. If the water setup doesn't exactly rival the gardens of the Villa d'Este, it is ingenious enough to keep us digging and exploring for many days. The elaborate underground system makes us understand precisely how precious water is in the country. When it flows, you figure out ways to save it; when it is plentiful, as now, you must respect it. St. Francis of Assisi must have known this. In his poem "The Canticle of the Creatures," he wrote, "Be praised, O Lord, for Sister Water, the which is so useful, humble, precious and chaste." We convert instantly to short showers, to turning off the water quickly when washing dishes and brushing our teeth.

Interesting that this oldest well has channels on either side of it to divert runoff so that any extra water flows into the cistern. As we clean around the cistern, we find two stone tubs for washing clothes and more hooks in the stone wall above it, where another pump must have hung. Do not waste a drop. And there, not five feet away from the natural well, the old one that went dry last summer—now replenished fully by the winter rains. The hand pump for potted plants, Ed decides, the old well for the grass, and for the house, our fine new *pozzo*, a hundred meters deep, drilled through solid rock.

"Wonderful water," the *pozzoaiolo*, the well driller, assures us as we pay him a fortune, "down to inferno but cold as ice." We count out the cash. He does not want a check; why would anyone use a check unless they didn't actually have the money? *"Acqua, acqua,"* he says, gesturing over the entire property. "Enough water for a swimming pool."

* * *

We noticed, vaguely, when we bought the house that a stone wall perpendicular to the front had tumbled down in a few places. Weeds, sumac, and fig sprouted along the fallen rocks. The first time we saw the house the section of the yard above that wall was topped with forty feet of rose-covered pergola lined with lilacs. When we returned to negotiate for the purchase, the pergola was gone, torn down in a zeal to clean up the place. The roses and lilacs were leveled. When I lifted my eyes from that debacle to the house, I saw that the faded green shutters were repainted a glossy dark brown. Stunned, we hardly noticed the heaps of stones. Later, we realized that a 120-foot-long wall of immense stone would have to be rebuilt. We forgot about the romantic pergola with its climbing roses.

During those few weeks here last summer after buying the house, Ed started to take down parts of the wall adjacent to the tumbled sections. He thought stone building sounded gratifying— finding just the right stone to slide into place, tapping it in with a mallet, scoring stone surfaces, hitting them precisely to direct the split. The ancient craft is appealing; so is the good hard labor. An alarming pile of stones grew daily, as did his muscles. He became a little obsessed. He bought thick leather gloves. Big rocks went in one line, small ones in another, and flat ones in another. Like all the terrace walls on the property, this was drywall, with a depth of more than a yard: nicely fitted and stacked stones in front, neat as a jigsaw, with smaller ones behind. The structure leaned backward, to counteract the natural downward heave of the hillside. Unlike the lovely stone fences of New England, which cleared the fields of stone, these actually are structural; only with braced terraces is a hillside like ours an olive farm or vineyard. On one terrace where the stones fell, a large almond tree also toppled.

When we had to leave, about thirty feet of the wall lay in orderly piles. Ed was enthusiastic about stonework, though slightly daunted by the excavation and the surprising depth of stonework behind the facade of the wall. But instead of the miles to go, we noticed the huge heaps of stones he'd stacked.

Over the winter we read *Building with Stone* by Charles McRaven. Ideas such as sealing out moisture and foundations and frost lines started to crop up. The height of the remaining wall was not the actual height the rebuilt wall would have to be to support the broad terrace leading up to the house. Besides being 120 feet long, the wall must be fifteen feet high, buttressed from behind. As we read about packed fill, thrust, balance, and all the ways the earth shifts when it freezes, we began to think we had the Great Wall of China on our hands.

We were absolutely right. We've just had several experienced *muratori,* masons, out to view the remains. This job is a monster. Restoration work inside seems dwarfed beside this project. Still, Ed envisions himself apprenticed to a rugged man in a cap, a stone artist. *Santa Madonna, molto lavoro,* much work, each *muratore* exclaims in turn. *Molto. Troppo,* too much. We learn that Cortona recently adopted codes for walls such as this one because we're in an earthquake zone. Reinforced concrete will be required. We are not prepared to mix concrete.

We have five acres of blackberry and sumac jungle to deal with, trees that need pruning. Not to mention the house. The wall estimates are astronomical. Few even want to tackle the job.

This is how in Tuscany we build the Great Wall of Poland.

Signor Martini sends a couple of his friends by. I forewarn him that we are interested in getting the work done immediately and that we want a price for *fratelli*, brothers, not for *stranieri*, foreigners. We are recovering from the new well and still awaiting permits so the major house work can begin. His first friend says sixty days of labor. For his price we could buy a small steamer and motor around Greece. The second friend, Alfiero, gives a surprisingly reasonable estimate, plus has the terrific idea that another wall should run along the row of linden trees on an adjacent terrace. When you don't speak a language well, many of your cues for judging people are missing. We both think he is fey—an odd quality for a mason—but Martini says he is *bravo*. We want the work done while we are in residence, so we sign a contract. Our *geometra* doesn't know him and cautions us that if he's available he probably is not good. This kind of reasoning doesn't sink in with us.

The schedule calls for work to begin the following Monday. Monday, Tuesday, and Wednesday pass. Then a load of sand arrives. Finally, at the end of the week, Alfiero appears with a boy of fourteen and, to our surprise, three big Polish men. They set to work and by sundown, amazingly, the long wall is down. We watch all day. The Poles lift one-hundred-pound stones as though they were watermelons. Alfiero speaks not a word of Polish and they speak about five words of Italian. Fortunately, the language of manual labor is easy to act out. "*Via, via,*" Alfiero waves at the stones and they have at them. The next day they excavate dirt. Alfiero exits, to go to other jobs, I suppose. The boy, Alessandro, purely pouts. Alfiero is his stepfather and evidently is trying to teach the boy about work. He looks like a little Medici prince, petulant and bored as he stands around listlessly kicking stones with the toe of his tennis shoe. The Poles ignore him. From seven until twelve they don't stop. At noon they drive off in their Polski Fiat, returning at three for five more solid hours of labor.

The Italians, who have been "guest workers" at many times and in many countries, are thrown by the phenomenon happening in their own country. During this second summer at Bramasole, the newspapers are tolerant to indignant about Albanians literally washing up on the shores of southern Italy. Living in San Francisco, a city where immigrants arrive daily, we cannot get excited about their problem. Americans in cities have realized that migrations are on the increase; that the whole demographic tapestry is being rewoven on a vast scale in the late twentieth century. Europe is having a harder time coming to grips with this fact. We have our own poor, they tell us incredulously. Yes, we say, we do, too. Italy is amazingly homogeneous; it is rare to see a black or Asian face in Tuscany. Recently, Eastern Europeans, finding the German work force at last full of people like themselves, began arriving in this prosperous part of northern Italy. Now we understood Alfiero's estimate for the work. Instead of paying the normal Italian twenty-five thousand to thirty thousand lire per hour, he is able to pay nine thousand. He assures us they are legal workers and are covered by his insurance. The Poles are pleased with the hourly wage; at home, before the factory went kaput, they barely earned that much in a day.

Ed grew up in a Polish-American Catholic community in Minnesota. His parents were born of Polish immigrants and grew up speaking Polish on farms on the Wisconsin-Minnesota border. Of course, Ed knows no Polish. His parents wanted the children to be All American. The three words he tried out with the Poles they couldn't understand. But these men he can't understand seem very familiar. He's used to names like Orzechowski, Cichosz, and Borzyskowski. Passing in the yard, we nod and smile. The way we finally make contact with them comes through poetry. One afternoon I come across a poem by Czeslaw Milosz, long exiled in America but quintessentially a Polish poet. I knew he'd made a triumphant journey back to Poland a few

years ago. When Stanislao crossed the front terrace with the wheelbarrow, I asked, "Czeslaw Milosz?" He lit up and shouted to the two
others. After that, for a couple of days, when I passed one or the other
of them, he would say, "Czeslaw Milosz," as though it were a greeting,
and I would answer, "*Sì*, Czeslaw Milosz." I even knew I was pro-
nouncing the name correctly because I'd once practiced his name
when I had to introduce the poet at a reading. For several days before
that, I'd referred to him to myself as "Coleslaw" and had anxiety that
I would stand up before the audience and introduce him that way.

     Alfiero becomes a problem. He lights like a butterfly on one
project after another, starting something, doing a sloppy job, then taking off. Some days he just doesn't show up at all. When reasonable
questioning doesn't work, I revert to the old Southern habit of throwing a fit, which I find I still can do impressively. For a while, Alfiero
straightens up and pays attention, then like the whimsical child that
he is, he loses his focus. He has a charm. He throws himself into playful descriptions of frog races, fast Moto Guzzis, and quantities of
wine. Patting his belly, he speaks in the local dialect and neither of us
understands much of what he says. When it's time to throw a fit,
I call Martini, who does understand. He nods, secretly amused, Alfiero
looks abashed, the Poles let no expression cross their faces, and Ed is
mortified. I say that I am *malcontenta*. I use waving gestures and shake
my head and stamp my foot and point. He has used rows of tiny stones
under rows of big stones, there are vertical lines in the construction,
he has neglected to put a foundation in this entire section, the cement
is mostly sand. Martini begins to shout, and Alfiero shouts back at him,
since he dares not shout at me. I hear the curse *"Porca Madonna"* again,
a serious thing to say, and *"Porca miseria,"* pig misery, one of my favorite
curses of all times. After a scene, I expect sulking but, no, he turns up
sunny and forgetful the next day.

     "Buttare! Via!" Take it down, take it away. Signor Martini starts
to kick at Alfiero's work. "Where did your mother send you to school?

Where did you learn to make cement like sand castles?" Then they both turn and shout at the Poles. Now and then Martini rushes in the house and calls Alfiero's mother, his old friend, and we hear him shouting at her, then subsiding into soothing sounds.

They must think, privately, that we are brilliant to know so much about wall building. What neither Signor Martini nor Alfiero realizes is that the Poles let us know when something is not right. *"Signora,"* Krzysztof (we call him Cristoforo, as he wishes) says, motioning to me, *"Italia cemento."* He crumbles too-dry cement between his fingers. *"Polonia cemento."* He kicks a rock-hard section of the retaining wall. This has become a nationalistic issue. "Alfiero. *Poco cemento."* He puts his fingers to his lips. I thank him. Alfiero is using too little cement in his mixture. Don't tell. They begin to roll their eyes as a signal, or, after Alfiero departs, which usually is early in the day, to show us problems. Everything Alfiero touches seems bad, but we have a contract, they work for him, and we are stuck with him. However, without him, we would not have met the Poles.

Near the top of the wall, they uncover a ground-level stump. Alfiero maintains it is *non importa.* We see Riccardo shake his head quickly, so Ed says authoritatively that it will have to be dug out. Alfiero relents but wants to pour on *gasolio* to kill it. We point to the pristine new well not twenty feet away. The Poles began to dig and two hours later are still digging. Beneath the exposed stump, a mammoth three-legged root has wrapped itself around a stone as big as an automobile tire. Hundreds of inveigling roots shoot out in all directions. Here is the reason much of the wall had fallen in the first place. When they finally wrench it out, they insist on evening the legs and top, the stone still entwined. They load it in a wheelbarrow and take it up to the lime tree bower, where it will remain, the ugliest table in Tuscany.

They sing while they heave stone and their voices begin to sound like the way the work of the world should sound. Sometimes Cristoforo sings in a falsetto, a strangely moving song, especially coming from his big brown body. They never skimp on a minute's work, even though their boss is gone all the time. On days when their supplies are gone because Alfiero forgets to reorder, he capriciously tells them not to work. We hire them to help clear the terraces of weeds. Finally we have them sanding all the inside shutters. They seem to know how to do everything and work about twice as fast as anyone I've ever seen. At the end of the day, they strip and rinse off with the hose, dress in clean clothes, then we have a beer.

57

Don Fabbio, a local priest, lets them live in a back room of the church. For about five dollars apiece, he feeds all three of them three meals a day. They work six days a week—the priest does not allow them to work on Sunday—exchanging all the lire they make into dollars and stashing it away to take home for their wives and children. Riccardo is twenty-seven, Cristoforo thirty, and Stanislao forty. During the weeks they work, our Italian deteriorates. Stanislao has worked in Spain, so our communication begins to be an unholy mixture of four languages. We pick up Polish words: *jutro*, tomorrow; *stopa*, foot; *brudny*, dirty; *jezioro*, lake. Also something that sounds like *grubbia*, which was their name for Signor Martini's sloping stomach. They learned "beautiful" and "idiot" and quite a few Italian words, mostly infinitives.

Despite Alfiero, the wall is strong and beautiful. A curving flight of stairs, with flat tops on either side for pots of flowers, connects the first two terraces. The well and cistern have stone walls around them. From below, the wall looks immense. It's hard to get used to, since we liked the tumbled look, too. Like the other walls, soon it will have tiny plants growing in the cracks. Because the stone is old, it already looks natural in the landscape, if a bit tall. Now comes the pleasure of planning the walkway from the driveway around the well to the stone steps, the flowers and herbs for the border, and the flowerings and shadows of small trees along the wall. First we plant a white hibiscus, which pleases us by blooming immediately.

On a Sunday morning the Poles arrive after church, dressed in pressed shirts and trousers. We've seen them only in shorts. They've bought identical sandals at the local supermarket. Ed and I are clipping weeds when they arrive. We're dirty, wearing shorts, sweaty—reversed roles. Stanislao has a Soviet Union camera that looks to be from the thirties. We have Coca-Cola and they take several pictures. Anytime we serve them Coke, they always say, "Ah, America!" Before changing for work, they take us down to the wall and dig the dirt away from a few feet of the foundation. In large letters, they've written POLONIA in the concrete.

✳

Bramasole's staircase ascends three floors with a hand-made wrought-iron railing, whose symmetrical curves add a little rhythm to climbing. The fanlight, the bedroom terrace railing, only slightly rusted, and the railing around the balcony above the front door all employed some blacksmith for a long winter. The gate at the bottom of the driveway once was a stately entrance but like most things here, has been left to time far too long. The bottom bulges where lost tourists banged into it while turning around, after realizing they were on the wrong road to the Medici fortress. The lock has long since rusted and the hinges on one side have given way at the top, letting the gate drag.

Giuseppe has brought a friend, a maestro of iron, to see if our front gate can be salvaged. Giuseppe thinks not. We need something more suitable for the *bella villa*. The man who unfolds from Giuseppe's *cinque cento* could have stepped from behind a time shield of the Middle Ages. He is as tall and gaunt as Abraham Lincoln; he wears black overalls and his unusually black hair has no gleam. Hard to account for his strangeness; somehow he looks as though he's made out of something else. He uses few words but smiles shyly. I like him at once. Silently, he fingers the gate all over. Everything he has to say runs through his hands. It's easy to sense that he has given his life to this craft out of love. Yes, he nods, the gate can be repaired. The question is time. Giuseppe is disappointed. He envisions something grander. He draws shapes in the air with his arms, an arching top with arrows. A new one, more elaborate, with lights and an electronic device so we can be buzzed in the house and merely press a button for the gate to swing open. He has brought us this artist and we want him to *repair*?

We go to the shop to see the possibilities. En route, Giuseppe careens to the roadside and we leap out to see other gates this maestro has made. Some with swordlike designs, some with complex interlinking circles and wheat sheaves. One is topped with the initials of the owner, one, oddly, with a crown. We like the curved tops, the hoops and rings more than the more formidable arrow-topped ones, which seem like remnants of the time when the Guelfs and Ghibellines were looting and burning each other. All are obviously made to last forever. He rubs each one, saying nothing, letting the quality of his work speak for itself. I begin to imagine a small stylized sun at the center of ours, with twisted rays.

Ferro battuto, wrought iron, is an ancient craft in Tuscany. Every town has intricate locks on medieval doors, curly lanterns, holders for standards, garden gates, even fanciful iron animals and serpents shaped into rings for tying horses to the wall. Like other artisan traditions, this one is fast disappearing and it's easy to see why. The key word in blacksmith is black. His shop is charred, soot covers him, the antiquated equipment, and the forges that seem to have changed very little since Hephaestus lit the fire in Aphrodite's stove. Even the air seems hung with a fine veil of soot. All his neighbors have gates made by him. It must be satisfying to see one's work all around like that. His own house has a square patterned balcony, a flirtation, no doubt, with *moderne,* redeemed by attached baskets for flowers. The shop faces the house and between them are hens, ten or so cages of rabbits, a vegetable garden, and a plum tree with a handmade wooden ladder leaning up into the laden branches. After supper, he must climb up a few rungs and pick his dessert. My impression that he stepped out of time strengthens. Where *is* Aphrodite, surely somewhere near this forge?

"Time. Time is the only thing," he says. "I am *solo*. I have a son but . . ."

I can't imagine, at the end of the twentieth century, someone choosing this dark forge with traffic whizzing by, this collection of bands for wine barrels, andirons, fences, and gates. But I hope his son does step into it, or someone does. He brings over a rod that ends with a squared head of a wolf. He just holds it out to me, without a word. It reminds me of torch holders in Siena and Gubbio. We ask for an estimate to repair the *cancello*, also for an estimate for a new gate, rather simple but with a running form similar to the iron stair railing in the house, maybe a sun shape at the top closing, to go with the house's name. For once, we don't start asking for the date of completion, the one thing we've learned to insist on to counter the enviable Latin sense of endless time.

Do we really need a handmade gate? We keep saying, Let's keep it simple, this is not our real home. But somehow I know we'll want one he makes, even if it takes months. Before we leave, he forgets us. He's picking up pieces of iron, holding them in both hands for the heft or balance. He wanders among the anvils and hot grates. The gate will be in good hands. Already I can imagine its clank as I close it behind me.

✳

The well and the wall feel like significant accomplishments. The house, however, still is untouched. Until the main jobs are finished, there is little to do. No point in painting, when the walls will have to be opened for the heating pipes. The Poles have stripped the windows and have begun scrubbing down the whitewash in preparation for painting. Ed and I work on the terraces or travel around selecting bathroom tile, fixtures, hardware, paint; we look, too, for the old thin bricks for

the new kitchen's floor. One day we buy two armchairs at a local furniture store. By the time they're delivered, we realize they're awkward
and the dark paisley fabric rather weird, but we find them sumptuously
comfortable, after sitting upright in the garden chairs for weeks. On
rainy nights we pull them face-to-face with a cloth-covered crate
between them, our dining table with a candle, jam jar with wildflowers, and a feast of pasta with eggplant, tomatoes, and basil. On cool
nights we build a twig fire for a few minutes, just to take the damp chill
off the room.

  Unlike last summer, this July is rainy. Impressive storms hit frequently. In the daytime, I'm thrilled because of my childhood in the
South, where they really know how to put on the sound and light. San
Francisco rarely has thunderstorms and I miss them. "This heat has to
break," my mother would say, and it would, with immense cracks and
bolts followed by sheet lightning when the whole sky flashes on a million kilowatts. Often the storms seem to arrive at night. I'm sitting up
in bed, drawing kitchen and bathroom plans on graph paper; Ed is
reading something I never expected to see him reading. Instead of the
Roman poets, tonight it's *Plastering Skills*. Beside him is *The Home Water
Supply*. Rain starts to clatter in the palm trees. I go to the window and
lean out, then quickly step back. Bolts spear into the ground—jagged
like cartoon drawings of lightning—four, five, six at once, surrounding
the house. Thunderheads swarm over the hills and the quiet rolling
suddenly changes its tune and starts to explode so close it feels like my
own backbone snapping. The house shakes; this is serious. The lights
go out. We fasten the windows inside and still the wind whips rain
through cracks we didn't know were there. Spooky wind sucks in and
out of the chimney. Wild night. Rain lashes the house and the two silly
palms give and give in the wind. I smell ozone. I am certain the house
has been struck. This storm has selected our house. It won't move on;
we're the center and may be washed downhill to Lake Trasimeno.
"Which would you prefer," I ask, "landslide or direct hit by lightning?"

We get under the covers like ten-year-olds, shouting "Stop!" and "No!" each time the sky lights up. Thunder enters the walls and rearranges the stones.

When the big storm starts passing to the north, the black sky is left washed clean for stars. Ed opens the window and the breeze sends in pine scent from blown-down limbs and scattered needles. The electricity still is out. As we sit propped up on pillows, waiting for our hearts to slow down, we hear something at the window. A small owl has landed on the sill. Its head swivels back and forth. Perhaps its perch was blown down or it is disoriented by the storm. When the moon breaks through the clouds, we can see the owl staring inside at us. We don't move. I'm praying, Please don't come in the room. I am deathly afraid of birds, a holdover phobia from childhood, and yet I am entranced by the small owl. Owls seem always to be more than themselves, totemic in America, symbolic at least, and here, mythological as well. I think of Minerva's owl. But really it's just a small creature that belongs to this hill. We have seen its larger forebears several times at evening. Neither of us speaks. Since it stays, we finally fall asleep and wake in the morning to see that it has flown. At the window, only the quarter of six light—raked gold angling across the valley, suffusing the air briefly before the sun clears the hills and lifts into the absolved, clear day.

THE WILD ORCHARD

THE WATERMELON HOUR—A FAVORITE PAUSE IN THE AFTER-
noon. Watermelon is arguably the best taste in the world, and I must
admit that the Tuscan melons rival in flavor those Sugar Babies we
picked hot out of the fields in South Georgia when I was a child.
I never mastered the art of the thump. Whether the melon is ripe or
not, the thump sounds the same to me. Each one I cut, however, seems
to be at its pinnacle—toothy crispness, audacious sweetness. When
we're sharing melon with the workers, I notice that they eat the white
of the melon. When they finish, their rind is a limp green strip. Sitting
on the stone wall, sun on my face, big slice of watermelon—I'm seven
again, totally engrossed in shooting seeds between my fingers and
spooning out circles from the dripping quarter moon of fruit.

Suddenly, I notice the five pine trees edging the driveway are
full of activity. It sounds as though squirrels are pulling Velcro apart, or
biting into *panini*, those hard Italian rolls. A man leaps from his car,
quickly picks up three cones, and speeds off. Then Signor Martini
arrives. I expect he's bringing news of someone who can plow the
terraces. He picks up a cone and shakes it against the wall. Out come
black nubs. He cracks one with a rock and holds up a husk-covered

oval. "*Pinolo,*" he announces. Then he points to the dusky beads scattered all over the driveway. "*Torta della nonna,*" he states, in case I missed the significance. Better still, I think, pesto to make with all the proliferating basil that resulted from sticking six plants in the ground. I love pine nuts on salads. Pine nuts! And I've been stepping on them.

64

Of course I knew that *pinoli* come from pine trees. I've even inspected trees in my yard at home to see if, somewhere hidden in the cone, I would find pine nuts. I never thought of the trees lining the driveway as the bearers; thus far they simply have been trees that need no immediate attention. They're those painterly-looking pines, sometimes stunted by coastal winds, that line many Mediterranean beach towns, the kind Dante wandered among at Ravenna when he was in exile there. These along the driveway are feathery and tall. Imagine that plain *pino domestico* (I see in my tree book) will yield those buttery nuts, so delicious when toasted. One of the *nonnas* who make all those heavy *pinolo* studded tarts must have lived here. She must have made delectable ravioli with ground *noccioli,* hazelnut, stuffing, and macaroons and other *torte,* too, because there also are twenty almonds and a shady hazelnut tree that droops with its crop of nuts. The *nocciolo* grows with a chartreuse ruff around the nut, as though each one is ready to be worn in a lapel. The almonds are encased in tender green velvet. Even the tree that collapsed over the terrace and must be dying has sent out a plentiful crop.

Perhaps Signor Martini should be back at the office, prepared to show more foreign clients houses without roofs or water, but he joins me picking up the *pinoli.* Like most Italians I've met, he seems to have time to give. I love his quality of becoming involved in the moment. The sooty covering quickly blackens our hands. "How do you know so many things—were you born in the country?" I ask. "Is this the one day the cones fall?" He has told me previously that the hazelnuts are ripe on August 22, feast day of the foreign St. Filbert.

He tells me he grew up in Teverina, on down the road from Bramasole's *località*, and lived there until the war. I would love to know if he turned partisan or if he stuck to Mussolini until the end, but I merely ask if the war came near Cortona. He points up to the Medici fortress above the house. "The Germans occupied the fort as a radio communication center. Some of the officers quartered in the farmhouses came back after the war and bought those places." He laughs. "Never understood why the peasants weren't helpful." We've piled twenty or so cones on the wall.

65

I don't ask if this house was occupied by Nazis. "What about the partisans?"

"Everywhere," he says, gesturing. "Even thirteen-year-old boys—killed while picking strawberries or tending sheep. Shot. Mines everywhere." He does not continue. Abruptly, he says his mother died at ninety-three a few years ago. "No more *torta della nonna*." He is in a wry mood today. After I squash several *pinoli* flat with a stone, he shows me how to hit so that the shell releases the nut whole. I tell him my father is dead, my mother confined since a major stroke. He says he is now alone. I don't dare ask about wife, children. I have known him two summers and this is the first personal information we have exchanged. We gather the cones into a paper bag and when he leaves he says, *"Ciao."* Regardless what I've learned in language classes, among adults in rural Tuscany *ciao* is not tossed about. *Arrivederla* or, more familiarly, *arrivederci* are the usual good-byes. A little shift has occurred.

After half an hour of banging pine nuts, I have about four tablespoons. My hands are sticky and black. No wonder the two-ounce cellophane bags at home are so expensive. I have in mind that I will make one of those ubiquitous *torta della nonnas*, which seem sometimes to be the beginning and end of Italian desserts. The French and American variety of desserts is simply not of interest in the local cuisine. I'm convinced you have to have been raised on most Italian sweets to appreciate them; generally, their cakes and pastries are too dry for my palate. *Torta della nonna*, fruit tarts, perhaps a *tiramisu* (a dessert I loathe)—that's it, except in expensive restaurants. Most pastry shops and many bars serve this grandmother's torte. Though they can be pleasing, sometimes they taste as though *intonoco*, plaster, is one of the ingredients. No wonder Italians order fruit for dessert. Even gelato, which used to be divine all over Italy, is not dependably good anymore. Though many advertise that the gelato is their own, they neglect to say it's sometimes made with envelopes of powdered mix. When you find the real peach or strawberry gelato, it's unforgettable. Fortunately, fruit submerged in bowls of cool water seems perfect at the end of a summer dinner, especially with the local *pecorino*, Gorgonzola, or a wedge of *parmigiano*.

Translating grams into cups as best I can, I copy a recipe from a cookbook. Hundreds of versions of *torta della nonna* exist. I like the kind with polenta in the cake and a thin layer of filling in the middle. I don't mind the extra hour to pound open the pine nuts that at home I would have pulled from the freezer. First, I make a thick custard with two egg yolks, 1/3 cup flour, 2 cups milk, and 1/2 cup sugar. This makes too much, for my purposes, so I pour two servings into bowls to eat later. While the custard cools, I make the dough: 1-1/2 cups polenta, 1-1/2 cups flour, 1/3 cup sugar, 1-1/2 teaspoons baking powder, 4 oz. butter cut into the dry ingredients, one whole egg plus one yolk stirred in. I halve the dough and spread one part in a pie pan, cover with custard, then roll out the other half of the dough and cover the custard, crimping the edges of the dough together. I sprinkle a handful of toasted pine nuts on top and bake at 350° for twenty-five minutes. Soon the kitchen fills with a promising aroma. When it smells done, I place the golden *torta* on the kitchen windowsill and dial Signor Martini's number. "My *torta della nonna* is ready," I tell him.

When he arrives I brew a pot of espresso, then cut him a large piece. With the first forkful, he gets a dreamy look in his eyes.

"*Perfetto*" is his verdict.

❋

Besides the nuts, the original *nonna* planned more of an Eden here. What's left: three kinds of plums (the plump Santa Rosa type are called locally *coscia di monaca*, nun's thigh), figs, apples, apricots, one cherry (half dead), apples, and several kinds of pears. Those ripening now are small green-going-to-russet, with a crisp sweetness. Her gnarly apples—I'd love to know what varieties they are—may not be salvageable, but they're now putting forth dwarfish fruit that looks like the before pictures in ads for insect sprays. Many of the trees must be volunteers; they're too young to have been alive when someone lived here, and often they're in odd places. Since four plums are directly below a line of ten on a terrace, they obviously sprang from fallen fruit.

I'm sure she gathered wild fennel, dried the yellow flowers, and tossed the still-green bunches onto the fire when she grilled meat. We uncover grapes buried in the brush along the edges of the terraces. Some aggressive ones still send out long tangles of stems. Tiny bunches are forming. Along the terraces like a strange graveyard, the ancient grape stones are still in place—knee-high stones shaped like headstones, with a hole for an iron rod. The rod extends beyond the edge of the terrace, thereby giving the grower more space. Ed strings wire from rod to rod and lifts the grapes up to train them along the wire. We're amazed to realize that the whole place used to be a vineyard.

At the huge *enoteca* in Siena, a government-sponsored tasting room where wines from all over Italy are displayed and poured, the waiter told us that most Italian vineyards are less than five acres, about our size. Many small growers join local cooperatives in producing various kinds of wine, including *vino da tavola,* table wine. As we hoe weeds around the vines, naturally, we begin to think of a year 2000 Bramasole Gamay or Chianti. The uncovered grapes explain the heaps of bottles we inherited. They may yield the rough-and-ready red served in pitchers in all the local restaurants. Or perhaps the flinty Grechetto, a lemon white wine of this area. Ah, yes, this land was waiting for us. Or we for it.

Nonna's most essential, elemental ingredient surely was olive oil. Her woodstove was fired with the prunings; she dipped her bread in a plate of oil for toast, she doused her soups and pasta sauces with her lovely green oil. Cloth sacks of olives hung in the chimney to smoke over the winter. Even her soap was made from oil and the ashes from her fireplace. Her husband or his employee spent weeks tending the olive terraces. The old lore was to prune so that a bird could fly through the main branches without brushing its wings against the leaves. He had to know exactly when to pick. The trees can't be wet or the olives will mildew before you can get them to the mill. To prepare olives to eat, all the bitter glucoside must be leached out by curing them in salt or soaking them in lye or brine. Besides the practical, a host of enduring superstitions determine the best moment to pick or plant; the moon has bad days and good. Vergil, a long time ago, observed farmers' beliefs: Choose the seventeenth day after the full moon to plant, avoid the fifth. He also advises scything at night, when dew softens the stubble. I'm afraid Ed might veer off a terrace if he tried that.

Of our olives, some are paradigms—ancient, twisted, gnarled. Many are clusters of young shoots that sprang up in a circle around damaged trunks. In this benign crescent of hillside, it's hard to imagine the temperature dropping to minus six degrees, as it did in 1985, but gaps between trees reveal huge dead stumps. The olives will have to be revived from their long neglect. Each tree needs to be cleared of encroaching sumac, broom, and weeds, then pruned and fertilized. The terraces must be plowed and cleaned. This is major work but it will have to wait. Since olives are almost immortal, another year won't hurt.

"An olive leaf he brings, pacific sign," Milton wrote in *Paradise Lost*. The dove that flew back to the ark with the branch in its beak made a good choice. The olive tree does impart a sense of peace. It must be, simply, the way they participate in time. These trees are here and will be. They were here. Whether we are or someone else is or no one, each morning they'll be twirling their leaves and inching up toward the sun.

A few summers ago, a friend and I hiked in Majorca above Soller. We climbed across and through miles of dramatic, enormous olives on broad terraces. Up high, we came upon stone huts where the grove tenders sheltered themselves. Although we got lost and encountered a pacing bull in a meadow, we felt this immense peace all day, walking among those trees that looked and may have been a thousand years old. Walking these few curving acres here gives me the same feeling. Unnatural as it is, terracing has a natural feel to it. Some of the earliest methods of writing, called boustrophedon, run from right to left, then from left to right. If we were trained that way, it probably is a more efficient way to read. The etymology of the word reveals Greek roots meaning "to turn like an ox plowing." And that writing is like the rising terraces: The U-turn space required by an ox with plow suddenly loops up a level and you're going in the other direction.

✳

The five *tiglio* trees, old world lindens or limes, bear no fruit. They provide shade along the broad terrace beside the house when the sun will not allow us on the front terrace. We have lunch under the *tigli* almost every day. Their blossoms are like pearly earrings dangling from the leaves, and when they open—all it seems on the same day—fragrance envelopes the whole hillside. At the height of bloom, we sit on the upstairs patio, just adjacent to the trees, trying to identify the fragrance.

69

I think it smells like the perfume counter in the dime store; Ed thinks it smells like the oil his uncle Syl used to slick back his hair. Either way, it attracts every bee in town. Even at night, when we take our coffee up to the patio, they are working the flowers over. Their collective buzz sounds like a major swarm approaching. It's both lulling and alarming. Ed stays in the doorway at first because he's allergic to bee sting, but they aren't interested in us. They have their honey sacs to fill, their legs to dust with pollen.

Allergic or not, Ed longs for beehives. He tries to get me interested in being the beekeeper. He takes the fact that I never have been stung by a bee to mean that they won't sting me. I point out that I once was stung by a whole nest of wasps but somehow that doesn't count. He imagines a row of hives at the end of the lime trees. "You'll be fascinated when you look in the hive," he says. "When it's hot, dozens of workers stationed at the door whir their wings to cool the queen." I've noticed that he has collected lots of local honeys. Frequently there's a pot of hot water on the stove with a jar of waxy, stiff honey softening in it. The acacia is pale and lemony; the dark chestnut is so thick a spoon will stand up straight in it. He has a jar of *timo*, thyme honey, and, of course, the *tiglio*. The wildest is *macchia*, from the salty coastal shrubs of Tuscany. "The queen bee's life is totally overrated. All she does is lay eggs, lay eggs. She takes *one* nuptial flight. That one stuns her with enough fertile power to be trapped in the hive forever. The workers—the sexually undeveloped females—have the best life. They have fields of flowers to roll in. Imagine turning over and over inside a rose." I can tell he's carried away with the idea. I'm getting interested myself.

"What do they eat inside the hive all winter?"

"Beebread."

"Beebread? Are you serious?"

"It's a mixture of pollen and honey. And the worker excretes gold wax from her stomach for the comb. Those neat hexagons!"

I try to imagine the size of a worker bee's intestinal system, how many times she must fly from the hive to the *tiglio* to make even a tablespoon of honey. A thousand times? A jar must represent a million flights of bees carrying a heavy cargo of honeydew, their legs sticky with pollen. In *The Georgics*, which is sort of an ancient farmer's almanac, Vergil writes that bees lift small stones to ballast themselves as they fly through boisterous east winds. He is wise on the subject of bees but not entirely to be trusted; he thought they would generate spontaneously from the decayed carcass of a cow. I like the image of a bee clutching a small stone, like a football player holding the ball to his chest as he barrels down the field. "Yes, I can see four hives painted green. I like the beekeeper's gear, that medieval-looking veil, lifting the dark combs—we could roll our own candles from the wax." Now I'm drawn into this idea.

But he stands up and leans out into the dizzying fragrance. Practicality has left him. "The wasps are anarchistic, whereas the bees . . ."

I gather up the coffee cups. "Maybe we should wait until the house is done."

✳

Figs reveal water. On the terraces they grow near the stone chutes we discovered. The natural well has webby roots crawling down into it from the fig above. I'm mixed on figs. The fleshy quality feels spooky. In Italian, *il fico*, fig, has a slangy turn into *la fica*, meaning vulva. Possibly because of the famous fig leaf exodus from Eden, it seems like the most ancient of fruits. Oddest, too—the fig flower is inside the fruit. To pull one open is to look into a complex, primitive, infinitely sophisticated life cycle tableau. Fig pollination takes place through an interaction with a particular kind of wasp about one eighth of an inch long. The female bores into the developing flower inside the fig. Once in, she delves with her oviposter, a curved needle nose, into the female flower's ovary, depositing her own eggs. If her oviposter can't reach the ovary (some of the flowers have long styles), she still fertilizes the fig flower with the pollen she collected from her travels. Either way, one half of this symbiotic system is served—the wasp larvae develop if she has left her eggs or the pollinated fig flower produces seed. If reincarnation is true, let me not come back as a fig wasp. If the female can't find a suitable nest for her eggs, she usually dies of exhaustion inside the fig. If she can, the wasps hatch inside the fig and all the males are born without wings. Their sole, brief function is sex. They get up and fertilize the females, then help them tunnel out of the fruit. Then they die. The females fly out, carrying enough sperm from the tryst to fertilize all their eggs. Is this appetizing, to know that however luscious figs taste, each one is actually a little graveyard of wingless male wasps? Or maybe the sensuality of the fruit comes from some flavor they dissolve into after short, sweet lives.

✳

The women in my family always have made bread and butter pickles and muscadine jellies and watermelon rind pickles and peach preserves and plum butters. I feel drawn to the scalding kettle, with a flat of rapidly softening raspberries leaking juice on the counter, to the syrupy clove-scented bowls of sweet peaches about to be poured into an astringent vinegar bath, to ring-finger-sized cucumbers. In California, I've cried over rubber sealing rings that turned to gum, over jams that wouldn't jam, over a cauldron of guavas that made two dozen jars of gray jelly instead of the clear exotic topaz I expected. I don't have the gene my mother had for laying-by rows of crimson and emerald jars of fruit preserves and the little pickled things called *sottaceto* (under vinegar) here. When I look at the product of a sweating afternoon, all I can think is "Botulism?"

This long-lost owner who placed the fruit trees on a terrace so they sweetly dangle over a grassy walk, she, I'm sure, had a shelf under the stairs for her confitures, and no qualms about breaking open her spicy plums on a January morning. Here, I think, I'll master the art my mother should have passed to me as easily as she passed her taste for hand-painted china and expensive shoes.

From the Saturday market I lug a box of prime peaches down-hill to the car. They are so beautiful all I really want to do is pile them in a basket and look at the delicious colors. In the one cookbook I have here so far, I find Elizabeth David's recipe for peach marmalade. Nothing could be simpler: The halved peaches simply are cooked with a little sugar and water, cooled, then cooked again the next day, until the preserves set when ladled onto a saucer. Elizabeth David notes, "This method makes a rather extravagant but very delicious preserve. Unfortunately it tends to form a skin of mold within a very short time, but this does not affect the rest of the jam, some of which I have kept for well over a year, even in a damp house." I'm a little bothered by this mold note, and she's vague about sterilizing jars and never mentions listening for the *whoosh* of the seal I heard as Mother's green tomato pickles cooled. I remember my mother tapping the tops to make sure the lid had sucked down. It sounds as though Elizabeth David just dishes it up into the jars then forgets it, scraping off mold with impunity before spreading some on her toast. Still, she says "rather extravagant but very delicious," and if Elizabeth David says that, I believe her. Since I have all these peaches, I decide to make seven pounds and just eat the rest. We'll use the preserves this summer before any unappetizing mold can form in this damp house. I'll give some to new friends, who will wonder why I'm not painting shutters instead of stirring fruit.

I drop the peaches into boiling water for a moment, watching the rosy colors intensify, then spoon them out and slide the skins off as easily as taking off a silk slip. This recipe is simple, not even a few drops of lemon juice or a grating of nutmeg or a clove or two. I remember my mother putting in a kernel from inside the peach pit, an almond-scented secret nut. Soon the kitchen fills with a fly-attracting sweetness. The next day, I boil the jars for good measure, while the fruit cooks down again, then spoon it in. I have five lovely jars of jam, peachy but not too sweet.

74

The *forno* in Cortona bakes a crusty bread in their wood oven, a perfect toast. Breakfast is one of my favorite times because the mornings are so fresh, with no hint of the heat to come. I get up early and take my toast and coffee out on the terrace for an hour with a book and the green-black rows of cypresses against the soft sky, the hills pleated with olive terraces that haven't changed since the seasons were depicted in medieval psalters. Sometimes the valley below is like a bowl filled up with fog. I can see hard green figs on two trees and pears on a tree just below me. A fine crop coming in. I forget my book. Pear cobbler, pear chutney, pear ice, green figs (would the wasps already be in green figs?) with pork, fig fritters, fig and *nocciolo* tart. May summer last a hundred years.

THE HOUSE, ONLY TWO KILOMETERS FROM TOWN, FEELS like a deep country place. We can't see any neighbors, although we hear the man way above us calling *vieni qua*, come here, to his dog. The summer sun hits like a religious conviction. I can tell time by where the sun strikes the house, as though it were a gigantic sundial. At five-thirty, the first rays smack the patio door, routing us out of bed and giving us the pleasure of dawn. At nine, a slab of sunlight falls into my study from the side window, my favorite window in the house for its framed view over the cypresses, the groves in the valley, and out into the Apennines. I want to paint a watercolor of it but my watercolors are awful, fit only to be stored on a closet shelf. By ten, the sun swings high over the front of the house and stays there until four, when a cut of shadow across the lawn signals that the sun is heading toward the other side of the mountain. If we walk to town that way in late afternoon, we see a prolonged, grandiose sunset over the Val di Chiana, lingering until it finally just dissolves, leaving enough streaked gold and saffron behind to light a way home until nine-thirty, when indigo dark sets in.

On moonless nights it is as black as inside an egg. Ed has gone back to Minnesota for his parents' fiftieth wedding anniversary. A shutter bangs; otherwise, the silence reverberates so strongly that I think I can hear my own blood circulating. I expect to lie awake, to imagine a drug-crazed intruder with an Uzi creeping up the stairs in the dark. Instead, in the wide bed with flowered sheets, I spread my books, cards, and notepaper around me and indulge in the rare act of writing letters to friends. A second indulgence goes straight back to high-school days—consuming a plate of brownies and a Coke while copying paragraphs and verses I like into my notebook. If only Sister, my black long-haired cat, were here. She is truly a good companion for solitude. It's far too hot for her to sleep against my feet, as she likes to do; she would have to stay on a pillow at the foot of the bed. I sleep like óne newly born and in the morning have coffee on the patio, walk to town for groceries, work on the land, come in for water, and it is only ten o'clock. Hours go by without the need to speak.

After a few days, my life takes on its own rhythm. I wake up and read for an hour at three A.M.; I eat small snacks—a ripe tomato eaten like an apple—at eleven and three rather than lunch at one. At six I'm up, but by siesta time, the heat of the day, I'm ready for two hours in bed. Slumber sounds heavier than sleep, and with the hum of a small fan, it's slumber I fall into. At last, I have time to take a coverlet outside at night and lie on my back with the flashlight and the star chart. With the Big Dipper easily fixed right over the house, I finally locate Pollux in Gemini and Procyon in Canis Minor. I forget the stars and here they are, so alive all along, pulsing and falling.

A French woman and her English husband walk up the driveway and introduce themselves as neighbors. They've heard Americans bought the place and are curious to meet those mad enough to take on this ordeal of restoration. They invite me to lunch the next day. Since both are writers and are restoring their small farmhouse, we fall into instant camaraderie. Should they have the staircase here or there, what to do with this tiny room, would a bedroom in the animal stall downstairs be too dark? The *comune* won't allow you to cut windows, even in almost airless farmhouses; exteriors must remain intact on historical property. They invite me to dinner the next night and introduce me to two other foreign writers, French and Asian-American. By the time Ed returns in a week, we're invited to the house of these writers.

The table is set under a shady grape arbor. Cold salads, cold wine, fruit, a grand cheese soufflé somehow steamed on top of the stove. Heat shimmers around the olive trees in the distance. On the stone patio, we're cool. We're introduced to the other guests: novelists, journalists, translators, a nonfiction writer—all older expatriates who've settled in these hills and restored properties. To live wholly in another country fascinates me. I'm curious how the trip or assignment to Italy turned into a lifetime for each of them and I ask Fenella, the international journalist, on my right, about this. "You can't imagine what Rome was in the fifties. Magic. I simply fell in love—like you fall in love with a person—and schemed to find a way to stay there. It wasn't easy. I got on as a stringer for Reuters. Look at the old movies and you'll see there were almost no cars. This was not long after the war and Italy was devastated, but the *life*! It was unbelievably cheap, too. Of course we didn't have much money but we lived in enormous apartments in grand *palazzi* for nothing. Every time I went back to America, I just couldn't wait to get back. It wasn't a rejection—or maybe it was. Anyway, I've never wanted to be anywhere else."

"We feel the same way," I say, and then realize that's not really the truth. I succumb totally to the "magic" of this place, but I know the appeal to me is partly the balance it restores to my life in America. I'm not about to leave there, even if I could. I try to amend what I've said. "My job at home is hard but I really love it—I'm pushed by it.

And San Francisco is not home at the blood root, but it's a lucky, very beautiful place to live, earthquakes and all. Spending time here lets me escape the craziness and violence and downright surreal aspects of America, and my own overscheduled life. Three weeks after arrival, I realize I've let down some guard that is so instinctive to me, living in an American city, that I don't realize I have it." She looks at me with sympathy. At this point, the violence in America is hard for anyone to comprehend. "Literally, my pulse slows," I continue. "Even so, I sense that I can best develop my thinking there—it's my culture, my rough edge, my past." I'm not sure I've explained myself well. She raises her glass to me.

"*Esatto,* my daughter feels the same. You didn't come along in time to know Rome back then. It's terrible now. But then it was irresistible." I suddenly realize they're in double exile, from the United States and from Rome.

Max joins in. He had to go to Rome last week and the traffic was horrendous, then the gypsies accosted him, as if he were a tourist, pressing their cardboard against him in an effort to distract him while they tried to pick his pocket. "Long ago, I learned to put the evil eye on them," he tells Ed and me. "They scatter then." They all agree, Italy is not what it used to be. What is? All my adult life I've heard how Silicon Valley used to be all orchards, how Atlanta used to be genteel, how publishing used to be run by gentlemen, how houses used to cost what a car costs now. All true, but what can you do but live now? Our friends who've recently bought a place in Rome are wild about the city. We love it. Maybe living with Bay Bridge traffic and San Francisco prices prepares us for anything.

One guest is a writer I have long admired. She moved here about twenty years ago, after living for years in the postwar wild south of Italy and then in Rome. I knew she lived here and even had been given her telephone number by a mutual acquaintance in Georgia, where she now spends a part of every year. Cold calls always have been hard for me to make and I am a little awed by the woman who wrote, in luminous, austere prose, about the dark, raucous, convoluted lives of women down in ravaged Basilicata.

Elizabeth is across the table and down from me. I see her cover her glass with her hand as Max starts to pour wine. "You know I never drink wine at lunch." Ah, the austerity. She wears a blue cotton shirt with some vaguely religious-looking medallion around her neck. She has a dead-level blue gaze, fair skin, and a voice I think has a touch of my own accent.

I lean forward and venture, "Is that a trace of a Southern accent?"

"I certainly hope not," she snaps—do I see a hint of a smile?—and quickly turns back to the famous translator beside her. I look down into my salad.

By the time Richard serves his lemon gelato made with mascarpone, the gathering is mellowing. Several empty wine bottles stand on a side table. The intense sun is now caught in the limbs of a chestnut. Ed and I join in where we can but this is a lively group of old friends with years of shared experiences. Fenella talks about her research trips to Bulgaria and Russia; her husband, Peter, tells a story about bringing a gray parrot in his coat pocket when he came back from an assignment in Africa. Cynthia talks about a family dispute over her famous mother's notebooks. Max makes us laugh over his unbelievable luck in sitting next to a film producer on a flight to New York, launching into a description of his script to this captive, who finally said to send him the script. Now the producer is coming to visit and has bought the option. Elizabeth looks bemused.

As the party breaks up she says, "You were supposed to call me. I've tried to get your number but there's no listing. Irby [a friend of my sister's] told me you've bought a house here. In fact, I met your sister at a dinner in Rome—Georgia, that is." I make excuses about the confusions of the house, then impulsively ask her to dinner on Sunday.

Impulsively, because we don't have furniture, dishes, linen—only the rudimentary kitchen with a few pots and plates.

✳

I pick up a linen cloth at the market to cover the ramshackle table left behind in the house, arrange wildflowers in a jar and place it in a flowerpot, plan dinner carefully but keep it simple: ravioli with sage and butter, sautéed chicken and *prosciutto* rolls, fresh vegetables and fruit. As Elizabeth arrives, Ed is moving the table out to the terrace. The entire top and one leg fall off—either an icebreaker or a disaster. She helps us piece the table together and Ed pounds in a few nails. Covered and set, it looks quite nice. We tour the big empty house and begin to talk drainpipes, wells, chimneys, whitewash. She completely restored a noble *casa colonica* when she moved here. As a wall came down the first day, she found an angry sow left behind by the peasants. Quickly, it becomes clear that she knows *everything* about Italy. Ed and I begin what is to become the ten thousand questions. Where do you get your water tested? How long was a Roman mile? Who's the best butcher? Can you buy old roof tiles? Is it better to apply for residency? She has been an intense observer of Italy since 1954 and knows an astonishing amount about the history, language, politics, as well as the telephone numbers of good plumbers, the name of a woman who prepares *gnocchi* with the lightest touch north of Rome. Long dinner under the moon, hoping the table won't keel over. Suddenly we have a friend.

Every morning, Elizabeth goes into town, buys a paper, and takes her espresso at the same café. I'm up early, too, and love to see the town come alive. I walk in with my Italian verb book, memorizing conjugations as I walk. Sometimes I take a book of poetry because walking suits poetry. I can read a few lines, savor or analyze them, read a few more, sometimes just repeat a few words of the poem; this meditative strolling seems to free the words. The rhythm of my walking matches the poet's cadence. Ed finds this eccentric, thinks I will be known as the weird American, so when I get to the town gate, I put away my book and concentrate on seeing Maria Rita arranging vegetables, the shopkeeper sweeping the street with one of those witch brooms made of twigs, the barber lighting his first smoke, leaning back in his chair with a tabby sleeping on his lap. Often I run into Elizabeth. Without plan, we begin to meet a morning or two a week.

81

❋

In town, too, Ed and I are beginning to feel more at home. We try to buy everything right in the local shops: hardware, electrical transformers, contact lens cleaner, mosquito candles, film. We do not patronize the cheaper supermarket in Camucia; we go from the bread store to the fruit and vegetable shop, to the butcher, loading everything into our blue canvas shopping bags. Maria Rita starts to go in back of her shop and bring out the just-picked lettuces, the choice fruit. "Oh, pay me tomorrow," she says if we only have large bills. In the post office, our letters are affixed with several stamps by the postmistress then individually hand-canceled with vengeance, *whack, whack, "Buon giorno, signori."* At the crowded little grocery store, I count thirty-seven kinds of dried pasta and, on the counter, fresh *gnocchi, pici*, thick pasta in long strands, fettuccine and two kinds of ravioli. By now they know what kind of bread we want, that we want the *bufala*, buffalo milk mozzarella, not the *normale*, regular cow's milk kind.

We buy another bed for my daughter's upcoming visit. Box springs don't exist here. The metal bed frame holds a base of woven wood on which the mattress rests. I thought of the slats in my spool bed when I was growing up, how the mattress, springs and all, collapsed when I jumped up and down on the bed. But this is securely made, the bed firm and comfortable. A very young woman with tousled black curls and black eyes sells old linens at the Saturday market. For Ashley's bed I find a heavy linen sheet with crocheted edges and big square pillowcases of lace and embroidery. Surely these accompanied a bride to her marriage. The condition is so good I wonder if she ever took them from her trunk. They have dusty lines where they've been folded, so I soak them in warm suds in the hip bath, then hang them out to dry in the midday sun, a natural strong bleach that turns them back to white.

Elizabeth has decided to sell her house and rent the former priest's wing attached to a thirteenth-century church called Santa Maria del Bagno, Saint Mary of the Baths. Although she won't move until winter, she begins to sort her belongings. Perhaps out of memory of that first dinner, she gives us an iron outdoor table and four curly chairs. Years ago, when she worked on a TV show about Moravia, he demanded a place to rest between shoots. She bought the set then. I give the "Moravia table" a fresh coat of that blackish green paint you see on park furniture in Paris. We also are the recipients of several bookcases and a couple of shopping bags full of books. The fourteenth-century hermits who lived on this mountain still might approve of our white rooms so far: beds, books, bookcases, a few chairs, a primitive table. Big willow baskets hold our clothes.

On the third Saturday of each month, a small antique market takes place in a piazza in the nearby castle town of Castiglione del Lago. We find a great sepia photograph of a group of bakers and a couple of chestnut coatracks. Mostly we browse around, astonished at the crazy prices on bad garage sale furniture. On the way home, we come upon an accident—someone in a tiny Fiat tried to pass on a curve—the Italian birthright—and rammed into a new Alfa Romeo. The upside-down Fiat still has one spinning wheel and two passengers are being extracted from the crumpled car. An ambulance siren blares. The smashed Alfa is standing, doors open, no passengers in the front seat. As we inch by, I see a dead boy, about eighteen, in the backseat. He is still upright in his seat belt but clearly is dead. Traffic stops us and we are two feet from his remote blue stare, the trickle of blood from the corner of his mouth. Very carefully, Ed drives us home. The next day, when we are back in Castiglione del Lago for a swim in the lake, we ask the waiter at the bar if the boy killed in the accident was local. "No, no, he was from Terontola." Terontola is all of five miles away.

✳

We're expecting the permits soon. Meanwhile, the main project we hope to finish before we go home at the end of August is the sand-blasting of the beams. Each room has two or three large beams and twenty-five or thirty small ones. A big job.

Ferragosto, August 15, is not just a holiday for the Virgin, it is a signal for work to cease and desist all over Italy both before and after that day. We underestimated the total effect of this holiday. When we began calling for a *sabbiatrice*, sandblaster, after the wall was finished, we found only one who would think of taking the job in August. He was to arrive on the first, the job to last three days. On the second we began to call and have been calling ever since. A woman who sounds very old shouts back that he is on *vacanze al mare*, he's over on the coast walking those sandy beaches instead of sandblasting our sticky beams. We wait, hoping he will appear.

Although we can't paint until after the central heating is installed, we begin to scrub down the walls in preparation. On Saturdays and odd days when they're not working elsewhere, the Poles come over to help us. The flaky whitewash brushes off on our clothes if we rub against it. As they clean the walls with wet cloths and sponges, they uncover the earlier paints, most prevalent a stark blue that must have been inspired by Mary's blue robes. Renaissance painters could get that rare color only from ground lapis lazuli brought from quarries in what is now Afghanistan. Faintly, we see a far-gone acanthus border around the top of the walls. The *contadina* bedroom used to be painted in foot-wide blue and white stripes. Two upstairs bedrooms were clear yellow, like the *giallorino* Renaissance painters favored, made from baked yellow glass, red lead, and sand from the banks of the Arno.

From the third floor, I hear Cristoforo calling Ed, then he calls me. He sounds urgent, excited. He and Riccardo talk at once in Polish and point to the middle of the dining room wall. We see an arch, then he rubs his wet cloth around it and scumbles of blue appear, then a farmhouse, almond green feathery strokes of what may be a tree. They have uncovered a fresco! We grab buckets and sponges and start gently cleaning the walls. Every swipe reveals more: two people by a shore, water, distant hills. The same blue that's on the walls was used for the lake, a paler blue for sky and soft coral for clouds. The biscuit-colored houses are the same colors we see all around us. Vibrant when wet, the colors pale as they dry. An electrical line, buried at some point in the wall, mars a faux-framed classical scene of ruins in a panel over the door. We rub all afternoon. Water runs down our arms, sloshes on the floor. My arms feel like slack rubber bands. The lake scene continues on the adjoining wall and it is vaguely familiar, like the villages and landscape around Lake Trasimeno. The naive style reveals no newly discovered Giotto but it's charming. Someone didn't think so and whitewashed it. Luckily, they didn't use tougher paint. We will be able to live with this soft painting surrounding our dinners indoors.

*

A hundred years may not be long enough to restore this house and land. Upstairs I rub the windows with vinegar, shining the green scallop of the hills along the sky. I spot Ed on the third terrace, waving a long spinning blade. He's wearing red shorts as bright as a banner, black boots against the locust thorns, and a clear visor to shield his eyes from flying rocks. He could be a powerful angel, coming to announce a late annunciation, but he is only the newest in an endless line of mortals who've worked to keep this farm from sliding back into the steep slope it once was, perhaps long before the Etruscans, when Tuscany was a solid forest.

The ugly whine of the weed machine drowns out the whinnies of the two white horses across the road and the multicultural birds that wake us up every morning. But the dry weeds must be cut in case of fire, so he works in the fiery sun without his shirt. Each day his skin darkens. We've learned the gravity of the hillside, the quick springs pulling down dirt and the thrust of the stone walls which must be sluices and must push back harder than the downward pull of the soil. He bends and slings olive prunings to a stack he's building for fires on cool nights. What a body of work this place is. Olive burns hot. The ashes then are returned to the trees for fertilizer. Like the pig, the olive is useful in every part.

The old glass sags in places—strange that glass which looks so solid retains a slow liquidity—distorting the sharp clarity of the view into watery Impressionism. Usually, if I am polishing silver, ironing, vacuuming at home, I am highly conscious that I am "wasting time," I should be doing something more important—memos, class preparation, papers, writing. My job at the university is all-consuming. Housework becomes a nuisance. My houseplants know it's feast or famine. Why am I humming as I wash windows—one of the top ten dreaded chores? Now I am planning a vast garden. My list includes sewing! At least a fine handkerchief linen curtain to go over the glass bathroom door. This house, every brick and lock, will be as known to me as my own or the loved one's body.

Restoration. I like the word. The house, the land, perhaps ourselves. But restored to what? Our lives are full. It's our zeal for all this work that amazes me. Is it only that once into the project, what it all means doesn't come up? Or that excitement and belief reject questions? The vast wheel has a place for our shoulders and we simply push into the turning? But I know there's a taproot as forceful as that giant root wrapped around the stone.

I remember dreaming over Bachelard's *The Poetics of Space*, which I don't have with me, only a few sentences copied into a notebook. He wrote about the house as a "tool for analysis" of the human soul. By remembering rooms in houses we've lived in, we learn to abide (nice word) within ourselves. I felt close to his sense of the house. He wrote about the strange whir of the sun as it comes into a room in which one is alone. Mainly, I remember recognizing his idea that the house protects the dreamer; the houses that are important to us are the ones that allow us to dream in peace. Guests we've had stop in for a night or two all come down the first morning, ready to tell their dreams. Often the dreams are way-back father or mother dreams. "I was in this car and my father was driving, only I was the age I am now and my father died when I was twelve. He was driving fast . . . ." Our guests fall into long sleeps, just as we do when we arrive each time. This is the only place in the world I've ever taken a nap at nine in the morning. Could this be what Bachelard meant by the "repose derived from all deep oneiric experience"? After a week or so, I have the energy of a twelve-year-old. For me, *house*, set in its landscape, always has been crypto-primo image land. Bachelard pushed me to realize that the houses we experience deeply take us back to the *first* house. In my mind, however, it's not just to the first house, but to the first concept of self. Southerners have a gene, as yet undetected in the DNA spirals, that causes them to believe that place is fate. Where you are is who you are. The further inside you the place moves, the more your identity is intertwined with it. Never casual, the choice of place is the choice of something you crave.

An early memory: Mine is a small room with six windows, all open on a summer night. I'm three or four, awake after everyone has gone to bed. I'm leaning on the windowsill looking out at the blue hydrangeas, big as beach balls. The attic fan pulls in the scent of tea olive and lifts the thin white curtains. I'm playing with the screen latch, which suddenly comes undone. I remember the feel of the metal hook and the eye I almost can stick my little finger into. Next, I'm climbing up on the sill and jumping out the window. I find myself in the dark backyard. I start running, feeling a quick rush of what I now know as freedom. Wet grass, glow of white camellias on the black bush, the new pine just my height. I go out to my swing in the pecan tree. I've just learned to pump. How high? I run around the house, all the rooms of my sleeping family, then I stand in the middle of the street I am not allowed to cross. I let myself in the back door, which never was locked, and into my room.

That pure surge of pleasure, flash flood of joy—to find the electric jolt of the outside place that corresponds to the inside—that's it.

In San Francisco, I go out on the flower-filled tiny back deck of my flat and look three stories down at the ground—a city-sized terrace surrounded with attractive low-maintenance flower beds on a drip system, cared for by a gardener. It does not lure me. That the jasmine on the high fences has climbed to my third floor and blooms profusely around the stair railing, I am thankful for. At night after work, I can step out to water my pots and watch for stars and find the tumbling vines sending out their dense perfume. Such flowers—jasmine, honeysuckle, gardenia—spell South, metabolic home, to my psyche. A fragmental connection though—my feet are three stories off the earth. When I leave my house, concrete separates my feet from the ground. The people who have bought the flats on the first and second floors are friends. We have meetings to discuss when to repair the steps or when to paint. I look into or onto the tops of trees, wonderful trees. My house backs onto the very private gardens unhinted at by the joined fronts of Victorian houses in my neighborhood. The center of the block is green. If all of us took down our fences, we could wander in a blooming green sward. Because I like my flat so much, I didn't know what I missed.

Was there really a *nonna*, a presiding spirit who centered this house? This three-story house rooted to the ground restores some levels in my waking and sleeping hours. Or is it the house? A glimmer: *Choice* is restorative when it reaches toward an instinctive recognition of the earliest self. As Dante recognized at the beginning of *The Inferno*: What must we do in order to grow?

At home I dream of former houses I've lived in, of finding rooms I didn't know were there. Many friends have told me that they, too, have this dream. I climb the stairs to the attic of the eighteenth-century house I loved living in for three years in Somers, New York, and there are three new rooms. In one, I find a dormant geranium, which I take downstairs and water. Immediately, Disney-style, it leafs and breaks into wild bloom. In house after house (my best friend's in high school, my childhood home, my father's childhood home), I open a door and there is more than I knew. All the lights are on in the New York house. I am walking by, seeing the life in every window. I never dream of the boxy apartment I lived in at Princeton. Nor do I dream of my flat I am so fond of in San Francisco—but perhaps that is because I can hear from my bed before I fall asleep foghorns out on the bay. Those deep voices displace dreams, calling from spirit to spirit, to some underlying voice we all have but don't know how to use.

In Vicchio, a house I rented a few summers ago brought the recurrent dream to reality. It was a huge house with a caretaker in a side wing. One day I opened what I'd assumed was a closet in an unused bedroom and found a long stone corridor with empty rooms on either side. White doves flew in and out. It was the second floor of the housekeeper's wing and I hadn't realized it was uninhabited. In many waking moments since, I've opened the door to the stony light of that hallway, oblong panels of sunlight on the floor, caught a glimpse and flutter of white wings.

Here, I am restored to the basic pleasure of connection to the outdoors. The windows are open to butterflies, horseflies, bees, or anything that wants to come in one window and out another. We eat outside almost every meal. I'm restored to my mother's sense of preserving the seasons and to *time*, even time to take pleasure in polishing a pane of glass to a shine. To the house safe for dreaming. One end of the house is built right against the hillside. An omen of reconnection? Here, I don't dream of houses. Here, I am free to dream of rivers.

✳

Though the days are long, the summer is somehow short. My daughter, Ashley, arrives and we have mad, hot days driving around to sights. When she first walked up to the house, she stopped and looked up for a while, then said, "How strange—this will become a part of all our memories." I recognized that knowledge we sometimes get in advance when travelling or moving to a new city—here's a place that will have its way with me.

Naturally, I want her to love it but I don't have to convince her. She begins talking about Christmas here. She chooses her room. "Do you have a pasta machine?" "Can we have melon every meal?" "A swimming pool could go up on that second terrace." "Where's the train schedule to Florence? I need shoes."

The minute she graduated from college, she lit out for New York. The artist's life, the odd-job life, the long hot summer, health problems—she's ready for the icy mountain-fed pool run by a priest back in the hills, for trips to the Tyrrhenian coast, where we rent beach chairs and bake all day, for strolls in stony hill towns at night after dinner in a strictly local *trattoria*.

The days stream by and soon it is time for both of us to leave. I must be at work but Ed will stay another ten days. Maybe the sandblaster will come.

FESTINA TARDE (MAKE HASTE SLOWLY)

WALKING OUT OF THE SAN FRANCISCO AIRPORT, I'M
shocked by cool foggy air, smelling of salt and jet fumes. A taxi driver
crosses the street to help with luggage. After a few pleasantries, we lapse
into silence and I'm grateful. I have been travelling for twenty-four
hours. The last leg, from JFK, where Ashley and I said good-bye, to SF
seems cruel and unusual, especially the extra hour it takes because of
the prevailing wind. The houses on the hills are necklaces of light, then
along the right, the bay almost laps the freeway. I watch for a certain
curve coming up. After rounding it, suddenly the whole city rises, the
stark white skyline. As we drive in, I anticipate the breath-stopping
plunges over hills and glimpses between buildings where I know there's
a wedge or slice or expanse of rough blue water.

     Still, imprinted on my eyes are the stone towns, mown fields,
and sweeping hills covered with vineyards, olives, sunflowers; this landscape looks exotic. I start to look for my house key, which I thought was
in the zippered inside pocket of my bag. If I've lost it—what? Two friends
and a neighbor have keys to my place. I imagine getting their answering machines, "I'm out of town until Friday . . ." We pass Victorian
houses discreetly shuttered and curtained, porch lights shining on

wooden banisters and pots of topiary. No one, not even a dog walker or someone running to the store for milk, is out. I feel a pang for the towns full of people who leave their keys dangling in their locks, for the evening *passeggiata* when everyone is out and about, visiting, shopping, taking a quick espresso. I've left Ed there because his university starts later than mine and the sandblasting still is a dream of accomplishment for the summer. The taxi lets me out and speeds off. My house looks the same; the climbing rose has grown and tried to wind around the columns. Finally I find the key mixed in with my Italian change. Sister comes to greet me with a plaintive meow and a quick brush of her sides against my ankles. I pick her up to smell her earthy, damp leaf smell. In Italy, I often wake up thinking she has leapt on the bed. She jumps on top of my bag and curls down for a nap. So much for having suffered in my absence.

Lamps, rugs, chests, quilts, paintings, tables—how amazingly comfortable and cluttered this looks after the empty house seven thousand miles away. Bookshelves, crammed, the glass kitchen cabinets lined with colorful dishes, pitchers, platters—so much of everything. The long hall carpet—so soft! Could I walk out of here and never look back? Virginia Woolf, I remember, lived in the country during the war. She rushed back to her neighborhood in London after a bombing and found her house in ruins. She expected to be devastated but instead felt a strange elation. Doubtless, I would not. When the earth quaked, I was shaken for days over my whiplashed chimney, broken vases, and wineglasses. It's just that my feet are used to the cool *cotto* floors, my eyes to bare white walls. I'm still *there*, partly here.

There are eleven messages on the answering machine. "Are you back?" "I need to get your signature on my graduation form . . ." "Calling to confirm your appointment . . ." The housesitter has left a list of other calls on a pad and stacked the mail in my study. Three knee-high stacks, mostly junk, which I compulsively begin to go through.

Because I have stayed away as long as possible, I must return to the university immediately. Classes begin in four days, and regardless of faxes from Italy and the good offices of an excellent secretary, I am chair of the department and need to be bodily present. By nine, I'm there, dressed in gabardine pants, a silk print blouse. "How was your summer?" we all say to one another. The start-up of a school year always feels exhilarating. Everyone feels the zest in the air. If the book-store were not crowded with students buying texts, I probably would go over and buy a supply of fine-point pens, a notebook with five-subject index, and a few pads. Instead, I sign forms, memos, call a dozen people. I go into racing gear, ignoring jet lag.

Stopping for groceries after work, I see that the organic store has added a masseuse to the staff. I could pause in a little booth and get a seven-minute massage to relax me before I begin selecting pota-toes. I'm temporarily overwhelmed by the checkout rows, the aisles and aisles of bright produce and the tempting cakes at the new bakery just installed in the front of the store. Mustard, mayonnaise, plastic wrap, baking chocolate—I buy things I haven't seen all summer. The deli has crab cakes and stuffed baked potatoes with chives, and corn salad and tabouli. So much! I buy enough "gourmet takeout" for two days. I'm going to be too busy to cook.

It's eight A.M. at Bramasole. Ed probably is chopping weeds around an olive tree or pacing around waiting for the sandblaster. As I turn in my garage I see Evit, the one-toothed homeless man, rifling through our recycle bin for bottles and cans. My neighbor has posted a VISUALIZE BEING TOWED sign on his garage door.

The last message on the machine starts with static, then I hear Ed's voice; he sounds raspy. "I was hoping to catch you, sweetheart; are you *still* at work? The sandblaster was here when I got home from the airport." Long pause. "It's hard to describe. The noise is deafening. He's got this huge generator and the sand really does *blast* out and fall into every crack. It's like a storm in the Sahara. He did three rooms yester-day. You can't believe how much sand is on the floors. I took all the furniture out on the patio and I'm just camped in one room, but the sand is *all* over the house. The beams look *very good*; they're chestnut, except for one elm. I don't know *how* I'm going to get rid of this sand. It's in my *ears* and I'm not even in the room with him. Sweeping is out of the question. I *wish* you were here." He usually doesn't speak with so many italics.

When he calls next, he's on the *autostrada* near Florence, en route to Nice and home. He sounds exhausted and elated. The permits have come through! The blasting is over. Primo Bianchi, however, won't be able to do our work because he must have a stomach operation. Ed met again with Benito, the yellow-eyed Mussolini look-alike, and has worked out a contract with him. Work is to start immediately and to finish in early November, easily in time for Christmas. The clean-up goes slowly; the sandblaster says to expect sand to trickle down for five years!

Ian, who helped us with the purchase, will oversee the work. We left diagrams of where electrical outlets, switches, and radiators should go, how the bathroom should be laid out, how the kitchen should be installed—even the height of the sink and the distance between the sink and the faucet—where to pick up the fixtures and tile we selected for the bathroom, everything we can think of. We are anxious for word that work is under way.

The first fax arrives September 15; Benito has broken his leg on the first day of the job and start-up will be delayed until he is able to walk.

✳

Festina tarde was a Renaissance concept: Make haste slowly. Often it was represented by a snake with its tail in its mouth, by a dolphin entwined with an anchor, or by the figure of a seated woman holding wings in one hand and a tortoise in the other: The great wall of Bramasole in one, the central heating, kitchen, patio, and bathroom in the other. The second fax, October 12, warns that "delays have occurred" and that "some changes in installation can be expected" but he has full confidence and not to worry.

We fax back our encouragement and ask that everything be covered well with plastic and taped.

Another fax, just after, says the opening of the three-foot-thick wall between the kitchen and dining room has begun. Two days later, Ian faxes us the news that when a very large boulder was pulled out, the whole house creaked and all the workers ran out because they feared a collapse.

We called. Didn't they brace the rooms? Had Benito used steel? Why hadn't they known what to do? How could this happen? Ian said stone houses were unpredictable and couldn't be expected to react the way American houses react and the door is now in and looks fine, although they didn't make it as wide as we wanted because they were afraid to. I vacillated between thinking that the workers were incompetent and fearing that they might have been crushed by an unstable house.

By mid-November, Benito has finished the upstairs patio and the opening of the infamous door, plus they've opened the two upstairs doors that connect to the *contadina* apartment. We decide to cancel the opening of the other large door that would join the living room to the *contadina* kitchen. The image of all Benito's men fleeing the premises does not inspire confidence. The next delays Ian mentions concern the new bath and the central heating. "Almost certainly," he advises, "there will be no heat when you come for Christmas. In fact, the house will not be habitable due to the fact that the central heating pipes must be inside the house, not on the back as we were originally told." Benito asks him to relay that his charges are higher than anticipated. Items listed on the contract have been farmed out to electricians and plumbers and their overlapping bills have become incomprehensible. We have no way of knowing who did what; Ian seems as confused as we are. Money we wire over takes too long to get there and Benito is angry. What is clear is that we are not there and our house's work is done between other jobs.

❋

Hoping for miracles, we go to Italy for Christmas. Elizabeth has offered us her house in Cortona, which is partly packed for her move. She also wants to give us a great deal of her furniture, since her new house is smaller. As we drive out of the Rome airport, rain hits the windshield like a hose turned on full blast. All the way north we face foggier and foggier weather. When we arrive in Camucia, we head straight to the bar for hot chocolate before we go to Elizabeth's. We decide to unpack, have lunch, and face Bramasole later.

The house is a wreck. Canals for the heating pipes have been cut into the inside walls of every room in the house. The workers have left rock and rubble in piles all over the unprotected floors. The plastic we'd requested was simply tossed over the furniture so every book, chair, dish, bed, towel, and receipt in the house is covered in dirt. The jagged, deep, floor-to-ceiling cuts in the wall look like open wounds. They are just beginning on the new bathroom, laying cement on the floor. The plaster in the new kitchen already is cracking. The great long sink has been installed and looks wonderful. A workman has scrawled in black felt-tip pen a telephone number on the dining room fresco. Ed immediately wets a rag and tries to rub it clean but we're stuck with the plumber's number. He slings the rag onto the rubble. They've left windows open all over and puddles have collected on the floor from this morning's rain. The carelessness apparent everywhere, such as the telephone being completely buried, makes me so angry I have to walk outside and take gulps of cold air. Benito is at another job. One of his men sees that we are extremely upset and tries to say that all will be done soon, and done well. He is working on the opening between the new kitchen and the cantina. He's shy but seems concerned. A beautiful house, beautiful position. All will be well. His bleary old blue eyes look at us sadly. Benito arrives full of bluster. No time to clean up before we arrived, and anyway it's the plumber's responsibility, he has been held up himself because the plumber didn't come when he said he would. But everything is *perfetto, signori*. He'll take care of the cracked plaster; it didn't dry properly because of the rains. We hardly answer. As he gestures, I catch the worker looking at me. Behind Benito's back he makes a strange gesture; he nods toward Benito, then pulls down his eyelid.

The upstairs patio seems perfect. They've laid rose-colored brick and reattached the rusty iron railings so that the patio is secure but still looks old. Something was done well.

By four, twilight begins; by five, it's night. Still, the stores are opening after siesta. A morning of work, siesta, reopening at dark for several hours: the winter rhythm unchanged from the massively hot summer days. We stop by and greet Signor Martini. We're cheered to see him, knowing he'll say, *"Boh,"* and *"Anche troppo,"* one of his all-purpose responses that means yes, it's too bloody much. In our bad Italian we explain what's going on. As we start to go, I remember the strange gesture. "What does this mean?" I ask, pulling down my eyelid.

"Furbo," cunning, watch out, he answers. "Who's *furbo?"*

"Apparently our contractor."

＊

Warm house. Thank you, Elizabeth. We buy red candles, cut pine boughs and bring them in for some semblance of Christmas. Our hearts are not into cooking, although all the winter ingredients in the shops almost lure us to the kitchen. We love the furniture Elizabeth has given us. Besides twin beds, coffee table, two desks, and lamps, we'll have an antique *madia*, whose top part was used to knead bread and let it rise. Beneath the coffin-shaped bread holder are drawers and cabinet. The chestnut's warm patina makes me rub my hand over the wood.

On the list she's left for us, we find her immense *armadio*, large enough to hold all the house linens, a dining room table, antique chests, a *cassone* (tall storage chest), two peasant chairs, and wonderful plates and serving pieces. Suddenly we will live in a furnished house. With all our rooms, there will be plenty of space, still, for acquiring our own treasures. Amid all the restoration horrors, this great act of generosity warms us tremendously. Right now, the pieces seem to belong to her orderly house, but before we leave we must move everything over to the house full of debris.

97

As Christmas nears, work slows then stops. We had not anticipated that they would take off so many holidays. New Year's has several holidays attached to it. We'd never heard of Santo Stefano, who merits one day off. Francesco Falco, who has worked for Elizabeth for twenty years, brings his son Giorgio and his son-in-law with a truck. They take apart the *armadio*, load everything into the truck except the desk, which is too wide to exit the study. Elizabeth has written all her books at that desk and it seems that it was not meant to leave the house. I'm taking boxes of dishes to our car when I look up and see them lowering a desk by rope out the second-floor window. Everyone applauds as it gently lands on the ground.

At the house, we cram all the furniture into two rooms we've shoveled out and swept. We cover everything with plastic and shut the doors.

There is absolutely nothing we can do. Benito does not answer our calls. I have a sore throat. We've bought no presents. Ed has grown silent. My daughter, sick with flu in New York, is spending her first Christmas alone because the construction debacle threw off her plans to come to Italy. I stare for a long time at an ad for the Bahamas in a magazine, the totally expected photo of a crescent of sugar-sand beach along clear, azure water. Someone, somewhere, drifts on a yellow striped float, trailing her fingers in a warm current and dreaming under the sun.

On Christmas Eve we have pasta with wild mushrooms, veal, an excellent Chianti. Only one other person is in the restaurant, for *Natale* is above all a family time. He wears a brown suit and sits very straight. I see him slowly drink wine along with his food, pouring out half glasses for himself, sniffing the wine as though it were a great vintage instead of the house carafe. He proceeds through his courses with care. We're through; it's only nine-thirty. We'll go back to Elizabeth's, build a fire, and share the *moscato* dessert wine and cake I bought this afternoon. While Ed waits for coffee, our dinner partner is served a plate of cheese and a bowl of walnuts. The restaurant is silent. He cracks a shell. He cuts a bit of cheese, savors it, eats a walnut, then cracks another. I want to put my head down on the white cloth and weep.

❋

According to Ian, the work finished satisfactorily at the end of February. We paid for the amount contracted but not for the exorbitant extra amount Benito tacked on. He listed such charges as a thousand dollars for hanging a door. We will have to be there to determine exactly what extra work he did. How we'll settle the final amount is a mystery.

In late April, Ed returns to Italy. He has the spring quarter off. His plan is to clear the land and treat, stain, and wax all the beams in the house before I arrive on June first. Then we will clean, paint all rooms and windows, and restore the floors to the condition they were in before Benito's restoration. The new kitchen has in it only the sink, dishwasher, stove, and fridge. Instead of cabinets, we plan to make plastered brick columns with wide plank shelves and have marble cut for countertops. We have a major incentive: At the end of June, my friend Susan has planned to be married in Cortona. When I asked why she wanted her wedding in Italy, she replied cryptically, "I want to get married in a language I don't understand." The guests will stay with us and the wedding will take place at the twelfth-century town hall.

Ed tells me he's confined to the room on the second floor that opens onto the patio, his little haven amid the rubbish. He cleans one bathroom, unpacks a few pots and dishes, and sets up rudimentary housekeeping. Benito hauled several loads out of the house but only made it as far as the driveway, now a dump. On the front terrace he left a small mountain of stone that was taken out of the wall. The patio and bedroom brick form another small mountain. Even so, Ed is elated. They're gone! The new bathroom, with its foot square tiles, *belle époque* pedestal sink, and built-in tub, feels large and luxurious, a stark contrast to the former bucket-flush bathroom. Spring is astonishingly green and thousands of naturalized irises and daffodils bloom in long grass all over our land. He finds a seasonal creek pouring over mossy rocks where two box turtles sun themselves. The almond and fruit trees are so outrageously beautiful that he has to tear himself away from working outside.

We try not to call; we tend to get into long conversations, then decide that we could have done x at the house for the money the call has cost. But there is a great need to recount what you've done when you're working on a house. Someone needs to hear that the beams look really great after their final waxing, that your neck is killing you from working above your head all day, that you're on the fourth room. He relates that each room takes forty hours: beams, ceiling, walls. Floors will come last. Seven to seven, seven days a week.

Finally, finally, June—I can go. With all the work Ed has described, I expect the house to glow when I arrive. But, naturally enough, Ed has concentrated on telling me his progress.

When I first arrive, it's hard to focus on how far he has come. The beams look beautiful, yes. But the grounds are full of rubbish, plaster, the old cistern. The electrician has not shown up. Six rooms haven't

99

been touched. All the furniture is piled into three rooms. It's strictly a war zone. I try not to show how horrified I am.

I'm ready for r & r. Unfortunate, because there's nothing to do but launch into this work. We have about three weeks to get ready for our first major onslaught of guests. The wedding! It seems ludicrous that anyone could stay here.

Ed is 6'2". I am 5'4". He takes the ceiling: I take the floor. Biology is destiny—but which is better? He actually loves finishing the beams. Painting the brick ceiling is less fun but is rewarding. Suddenly the gunky beams and flaking ceiling are transformed into dark substantial beams, pristine white-brick ceiling. The room is defined. Painting goes quickly with the big brushes made of wild boar hair. Pure white walls—white on plaster is whiter than any other white. As each room is finished, my job is to paint the *battascopa*, a six-inch-high gray strip along the bases of the walls, a kind of pseudo-moulding that is traditional in old houses of this area. Usually it's a brick color but we prefer the lighter touch. The word means broom-hit. The darker paint doesn't show the marks of the mops and brooms that must constantly pass over these floors. Almost upside down, I measure six inches in several places, tape the floor and wall, then quickly paint and pull off the tape. Naturally, the tape pulls off some white paint, which then has to be retouched. Twelve rooms, four walls each, plus the stairwell, landings, and entrance. We're leaving the stone cantina as is. Next, I decalcify the floor. The first step is to sweep up all the large chunks and dirt, then vacuum. With a special solution I spread, the residue from dirt, plaster, and paint drippings is dissolved. After that, I rinse the floor with a wet mop three times, the middle time with a mild soap solution. I'm on my knees. Next: mop again with water and a little muriatic acid. Rinse, then paint the floor with linseed oil, letting it soak in and dry. After it dries for two days, I wax. On the floor again, char style. My knees, totally unused to this, rebel and I suppress groans when I stand up. Last step: buff with soft cloth. The floors come back, rich and dark and shiny. Each room pops into place, looking very much as they did when we bought the house, only now the beams are right and the radiators are in place. *"Brutto,"* ugly, I said to the plumber when I saw them. "Yes," he replied, "but beautiful in winter."

As Ed told me, seven to seven: seven days a week. We spread the rubble down the driveway, which is chewed up anyway from all the trucks. We dig in the larger stones and bricks, spread grass cuttings on top. Gradually, it will settle in. We hire someone to take away a truckload that Benito failed to haul. On a walk a few days later, we see a pile of awful rubble dumped along a road about a mile from our house, and to our horror, spot our plaster with the madonna blue coat of paint underneath.

From high school through graduate school, Ed worked as a house mover, busboy, cabinetmaker, refrigerator hauler. A friend calls him "the muscular poet." He's thriving on this work, though he, too, is sapped at night. I never have done manual labor, except spurts of refinishing furniture, pruning, painting, and wallpapering. This is an order of bodily exertion to shock my system. Everything aches. What *is* water on the knee? I think I may get it. I die at night. In the mornings, we both have surges of new energy that come from somewhere. We plug right back in. We're consumed. I'm amazed: the relentlessness we've developed. I never will feel the same toward workers again; they should be paid fortunes.

When I seal the patio bricks with linseed oil, the sun feels especially deadly. I'm determined to finish and keep working until I start to reel with the fumes and the heat. Now and then I stand up and breathe in great draughts of the honeysuckle we've planted in an enormous pot, stare off into the great view, then dip the brush into the pot again. Who would think to ask, when paying a lot for a new patio, whether the job included finishing the brick's surface? It never occurred to either of us that we would have to treat the kitchen and patio bricks to several coats of this gloppy stuff.

After we clean up late in the day, we walk around assessing what's left, how we've done. We will not have any children together but decide that this is the equivalent of having triplets. As each room is finished, we get to bring in the furniture for it. Gradually, rooms are set up, still spare but basically furnished. I've brought over white bedspreads for the twin beds. We take a morning in Arezzo and buy a few lamps from a place that still makes the traditional majolica vases of the area into lamps. A fabulous feeling—things are shaping up, they're done, it's clean, we'll be warm in winter—we've done it! This feels giddy and fuels us to keep going.

A week before the wedding, our friends Shera and Kevin arrive from California. We see them get off the train way down the track. Kevin is maneuvering something enormous that looks like a coffin for two. His bicycle! We keep working while they go to Florence, Assisi, and on the Piero della Francesca trail. At night we make great meals together and they tell us all the wonders they've seen and we tell them about the new faucet we want to install for the hip bath. They fall instantly in love with the whole area and seem to want to hear our daily saga of cleaning the new bricks on the kitchen floor. When they're not travelling, Kevin is off on long bicycle trips. Shera, an artist, is captive here. She is painting milky blue half circles over the windows in a bedroom. We've picked a star from one of Giotto's paintings and she makes a stencil of it and fills the half domes with gold leaf stars. A few stars "fall" out of the dome and onto the white walls. We're preparing the bridal chamber. At an antique shop near Perugia, I buy two colored prints of the constellations with mythological beasts and figures. At the Cortona market, I find pretty linen and cotton sheets in pale blue with cutwork in white. We're preparing, too, for our first houseparty. We buy twenty wineglasses, linen tablecloths, pans for baking the wedding cake, a case of wine.

There is no way everything can be finished in time for the wedding (or ever?), but we manage an extraordinary amount. The day before everyone arrives, Kevin comes downstairs and asks, "Why does the toilet steam? Is there something peculiar about Italian toilets?" Ed brings in the ladder, climbs up to the wall-mounted tank, and dips in his hand. Hot water. We check the other bathrooms. The new one is O.K. but the other old one also has hot water. We hardly have used those bathrooms and had not let water run long enough for the hot water to arrive, so we had not noticed that neither bathroom had cold water at all. As soon as guests started using the baths, it became noticeable. Shera says she thought the shower was awfully hot, once it finally warmed up, but hadn't wanted to complain. The plumber cannot come for a few days, so we will go through the wedding with quick showers and smoking toilets!

The front terrace is still rough but we have potted geraniums along the wall to distract from the torn-up ground. At least we removed the rubble. Four rooms have beds. Susan's two cousins from England and Cole's brother and sister-in-law are arriving. Shera and Kevin will move to a hotel in town for a couple of days. Other friends are coming from Vermont.

By day, we are twelve in the house. Many hands to help with drinks and lunch. The cake must be improvised because the oven is small. I envisioned three tiers of sponge cake with a hazelnut butter-cream frosting, to be served with whipped cream and cherries steeped in sugared wine. We couldn't find a large pan for the bottom and finally bought a tin dog dish to bake it in. The cake is lovely, if a bit lopsided. We decorate it with flowers all around. Everyone is running off in different directions sightseeing and shopping.

We're having the prenuptial dinner here on a clear warm night, everyone in pale linens and cottons. Many photos are taken of us arm in arm on the steps and leaning over the balcony. Susan's cousin brings out champagne he has brought from France. After drinks with *bruschette* and dry olives, we start with cool fennel soup. I've made a rustic casserole of chicken, white beans, sausage, tomatoes, and onions. There are tiny green beans, baskets of bread, and a salad of arugula, radicchio, and chicory. Everyone tells wedding stories. Mark was to have married a Colorado girl who ran away on the wedding day and married someone else in a week. Karen was a bridesmaid on a boat wedding and the bride's mother, in teal chiffon, tipped into the drink. When I married at twenty-two, I wanted a midnight wedding with everyone wearing robes and carrying candles. The minister said absolutely not, that midnight was a "furtive hour." Nine was as late as he'd go. And instead of a robe, I wore my sister's wedding dress and carried a leatherbound Keats down the aisle. My mother pulled my skirt and I leaned over for her words of wisdom. She whispered, "It won't last six months." But she was wrong.

We should have an accordion player, à la Fellini, and maybe a white horse for the bride to ride, but we do well with the fabulous night, and the CD player inspires a little dancing in the dining room. The white peach tart with pine nuts should end this dinner but Ed's description of the *crema* and the hazelnut *gelati* in town sends everyone to the cars. They're amazed that such a small town is still hopping at eleven, everyone outdoors with coffee, ice cream, or perhaps an *amaro*, an after-dinner bitter. Babies in strollers still as wide-eyed as their parents, teenagers sitting on the town hall steps. The only thing sleeping is a cat on top of the police car.

The morning of the wedding Susan, Shera, and I pick a bouquet of lavender, pink, and yellow wildflowers for Susan to carry. When we're all dressed in silks and suits, we walk into town over the Roman road. Ed carries our good shoes in a shopping bag. Susan has brought Chinese painted paper parasols for everyone because of the midday sun. We walk through town and up the steps of the twelfth-century town hall. It's a dark, high-ceilinged room with tapestries and frescoes and high judicial-looking chairs, an impressive room to sign a treaty in. The city of Cortona has sent red roses and Ed has arranged for Bar Sport to come over right after the ceremony with cold *prosecco*. Susan's cousin Brian runs all around with his video camera, getting shots from every angle. After the brief ceremony, we cross the piazza to La Logetta for a Tuscan feast beginning with a selection of typical *antipasti*: *crostini*, little rounds of bread topped with olives, peppers, mushroom, or chicken liver; *prosciutto e melone*, fried olives stuffed with *pancetta* and spicy bread crumbs; and the local *finocchiona*, a salami studded with fennel seeds. Next they bring out a selection of *primi*, first courses to try, including ravioli with butter and sage, and *gnocchi di patate*, little "knuckles" of potato served here with pesto. Course after course arrives, culminating in platters of roast lamb and veal and the famous grilled Val di Chiana steak. Karen notices the grand piano in the corner under a massive vase of flowers and prevails upon Cole, who is a pianist, to play. Ed is at the other end of the table but he catches my eye as Cole begins Scarlatti. Three weeks ago this was a dream, a long shot, a frightening prospect. "Cheers!" the English cousins call out.

105

Back at home, we're all stunned by the food and heat and decide to postpone the wedding cake until late afternoon. I hear someone snoring. In fact, I hear two people snoring.

Though the cake lacks that professional touch, it may be the best cake I ever tasted. I'll credit our tree for the nuts. Shera and Kevin are dancing in the dining room again. Others stroll out to the point where our land ends for the view of the lake and valley. We can't decide whether to eat again or forget it. Finally we run down to Camucia for pizza. Our favorite places are closed, so we end up in a definitely downscale, unatmospheric place. The pizza is excellent, however, and no one seems to notice the dust gray curtains or the cat who has leapt on the adjoining table and is polishing off the remains of someone's dinner. At the end of the table our bride and groom, holding hands, are in a charmed circle of two.

Susan and Cole have headed to Lucca then back to France; their family guests are gone.

Shera and Kevin are here for a few more days. Ed and I visit the *marmista* and choose thick white marble for the countertops. The next day he cuts and bevels them and Ed and Kevin load them into the back of the car. Suddenly the kitchen looks the way I thought it would: brick floor, white appliances, long sink, plank shelves, marble counters. I sew a blue plaid curtain to go under the sink and hang a braid of garlic and some dried herbs from the wall shelves. In town we find an old peasant dish and cup rack. The dark chestnut looks great against the white walls. At last, a place for all the cups and bowls we're buying in the local ceramic patterns.

Everyone has gone. We eat the last of the wedding cake. Ed begins one of his many lists—we should paper a room with them—of projects he hopes to accomplish now. The kitchen is looking irresistible and we're moving into high season for vegetables and fruit. July fourth: Much of summer is left. My daughter is coming. Travelling friends will stop in for lunch or for a night. We're ready.

MARKET DAY FALLS ON THURSDAYS IN CAMUCIA, THE lively town at the bottom of Cortona's hill, and I'm there early before the heat sets in. Tourists pass right through Camucia; it's just the modern spillover from the venerable and dominant hill town above it. But modern is relative. Among the *frutta e verdura* shops, the hardware and seed stores, you happen on a couple of Etruscan tombs. Near the butcher's shop are remnants of a villa, an immense curly iron gate and swag of garden wall. Camucia, bombed in World War II, has its share of chestnut trees, photographable doors, and shuttered houses.

On market day, a couple of streets are blocked to traffic. The vendors arrive early, unfolding what seems like whole stores or supermarket aisles from specially made trucks and wagons. One wagon sells local *pecorino*, the sheep's milk cheese that can be soft and almost creamy, or aged and strong as a barnyard, along with several wheels of *parmigiano*. The aged cheese is crumbly and rich, wonderful to nibble as I walk around the market.

I'm hunting and gathering food for a dinner for new friends. My favorite wagons belong to the two *porchetta* maestros. The whole pig, parsley entwined with the tail, apple—or a big mushroom—in its mouth, stretches across the cutting board. Sometimes the decapitated head sits aside at an angle, eyeing the rest of its body, which has been stuffed with herbs and bits of its own ears, etc. (best not to inquire too closely), then roasted in a wood oven. You can buy a *panino* (a crusty roll) with nothing on it but slabs of *porchetta* to take home, lean or with crispy, fatty skin. One of the lords of the *porchetta* wagons looks very much like his subject: little eyes, glistening skin, and bulbous forearms. His fingers are short and porky, with bitten-down nails. He's smiling, extolling his pig's virtues, but when he turns to his wife, he snarls. Her lips are set in a permanent tight half smile. I've bought from him before and his *porchetta* is delicious. This time I buy from the milder man in the next stand. For Ed, I ask for extra *sale,* salt, which is what the indefinable stuffing is called. I like it but find myself picking through to see if there's something peculiar in it. Though the pig is useful and tasty in all its parts and preparations, the slow-roasted *porchetta* must be its apogee. Before I move on to the vegetables, I spot a pair of bright yellow espadrilles with ribbons to wind around the ankles; I balance my shopping bags while I try on one. Perfect, and less than ten dollars. I drop them in with the *porchetta* and *parmigiano*.

Scarves (bright Chanel and Hermès copies) and linen tablecloths float from awnings; toilet cleaners, tapes, and T-shirts are stacked in bins and on folding tables. Besides buying food, you can dress, plant a garden, and stock a household from this market. There are a few local crafts for sale but you have to look for them. The Tuscan markets aren't like those in Mexico, with wonderful toys, weaving, and pottery. It's a wonder these markets continue at all, given the sophistication of Italian life and the standard of living in this area. I find the iron-working traditions still somewhat in evidence. Occasionally, I see good andirons and handy fireplace grills. My favorite is a holder for whole *prosciutto*, an iron grip with handle mounted on a board for ease in slicing; maybe someday I'll find I need that much *prosciutto* and buy one. One week I bought handwoven baskets made from dark supple willow twigs, the large ones perfect for kitchen supplies and the small round ones for the ripe-right-now peaches and cherries. One woman sells old table and bed linens with thick monograms, all of which must have been gathered from farms and villas. She has three mounds of yellowed lace. Perhaps some of it was made on the nearby island, Isola Maggiore in Lake Trasimeno. Women still sit in the doorways there, hooking lace in the afternoon light. I find two enormous square linen pillowcases with miles of inset lace and ribbons—ten thousand lire, same as the sandals, seems to be the magic number today. Of course, I will have to have the pillows especially made. When I buy some striped linen dishtowels, I notice several goat skins hanging from a hook. I have in mind that they would look terrific on the *cotto* floors at my house. The four the man has are too small but he says to come back next week. He tries to convince me that his sheepskins would be better anyway, but they don't appeal to me.

I'm wending my way toward the produce, but walk up to the bar for a coffee. Actually, I stop with an excuse to stare. People from surrounding areas come not only to shop but to greet friends, to make business arrangements. The din around the Camucia market is a lovely swarm of voices, many speaking in the local Val di Chiana dialect; I don't understand most of what they're saying but I do hear one recurring habit. They do not use the *ch* sound for *c*, but slide it into an *s* sound. "Shento," they say for *cento* (one hundred), instead of the usual pronunciation "chento." I heard someone say "cappushino," for cappuccino, though the usual affectionate shortening of that is "cappuch." Their town is pronounced not "Camuchia," but "Camushea." Odd that the *c* is often the affected letter. Around Siena, people substitute an *h* sound for *c*—"hasa" and "Hoca-Hola." Whatever the local habit with *c*, they're all talking. Outside the bar, groups of farmers, maybe a hundred men, mill about. Some play cards. Their wives are off in the crowd, loading their bags with tiny strawberries, basil plants with dangling roots, dried mushrooms, perhaps a fish from the one stand that sells seafood from the Adriatic. Unlike the Italians who take their thimbleful of espresso in one quick swallow, I sip the black, black coffee.

A friend says Italy is getting to be just like everywhere else—homogenized and Americanized, she says disparagingly. I want to drag her here and stand her in this doorway. The men have the look of their lives—perhaps we all do. Hard work, their faces and bodies affirm. All are lean, not a pound of extra fat anywhere. They look cured by the sun, so deeply tan they probably never go pale in winter. Their country clothes are serviceable, rough—they don't "dress," they just get dressed. They wear, as well, a natural dignity. Surely some are canny, crusty, cruel, but they look totally present, unhidden, and alive. Some are missing teeth but they smile widely without embarrassment. I look in one man's eyes: The left one is white with milky blue veins like those in an exploded marble. The other is black as the center of a sunflower. A retarded boy wanders among them, neither catered to nor ignored. He's just there, living his life like the rest of us.

At home I plan a menu ahead, though I frequently improvise as I shop. Here, I only begin to think when I see what's ripe this week. My impulse is to overload; I forget there are not ten hungry people at home. At first I was miffed when tomatoes or peas had spoiled when I got around to cooking them a few days later. Finally I caught on that what you buy today is ready—picked or dug this morning at its peak. This also explained another puzzle; I never understood why Italian refrigerators are so minute until I realized that they don't store food the way we do. The Sub-Zero giant I have at home begins to seem almost institutional compared to the toy fridge I now have here.

Two weeks ago, small purple artichokes with long stems were in. We love those, quickly steamed, stuffed with tomatoes, garlic, yesterday's bread, and parsley, then doused with oil and vinegar. Today, not a one. The *fagiolini*, slender green beans, are irresistible. Should I have two salads, because the beans also would be good with a shallot vinaigrette? Why not? I buy white peaches for breakfast but for tonight's

dessert, the cherries are perfect. I take a kilo, then set off to find a pitter back in the other part of the market. Since I don't know the word,
I'm reduced to sign language. I do know *ciliegia*, cherry, which helps.
I've noticed in French and Italian country desserts that the cooks don't
bother to pit the cherries, but I like to use the pitter when they're
served in a dish. These I'll steep in Chianti with a little sugar and   *111*
lemon. I decide on some tiny yellow potatoes still half covered with
dirt. Just a scrubbing, a dribble of oil and some rosemary and they'll
roast in the oven.

I could complete my shopping for this meal right here. I pass
cages of guinea hens, ducks, and chickens, as well as rabbits. Since my
daughter had a black angora rabbit as a pet once, I can't look with cold
eyes on the two spotted bunnies nibbling carrots in the dusty Alitalia
flight bag, can't imagine them trembling in the trunk of my car. I
intend to stop at the butcher's for a veal roast. The butcher's is bad
enough. I admit it's not logical. If you eat meat, you might as well recognize where it comes from. But the drooped heads and closed eyelids
of the quail and pigeon make me stop and stare. Rooster heads, chicken
feet (with yellow nails like Mrs. Ricker's, my grandmother's Rook
partner), the clump of fur to show the skinned rabbit is not a cat, whole
cows hanging by their feet with a square of paper towel on the floor
to catch the last drops of blood—all these things make my stomach flip.
Surely they're not going to eat those fluffy chicks. When I was a child,
I sat on the back steps and watched our cook twist a chicken's neck
then snap off the head with a jerk. The chicken ran a few circles, spurt-
ing blood, before it keeled over, twitching. I love roast chicken. Could
I ever wring a neck?

I have as much as I can carry. The other stop I'll make is at
the cooperative cantina for some local wine. Near the end of the sin-
uous line of market stalls, a woman sells flowers from her garden.
She wraps an armful of pink zinnias in newspaper and I lay them under
the straps of my bag. The sun is ferocious and people are beginning

to close down for siesta. A woman who has not sold many of her striped lime and yellow towels looks weary. She dumps the dog sleeping in her folding chair and settles down for a rest before she begins to pack up.

On my way out, I see a man in a sweater, despite the heat. The trunk of his minuscule Fiat is piled with black grapes that have warmed all morning in the sun. I'm stopped by the winy, musty, violet scents. He offers me one. The hot sweetness breaks open in my mouth. I have never tasted anything so essential in my life as this grape on this morning. They even smell purple. The flavor, older than the Etruscans and deeply fresh and pleasing, just leaves me stunned. Such richness, the big globes, the heap of dusty grapes cascading out of two baskets. I ask for *un grappolo*, a bunch, wanting the taste to stay with me all morning.

❋

As I unload my cloth sacks, the kitchen fills with the scents of sunny fruits and vegetables warmed in the car. Everyone coming home from market must feel compelled to arrange the tomatoes, eggplants (*melanzane* sounds like the real name and even aubergine is better than dreary-sounding eggplant), zucchini, and enormous peppers into a still life in the nearest basket. I resist arranging the fruit in a bowl, except for what we'll eat today, because it's ripe this minute and all we're not about to eat now must go in the fridge.

I'm still amazed that the kitchen is finished. Though there still is the ghost of a circle above the outside door, where a saint or cross hung in a niche when this was the chapel for the house, there is no sign at all of the room's later inhabitants, oxen and chickens. When the mangers were ripped out, we found the remains of elaborate scroll designs on the crumbling plaster. As the nasty pen came down, we saw green faux marble designs. Now and then in the restoration we stopped and said, "Did you ever expect to be scraping decades of mold from animal's uric acid off a wall?" and "You realize we'll be cooking in a *chapel*?"

Now, oddly, it looks as though the kitchen always could have been this way. Like those in the rest of the house, the floors are waxed brick, the walls white plaster, and the ceiling has (oh, Ed's neck and back!) dark beams. We avoided cabinets. It was easy to construct the plaster-covered brick supports built for thick plank shelves we envisioned when we spent our evenings drawing on tablets of grid paper. Ed and I cut and painted them white. The baskets from the market hold utensils and staples. The two-inch-thick white Carrara marble tops are smooth to my eye and always cool to the touch or to the pizza dough and pastry I roll on it. We hung the same rough shelves on another wall for glasses and pasta bowls. To secure the brackets, Ed drilled toggle bolts into solid rock, spewing stones and straining the drill to its highest whine.

113

*

The *signora* who lived here a hundred years ago could walk in now and start to cook. She'd like the porcelain sink, big enough to bathe a baby in, its drain board and the curved chrome faucet. I imagine her with a pointed chin and shiny black eyes, her hair swept up and twisted in a comb. She's in sturdy shoes that tie and a black dress with the sleeves pushed up, ready to roll out the ravioli. She'd be ecstatic, no doubt, to see appliances—the dishwasher, stove, and frost-free fridge (still a novelty in Tuscany), but otherwise, she'd feel quite at home. In my next life, when I am an architect, I always will design houses with kitchens that open to the outdoors. I love stepping out to head and tail my beans while sitting on the stone wall. I set dirty pots out to soak, dry my dishcloths on the wall, empty excess clean water on the arugula, thyme, and rosemary right outside the door. Since the double door is open day and night in summer, the kitchen fills with light and air. A wasp—is it the same one?—flies in every day and drinks from the faucet, then flies right out.

The one absolutely American feature is the lighting. Terrifically high utility costs explain the prevalence of forty-watt bulbs hanging in so many houses. I cannot bear a dim kitchen. We chose two bright fixtures and a rheostat, causing Lino, the electrician, extreme consternation. He'd never installed a rheostat, which intrigued him. But the lights! "One is enough. You are not performing surgery in here," he insisted. He needed to warn us that our electrical bill—he had no words, only the gesture of loosely shaking both hands in front of him and shaking his head at the same time. Clearly, we are headed for ruin.

On the brick ledge behind the sink, I've begun to accumulate local hand-painted majolica platters and bowls. I've thought of luring Shera back to paint a stencil of grapes, leaves, and vines around the top of the walls. But for the moment, the kitchen is *finito*.

❋

We poured so much energy into the kitchen because a dominant gene in my family is the cooking gene. No matter what occasion, what crisis, the women I grew up among could flat out hold forth in the kitchen, from delicate timbales and pressed chicken to steaming cauldrons of Brunswick stew. In summer, my mother and our cook, Willie Bell, went into marathons of putting up tomatoes, pickling cucumbers, stirring vats of scuppernongs for jelly. By early December they had made brandied cakes and shelled mountains of pecans for roasting. Never was our kitchen without tins of brownies and icebox cookies. Or without a plate of cold biscuits left over from dinner. I still miss toasted biscuits for breakfast. At one meal we already were talking about the next.

My daughter showed every sign of breaking the legacy of my mother and Willie, whose talents destined my sisters and me to shelves of cookbooks, constant plans for the next party, and—ultimate test—even the fate to cook when eating alone. Throughout her childhood, except for an occasional batch of obsidian-like fudge, Ashley disdained the kitchen. Shortly after she graduated from college, she began to cook and immediately started calling home for recipes for chicken with forty cloves of garlic, profiteroles, risotto, chocolate soufflé, potatoes Anna. Without meaning to, she seemed to have absorbed certain knowledge. Now, when we're together, we, too, go into paroxysms of planning and cooking. She has taught me a great marinated pork tenderloin recipe and a buttermilk lemon cake. These familial connections give me a helpless feeling: Cooking is destiny.

This inexorable inheritance notwithstanding, in recent years, I've worked more and more. In our normal life in San Francisco, everyday cooking becomes, at times, a chore. I confess to an occasional supper of ice cream from the carton, eaten with a fork while leaning against the kitchen counter. Sometimes we both get home late and find in the fridge celery, grapes, withered apples, and milk. No problem, since San Francisco has great restaurants. On weekends we try to roast two chickens or make minestrone or a big pasta sauce to get us to Tuesday. On Wednesday: a stop at Gordo's for super carnitas burritos with sour cream, guacamole, extra hot sauce, and a thousand grams of fat. In rushes of super organization, I freeze plastic tubs of soup and chili and stew and stock.

The leisure of a summer place, the ease of prime ingredients, and the perfectly casual way of entertaining convince me that this is the kitchen as it's meant to be. I think of my mother's summer tables often. She *launched* meals, seemingly with ease. Finally it dawns on me—maybe I'm not simply inadequate. It was easier then. She had people around her, as we do here. I sat on the ice cream churn while my sister turned the handle. My other sister shelled peas. Willie was totally capable. My mother directed kitchen traffic, arranged the table. I use her recipes often, and have a measure of her ease with guests but, please, no fried chicken. Here, I have that prime ingredient, time. Guests really do want to pit the cherries or run into town for another wedge of *parmigiano*. Also, cooking seems to take less time because the quality of the food is so fine that only the simplest preparations are called for. Zucchini has a real taste. Chard, sautéed with a little garlic, is amazing. Fruit does not come with stickers; vegetables are not waxed or irradiated, and the taste is truly different.

Nights turn cool at fifteen hundred feet. That suits us because we can prepare some of the hearty foods that are not at all suitable in the sun. While *prosciutto* with figs, chilled tomato soup, Roman artichokes, and pasta with lemon peel and asparagus are perfect at one, the fresh evenings fuel the appetite. We serve spaghetti with *ragù* (I finally learned that the secret ingredient of a *ragù* is chicken liver), minestrone with globes of pesto, *osso buco*, grilled polenta, baked red peppers stuffed with ricotta and herb custard, warm cherries in Chianti with hazelnut pound cake.

When tomatoes are ripe, nothing is better than cold tomato soup with a handful of basil and a garnish of polenta croutons. *Panzanella*, little swamp, is another tomato favorite, a salad of oil, vinegar, tomatoes, basil, cucumber, minced onion, and stale bread soaked in water and squeezed dry—a true invention from necessity. Since bread must be bought every day, Tuscan cooking makes good use of leftovers. The rough loaves work perfectly for bread puddings and for the best French toast I've ever had. We go for days without meat and don't even miss it, then a roasted *faraona* (guinea hen) with rosemary, or sage-stuffed pork loin, remind us of how fabulous the plainest meats can be. I cut a small basketful of thyme, rosemary, and sage, wishing I could beam one of each plant to San Francisco, where I keep a window box of faltering herbs going. Here, the sun doubles their size every few weeks. The oregano near the well quickly spreads to a circle about three feet wide. Even the wild mint and lemon balm I dug up on the hill and moved have taken off. Mint thrives. Vergil says deer wounded by hunters seek it for wounds. In Tuscany, where hunters long since have driven out most wild life, the mint is more plentiful than deer.

Maria Rita, at the *frutta e verdura*, tells me to use lemon balm in salads and vegetables, as well as in my bathwater. I think I would like cutting herbs even if I weren't cooking. The pungency of just-snipped herbs adds as much to the cook's enjoyment as to taste. After weeding the thyme, I don't wash my hands until the fragrance fades from my hands. I planted a hedge of sage, more than I ever could use, and let most flower for the butterflies. Sage flowers, along with lavender, look pretty in wildflower bouquets. The rest I dry or use fresh, usually for white beans with chopped sage and olive oil, a favorite of Tuscans, who are known as "bean eaters."

117

Anytime we grill, Ed tosses long wands of rosemary on the coals and on the meat. The crispy leaves not only add flavor, they're good to nibble, too. When he grills shrimp, he threads them on rosemary sticks.

I have pots of basil by the kitchen door because it is supposed to keep out flies. During the wall-building and well-drilling weeks, I saw a worker crush leaves in his hand and smear his wasp sting. He said it took away all the pain. A larger patch grows a few feet away. The more I cut off, the more seems to grow. I use whole leaves in salad, bunches for pesto, copious amounts in sautéed summer squashes and tomato dishes. Of all herbs, basil holds the essence of Tuscan summer.

❃

The long stretch of summer lunches calls for a long *tavola*. Now that the kitchen is finished, we need a table outdoors, the longer the better, because inevitably the abundance at the weekly market incites me to buy too much and because inevitably guests gather—friends from home, a relative's friends from somewhere who thought they'd say hello since they were in the area, and new friends, sometimes with friends of *theirs*. Add another handful of pasta to the boiling pot, add a plate, a tumbler, find another chair. The table and the kitchen can oblige.

I have considered my table, its ideals as well as its dimensions. If I were a child, I would want to lift up the tablecloth and crawl under the unending table, into the flaxen light where I could crouch and listen to the loud laughs, clinks, and grown-up talk, hear over and over *"Salute"* and *"Cin-cin"* travelling around the chairs, stare at kneecaps and walking shoes and flowered skirts hiked up to catch a breeze, the table steady under its weight of food. Such a table should accommodate the wanderings of a large dog. At the end, you need room for an enormous vase of all the flowers in bloom at the moment. The width should allow platters to meander from hand to hand down the center, stopping where they will, and numerous water and wine bottles to accumulate over the hours. You need room for a bowl of cool water to dip the grapes and pears into, a little covered dish to keep the bugs off the Gorgonzola (*dolce* as opposed to the *piccante* type, which is for cooking) and *caciotta*, a local soft cheese. No one cares if olive pits are flung into the distance. The best wardrobe for such a table runs to pale linens, blue checks, pink and green plaid, not dead white, which takes in too much glare. If the table is long enough, everything can be brought out at once, and no one has to run back and forth to the kitchen. Then the table is set for primary pleasure: lingering meals, under the trees at noon. The open air confers an ease, a relaxation and freedom. You're your own guest, which is the way summer ought to be.

In the delicious stupor that sets in after the last pear is halved, the last crust scoops up the last crumbles of Gorgonzola, and the last drop empties into the glass, you can ruminate, if you are inclined that way, on your participation in the great collective unconscious. You are doing what everyone else in Italy is doing, millions of backsides being shined by chairs at millions of tables. Over each table, a miniature swarm of gnats is gathering. There are exceptions, of course. Parking attendants, waiters, cooks—and thousands of tourists, many of whom made the mistake of eating two wedges of great sausage pizza at eleven and now have no inclination to eat anything. Instead, they wander under the unbearable sun, peeking through metal grates covering shop windows, pushing at the massive doors of locked churches, sitting on the sides of fountains while squinting into minuscule guidebooks. Give it up! I've done the same thing. Then, later, it's hard to deny yourself the luscious *melone* ice cream cone at seven, when the air is still hot and your sandals have rubbed your heels raw. Those weak ones (*mea culpa*) who succumb possibly will have another wedge, artichoke this time, on the way to the hotel; then, when Italy begins eating at nine, the foreign stomach doesn't even mumble. That happens much later, when all the good restaurants are full.

The rhythm of Tuscan dining may throw us off but after a long lunch outside, one concept is clear—siesta. The logic of a three-hour fall through the crack of the day makes perfect sense. Best to pick up that Piero della Francesca book, wander upstairs and give in to it.

I know I want a wooden table. When I was growing up, my father had dinners for his men friends and a few employees on Fridays. Our cook, Willie Bell, and my mother spread a long white table under a pecan tree in our yard with fried chicken cooked right there on our brick barbecue, potato salad, biscuits, iced tea, pound cake, and bottles of gin and Southern Comfort. The noon meal often lasted most of the day, sometimes ending with the swaying men, arm in arm singing "Darktown Strutter's Ball" and "I'm a Ramblin' Wreck from Georgia Tech" slowly as if on a tape that warped in the sun.

From the very first weeks we lived in the house, we used the abandoned worktable, a crude prototype of the table I imagined us eventually setting under the line of five *tigli* trees. At a market stall, I bought tablecloths, long to keep splinters from digging into our knees. With napkins to match, a jar of poppies, Queen Anne's lace, and blue bachelor's buttons on the table, our yellow plates from the COOP, we served forth, mainly to each other.

My idea of heaven is a two-hour lunch with Ed. I believe he must have been Italian in another life. He has begun to gesture and wave his hands, which I've never seen him do. He likes to cook at home but simply throws himself into it here. For a lunch he prepares, he gathers *parmigiano*, fresh mozzarella, some *pecorino* from the mountains, red peppers, just-picked lettuces, the local salami with fennel, loaves of *pane con sale* (the bread that isn't strictly traditional here since it has salt), *prosciutto*, a glorious bag of tomatoes. For dessert, peaches, plums, and, my favorite, a local watermelon called *minne di monaca*, nun's tits. He piles the bread board with our cheeses, salami, peppers, and on our plates arranges our first course, the classic *caprese*: sliced tomatoes, basil, mozzarella, and a drizzle of oil.

In the *tigli* shade, we're protected from the midday heat. The cicadas yammer in the trees, that deeply heart-of-summer sound. The tomatoes are so intense we go silent as we taste them. Ed opens a celebratory bottle of *prosecco* and we settle down to recap the saga of buying and restoring the house. Oddly, we now omit the complications and panic; we've begun the selection process, the same one that insures the continuance of the human race: forgetting the labor. Ed starts drawing up plans for a bread oven. We dream on about other projects. The sun through the flowering trees bathes us in gold sifted light. "This isn't real; we've wandered into a Fellini film," I say.

Ed shakes his head. "Fellini is a documentary filmmaker—I've lost my belief in his genius. There are Fellini scenes everywhere. Remember the brilliant motorcycle that comes around and around in *Amarcord*? It happens *all* the time. You're nowhere in a remote village, no one in sight, and suddenly a huge Moto Guzzi streaks by." He peels a peach in one long spiral and just because this was all too pleasant we open a second bottle of *prosecco* and wile away another hour before we

120

drift in to rest and revive our energy for a walk into town to case out the restaurants, stroll along the parterre overlooking the valley, and, hard to contemplate, begin the next meal.

✳

We have called the shy and silent carpenters, Marco and Rudolfo. They seem amused no matter what work they do here. The idea of a painted table seating ten seems to stun them. They're used to chestnut stain. Are we certain? I see them swap a glance with each other. But it will have to be repainted in two years. Too impractical. We've sketched what we want and have the paint sample, too—primary yellow.

They return four days later with the table, sealed and painted—a miracle turnaround time anywhere but especially for two as busy as they are. They laugh and say the table will glow in the dark. It does pulsate with color. They haul it to the spot with the broadest view into the valley. In the deep shade, the yellow shines, luring us to come forth from the house with jugs and steaming bowls, baskets of fruit and fresh cheeses wrapped in grape leaves.

✳

Dinner tonight is for an Italian couple, their baby, and our compatriot writers. This Italian baby girl, at seven months, chews on piquant olives and looks longingly at the food. Our friends have been amused by our adventures in restoration, safely amused since their houses were restored before workmen disappeared and before the dollar dove. Each knows an astonishing amount about wells, septic systems, gutters, pruning—minute technical knowledge acquired by years under the roofs of quirky old farmhouses. We're awed by their fluency with Italian, their endless knowledge of the intricacies of telephone bills. Though I imagine conversations about the currents in Italian literature, opera, and controversial restorations, we seem to discuss most passionately olive pruning, grease traps, well testing, and shutter repair.

The menu: with drinks, *bruschette* with chopped tomatoes and basil, *crostini* with a red pepper confit. The first course, *gnocchi*, not the usual potato but light semolina *gnocchi* (small servings—it's rich), followed by veal roasted with garlic and potatoes, then garnished with fried sage. The little green beans, still crisp, warm, with fennel and olives. Just before they arrive, I pick a huge basket of lettuces. At the start of summer, I scattered two envelopes of mixed lettuces as an edging along a flower bed. They were up in a week and in three, bolted the border. Now they're everywhere; it feels odd to be weeding the flower bed and accumulating dinner at the same time. Some look unfamiliar; I hope we're not eating just-sprouting calendula or hollyhocks. The cherries, simmered and cooled, have attracted bees to them all afternoon. One of the tiny hummingbirds made a quick foray into the kitchen, drawn possibly by the scent of the deep red wine syrup.

When they arrive it will be the soft, slow Tuscan twilight, fading after drinks from transparent to golden to evening blue, then, by the end of the first course, into night. Night happens quickly, as though the sun were pulled in one motion under the hill. We light candles in hurricane shades all along the stone wall and on the table. For background music, a hilarious chorus of frogs tunes up. *Molte anni fa*, many years ago, our friends begin. Their stories weave an Italy around us that we know only through books and films. *In the sixties . . . In the seventies . . . A true paradise.* That's why they came—and stayed. They love it but it's downhill now in comparison to the four armoires from that nutty contessa. *How alive the streets of Rome were with people, and remember the theater with the roof that rolled back, how sometimes it would rain?* Then the talk shifts to politics. They know everyone. We're all horrified at the car bombing in Sicily. Is there a Mafia here? Our questions are naive. The fascist leaning in recent elections disturbs everyone. Could Italy go back? I tell them about the antique dealer in Monte San Savino. I saw a photo of Mussolini over his shop door and he saw me looking at it. With a big smile he asks if I know who that is. Not knowing if the photo is a campy object or one of veneration, I give him the fascist salute. He goes crazy, thinking I approve. He's all over me, talking about what a bold and *bravo* man Il Duce was. I want to get out with my strange purchases—a big gilt cross and the door to a reliquary—but now the prices come down. He invites me back, wants me to meet his family. Everyone advises me to take full advantage.

I feel immersed here; my "real life" seems remote. Odd that we're all here. We were given one country and we've set ourselves up in another—they much more radically than we; they defined their lives and work by *this* place, not *that*. We feel so much at home, pale and American as we are. We could just stay here, go native. Let my hair grow long, tutor local kids in English, ride a Vespa into town for bread. I imagine Ed on one of those tiny tractors made for terraced land. Imagine him starting a little vineyard. Or we could make tisanes of lemon balm. I look at him but he is pouring wine. I almost feel our strange voices—English, French, Italian—spreading out around the house, over the valley. Sound carries on the hills. (*Stranieri*, foreigners, we're called, but it sounds more dire, more like strangers, an oddly chilling word.) Often we hear parties of invisible neighbors above us. We've shifted an ancient order of things on this hillside, where the tax collector, the police captain, and the newsstand owner (our nearest neighbors although we can't see any of them) heard only Italian until we encamped here.

The Big Dipper, clear as a dot-to-dot drawing, seems about to pour something right on top of the house, and the Milky Way, so pretty in Latin as the *via lactia,* sweeps its bridal train of scattered stars over our heads. The frogs go silent all at once, as if someone shushed them. Ed brings out the *vin santo* and a plate of *biscotti* he made this morning. Now the night is big and quiet. No moon. We talk, talk, talk. Nothing to interrupt us except the shooting stars.

ONE SPRING WHEN I STUDIED COOKING WITH SIMONE Beck at her house in Provence, she said some things I never forgot. Another student, a caterer and cooking teacher, kept asking Simca for the technique for everything. She had a notebook and furiously wrote down every word Simca said. The other four of us were mainly interested in eating what we'd prepared. When she asked one time too many, Simca said crisply, "There *is* no technique, there is just the way to do it. Now, are we going to measure or are we going to cook?"

I've learned here that simplicity is liberating. Simca's philosophy applies totally to this kitchen, where we no longer measure, but just cook. As all cooks know, ingredients of the moment are the best guides. Much of what we do is too simple to be called a recipe—it's just the way to do it. I vary the ubiquitous *prosciutto e melone* with halved figs. The cold tomato soup I make is simply chopped herbs—mainly basil—and ripe tomatoes stirred into clear chicken stock and popped in the freezer until chilled. I roast whole heads of garlic in a terra-cotta dish with a little olive oil—great to squeeze the cloves onto bread. One of the best pastas is spaghetti tossed with chopped arugula, cream, and minced *pancetta*, then sprinkled with *parmigiano*. Green beans served with black olives, sliced raw fennel, spring onions, and a light vinaigrette or lemon juice must be one of the nicest things ever to happen to a bean. Ed's invention couldn't be easier: He splits figs, pours on a little honey, runs them under the broiler, then drizzles them with cream. Sliced peaches with sweetened mascarpone and a crumbling of *amaretti* cookies have become a standby. Some favorites are a bit more involved, though nothing to make me wonder what madness led me to get involved.

Growing such a plethora of herbs induces me to squander them. All platters are garnished with what's left in the basket: a bunch of flowering thyme scattered over vegetables, the roast presented on a bed of sage, sprigs of oregano around the pasta. Lavender, grape and fig leaves, and airy fennel greens are fun to use as garnishes, too. With a few wildflowers, cut herbs in a terra-cotta pot look right at home on the table.

Here are a few quick, personal recipes that guests have raved over or that have sent us secretly to the fridge the next morning to taste the leftovers. Italians wouldn't consider risotto or pasta a main course, but for us, often it is. The oil of choice is, of course, olive oil, unless otherwise specified. All herbs in these recipes are fresh.

ANTIPASTI

*

Red Peppers (or Onions) Melted with Balsamic Vinegar

The immense, convoluted, lustrous peppers in primary red, green, and yellow are my favorite vegetable of summer because they wake up so many dishes. A quick sauté of a mixture of the three adds zip to any plate. And there's red pepper soup, mousse of yellow peppers, old-fashioned stuffed green ones . . .

Seed and slice 4 peppers thinly and cook slowly in a little olive oil and 1/4 cup of balsamic vinegar until very soft, about an hour. Stir occasionally; peppers should almost "melt." Season with salt and pepper. Add oil and balsamic vinegar once or twice if they look dry. Run under the broiler (or grill) about 25 rounds of bread sprinkled with olive oil. Rub a cut clove of garlic over each piece. Spoon peppers onto bread and serve warm. Try the same method with thinly sliced onions, adding a teaspoon of brown sugar to the balsamic and letting the onions slowly caramelize. Both versions of this are rich accompaniments for roast chicken. Leftovers are good on pasta or polenta. With cheese and/or grilled eggplant, very savory sandwiches can be made quickly.

❋

Pea and Shallot Bruschetta

New peas pop right out of the crisp pods. I thought shelling them was a meditative act until I saw a woman in town sitting outside her doorway with her cat sleeping at her ankles. She was shelling an immense pile of peas and already had filled a large dishpan. She looked up and said something rapidly in Italian and I smiled, only to realize as I walked on that she'd said, "It shouldn't happen to a dog."

Mince 4 shallots. Shell enough peas to fill 1 cup. Mix and sauté in butter until the peas are done and the shallots are wilted. Add a little chopped mint, salt, and pepper. Chop coarsely in a food processor or by hand and spoon onto 25 rounds of bread as prepared in the recipe above.

❋

Basil and Mint Sorbet

I tasted this unlikely but tantalizing sorbet at the ancient fattoria-turned-restaurant Locanda dell'Amorosa in nearby Sinalunga. The next day I tried to duplicate it at home. At the restaurant, it was served after the pasta and fish courses and before the main course. More informally, it starts out a dinner on a warm summer night.

Make a sugar syrup by boiling together 1 cup of water and 1 cup of sugar, then simmering it for about 5 minutes, stirring constantly. Cool in the fridge. Purée 1/2 cup of mint leaves and 1/2 cup of basil leaves in 1 cup of water. Add another cup of water, 1 tablespoon of lemon juice, and chill. Mix the sugar syrup and the herbal water well and process in an ice cream maker according to manufacturer's instructions. Scoop into martini glasses or any clear glass dishes and garnish with mint leaves. Serves 8.

PRIMI PIATTI

❋

Cold Garlic Soup

As in chicken with 40 cloves of garlic, the amount of garlic in this recipe is no cause for alarm. The cooking process attenuates the strength but leaves the flavor.

Peel 2 whole heads of garlic. Chop 1 small onion and peel and dice 2 medium potatoes. Sauté the onion in 1 tablespoon of olive oil and, when it begins to turn translucent, add the garlic. The garlic should soften but not brown; cook gently. Steam the diced potatoes and add to the onion and garlic, along with 1 cup of chicken stock. Bring just to a boil, then quickly lower heat and simmer for 20 minutes. Purée in a food processor, then pour back into the pot and add 4 more cups of stock and 1 tablespoon of chopped thyme. (If you don't have a food processor, mince the garlic and onion before you cook them; after steaming, put the potatoes through a ricer.) Whisk in 1/2 cup of heavy cream. Season with salt and pepper, then chill. Stir before serving with chopped thyme or chives on top. Serves 6.

❋

Fennel Soup

Thinly slice 2 fennel bulbs and 2 bunches of spring onions. Sauté briefly in a little olive oil. Add 2 cups of chicken stock to the pan and simmer until the fennel is cooked. Stir frequently. Purée until smooth. Whisk in 2-1/2 more cups of stock. Season with salt and pepper and cover. Bring to a boiling point, then lower the heat and simmer for 10 minutes. Whisk in 1/2 cup of mascarpone or heavy cream. Remove from heat immediately. Serve cold or warm, garnished with toasted fennel seeds. Serves 6.

❋

Pizza with Onion Confit and Sausage

Pizza is endless in variety. Ed's favorite is Napoli: capers, anchovies, mozzarella. I like fontina, olives, and *prosciutto*. Another favorite is arugula and curls of *parmigiano*. We're also enamored of potato pizza, as well as all the standard ones. When we cook outside, we always grill lots of extra vegetables and sausages for salads and pizza the next day. A great vegetarian combination is grilled eggplant with sundried tomatoes, olives, oregano, basil, and mozzarella.

Thinly slice 3 onions and "melt" in a frying pan on low heat, using a small amount of olive oil and 3 tablespoons of balsamic vinegar. Onions should be caramel colored and limp. Season with marjoram, salt and pepper. Grill or sauté 2 large sausages. Here we use the local pork sausage seasoned with fennel seeds. Slice. Grate 1 cup of mozzarella or parmigiano.

Dough: Dissolve 1 package of yeast in 1/4 cup of warm water for 10 minutes. Mix the following: 1/2 teaspoon of salt, 1 teaspoon of sugar, 3 tablespoons of olive oil, 1 cup of cool water, and pour into a mound of 3-1/4 cups of flour. Knead on a flat surface until elastic and smooth. If you're using a food processor, pulse until the dough forms a ball, then remove and knead by hand. Place dough in a buttered and floured bowl and let rest for 30 minutes. Roll into 1 large or 2 smaller circles and brush with oil. Scatter cheese, onions, and sausage over the surface and bake at 400° for 15 minutes. Cut into 8 pieces.

❋

Semolina Gnocchi

Gnocchi's usual knuckle shape changes in this grand and rich dish. Unlike the potato *gnocchi* or the light spinach and ricotta *gnocchi*, the *gnocchi* made with semolina are biscuit-sized. I used to buy these from a woman down in the valley until I found out how easy they are to make.

Bring 6 cups of milk almost to a boil in a large saucepan. Pour in 3 cups of semolina in a steady stream, stirring constantly. Cook on low, as you would cook polenta, continuing to stir for 15 minutes. Remove from heat, beat in 3 egg yolks, 3 tablespoons of butter and 1/2 cup of grated parmigiano. Season with salt, pepper, and a little nutmeg. Beat briefly, lifting the mixture to incorporate air. Spread mixture in a circle 1 inch thick on the lightly floured counter or cutting board and let it cool. Cut into biscuit-sized circles with the rim of a glass or a cookie cutter. Place in a well-buttered baking dish. Pour 3 tablespoons of melted butter over the top, then sprinkle with 1/4 cup of parmigiano. Bake, uncovered, at 400° for fifteen minutes. Serves 6.

✹

Everything Pasta Salad with Baked Tomatoes

When making soups, ratatouille, or this salad, I steam everything separately. This keeps the flavors distinct and allows me to cook each vegetable to its first point of doneness. I've never seen pasta salad on an Italian menu, but it's a marvelous American import. This goes easily to a picnic in a big plastic container.

Prepare vinaigrette: 3/4 cup of olive oil, red wine vinegar to taste (about 3 tablespoons), 3 cloves of crushed garlic, 1 tablespoon of chopped thyme, salt, and pepper. Shake in a jar.

Fresh vegetables: 8 medium carrots, 5 slender zucchini, 2 big red peppers, 2 hot peppers, about one-half pound of green beans, and one bunch of spring onions. Cut in small pieces, except for hot peppers—mince these. Steam one by one until just done. Cool.

Chicken: Rub 2 whole breasts with olive oil and place in an oiled pan. Season with thyme, salt, and pepper. Roast at 350° for about 30 minutes. Cool and slice into julienne strips.

Pasta: Fusilli, *the short, spiraled pasta, is best for salad. Cook two 1-pound packages and drain; immediately toss with 2 tablespoons of olive oil. Season and cool.*

Mix everything well in a large container, such as a turkey roasting pan, and chill until an hour before serving. Toss again and divide between two large bowls.

For the tomatoes: Select one for each person (plus a few more for leftovers). Cut a cone-shaped hollow from the stem end and spoon out seeds. Trim off the bottom. Sprinkle with salt and pepper, then stuff tomato with a mixture of bread crumbs, chopped basil, and toasted pine nuts. Drizzle with olive oil. Bake at 350° for about 15 minutes.

To serve, place tomato in the center of the plate, surround with pasta salad, garnish with black olives and thyme sprigs and/or basil leaves. Makes 16-20 very pretty servings.

SECONDI

❋

Risotto with Red Chard

Risotto has become soul food to me. Like pasta, pizza, and polenta, it's another dish of infinite variety. In spring, barely cooked asparagus, tiny carrots, and a little lemon make a light risotto. I especially like it with fava beans that have been sautéed with minced shallots in a covered pan, then stirred into the risotto. Other good choices: chopped fennel, barely cooked, with rock shrimp; sautéed fresh mushrooms or dried *porcini* soaked in tepid water until plumped; grilled radicchio and pancetta. In Italy, you can buy *funghi porcini* bouillon cubes in grocery stores. They're excellent for risotto when no stock is at hand. Many recipes call for too much butter; if you have a good stock, butter is unnecessary and only a little olive oil is needed to start things off. If any risotto is left the next day, heat a tablespoon of olive oil in a non-stick pan, spread and pat down the risotto, and cook over a medium flame until crisp on the bottom. Flip over with a large spatula and crisp the other side. A fine lunch.

Chop, then sauté, 1 medium onion in 1 tablespoon of oil for about 2 minutes. Add 2 cups of Arborio rice and cook for a couple of minutes. Meanwhile, in another pot, heat 5-1/2 cups of seasoned stock (chicken, veal, or vegetable) and 1/2 cup of white wine to a boil and reduce heat to a simmer. Ladle the stock and wine gradually into the rice, stirring each ladle into the rice until it is absorbed before adding more. Keep both the stock mixture and the rice at a simmer. Stir and stir until rice is done. It should be al dente and rather soupy. Add 1/2 cup of grated parmigiano. Thoroughly wash a bunch of chard, preferably red. Chop in shreds and quickly sauté in a little olive oil and minced garlic. Stir into risotto. Serve and pass a bowl of grated parmigiano. Serves 6.

＊

Rich Polenta Parmigiana

This is more of a California polenta than a traditional Italian one. So much butter and cheese! Classic polenta is cooked by the same method—don't stop stirring—with two or even three more cups of water. You then pour the polenta out on a cutting board and let it rest until firm. Often it's served with a *ragù* or with *funghi porcini*. I've served this version to Italians and they've loved it. Leftover polenta, either plain or this richer one, is sublime when sautéed until crisp.

Soak 2 cups of polenta in 3 cups of cold water for 10 minutes. In a stock pot, bring 3 cups of water to a boil and stir in the polenta. Let it come to a boil again, then turn down the heat immediately and stir for 15 minutes on a gentle flame that is strong enough to keep slow, big bubbles rising. Add salt and pepper, 8 tablespoons of butter, and 1 cup of grated parmigiano. Add more water if the polenta is too thick. Stir well and pour into a large buttered baking dish. Run in the oven at 300° for about 15 minutes. Serves 6.

❋

A Sauce of Porcini

When available, fresh *porcini* are a treat. They're at their finest simply brushed with olive oil and grilled, a dish that is as substantial as steak, which they're often paired with on the grill. Out of season, the dried ones have many talents. Though they seem expensive, a little bit adds a lot of flavor. Spoon this sauce over polenta or serve as a risotto or pasta sauce.

Soften about 2 ounces of dried porcini in 1-1/2 cups of warm water. This takes about one half hour. Peel and dice five cloves of garlic and gently sauté in 2 tablespoons of olive oil. Add 1 tablespoon each finely chopped thyme and rosemary, 1 cup of tomato sauce, and salt and pepper. Strain the mushroom water through cheesecloth and add it to the tomato mixture. Chop and add the mushrooms and simmer the sauce until thick and savory, about twenty minutes. 6 servings for polenta, 4 for pasta.

❋

Chicken with Chickpeas, Garlic, Tomatoes, and Thyme

One of those recipes that can expand to accommodate any number.

Simmer 2 cups of dried chickpeas in water with 2 cloves of garlic, salt, and pepper until tender but with plenty of bite, about 2 hours. In hot olive oil, quickly brown 6 breasts that have been shaken in a bag of flour. Arrange pieces in a baking dish. Drain chickpeas and scatter over chicken. Add a little olive oil to the same pan and sauté 1 coarsely chopped onion and 3 cloves of minced garlic; add 4 ripe tomatoes, also chopped coarsely,

1 teaspoon of cinnamon, and 2 tablespoons of thyme. Simmer 10 minutes. Spread over the chicken. Season with salt, pepper, sprigs of fresh thyme, and 1/2 cup of black olives. Bake, uncovered, at 350° for about 30 minutes, depending on the size of the chicken breasts. This is attractive in a terra-cotta dish. Serves 6.

❋

Basil and Lemon Chicken

A last-minute favorite, this chicken, served with a platter of summer squash and sliced tomatoes, tempers the hottest July night.

     In a large bowl, mix 1/2 cup each of chopped spring onions and basil leaves. Add the juice of 1 lemon, salt and pepper. Mix and rub onto 6 chicken pieces and place in a well-oiled baking pan. Dribble with a little olive oil. Roast, uncovered, at 350° for about 30 minutes, depending on the size of the chicken. Garnish with more basil leaves and lemon slices. Serves 6.

❋

Turkey Breast with Green and Black Olives

Turkey is popular here, though the whole bird is rare except at Christmas. In this recipe, the breast is sliced into cutlets, like *scallopine*. You can use flattened chicken breasts instead of turkey. If you don't pit the olives, warn your guests. I use the rest of the breast for distinctly un-Tuscan stir-fry with peppers.

     In a large pan, sauté 6 turkey cutlets in olive oil until almost done and remove to a platter. Add a little more oil to the pan and sauté 1 finely chopped onion and 2 cloves of crushed garlic. Add 1 cup of vermouth and bring to a boil, then quickly reduce heat to a simmer. Cover for 2 or 3 minutes, then add the turkey again, as well as the juice of 1 lemon and 1 cup of mixed green and black olives. Cook for 5 minutes or until the turkey is done. Season with salt and pepper and stir in a handful of chopped parsley. Serves 6.

CONTORNI

✴

Fried Zucchini Flowers

When this is good it's very, very good and when it's limp it's a disaster. I've made it both ways. The mistake was in the oil, which must be hot. Peanut or sunflower are the best oils for these delicate summer flowers.

Choose a fresh bunch of flowers, about a dozen. If they're slightly droopy, don't bother. Don't wash the blossoms; if moist, pat dry. Place a thin strip of mozzarella inside each one, dip in batter. To prepare the batter, beat 2 eggs with 1/4 teaspoon of salt and pour in 1 cup of water and 1-1/4 cups of flour. Mix well, breaking any lumps with a fork. Make sure the oil is hot (350°) but not smoking. Fry until golden and crispy. Drain quickly on paper towels and serve immediately.

✴

Baked Peppers with Ricotta and Basil

Stuffed peppers were my favorite dorm food in college. This ricotta filling is the polar opposite of the "mystery meat" we faced at Randolph-Macon. Fresh ricotta, made from ewe's milk, is a treat. The special baskets for making it imprint the sides of the cheese with a woven pattern. We often buy it at farms around Pienza, which is sheep country and also the source of *pecorino*.

Singe 3 large yellow peppers quickly over a gas flame or a grill. The peppers should char all over, but don't cook them so long that they turn limp. Cool in a plastic bag, then slide off the burned skin. Cut in half and clean out ribs and seeds. Drizzle with olive oil. In a bowl, mix 2 cups of ricotta, 1/2 cup of chopped basil, 1/2 cup of finely sliced green onions, 1/2 cup minced Italian parsley, salt and pepper. Beat in 2 eggs. Fill peppers and bake at 350° for 30 minutes. Garnish with basil leaves. Serves 6.

Fried Sage

Too often sage is associated with that green dust that comes in little jars and makes you sneeze. Fresh sage has an assertive punch that complements meat.

Wash 20 or 30 sprigs of sage, pat with paper towels, and allow to dry completely. Heat 2 inches of sunflower or peanut oil until it is very hot but not smoking. Dip sprigs in batter (see recipe for Fried Zucchini Flowers, on page 134) and drop them in hot oil (350°) for about 2 minutes or until the leaves are crisp. Drain on paper towels. A splendid garnish for lamb, pork, or any meat.

Sage Pesto

I found a pestle of olive wood at the monthly antique market in Arezzo and put it to use with an old stone mortar rescued from a friend who used it as a copious ashtray. These big mortars, she explained, originally were used for grinding coarse salt. Until recently, salt, a heavily taxed and government-controlled monopoly, was sold only in tobacco shops. The cheaper coarse salt was widely used. The large old mortars are handy for pesto; the pestle and rough stone release oils from the herbs and bind the essences of all the ingredients. Extrapolating on the basic basil pesto, I've made a lemon-parsley pesto for fish, an arugula pesto for pasta and *crostini,* and a mint pesto for shrimp. I've come to prefer the texture of these pestos to the smoother ones I'm used to. Traditional Tuscan white beans with sage and olive oil taste even better with a daub of this sage pesto. I like it on *bruschetta.* Passed separately in a bowl, it's a good accompaniment for grilled sausages.

Chop a big bunch of sage leaves, 2 cloves of garlic, and 4 tablespoons of pine nuts. Grind together in the mortar (or food processor), slowly adding olive oil to form a thick paste. Transfer to a bowl, mix again, add salt and pepper and a handful of grated parmigiano. Makes about 1-1/2 cups.

DOLCI

✳

Hazelnut Gelato

Super rich, this gelato makes me want to give up my citizenship and decamp permanently. Even people who claim not to like ice cream slip into a swoon over this one.

Toast 1-1/2 cups of hazelnuts in a moderate oven for five minutes. Watch the nuts carefully; they burn easily. Remove, wrap in a dish towel, and rub off the fine brown skin. Chop coarsely. Beat 6 egg yolks and gradually stir in 1-1/2 cups of sugar, beating until nicely incorporated. Heat 1 quart of half-and-half until almost boiling, then remove from the heat and quickly whisk in the egg and sugar mixture. In a double boiler, cook the mixture gently until it thickens and coats a wooden spoon. Cool in the fridge. Whisk in 2 table-spoons Fra Angelico (hazelnut liqueur) or vanilla, and 2 cups of heavy cream. Add hazelnuts and the juice and zest of one lemon. Pour the mixture into an ice cream maker and process according to manufacturer's instructions. Makes about 2 quarts.

✳

Cherries Steeped in Red Wine

All through June we buy cherries by the kilo and start eating them in the car on the way home. Almost nothing you can invent improves the taste of the plain cherry. We've planted three cherry trees and have uncovered three more from the ivy and brambles. Two neighboring trees are necessary for fruit production.

Stem and pit 1 pound of cherries. Pour 1 cup of red wine and the zest of a lemon over them and simmer for 15 minutes, stirring occasionally. Cover and let stand for 2 or 3 hours. Serve in bowls with plenty of juice and a big dollop of sweetened whipped cream or mascarpone. Little slices of hazel-nut pound cake or cookies also might be served. You can use plums or pears instead of cherries. Serves 4.

✳

Folded Peach Tart with Mascarpone

I first learned to make folded pie crusts from a Paula Wolfert cookbook. On a cookie sheet, you spread the crust, pile the filling in the middle, then loosely fold the edges toward the center, forming a rustic tart with a spontaneous look. The peaches here—both the yellow and the white varieties—are so luscious that eating one should be a private act.

Roll out your favorite crust a little larger than you normally do for a pie pan. Slide to a nonstick cookie sheet or baking dish. Slice 4 or 5 peaches. Mix 1 cup of mascarpone, 1/4 cup of sugar, and 1/4 cup of toasted almond slices. Combine this gently with peaches. Spoon into the center of the crust, and flop the pastry edges over, pressing them down a bit into the fruit mixture. Don't seal over the top—leave a four- or five-inch hole. Bake at 375° for about 20 minutes. Serves 6.

✳

Pears in Mascarpone Custard

This is an Italian version of the fruit cobblers I must have first tasted at the age of six months in the South, where they almost always were made of peaches or blackberries.

Peel and slice 6 medium pears (or peaches or apples) and arrange in a buttered baking dish. Sprinkle with 1 teaspoon of sugar. Cream 4 tablespoons of butter and 1/2 cup of sugar until light. Beat in 1 egg, then 2/3 cup of mascarpone. Stir in 2 tablespoons of flour last and mix well. Spoon over the fruit. Bake at 350° until just set, about 20 minutes. Serves 6 generously.

ITALIANS ALWAYS HAVE LIVED OVER THE STORE. THE *palazzi* of some of the grandest families have bricked-in arches at ground level, with remains of waist-high stone counters where someone used to ladle out preserved briny fish from a vat to customers, or carve the stuffed pig, a job now performed in sleek open-sided trucks that ply the weekly markets or sell from roadsides. I run my hand over these worn stone counters when I pass them. From odd windows at ground level, the *palazzo*'s house wine was sold. First floors of some grand houses were warehouses. Today, my bank in Cortona is the bottom of the great Laparelli house, which rests on Etruscan stones. On the top floors, windows open to the night show antique chandeliers, big armfuls of light. Often the residents are leaning out, two, sometimes three to a window, watching one more day pass in the history of this piazza. The main shopping streets, lined with great houses, are everywhere converted on the ground floor to the businesses of hardware, dishes, food, and clothing. For many buildings, probably it always has been so.

On the facades, I notice how many times previous occupants have changed their minds. The door should be here—no, here—and the arch should be a window, and shouldn't we join this building to the next one or add a continuous new facade across all three medieval houses now that the Renaissance is here? The medieval fish market is a restaurant, the Renaissance private theater is an exhibition space, the stone clothes-washing sinks still just await the flow of water, the women with their baskets.

But the clock repairer in his four-by-six-foot shop under the eleventh-century stairway of the city offices has been there for all this time, though he may now be changing the battery on the Swatch watch of an exchange student. He used to blow the glass and sift the white sand from the Tyrrhenian at Populonia for his hourglasses. He studied the water clocks drip by drip. I never have seen him stand; his back must be a hoop from slouching over the tiny parts for so many centuries. His face is lost behind the lenses he wears, so thick that his eyes seem to lunge forward. As I stop in front of his shop, he is working by the light that always angles in just so on the infinitesimal wheels and gold triangles, the numbers of the hours that sometimes fall off the white face, four and five and nine sprinkled on his table.

Perhaps my own teaching activities are immortal and I just don't see it because the place doesn't have this backdrop of time; in fact, my building at the university is a prime earthquake hazard, slated to be demolished. We're to move to a new building next fall, one with a flexible structure suited to a foundation that is partly sand dune. A postwar structure, the current Humanities Building already is obsolete: fifty-year turnaround.

The cobbler, however, seems permanent in his cave-shaped shop, which expands around him only enough for his bench, his shelf of tools, the shoes to be picked up, and one customer to squeeze into. A red boot like one on an angel in the Museo Diocesano, Gucci loafers, a yard of navy pumps, and a worn work shoe that must weigh more than a newborn baby. A small radio from the thirties still brings in the weather from the rest of the peninsula as he polishes my repaired sandal and says it should last for years.

At the *frutta e verdura,* it is the same, the same white peaches at the end of July. The figs that are perfect now and overripe by the time I get them to the kitchen. Apricots, a little basket of rising suns, and bunches of field lettuce still wet with dew. The Laparelli girl, who became a saint and now lies uncorrupted in her venerated tomb, stopped here for her grapes before she gave up eating, in order to feel His suffering more clearly. "From my garden this morning," she heard, as I do when Maria Rita holds up the melon for me to smell the fruit's perfume and her clean hand so often in the earth. When she takes me in the back of her shop to show me how much cooler it is, I step back into the medieval rabbit warren many buildings still are, behind their facades and windows filled with camcorders, silk skirts, and Alessi gadgets. We're under stone stairs, where she has a sink to wash the produce, then, another step down, we're in a narrow stone room with a twist into darkness at the end. *"Fresca,"* she says, fanning herself, and she shows me her chair among the wooden crates, where she can rest between customers. She doesn't get much rest. People shop here for her cascades of laughter, as well as for the uncompromising quality of her produce. She's open six and a half days a week, plus she cares for a garden. Her husband has been ill this year, so she's shifting crates every day as well. By eight, she's smiling, washing down her stoop, wiping a speck off a pyramid of gargantuan red peppers.

We shop here every day. Every day she says, *"Guardi, signori,"* and holds up a misshapen carrot that looks obscene to her, a luscious basket of tomatoes, or a cunning little bunch of radishes. Every garlic head, lemon, and watermelon in her shop has been lavished with attention. She has washed and arranged. She makes sure her best customers get the most select produce. If I pick out plums (touching is a no-no in produce shops and I sometimes forget), she inspects each, points out any deficiency she detects, mumbles, takes another. Each purchase comes with cooking tips. You can't make minestrone without *bietola;* chard is what makes minestrone. And toss in a heel of *parmigiano* for flavor. Just melt these onions for a long time in olive oil, a dash of balsamic vinegar, serve them on *bruschetta.*

Many of her customers are tourists, stopping in for some grapes or a few peaches. A man buys fruit and makes motions of washing his hands. He points to the fruit. She figures out that he's asking her where he can wash it. She explains that it is washed, no one has touched it, but, of course, he can't understand, so she leads him by the elbow down the street and points to the public water fountain. She finds this amusing. "Where is he from that he thinks the fruit isn't clean?"

All along the streets, artisans open their shop doors to the front light. As I glimpse the work inside, I think medieval guilds might still be practicing their crafts. A young man works on elaborate fruit and flower marquetry of a seventeenth-century desk. As he trims a sliver of pear wood, he's as intent as a surgeon reattaching a severed thumb. In another shop near the Porto Sant'Agostino, Antonio of the dark intent gaze is framing botanical prints. I step in to look and spot a lovely old mirror on his shelf. *"Posso?"* May I, I ask before I touch it. When I lift it, the top of the frame comes loose in my hand and the fragile, silver-backed antique mirror crashes to the floor. I want to dissolve. But his main concern is my seven years of bad luck. I insist on paying for the mirror, over his protests. He will make a couple of small mirrors with the old foxed shards and he will repair my frame and put in a new mirror. As I leave, I see him carefully picking up the pieces.

Most fascinating to look into is the place where paintings are restored. Strong fumes emanate from this workshop where two women in white deftly clean layers of time off canvases and rework spots that have been punctured or damaged. Renaissance painters used marble dust, chalk, and eggshells as paint bases. Sometimes they applied gold leaf onto a mordant made of garlic. Their black paint came from lampblack, burned olive sticks, and nutshells; some reds from insect secretions, often imported from Asia. Ground stones, berries, peach pits, and glass yielded other colors, which were applied with brushes made from boar, ermine, feathers, and quills: spiritual art coming directly out of nature. To duplicate the colors of those mulberry dresses, mauve cloaks, azurite robes, modern alchemical processes must go on in this little shop.

In holes in the wall all over town, the refinishing of furniture goes on. Many men make tables and chests from old wood. There's no subterfuge involved, no attempt to pass them off as antiques; they know the aged wood won't crack, will take the stain and wax, in short, will look *right*, that is, old. We take our tools to be sharpened in a black-ened room where the *fabbro* apologizes because he can't get them back before tomorrow. When we pick up the ten hoes, scythes, sickles, etc., their knife edges gleam. Tempting, but I do not run my finger across the edge.

The tailor does not wear glasses and his stitches could be done by mice. In his dark shop with the sewing machine by the window and the spools lined up on the sill, I see a new white bicycle, a water bot-tle attached for long trips, nifty leather saddlebags over the back wheel. When I see him later, though, he is only in the town park, feeding three stray cats food from his saddlebags. He unwraps the scraps they are so clearly expecting. He and I are the only ones out on Sunday morning, when most people who live here are doing something else. When I gave him my pants to hem last week, he showed me a circle of photos tacked up on the back wall. His young wife with parted lips and wavy, parted hair. *Morta*. His mother like an apple doll, also dead. His sister. There was one of him, too, as a young soldier for the Pope, restored to youth, with black hair, his legs apart and shoulders back. He was twenty-five in Rome, the war just ended. Now fifty more years have passed, everyone gone. He pats the white bicycle. *I never thought I'd be the one left.*

※

Cortona merits almost seven pages in the excellent *Blue Guide: Northern Italy*. The writer meticulously directs the walker up each street, pointing out what's of interest. From the gates to the city, further excursions into the surrounding countryside are recommended. Each side altar in the *duomo* is described according to its cardinal orientation, so that, if you happen to know which way east is, after travelling the winding roads, you can locate yourself and self-guide through the nooks and crannies. The writer has even identified all the murky paintings in the choir area. Reading the guide, I'm overwhelmed once again by all the art, architecture, history in one little hill town. This is only one of hundreds of such former marauder lookouts, perched picturesquely for views now.

143

Now that I know this one place a little, I read with doubled perception. The guide directs me to the acacia-shaded lane along the inside wall of the town, and I immediately remember the modest stone houses on one side, the view over the Val di Chiana on the other. I see, too, the three-legged dog I know lives in the house that always has the enormous underpants drying on a line. I see the cane-bottomed chairs all the people who live along that glorious stretch of wall pull out at evening when they view the sunset and check in with the stars. Yesterday, walking there, I almost stepped on a still soft dead rat. Inside one of the doorways that opens right out onto the narrow street, I glimpsed a woman holding her head in her hands at the kitchen table. Whether she was weeping or catching a catnap, I don't know.

Whatever a guidebook says, whether or not you leave somewhere with a sense of the place is entirely a matter of smell and instinct. There are places I've been which are lost to me. When I was there, I followed the guide faithfully from site to site, putting check marks in the margins at night when I plotted my route for the next day. On my first trip to Italy, I was so excited that I made a whirlwind, whistlestop trip to five cities in two weeks. I still remember everything, the revelation of my first espresso under the arcades in Bologna, remarking that it stung my throat. Climbing *every* tower and soaking my blistered feet in the bidet at night. The candlelit restaurant in Florence where I first met ravioli with butter and sage. The pastries I bought to take to the room, all wrapped and tied like a present. The dark leather smell of the shoe store where I bought (inception of a life long predilection) my first pair of Italian shoes. Discovering Allori in a corner of the Uffizi. The room at the foot of the Spanish Steps where Keats died, and dipping my hand in the boat-shaped fountain just outside, thinking Keats had dipped his hand there. I kept no record of that trip. On later trips, I began to carry a travel journal because I realized how much I forgot over time. Memory is, of course, a trickster. I remember little of three days in Innsbruck—the first bite of autumn air, a beautiful woman with red hair at the next table in a restaurant—but I can still touch every stone of Cuzco; little is left of Puerto Vallarta but the Yucatan is bright in memory. I loved the Mayan ruins seen through waves of hallucinatory heat, a large iguana who slept on the porch of my thatched room, the dogged solitude of the people, crazy storms that blew out the lights, mosquito netting waving around the bed, and candles melting astonishingly fast.

Although a getaway weekend may be just that, most trips have an underlying quest. We're looking for something. What? Fun, escape, adventure—but then what? "This trip is life changing," my nephew said. Did he know that at the outset, come to Italy looking for affirmation of a change he felt rising in him? I suspect not; he discovered this in travelling. Another guest compared the water, the architecture, the landscape, the wine—all she saw to her home town's more excellent version. It irritated me to the point of surliness. I wanted to tape her mouth, point her to an eleventh century monastery and say "Look." I felt she went home having seen nothing. Shortly after, she wrote that she was getting a divorce (no word of this while she was here) after a fourteen-year marriage to a man who has decided he is gay. When I thought back on her attitudes here, I understood that she desperately had looked for the comfort of a home which was no longer there. A guest earlier in the summer was on one of those marathon seven countries in three weeks trips. It's tempting to mock that impulse but to me it's extremely interesting when one chooses to power through that many miles. First of all, it's very American. Just *drive*, please. And far and quickly. There's a strong "get me out of here" impetus behind such trips, even when they're disguised as "seeing the lay of the land so I'll know the places I want to come back to." It's not the destinations; it's the ability to be on the road, happy trails, out where no one knows or understands or cares about all the deviling things that have been weighing you down, keeping you frantic as a lizard with a rock on its tail. People travel for as many reasons as they don't travel. "I'm so glad I went to London," a friend told me in college, "Now I don't ever have to go again." The opposite end of that spectrum is my friend Charlotte who crossed China in the back of a truck, an alternate route into Tibet. In his poem "Words from a Totem Animal," W. S. Merwin cuts to the core:

> Send me out into another life
> lord because this one is growing faint
> I do not think it goes all the way.

Once *in* a place, that journey to the far interior of the psyche begins or it doesn't. Something must make it yours, that ineffable *something* no book can capture. It can be so simple, like the light I saw on the faces of the three women walking with their arms linked when the late afternoon sun slanted into the Rugapiana. That *light* seemed to fall

145

like a benison on everyone beneath it. I, too, wanted to soak my skin under such a sun.

*

The ideal approach to my new hometown is first to see the Etruscan tombs down in the flatland below the town. There are tombs from 800 to 200 B.C. near the train station in Camucia and on the road to Foiano, where the custodian never likes the tip. Maybe he's in a bad mood because he spends eerie nights. His small farmhouse, with a bean patch and yard-roaming chickens, coexists with this *tomba* that would appear strangely primordial in the moonlight. A little uphill, a rusted yellow sign is all that points to the so-called tomb of Pythagoras. I pull over and walk along a stream until I reach a short lane, cypress lined, leading to the tomb. There's a gate but it doesn't look as if anyone ever bothers to close it. So there it is, just sitting on a round stone platform. Niches for the upright sarcophagi look like the shrine at the bottom of my driveway. The ceiling is partially gone but enough of the curve is left that I can see the dome shape. I'm standing inside a structure someone put together at least two thousand years ago. One massive stone over the door is a perfect half moon.

The mysterious Etruscans! My knowledge of them, until I started to come to Italy, was limited to the fact that they preceded the Romans and that their language was indecipherable. Since they built with wood, little remained. I was almost all wrong. Not much of their written language has been found, but much has been translated by now, thanks to the crucial find of some strips of linen shroud from an Egyptian mummy that travelled to Zagreb as a curio and were preserved later in the museum there. How the Etruscan linen, inscribed with text in ink made from soot or coal, became the wrapping for a young girl is still unknown. Possibly Etruscans migrated to Egypt after they were conquered by Rome around the first century B.C. and the girl was actually Etruscan. Or perhaps the linen was simply a convenient remnant, torn into strips by embalmers who used whatever was at hand. The mummy carried enough Etruscan text to provide several key roots, although the language still isn't totally translated. It's too bad what they left written on stone is gravestone information and government fact. A friend told me that last year a local *geometra* discovered a bronze tablet covered with Etruscan writing. He kicked it up in the dirt of a farmhouse where he was overseeing a renovation and took it home. The police heard about this and called on him that night; presumably, it is in the hands of archaeologists.

147

Of the local Etruscan culture, an astonishing amount continues to be unearthed. Beside one of the local tombs, a seven-step stairway of stone flanked with reclining lions intertwined with human parts—probably a nightmare vision of the underworld—was discovered in 1990. Nearby Chiusi, like Cortona one of the original twelve cities of Etruria, only recently found its town walls. Both Cortona and Chiusi have extensive collections of Etruscan artifacts found both by archeological digs and by farmers turning up bronze figures in their furrows. In Chiusi, the museum custodian will take you out to see some of the dozens of tombs found in that area. The Romans considered Etruscans warlike (the Romans weren't?), so they come down to us with that rap on them, but the tombs, enormous clay horses, bronze figures, and household objects reveal them to be a majestic, inventive, humorous people. Certainly, they must have been strong. Everywhere they've left remains of walls and tombs constructed of stupendous stone.

In the land around Cortona, tombs that have been found are called *meloni* locally, for the curved shape of the ceilings. To stand under one of these for a few moments is all you need to absorb the sense of time that prepares you for Cortona.

Leaving the tombs, I start uphill, gently at first, then in a series of switchbacks, I begin to climb, glimpsing through the windshield terraced olives, the crenelated tower of Il Palazzone, where Luca Signorelli fell off scaffolding and died a few months later, a broken watchtower and tawny farmhouses. A soft palate: the mellow stone, olive trees flickering moss green to platinum; even the sky may be veiled by thin mist from the lake nearby. In July, small mown wheat fields bordering the olives turn the color of lion's fur. I glimpse Cortona, noble in profile as Nefertiti. At first I'm below the great Renaissance church of Santa Maria del Calcinaio, then, for a 280-degree loop of the road, level with its solid volumes, then above, looking down on the silvery dome and the Latin cross shape of the whole. The shoe tanners built this church, after the common occurrence of the appearance of the Virgin's face on their tannery wall. She is Saint Mary of the Lime Pits because they used lime in tanning leather and the church is erected on their quarry grounds. Odd how often sacred ground remains sacred: The church rests on Etruscan remains, possibly of a temple or burial ground.

A quick look back—I see how far I have climbed. The wide-open Val di Chiana spreads a fan of green below me. On clear days I can spot Monte San Savino, Sinalunga, and Montepulciano in the distance. They could have sent smoke signals: big *festa* tonight, come on over. Soon I've reached the high town walls, and to get one more brush with the Etruscans, drive all the way to the last gate, Porta Colonia, where the big boggling Etruscan stones support the base, with medieval and later additions built on top.

Whizzing past, I love the fast glimpses into the gates. In town, they sell old postcards of these views and they look exactly the same as now: the gate, the narrow street sloping up, the *palazzi* on either side. When I enter the town, the immediate sense is that I am *inside* the gates—a secure feeling if hoards of Ghibellines, Guelfs, or whoever the current enemy are spotted in the distance waving their lances, or even if I've only managed to survive the *autostrada* without getting my car mirror "kissed" by a demon passing in a car half the size of mine.

If I come by car, I walk in on Via Dardano, a name from deep in time. Dardano, believed to have been born here, was the legendary founder of Troy. Right away on the left, I pass a four-table trattoria, open only at midday. No menu, the usual choices. I love their thinly pounded grilled steak served on a bed of arugula. And love to watch the two women at the wood-fired stove in the kitchen. Somehow they never appear to be sweltering.

I'm fascinated by the perfect doors of the dead on this street. Traditionally, they're considered to be exits for the plague dead— bad juju for them to go out the door the living use. If this is so, the custom must have come from some superstition much older than Christianity, which was firmly the religious preference of that time. Some suggest that the raised, narrow doors were used in times of strife when the *portone*, the main door, was barricaded. I've wondered if they were not simply doors used when stepping out of a carriage or off a horse and right into the house in bad weather—rather than stepping down into the wet, probably filthy, street—or even in good weather to protect a long silk skirt. George Dennis, nineteenth-century archaeologist, described Cortona as "squalid in the extreme." That the doors are rather coffin shaped, however, lends a certain visual reinforcement to the door of the dead theory.

The *centro* consists of two irregular piazzas, joined by a short street. No town planner would design it this way but it is charming. A fourteenth-century town hall with twenty-four broad stone steps dominates the Piazza della Repubblica. The steps serve as ringside seats at night when everyone is out having *gelato*—a fine place to take in the evening spectacle below. From here, you can see a loggia on the level above across the piazza, where the fish market used to be. Now it's terrace seating for a restaurant and another perch for viewing. All around are harmonious buildings, punctuated by streets coming up from three gates. The life in the street buzzes, thrives. The miracle of no cars— how amazingly that restores human importance. I first feel the scale of the architecture, then see that the low buildings are completely geared to the body. The main street, officially named Via Nazionale but known locally as Rugapiana, the flat street, is only for walking (except for a delivery period in the morning) and the rest of the town is inhospitable to drivers, too narrow, too hilly. A street connects to a higher or lower one by a walkway, a *vicolo*. Even the names of the *vicoli* make me want to turn into each one and explore: Vicolo della Notte, night, Vicolo dell'Aurora, dawn, and Vicolo della Scala, a long rise of shallow steps.

In these stony old Tuscan towns, I get no sense of stepping back in time that I've had in Yugoslavia, Mexico, or Peru. Tuscans are of this time; they simply have had the good instinct to bring the past along with them. If our culture says burn your bridges behind you—and it does—theirs says cross and recross. A fourteenth-century plague victim, perhaps once hauled out of one of the doors of the dead, could find her house and might even find it intact. Present and past just coexist, like it or not. The old Medici ball insignia in the piazza until last year had a ceramic hammer and sickle of the Communist party right beside it.

I walk through the short connecting leg of street to Piazza Signorelli, named for one of Cortona's hometown boys. Slightly larger, this piazza swarms on Saturday, market day, year round. It hosts an antique fair on the third Sunday in summer months. Two bars' outdoor tables extend into the piazza. I always notice the rather forlorn-looking Florentine lion slowly eroding on a column. No matter how late I go into town, people are gathered there; one last coffee before the strike of midnight.

Here, too, the *comune* sometimes sponsors concerts at night. Everyone is out anyway, but on these nights the piazza fills up with people from the nearby *frazioni* and farms and country villas. In this town of dozens of Catholic churches, a black gospel choir from America is singing tonight. Of course, this is no spontaneous Baptist group from a Southern church but a highly produced, professional choir from Chicago, complete with red and blue floodlights and cassettes for sale for twenty-thousand lire. They belt out "Amazing Grace" and "Mary Don't You Weep." The acoustics are weird and the sound warps around the eleventh- and twelfth-century buildings surrounding this piazza, where jousts and flag throwers have performed regularly, and where on certain feast days, the bishops hold aloft the relics of saints, priests swing braziers of burning myrrh, and we walk through town on flower petals scattered by children. The sound engineer gets the microphones adjusted and the lead singer begins to pull the crowd to him. "Repeat after me," he says in English, and the crowd responds. "Praise the Lord. Thank you, Jesus." The English and American forces liberated Cortona in 1944. Until tonight, this many foreigners may never have gathered here since, certainly not this many black ones. The choir is big. The University of Georgia's students from the art program in Cortona are all out for a little down-home nostalgia. They, a smattering of tourists, and almost all the Cortonese are crushed into Piazza Signorelli. "Oh, Happy Day," the black singers belt out, pulling an Italian girl on stage to sing with them. She has a mighty voice that easily matches any of theirs, and her small body seems all song. What are they thinking, this ancient race of Cortonese? Are they remembering the tanks rolling in, oh happy, happy day, the soldiers throwing oranges to the children? Are they thinking, Mass in the duomo was never like this? Or are they simply swaying with the crude American Jesus, letting themselves be carried on his shoulders by the music?

The piazza's focus is the tall Palazzo Casali, now the Etruscan Academy Museum. The most famous piece inside is a fourth-century B.C. bronze candelabrum of intricate design. It's remarkably wild. A center bowl fed oil to sixteen lamps around the rim. Between them, in bold relief, are animals, horned Dionysus, dolphins, naked crouching men *in erectus*, winged sirens. One Etruscan word, *tinscvil*, appears between two of the lamps. According to *The Search for the Etruscans* by James Wellard, *Tin* was the Etruscan Zeus and the inscription translates "Hail to Tin." The candelabrum was found in a ditch near Cortona in 1840. In the museum, it is hung with a mirror above so you can get a good look. I once heard an English woman say, "Well, it is interesting,

I suppose, but I wouldn't buy it at a jumble sale." In glass cases, you see chalices, vases, bottles, a wonderful bronze pig, a two-headed man, many lead soldier-sized bronze figures from the sixth and seventh centuries B.C., including some in *tipo schematico*, an elongated style that reminds the contemporary viewer of Giacometti. Besides the Etruscan collection, this small museum has a surprising display of Egyptian mummies and artifacts. So many museums have excellent Egyptian exhibits; I wonder sometimes if anything from ancient Egypt ever was lost. I always visit several paintings I like. One, a portrait of the thoughtful Polimnia wearing a blue dress and a laurel crown, was long thought to be Roman, from the first century A.D. She's the muse of sacred poetry and looks quite pensive with the responsibility. Now she's believed to be an excellent seventeenth-century copy. The museum has not changed the more impressive date.

Appealing family crests emblazoned with carved swans, pears, and fanciful animals cover the side of the Palazzo Casali. The short street below leads to the Duomo and the Museo Diocesano, formerly the Chiesa del Gesù, which I sometimes pop into. Upstairs, the treasure is the Fra Angelico *Annunciation*, with a fabulous neon orange-haired angel. The Latin that comes out of the angel's mouth heads toward the Virgin; her reply comes back to him upside down. This is one of Fra Angelico's great paintings. He worked in Cortona for ten years and this triptych and a faded, painted lunette over the door of San Domenico are all that remain from his years here.

Just to the right of Palazzo Casali is Teatro Signorelli, the new building in town, 1854, but built in a quasi-Renaissance style with arched portico, perfect to shade the vegetable sellers from sun or rain. Inside is an opera house straight out of a Márquez novel: oval, tiered, little boxes and seats upholstered in red, with a small stage on which I once witnessed a ballet troupe from Russia thump around for two hours. It serves now as the movie theater in winter. Midway through the movie, the reel winds down. Intermission. Everyone gets up for coffee and fifteen minutes of talk. It's hard, when you really love to talk, to shut up for an entire two hours. In summer, the movies are shown *sotto le stelle*, under the stars, in the town park. Orange plastic chairs are set up in a stone amphitheater, kind of like the drive-in with no cars.

Off both of these piazzas, streets radiate. This way to the medieval houses, that to the thirteenth-century fountain, there to the tiny piazzas, up to the venerable convents and small churches. I walk along all of these streets. I never have not seen something new. Today, a *vicolo* named Polveroso, dusty, though why it should be more or less dusty than others was impossible to see.

If you're in great shape, you'll still huff a little on a walk to the upper part of town. Even in the mad-dog sun right after lunch, it's worth it. I pass the medieval hospital, with its long portico, saying a little prayer that I never have to have my appendix out in there. At meal times, women dash in carrying covered dishes and trays. If you're hospitalized, it's simply expected that your family will bring meals. Next is the interminably closed church of San Francesco, austerely designed by Brother Elias, pal of Saint Francis. At the side the ghost of a former cloister arcs along the wall. Up, up, streets utterly clean, lined with well-kept houses. If there are four feet of ground, someone has planted tomatoes on a bamboo tepee, a patch of lettuces. In pots, the neighborhood hands-down favorite, besides geraniums, is hydrangeas, which grow to bush size and always seem to be pink. Often, women are sitting outside, along the street on chairs, shelling beans, mending, talking with the woman next door. Once, as I approached, I saw a crone of a woman, long black dress, black scarf, hunched in a little cane chair. It could have been 1700. When I got closer, I saw she was talking on a cellular phone. At Via Berrettini, 33, a plaque proclaims it to be the birthplace of Pietro Berrettini; I finally figured out that's Pietro da Cortona. A couple of shady piazzas are surrounded by townhouse-style old houses, with pretty little gardens in front. If I lived here, I'd like *that* one, with the marble table under the arbor of Virginia creeper, the starched white curtain at the window. A woman with an elaborate swirl of hair shakes out a cloth. She is laying plates for lunch. Her rich *ragù* smells like an open invitation, and I look longingly at her green checked tablecloth and the capped bottle of farm wine she plunks down in the center of the table.

The church of San Cristoforo, almost at the top, is my favorite in town. It's ancient, ancient, begun around 1192 on Etruscan foundations. Outside, I peer into a small chapel with a fresco of the Annunciation. The angel, just landed, has chalky aqua sleeves and skirts still billowing from flight. The door to the church is always open. Actually, it's always half open, just ajar, so that I pause and consider before I go in. Basically a Romanesque plan, inside the organ balcony of curlicued painted wood is a touching country interpretation of Baroque. A faded fresco, singularly flat in perspective, shows Christ crucified. Under each wound, a suspended angel holds out a cup to catch his falling blood. They're homey, these neighborhood churches. I like the jars (six today) of droopy garden flowers on the altar, the stacks of Catholic magazines under another fresco of the Annunciation. This Mary has thrown up her hands at the angel's news. She has a you've-got-to-be-kidding look on her face. The back of the church is dark. I hear a soft honking snore. In the privacy of the last pew, a man is having a nap.

Behind San Cristoforo is one of the staggering valley views, cut into diagonally by a slice of fortress wall, amazingly high. What has held them up all these centuries? The Medici castle perches at the top of the hill, and this part of its extensive walls angles sharply down. I walk up the road to the Montanina gate, the high entrance to town. Etruscan, too; isn't this place ancient? I often walk this way into town. My house is on the other side of the hill and from there the road into this top layer of Cortona remains level. I like to go through the upper town without having to climb. One pleasure of my walk is Santa Maria

Nuova. Like Santa Maria del Calcinaio, this church is situated on a broad terrace below the town. From the Montanina road, I'm looking down at its fine-boned shape, rhythmic curves, and graceful dome, a deeply glazed aquamarine and bronze in the sun. Though Calcinaio is more famous, having been designed by Francesco di Giorgio Martini, Santa Maria Nuova pleases my eye more. Its lines counter a sense of weight. The church looks as though it alighted there and easily could fly, given the proper miracle, to another position.

Turning back from the gate toward town, I walk to the other treasure of a church, San Niccolò. It's newer, mid-fifteenth century. Like San Cristoforo's, the decorations are amateurish and charming. The serious piece of art is a Signorelli double-sided painting, a deposition on one side and the Madonna and baby on the other. Meant to be borne on a standard in a procession, it now can be reversed by the custodian. On a hot day, this is a good rest. The eye is entertained; the feet can cool on the stone floor. On the way out, almost hidden, I spot a small Christ by Gino Severini, another Cortona boy. As a signer of the Futurist manifesto and an adherent to the slogan "Kill the moonlight," Severini doesn't readily associate in my mind with religious art. The Futurists were down on the past, embraced velocity, machines, industry. Around town, in restaurants and bars, I've seen posters of Severini's paintings, all color, swirl, energy. Then, over a table in Bar Sport, I noticed that the modern Madonna nursing a baby is his. The woman, unlike any Madonna I've seen, has breasts the size of cantaloupes. Usually a Madonna's breasts look disassociated from the body; often they're as round as a tennis ball. The Severini original in the Etruscan museum just escapes being lugubrious by being tedious. A separate room devoted to Severini is filled with an interesting hodgepodge of his work. Nothing major, unfortunately, but a taste of the styles he ran through: Braque-like collages with the gears, pipes, speedometers the Futurists loved, a portrait of a woman rather in the style of Sargent, art school-quality drawings, and the more well-known

Cubist abstractions. A couple of glass cases hold his publications and a few letters from Braque and Apollinaire. None of this work shows the verve and ambition he was capable of. Of course, all the Futurists have suffered from their early enthusiasm for Fascism; baby went out with the bathwater. They've suffered more from the tendency we have had, until recently, to look to France for the news about art. Many astounding paintings from the Futurists are unknown. For whatever reasons, Severini, in his later years, returned to his roots for subjects. I think there's a microbe in Italian painters' bloodstreams that infects them with the compulsion to paint Jesus and Mary.

As I leave San Niccolò, walking down, I pass several almost windowless convents (they must have large courtyards), one of which is still cloistered. If I had lace needing repair, I could place it on a Catherine wheel, where it is spun in to a nun to mend. Two of the convents have chapels, strangely modernized. On down the hill, I encounter Severini again in a mosaic at San Marco; if I climb this street, I'm on a Crucifixion trail he designed. A series of stone-enshrined mosaics traces Christ's progress toward the Crucifixion and then the Deposition. At the end of that walk (on a hot day I feel I've carried a cross), I'm at Santa Margherita, a large church and convent. Inside, Margherita herself is encased in glass. She has shrunk. Her feet are creepy. Most likely, a praying woman will be kneeling in front of her. Margherita was one of the fasting saints who had to be coaxed to take at least a spoon of oil every day. She shouted of her early sins in the streets. She would be neurotic, anorectic today; back then they understood her desire to suffer like Christ. Even Dante, it is believed, came to her in 1289 and discussed his "pusillanimity." Margherita is so venerated locally that when mothers call their children in the park, hers is the name most often heard. A plaque beside the Bernada gate (now closed) proclaims that through it she first entered the city in 1272.

The major street off the Piazza della Repubblica leads to the park. The Rugapiana is lined with cafés and small shops. The proprietors often are sitting in chairs outside or grabbing an espresso nearby. From the *rosticceria*, tempting smells of roasting chicken, duck, and rabbit drift into the street. They do a fast business in lasagne at lunch and all day in *panzarotti*, which means rolled bread but loses something in the translation. It's rolled around a variety of stuffings, such as mushrooms or ham and cheese. Sausage and mozzarella is one of the best. Past the circular Piazza Garibaldi—almost every Italian town has one—you come to the proof, if you have not intuited it before, that this is one of the most civilized towns on the globe. A shady park extends for a kilometer along the parterre. Cortonese use it daily. A park has a timeless quality. Clothing, flowers, the sizes of trees change; otherwise it easily could be a hundred years ago. Around the cool splash of the fountain of upside-down nymphs riding dolphins, young parents watch their children play. The benches are full of neighbors talking. Often a father balances a tiny child on a two-wheeler and watches her wobble off with a mixture of fear and exhilaration on his face. It's a peaceful spot to read the paper. A dog can get a long evening walk. Off to the right, there's the valley and the curved end of Lake Trasimeno.

The park ends at the *strada bianca* lined with cypresses commemorating the World War I dead. After walking along that dusty road toward home for about a kilometer, I look up and see, at the end of the Medici walls, the section of Etruscan wall known as Bramasole. My house takes its name from the wall. Facing south like the temple at Marzabotto near Bologna, the wall may have been part of a sun temple. Some local people have told us the name comes from the short days in winter we have on this side of the hill. Who knows how old the name, indicating a yearning for the sun, might be? All summer the sun strikes the Etruscan wall directly at dawn. It wakes me up, too. Behind the pleasure and fresh beauty of sunrise, I detect an old and primitive response: The day has come again, no dark god swallowed it during the night. A sun temple seems the most logical kind anyone ever would build. Perhaps the name does go back twenty-six or so centuries to the ancient purpose of this site. I can see the Etruscans chanting orisons to the first rays over the Apennines, then slathering themselves with olive oil and lying out all morning under the big old Mediterranean sun.

Henry James records walking this road in his *The Art of Travel*. He "strolled forth under the scorching sun and made the outer circuit of the wall. There I found tremendous uncemented blocks; they glared and twinkled in the powerful light, and I had to put on a blue eye-glass in order to throw into its proper perspective the vague Etruscan past . . ." A blue eye-glass? The nineteenth-century equivalent of sunglasses? I can see Henry peering up from the white road, nodding wisely to himself, dusting off his uppers, then, no doubt, heading back to his hotel to write his requisite number of pages for the day. I take the same stroll and attempt the same mysterious act, to throw the powerful light of the long, long past into the light of the morning.

RIVA, MAREMMA: INTO WILDEST TUSCANY

FINALLY, WE'RE READY TO LEAVE BRAMASOLE, IF ONLY
for a few days. The floors are waxed and gleaming. All the furniture
Elizabeth gave us shines with beeswax polish and the drawers are lined
with Florentine paper. The market supplied us with antique white cov-
erlets for the beds. Everything works. We even oiled the shutters one
Saturday, took each one down, washed it, then rubbed in a coat of the
ubiquitous linseed oil that seems to get poured onto everything. The
can of mixed garden flowers I flung along the Polish wall bloom with
abandon, ready to bolt at any moment. We live here. Now we can begin
the forays into the concentric circles around us, Tuscany and Umbria
this year, perhaps the south of Italy next year. Our travels are still
somewhat housebased: We are ready to stock a wine cellar, to begin to
build up a collection of wines associated with places where we have
enjoyed them with local food. Many Italian wines are meant to be
drunk immediately; our "cellar" under the stairs will be for special
bottles. In the cantina off the kitchen, we'll keep our demijohn and
the cases of house wine.

   Along the way we plan to taste as much of the Maremma cuisine as possible, bake in the sun, track down other Etruscan sites. Ever

since reading D.H. Lawrence's *Etruscan Places* years ago, I have wanted to see the ancient diving boy, the flute player in his sandals, the crouching panthers, to experience the mysterious verve and palpable *joie de vivre* hidden underground all those centuries. For several days we've plotted our route. This seems like a journey into the far interior, though, in reality, it's only about a hundred miles from our house to Tarquinia, where acres and acres of Etruscan tombs are still being explored. Time keeps bending on me here. The *density* of things to see in Tuscany makes me lose sight of our California sense of distance and freeway training, where Ed drives fifty miles to work. A week will be short. The area called the Maremma, moorland, is no longer swampy. The last of the marshy waters were long since drained off. Its history of killing malaria, however, kept this southwestern stretch of Tuscany relatively unpopulated. It's the land of the *butteri,* cowboys, of the only unsettled piece of coast along the Tyrrhenian, and of wide-open spaces interrupted only by small stone huts where shepherds used to shelter.

Soon we arrive in Montalcino, a town built for broad views along a bony ridge of hills. The eye seems to stop before the waving green landscape does. Small wine shops line the street. A table with white cloth and a few wineglasses waits right inside each door, as though inviting you in for an intimate drink with the proprietor and a toast to the great vintages.

The hotel in town is modest, indeed, and I'm alarmed that the electrical switches for the bathroom are located in the shower. I aim the showerhead as far into the opposite corner as possible and splash as little as possible. I do not want to fry before tasting the local wines! Compensation is our panorama of the tile rooftops and into the countryside. The *belle époque* café in the center of town doesn't appear to have changed an iota since 1870—marble tables, red velvet banquettes, gold mirrors. The waitress polishing the bar has cupid-bow lips and a starchy white blouse with ribbons on the sleeves. What could be more sensuous than a lunch of *prosciutto* and truffles on *schiacciata*, a flat bread like *focaccia*, with salt and olive oil, along with a glass of Brunello? The utter simplicity and dignity of Tuscan food!

   After siesta, we walk to the fourteenth-century *fortezza*, now a fantastic *enoteca*. In the old lower part, which used to store crossbows and arrows, cannons and gunpowder, all the wines of the area are available for tasting. It's brilliantly sunny outside. In the *fortezza*, the light is dim, the stone walls musky and cool. Vivaldi is playing while we try a couple of good whites from Banfi and Castelgiocondo vineyards. Appropriately, the music changes to Brahms as we taste the dark Brunellos from several vineyards: Il Poggiolo, Case Basse, and the granddaddy of all Brunello, Biondi. Brilliant, totally evolved wines that make me want to rush to a kitchen and prepare the kind of hearty food they deserve. I can't wait to cook for these wines—rabbit roasted with balsamic vinegar and rosemary, chicken with forty cloves of garlic, pears simmered in wine and served with mascarpone. The man serving us insists that we try some dessert wines. We fall for one called simply "B" and another Moscadello from Tenuta Il Poggione. The enologist must have been a former perfume maker. No dessert would be needed with these, except perhaps a white peach, just ripe. On second thought, a lemon soufflé might be just the touch of heaven. Or my old Southern favorite, crème brûlée. We buy a few bottles of the luxurious Brunellos. Just the memory of the price at home makes us indulgent. At Bramasole, we have good wine storage in two spaces under the stone stairs. We can shove cases in, lock the door, and start taking them out in a few years. Since long-term planning is not a strong suit of either of us, we buy a couple of cases of less costly Rosso di Montalcino, drinkable now, in fact, smooth and full bodied. I doubt if the dessert wines will be around by the end of summer.

   In late afternoon we drive the few miles to Sant'Antimo, one of those places that feels as if it must be built on sacred ground. From a distance, you see it over in a field of manicured olives, a pale travertine Romanesque abbey, starkly simple and pure in style. It does not look Italian. When Charlemagne passed this way, his soldiers were struck by an epidemic and Charlemagne prayed for it to stop. He promised to found an abbey if his prayer was granted and in 781 he built a church. Perhaps it is the heritage that gives the present church, built in 1118, its slender French lines. We arrive as vespers begin. Only a dozen people are here and three of these are women fanning themselves and chatting just behind us. Usually, the habit of regarding the church as an extension of the living room or piazza charms me, but today I turn and stare at them because the five Augustinian monks who strode in and took up their books have begun the Gregorian chant of this hour. The lofty, unadorned church amplifies their voices and the late lambent sun turns the travertine translucent. The music is piercing to my ear, as some birds' songs that almost can hurt. Their voices seem to roll and break, then part and converge on downward humming tones. The chanting disengages my mind, releases it from logic. The mind goes swimming and swims through large silence. The chant is buoyant, basic, a river to ride. I think of Gary Snyder's lines:

> *stay together*
> *learn the flowers*
> *go light*

I glance at Ed and he is staring up into the pillars of light. But the women are unmoved; perhaps they come every day. In the middle, they saunter noisily out, all three talking at once. If I lived here, I'd come every day, too, on the theory that if you don't feel holy here, you never will. I'm fascinated by the diligence of the monks performing this plainsong for the six liturgical hours of every day, beginning with *lodi*, prayers of praise, at seven A.M., and ending with *compieta,* compline, at nine. I would like to come back for a whole day and listen. I see in the brochure that those on spiritual retreat can stay in guest quarters and eat at a nearby convent. We walk around the outside, admiring the stylized hooved creatures supporting the roof.

A cool evening to ride over dirt roads admiring the land, sniffing like a dog out the window the fresh country smells of dry hay. We arrive at Sant'Angelo in Colle, a restaurant operated by Poggio Antico vineyards. A wedding party is in uproarious progress and all the waitresses are enjoying the action. We're put in a back room alone, with the rousing party echoing around us. We don't mind. A stone sink is piled with ripe peaches, scenting the room. We order thick onion soup, roast pigeon, potatoes with rosemary, and what else, the house's Brunello.

*

Wildest Tuscany is somewhat of an oxymoron. The region, as a whole, has been tamed for centuries. Every time I dig in the garden, I'm reminded of how many have gone before me on the land. I have a big collection of fragments of dishes, dozens of patterns, so many that I wonder if other women fling their dishes into the garden. Crockery colanders, edges of lids, delicate cup handles, and assorted pieces of plates gradually have collected on an outdoor tabletop, along with jawbones of a boar and a hedgehog. The land has been trod and retrod. A glance at terraced farming shows how the hills have been reshaped for the convenience and survival of humans. Still, the Maremma area remained, until less than a hundred years ago, a low coastal plain inhabited by cowboys, shepherds, and mosquitoes. Its *mal aria* was definitely associated with chills and fever. Farmhouses are occasional whereas the rest of Tuscany is dotted with them. The Renaissance touched lightly here; towns, generally, are not permeated with monumental examples of architecture and adorned by the great names in painting. The bad air, now soft and fresh, probably kept the extensive Etruscan tombs safer. Although many were recklessly pillaged, an astonishing number remain. Were Etruscans immune to malaria? All evidence shows that the area was quite populated in their time.

Our next base is a villa, now a small hotel, on the Acquaviva vineyard property outside Montemerano. Ed has cased the *Gambero*

164

Rosso guide and spotted this tiny village with three excellent restaurants. Since it is central for most of what we want to see, we decide to stay put for a few days rather than checking in and out of hotels. A tree-lined drive leads to a park-sized garden with shady places to sit outside and look over the rolling vineyards. We have a room right on the garden. I push open the shutters and the window fills with blue hydrangea. We quickly unpack and take off again; we can relax later.

Pitigliano must be the strangest town in Tuscany. Like Orvieto, it sits on top of a tufa mass. But Pitigliano looks like a drip castle, a precipitous one looming above a deep gorge. Who could look down, while trying to see the town and the road at the same time? Tufa isn't the strongest rock in the world, and sections of it sometimes weaken, erode, or veer off. Pitigliano's houses rise straight up; they're literally living on the edge. The tufa beneath the houses is full of caves—perhaps for the storage of the area's Bianco di Pitigliano, a wine that must derive its astringent edge from the volcanic soil. In town, the bartender tells us that many of the caves were Etruscan tombs. Besides wine, oil is stored and animals are housed. Medieval towns have a dark and twisted layout; this town's feels darker, more twisted. Many Jews settled here in the fifteenth century; it was outside the realm of the Papal States, who were busy persecuting. The area where they lived is called a ghetto. Whether there was a strict ghetto here, as there was in Venice, where Jews had to keep to a curfew, had their own government and cultural life, I don't know. The synagogue is closed for reconstruction but it does not appear that anything much is happening. Almost everything seems to be for sale. In this life or the next, some of the rim houses are going to find themselves in the gorge. Perhaps this contributes to the gloomy feel the town gives me. On the way out, we buy a few bottles of the local white for our growing collection. I ask how many Jews lived there during World War II. "I don't know, signora, I'm from Naples." Winding downhill, I read in a guidebook that

the Jewish community was exterminated in the war. I'd never trust a
guidebook on a fact and hope that this is wrong.

Tiny Sovana, nearby, has the feeling of a ghost town in
California, except that the few houses along the main street are
immensely old. People are outnumbered, it seems, by Etruscan tombs
built into the hillsides. We spot a sign and pull over. A path takes us
into a murky wooded area with a stagnant stream just made for female
anopheles mosquitoes. Soon we're scrambling on slippery paths, up
along a steep hillside. We begin to see the tombs—tunnels into the
hills, stony passageways leading back, probably to vipers. The entrances
in that wildness look undisturbed for the centuries. Nothing is
attended—no tickets sold, no guides waiting; it is as though you discover these strange haunted sepulchers yourself. Vines dangle, as in the
Mayan jungles around Palenque, and the eroded carvings in the tufa
also have that strangely Eastern aspect that many of the Mayan carvings have, as though long ago art was the same everywhere. It's very
clear that becoming an Etruscan archaeologist is a good move. Endless
areas are awaiting further investigation. We climb for hours, encoun-
tering only a large white cow standing up to its knees in the stream.
When we emerge, I have bleeding scratches on my legs but not a single mosquito bite. I have the feeling that this is a place I will think
about on nights of insomnia. Down the road, we see another sign. This
points to the remains of a temple, which looks carved out of the tufa
hillside. We walk among eerie arches and columns, partly excavated and
looking quite abandoned. Those Etruscans are going to stay mysterious. What did they do here? An Art in the Park summer concert series?
Strange rites? The guidebooks refer to this as a temple, and perhaps
here in the center a wise person practiced haruspication, the art of
divining by reading a sheep's liver. A bronze model of one was found
near Piacenza, with the liver divided into sixteen parts. It is thought
that the Etruscans similarly divided the sky, and that the way the liver
was sectioned also determined the layout of Etruscan towns. Who

knows? Perhaps the forerunners of talk shows held forth here or it was the market for seafood. In places such as Machu Picchu, Palenque, Mesa Verde, Stonehenge, and now here, I always have the odd and somber consciousness of how time peels us off, how irretrievable the past really is, especially in these hot spots where you sense some matrix of the culture took place. We can't help but push our own interpretations on them. It's a deep wish of philosophers and poets to search for theories of eternal return and time past being time present. Bertrand Russell was closer when he said the universe was created five minutes ago. We can't recover the slightest gesture of those who chopped out this rock, not the placing of the first stone, the lighting of a fire to make lunch, the stirring of a pot, the sniffing of an underarm, the sigh after lovemaking, *niente*. We can walk here, the latest little dots on the time line. Knowing that, it always amazes me that I am intensely interested in how the map is folded, where the gas gauge is pointed, whether we have withdrawn enough cash, how everything matters intensely even as it is disappearing.

We've seen enough for the day but can't resist a walk through ancient Sorano, also poised on an endangered tufa mass. There seem to be no tourists in this whole area. Even the roads are empty. Sorano looks the same way it did in 1492, when Columbus found America. The last building must have gone up around then. There's a somber feel to the narrow streets, a gray light that comes off the dark stone, but the people seem extraordinarily friendly. A potter sees us looking in and insists that we visit his workshop. When we buy two peaches, the man rinsing off his crates of grapes with a hose gives us a bunch. *"Speciale!"* he tells us. Two people stop to help us out of a tight parking place, one gesturing come on, the other gesturing stop.

We're dusty and worn out as we pull into our parking spot near Acquaviva's garden. Before dinner, we shower, change, and take glasses of their own white wine, a Bianco di Pitigliano, out to the comfortable chairs and watch the sun drop behind the hill, just as two Etruscans might have in this exact place.

Montemerano is only a few minutes away, a high castle town, beautiful and small.

It has its requisite fifteenth-century church with the requisite Madonna—this one with a difference. It's entitled *Madonna della Gattaiola, Madonna of the Cat Hole.* The bottom part of the painting had a hole to let the cat out of the church. Everyone in town seems to be outside. A few local boys and men are playing some jazz right in the center of town. The woman running the bar slams the door. Apparently she's heard enough. Absolutely everyone stares when a tall and gorgeous man in riding boots and a tight T-shirt strides by. But he's aloof, takes no notice. I see him check out his image in the shop windows he passes.

We're ravenous. As soon as the magic hour of seven-thirty arrives and the restaurant opens the door, we rush in. We're the only ones in Enoteca dell'Antico Frantoio, a former olive mill, now remodeled to the extent that it looks like a reproduction of itself. Although it has lost its authentic feel, the result is rather like an airy Napa Valley restaurant, so we feel quite at home. The menu, however, reveals the Maremma roots: *Acquacotta,* served all over Tuscany, is a particular local specialty, the "cooked water" soup of vegetables with an egg served on top; *testina di vitella e porcini sott'olio,* veal head and porcini mushrooms under olive oil; *pappardelle al ragù di lepre,* broad pasta with *ragù* made of hare; *cinghiale in umido alle mele,* smoked boar with apples. In *trattorie* over most of Tuscany, menus are almost interchangeable: the usual pastas with *ragù,* butter and sage, pesto, or tomato and basil, the standard selection of grilled and roasted meats, the *contorni* usually consisting of fried potatoes, spinach, and salad. No one seems interested in varying the classics of the cuisine. In this less settled, less travelled region, the cuisine of Tuscany is closer to its origins, the hunter bringing home the kill, the farmer using every part of the animal, the peasant woman making soup with a handful of vegetables and an egg. Usually you do not find the above items; nor do you see *capretto*, kid, or *fegatello di cinghiale*, boar liver sausage, on menus. The Frantoio has its more delicate side, too: *ravioli di radicchio rosso e ricotta*, ravioli with red radicchio and ricotta, and *sformato di carciofi*, a mold of baked artichoke. We start with *crostini di polenta con pure di funghi porcini e tartufo*, polenta squares with a purée of porcini and truffles—rich and savory. Ed orders the rabbit, roasted with tomatoes, onions, and garlic, and I bravely order the kid. It's delicious. The wine of the region is the Morellino di Scansano, black as the wine of Cahors, a discovery for us. This enoteca's own is the Banti Morellino, big and accomplished. Now I'm really happy.

In the morning, I have one of the favorite experiences of my life. We get up at five and go to the hot waterfall near Saturnia. No one is there at that hour, although the hotel manager warned us of crowds later in the day. Pale blue but clear water cascades over tufa, which the falls have hollowed out in many places, forming perfect places to sit down and let the warm water flow over and around you. When I first heard of the falls, I thought we might emerge smelling like old Easter eggs, but the sulphur is mild. The current has enough force that you feel massaged, not enough to sweep you away. Bliss. Where are the water nymphs? Whatever it is supposed to cure, I'm sure it does. After an hour I feel as though I have no bones in my body. I am utterly relaxed, limp, speechless. We leave just as two cars pull up. Back at Acquaviva, we have breakfast on the terrace: fresh orange juice, nut bread, toast, something like pound cake, and pots of coffee and warm milk. It's hard to leave. Only the lure of the Etruscans stirs us to pick up our map and go.

Tarquinia is out of Tuscany, a few miles into Lazio. It gets ugly along the way, industrial and crowded. I'm less able to visualize the Etruscans here than in the green and dreamy Maremma. Traffic annoys us after so many empty roads. Soon we're in the busy town of Tarquinia, where hoards of items from the tombs are exhibited in a fifteenth-century palazzo. Staggering, amazing, fantastic, and worth the trip alone are two terra-cotta winged horses from the fourth or third century B.C. These were found in 1938 near the steps leading to a temple, now just a two-level base of square limestone blocks. The horses must have been ornaments. I wonder about their connection to Pegasus, who started the flow of the sacred Hippocrene with a dash of his hoof, who always is linked with poetry and the arts. These are fabulously vigorous horses with muscles, genitals, ribs, perky ears, and feathered wings. The chronological arrangement of the museum is useful for sorting out when there were Attic influences, when they began using stone sarcophagi, how design changed. Everything from cinerary urns to perfume burners makes you feel the creative energy and spirit behind these objects. Several tomb paintings have been brought here to prevent deterioration. The tomb of the Triclinium, with its prancing musician and young dancer swathed in what looks like a chiffon throw, would melt the heart of a stone. In almost any museum, I fade after a couple of hours and can wander by with a glance at something that would have stopped me for minutes when I first arrived. We resolve to come back, though, because there is so much to linger over.

The field of tombs could be any field, the necropoli like outhouses attached to sheds. The structures built over tombs open to the public are simply entrances with a flight of steps leading down. The tombs are lit. We're disappointed to find that only four a day are open. Why? No one seemed to know; they're on a rotation system, that's all. Now we know we'll come back because the Hunting and Fishing Tomb is not on view today. We see the Lotus Flower one, with decorations that have almost a Deco style, then the Lionesses one, famous for the reclining man holding up an egg—symbolic of resurrection, as in Christian belief, the shell like the tomb broken open. Dancers cavort here, too. I notice their elaborate sandals with straps crossed and wound around the ankles just like the ones I'm wearing—did the Italians always love shoes? We're lucky to see the Jugglers' tomb, rather Egyptian looking, except for what appears to be a Middle Eastern belly dancer about to go into her act. In the two-chambered tomb of the Orcas remains, amid much faded scenes of a banquet, a startling portrait of a woman in profile with a crown of olive leaves.

After a quick bite, we drive the few kilometers to Norchia, which we've heard is the site of many recent finds. It does not appear that anyone has been about in decades. The broken sign points up to the sky. After we wander about, a farmer points us in the right direction. At the end of a dirt road we park and set out along the edge of a wheat field. A few meters down the path, we encounter a severed goat head covered with flies. Here, indeed, is a sign—a primitive one of sacrifice. "This is getting spooky," I say as we step around it. The terrain becomes precipitous. We're climbing down and all I can think about is the climb back up. A few rusted hand railings indicate we're going in the right direction. The declivity becomes sharper; we're skidding, holding on to vines. Haven't we seen enough of these tombs? When it levels out, we start to see the openings into the hillside, dark mouths, vines, and brush. We venture into two, breaking through impressive spiderwebs with sticks. Inside, it's as black as, well, a tomb. We see slabs and pits where the bodies and urns lay. Vipers must coil here now. We walk about half a mile along this level. The tombs are more numerous than at Sovana and poke into the hillside at various levels. There's an oppressive feeling of danger I can't identify. I just want to leave. I ask Ed if he thinks this is a weird place and he says, "Definitely, let's go." The way out is as awful as I expected. Ed stops to empty dirt out of his loafer and a sliver of bone falls out. We come to the place where we saw the goat head; it is no longer there. When we get back to the car, another one is parked near us. A young couple is kissing and rolling around with such intensity that they don't hear us.

This dispels the bad aura and we head back to the hotel, saturated with Etruscan voodoo.

Ah, dinner, the favorite hour. Tonight it's Caino, which we expect to be the gastronomic highlight of our trip. Before driving into Montemerano, we take a little detour to Saturnia, perhaps the oldest town in Italy if Cortona isn't. It would have to be if, as legend has it, Saturn, son of sky and earth, founded it. The warm waterfall, legend also tells us, first poured forth when the horse of Orlando (Roland in English) pawed the ground with his hoof. A town on Via Clodia has to be older than anything I can grasp. I practice saying "I live on Via Clodia," imagining a life on such an ancient street. The town is shady and active, not at all lost in time. A few highly bronzed people from the expensive hotel near the falls seem to be looking for something to buy but the shops are plain. They settle at an outdoor café and order colorful drinks in tall glasses.

Caino, a jewel: two gracious small rooms with flowers on the tables, pretty china and wineglasses. With glasses of *spumante*, we settle into the menu. Everything looks good and I have a hard time deciding. They, too, have a combination of sophisticated choices and the rustic Maremma specialties, such as *zuppa di fagioli,* white bean soup, pasta with rabbit sauce, *cinghiale all'aspretto di mora*, boar with blackberry sauce. For our *antipasti,* we're attracted to *flan di melanzane in salsa tiepida di pomodoro,* eggplant flan with tepid tomato sauce, and *mousse di formaggi al cetriolo,* a mousse of cheeses and cucumber. We both want *tagliolini all'uovo con zucchine e fiori di zucca,* egg pasta with zucchini and squash blossoms, for first courses. After that, it's roast lamb for Ed and duck breast in a sauce of grape must vinegar for me. We take the waiter's suggestion for tonight's Morellino, the Le Sentinelle Riserva 1990 by Mantellassi. Praise Allah! What a wine. The dinner is superb, every bite, and the service attentive. Everyone in the small restaurant has noticed the young couple at the table in the middle from the moment they were seated. They look like twins. Both have that curly, magnificent black hair and hers has jasmine flowers caught in its ripples. Both have the sultry eyes my mother used to refer to as "bedroom eyes" and lips like those on archaic Greek statues. They're dressed out of Milan or Rome boutiques, he in a somewhat rumpled tan linen suit and she in a yellow puckered silk sundress that was melted onto her. The waiter pours champagne for them, an oddity in an Italian restaurant. We all avert our eyes as they toast each other and seem to disappear into each other's eyes. Our salads look as if someone picked them from a field this afternoon, and perhaps they did. We're falling into a deep relaxation and exhilaration by now, just what a vacation is supposed to be. "Would you like to go to Morocco?" Ed asks out of nowhere.

"What about Greece? I never intended not to go to Greece." Seeing new places always brings up the possibility of other new places. We're riveted again by the beautiful couple. I see the other diners discreetly staring, too. He has moved from his chair across from her to the one next to her and has taken her hand. I see him reach into his pocket and take out a small box. We turn back to our salads. We will have to forego *dolci* but with our coffee they bring a plate of little pastries anyway, which we manage to eat. This is one of the best dinners I've had in Italy. Ed proposes that we stay a few more days and eat here every night. The lustrous girl now is holding out her hand, admiring a square emerald surrounded by diamonds I can see from here. They both smile at everyone, they suddenly realize, who has followed this engagement. Spontaneously we all lift our glasses in a toast and the waiter, sensing the moment, rushes in to refill. The girl shakes back her long hair and little white flowers fall on the floor.

When we leave, the village is dark and silent until we get to the bar at the end of the street, where the whole town must be playing cards and having a last coffee.

In the morning we drive over to Vulci, another ancient-sounding name, with a humpbacked bridge and a castle turned museum. The bridge is Etruscan, with Roman and medieval repairs and additions. Why it's so highly arched is impossible to know because the Fiora, little more than a mighty stream, runs far below in a gorge. But humped it is. Whatever road it once joined has disappeared, so the bridge has a strangely surreal aspect. The castle fortress at one end was built much later. A Cistercian monastery surrounded by a moat, it now serves as a museum, like Tarquinia's, full of astonishing things. Too bad the glass separates us from the objects. They are extremely appealing to the touch. I want to pick up each little votive hand, fawn-shaped perfume bottle, to rub the monumental stone sculptures, such as the boy on the winged horse. Here's the real news about the Etruscans—their art is fortifying, the remains of people who lived in the moment. D. H. Lawrence certainly caught that—but who could not, having seen as much as he did. Rereading him along the way, I'm struck often with what an *ass* he was. The peasants are dullards because they do not immediately see to the wishes of this obnoxious foreigner. No one is just waiting to take him miles into the country to see ruins. No one is equipped with candles the minute he asks. What an inconvenient country! The train schedules are unlike those at Victoria Station; the food is not to his liking. I forgive him now and then, when he totally disappears from the text and just writes what he sees.

Remains of the Etruscan, then Roman, town lie out in the field—stone foundations and bits of floor, some with black and white mosaic, subterranean passageways and remnants of baths: a floor plan of the town, actually, so that you walk around imagining the walls around you, the activities, the views across to the bridge. Off to the side, we see the stark Roman remains of a brick building, walls, a few windows, and holes for beams to hold up a floor. Vulci, a lavish archeological area. Unfortunately, the area's painted tombs are closed today—another reason to return.

We're amazed by the restaurants, too. Enoteca Passaparola, on the road leading up to Montemerano, serves robust food in a very casual ambience—paper napkins, chalkboard menu, plank floors. If there are cowboys left in the Maremma, I think they would head here. We order big plates of grilled vegetables and wonderful green salads with a bottle of Lunaia, a Bianco di Pitigliano made by La Stellata, another gorgeous local wine. The waiter tells us about the area's Cantina Cooperativa del Morellino di Scansano, then brings over a glass for us to taste. We find our house wine for the rest of the summer. At about $1.70 a bottle, it has a deep mellifluous taste that surprises us. More straightforward than the *reserve* Morellinos we've tried, this wine definitely stands up to be counted. We still have the backseat where we can pile a couple of cases.

At the next table an artist draws caricatures of us. Mine looks like Picasso's Dora Maar. When we toast him and begin to chat, he opens a satchel and starts showing us catalogues of his shows. Soon we're nodding politely. He pulls out reviews, pours more wine. His wife looks not mortified but resigned; she's been to restaurants with him before. They're at the *terme*, taking the waters for his liver. I can imagine him cornering people there as they sip their measures of mineral water. He slides his chair over, leaving her at their table. I'm torn between the pleasure of the berry tart listed on the chalkboard and the pleasure of getting the check and leaving. Ed asks for the check and we exit. Up in town we have coffee, then on the way back to the car, we look in the window and see that Signor Picasso is gone. So we have the berry tart after all. The waiter brings us a complimentary *amaro*. "They come here every night," he complains. "We're counting the days until he goes back to Milano with his liver."

Saturated with the Etruscans, well fed, pleased with the hotel, we pack and take off for Talamone, a high-walled town over the sea.

The water must be pure here. It's clear as far out as I can wade and quite cold. At our modern hotel, there's no beach, just rocks jutting straight up, with concrete platforms on the water where you can sit in a striped chair and sunbathe. We chose Talamone because it is adjacent to the Maremma's preserved seashore, the only long stretch of Tuscan coast unblemished by development. Most sand beaches are a series of concessions for umbrellas and rows of chairs as deep as the beach is wide, leaving only a strip along the water for walking. Often these concessions have changing rooms, showers, and snack bars. Italians seem to like this way of being at the beach. So many people to talk to! And. usually, families or groups of friends are together. As a Californian, I'm unhappy to be surrounded. Beaches I grew up on in Georgia and my years of loving the raw windy stretches of sand at Point Reyes unequip me for the Old World beaches. Ed and my daughter like the umbrellas. They've dragged me to Viareggio, Marina di Pisa, Pietrasanta, insist it's just different; you have to get into it. I like to lie on the beach and listen to the waves, to walk with no one in sight. The Tuscan beaches are as crowded as streets. The Maremma preserve, however, even has wild horses, foxes, boar, and deer, according to the brochure. I love the smell of the *macchia*, the wild salty shrubs sailors say they can smell when still out of sight of land. Mostly there's nothing—trails with wild rosemary and sea lavender through sandy hills, the vacant beaches. We walk and sit on the beach all morning. Tyrrhenian, Tyrrhenian the waves say, that ancient sea. We've brought mortadella sandwiches, a hunk of *parmigiano*, and iced tea. Except for a small group of people down the beach, I have my wish to be in nature alone. What color is the sea? Cobalt is close. No, it's lapis lazuli, exactly the color of Mary's dress in so many paintings, with a tesselated sheen of silver. It's good to walk, after days of chasing sites in the car. I'm trying to read but the sun is blaring—perhaps an umbrella *would* be nice.

In the morning we move on to Riva degli Etruschi, coast of the Etruscans. We can't get away from them. This beach does have the rented chairs but, since it joins the preserve, it's not as crowded. We're able to take a long, long walk on the beach followed by a siesta in our tiny individual cottage. We're near San Vicenzo, where Italo Calvino summered. The town shops sell rubber beach balls, rafts, and sand pails. At evening, everyone strolls around buying postcards and eating ice cream. Beach towns are beach towns. We find an outdoor restaurant and order *cacciucco*, a big fish stew. Several kinds of fish, filleted at the cart, are piled in a large white bowl and a hot broth is poured over them. The waiter spreads creamy roasted garlic on slices of toasted bread and we float them in the soup, breathing in the heady aroma. Two fierce little bug-eyed lobsters eye us from our bowls. The waiter keeps coming around, ladling in enough to keep the bread afloat. When he brings the salad, he wheels over a cart of olive oils in crocks, clear bottles, colorful ceramic ones, dozens of choices for our salad. We ask him to select for us and he pours from on high a thin stream of pale green oil onto a bowl of red and green radicchio.

En route to Massa Marittima, we detour to Populonia, simply because it is close and it sounds too ancient to miss. Every little pause makes me want to linger for days. In a café where we stop for coffee, two fishermen bring in buckets of fish, their night's catch. Lunch is not for hours, unfortunately. A woman from the kitchen starts writing up the menu of the day on a blackboard. We drive on into town and park under an immense fortress, the usual castle and wall like those in old books of hours. Ah, another Etruscan museum and I must see every object. Ed is through, for now, with anything that happened before the last millennium, so he goes off to buy honey from bees that have buzzed around in the coastal shrubs. We meet in a shop where I find an Etruscan clay foot for sale. Whether it's genuine or fake, I don't know. I decide to think about it while we take a walk but when we come back to buy it, the shop is closed. As we leave, I see a sign to an Etruscan site but Ed presses on the accelerator; he's tombed out.

Last overnight—the town I have chronically mispronounced. The accent, I find, is on Marit' tima. I've said Maritti' ma. Will I ever, ever learn Italian? Still so many basic errors. Once close to the sea, the town gradually became surrounded by silt, which eventually filled in, leaving Massa Marittima far inland but with a sense of outlook as it rises high over the grassy plain. We could be in Brazil, a remote outpost that appeals to magic realist novelists. It's two towns really, the old town and the older town, both austere, with deep shadows and sudden sunlight. We're a little tired. We check in and for the first time, our room has a TV. A World War II film, faded and in odd Italian, is on and we get hooked. A village, occupied by Germans, depends on an American soldier hiding in the countryside to help them. They must evacuate. They pile everything on a few donkeys and set out, for where we don't know. I doze. Someone is trying to open the shutters at Bramasole. I wake up. Another soldier is in the hayloft. Something is burning. Is Bramasole all right? Suddenly I realize this is our one day in Massa Marittima.

In two hours, we've covered every street. The Maremma keeps reminding me of the American West, its little out of the way towns the freeway missed by fifty miles, the shop owner staring out the window, the wide sky in his gaze. Certainly the piazza and fabulous cathedral are nothing like the West—the similarity is under the skin of the place: a loneliness, an eye on the stranger.

✳

En route home, we pause at San Galgano, loveliest of ruins, a graceful French Gothic church that lost its floor and roof centuries ago, leaving the open-windowed skeleton to grass and clouds. A romantic wedding could take place here. Where the large rose window was, only the imagination can color the space scarlet and blue; where monks lit candles at side altars, birds nest in the corners. A stone stairway leads nowhere. A stone altar remains, so disassociated from Christian function that human sacrifice could have taken place on it. The place fell into ruin when an abbot sold the lead in the roof for some war. Now it's a home for several cats. One has a litter of multicultural kittens; several fathers must have contributed to the ginger, black, and striped pile curled around the large white mother.

Home! Hauling in the wine, throwing open the shutters, running to water the drooping plants. We settle the wine into crates in the dark wedge of closet under the stairs. The spirit of all the grapes we saw ripening, now bottled and mellowing for those occasions we hope to celebrate. Ed closes the door, leaving them to dust and scorpions for now. Only a week away. We missed the house and come back understanding the next few circles around us. Qualities those of us with northern blood envy—that Italian insouciance and ability to live in the moment with gusto—I now see came down straight from the Etruscans. All the painted images from the tombs seem charged with meaning, if we only had the clues to read it. I close my eyes and look at the crouching leopards, the deft figure of death, the endless banqueting. Sometimes Greek myths come to mind, Persephone, Actaeon and the dogs, Pegasus, but the instinct I have is that the tomb images—and the Greek ones—each came from further back, and those further back came from something even earlier. The archetypes keep appearing and we find in them what we can, for they speak to our oldest neurons and synapses.

When I lived in Somers, New York, I had a large herb garden beside the eighteenth-century house I still dream of. Often I turned up brown and amber medicine bottles. As I was planting a border of santolina, the branches of which used to be spread on church floors in the Middle Ages to keep the human scents down, my trowel unearthed a small iron horse, rusty, stretched into full-out running position. I propped the horse on my desk as my private totem. Earlier this summer, I was digging up stones and my shovel sent flying a small object. When I picked it up, I was stunned to find that it was a horse. Is it Etruscan or is it a toy from a hundred years ago? This horse, too, is running.

A few years ago I read a section in the *Aeneid* about the decision to found Carthage on the spot where the wanderers dug up an omen:

179

> the head of a spirited horse, for by this sign
> it was shown that the race would be distinguished
> in war and abound with the means of life
>
> (I, 444)

The war in the line doesn't thrill me but "means of life" does. The hoof of Orlando opened the hot spring. The winged horses at Tarquinia, unearthed from stone rubble and dirt, keep appearing in my vision. I prop a postcard photo of them next to my own two horses. Means of life. The Etruscans had it. In certain times and places, we find it. We can run full out, if not fly.

THE ITALIAN ED IS A LIST MAKER. ON THE DINING ROOM table, the bedside table, the car seat, in shirt and sweater pockets, I find folded pieces of notepaper and crumpled envelopes. He makes lists of things to buy, things to accomplish, long-range plans, garden lists, lists of lists. They're in mixed English and Italian, whichever word is shorter. Sometimes he knows only the Italian word if it's a special tool. I should have saved the lists during the restoration and papered a bathroom with them, as James Joyce did with his rejection slips. We've exchanged habits; at home, he rarely makes even a grocery list—I make lists there, letters to write, chores, and especially of my goals for each week. Here, I usually don't have any goals.

It is hard to chart such changes of one's own in response to a new place but shifts are easy to spot in another person. When we first started coming to Italy, Ed was a tea drinker. As an undergraduate, he took a semester off to study on his own in London. He lived in a cold-water bed-sitter near the British Museum and sustained himself on cups of tea with milk and sugar while reading Eliot and Conrad. Espresso, of course, is pandemic in Italy; the *whoosh* of steam is heard in every piazza. During our first summer in Tuscany, I remember seeing him eye the Italians as they stepped up to the bar and ordered, in a clipped voice, *"un caffè."* At that time, espresso was rarely seen in America. When he ordered like the Italians, at first the bartenders asked him, *"Normale?"* They thought surely a tourist was making a mistake. We require big cups of brown coffee, as the Italians, with a touch of wonder, call it.

"Sì, sì, normale," he answered, with a slight tone of impatience. Soon he was ordering with authority; no one asked again. He saw the locals down it at once, instead of sipping. He noticed the brands different bars used: Illy, Lavazza, Sandy, River. He began commenting on the *crema* on top. Always he took it black.

"Your life must be sweet," one *barista* told him, "to take your coffee so bitter." Then Ed began to notice the sugar boats all the bars have, to notice how when the bartender put down the saucer and spoon, the sugar bowl would be pushed over and opened with a flourish. The Italians shoveled in an incredible amount—two, three mounded spoons. One day, I was shocked to see Ed, too, pouring in the sugar. "It makes it almost a dessert," he explained.

The second year we visited Italy, he went home at the end of the summer carrying a La Pavoni, purchased in Florence, a gleaming stainless-steel machine with an eagle on top, a hand-operated classic. I was the beneficiary of cappuccino in bed, our guests of after dinner espresso served in tiny cups he bought in Italy.

Here, he also has bought a La Pavoni, this one automatic. Before going to bed, he has his final cup of elixir, either at home or in town. There is something he likes about ordering in bars. Sometimes they have curvy Deco-era La Faema machines, sometimes chic Ranchillios. He examines the *crema*, swirls the cup once, and gulps it down. It gives him, he says, the strength to sleep.

The second major cultural experience he took to with zest is driving. Most travellers here feel that driving in Rome qualifies as an experience that can be added to one's *vita*, that everyday *autostrada* trips

181

are examinations in courage and that the Amalfi coast drive is a definition of hell. "These people really know how to drive," I remember him saying as he swung our no-power rented Fiat into the passing lane, turn signal blinking. A Maserati zooming forward in the rearview mirror blasted us back to the right lane. Soon he was admiring daring maneuvers. "Did you see *that*? He had two wheels dangling in thin air!" he marveled. "Sure, they have their share of duffers riding the center lane but most people keep to the rules."

"What rules?" I asked as someone in a tiny car like ours whizzed by going a hundred. Apparently there *are* speed limits, according to the size of the engine, but I never have seen anyone stopped for speeding in all my summers in Italy. You're dangerous if you're going sixty. I'm not sure what the accident rate is; I rarely see one but I imagine many are caused by slow drivers (tourists perhaps?) who incite the cars behind them.

"Just watch. If someone starts to pass and it's at all dicey, the person behind him won't pull out until the person has passed—he gives him the chance to drop back. No one ever passes on the right, ever. And they stay out of the left lane entirely except to pass. You know how at home someone figures he's going at the speed limit, he can stay in whatever lane he wants."

"Yes, but—look!—they pass on curves all the time. Here comes a curve, time to pass. They must learn that in driving school. I bet the instructor has an accelerator instead of a brake on his side of the car. You just *know*, if someone is behind you, he's planning to pass—it's his obligation."

"Yes, but all the oncoming traffic knows that. They adjust because they know cars are coming out."

He's delighted to read what the mayor of Naples says about driving there. Naples is the most chaotic city for drivers on earth. Ed loved it—he got to drive on the sidewalk while the pedestrians filled the street. "A green light is a green light, *avanti, avanti*," the mayor explained. "A red light—just a suggestion." And yellow? he was asked. "Yellow is for gaiety."

In Tuscany, people are more law abiding. They may jump the gun but they do stop for signals. Here, the challenge is the medieval streets with inches to spare on either side of the car and the sudden turn a bicycle barely could make. Fortunately, most towns have closed their historic centers to cars, a boon all around because the scale of piazza life is restored. A boon for my nerves, too, as the twisted streets lured Ed and we have backed out of too many when they became impassable, all the locals stopping and staring as we reverse through their town.

He was most impressed that the police drove Alfa Romeos. The first year after we went home he bought a twenty-year-old silver GTV in perfect condition, surely one of the prettiest cars ever made. He got three speeding tickets in six weeks. One he protested. He was harassed, he told the judge. The highway patrol picks on sports cars and this time he was not speeding. In a simple miscarriage of justice, the judge told him to sell the car if he didn't like the system and he doubled the fine on the spot.

For a while, we exchanged cars. We had to. He was in danger of losing his license. I drove the silver arrow to work and never got a ticket; he drove my vintage Mercedes sedan, unaffectionately known as the Delta Queen. "It lumbers," he complained.

"It's very safe, though—and you haven't been stopped."

"How could I in the gutless wonder?"

When we returned to Italy, he was back in his element. Most of our trips are on small roads. We've learned not to hesitate to take the unpaved roads if the route looks appealing. Usually, they're well maintained or at least navigable. We've been known to go off road to get to an abandoned thirteenth-century church and, as in the tiny towns, to back up when necessary. No problem to one who has ice water in his veins. To back uphill on a curvy one-lane road is an experience to delight the manic driver. "Whoa!" he shouts. He's turned around, one hand on the back of my seat, the other on the wheel. I'm looking down—straight down—into a lovely valley far below. There are perhaps five inches between the wheel and the edge. We encounter a car coming down. They jump out to confer, then they, too begin to back up; now we are a convoy of idiots. They're in a red Alfa GTV like Ed's at home. We all get out where the road widens and they discuss the car at length, going over its particular kind of mirror, the problem with the turn signal, value today, ad infinitum. I've spread the ordinance map on the hot hood of the Fiat, trying to figure how we can escape this ravine where, obviously, the collapsed monastery is not located.

One reason Ed likes the *autostrada* so much is that he gets to combine his pleasures. Autogrills appear every thirty or so miles. Sometimes they're quick stop places with a bar and gas. Others arch over the freeway and have a restaurant and shop, even a motel. He appreciates the clean efficiency of the bars. He nips his espresso, often has a quick *panino* of thick bread and mortadella. I will have a cappuccino, unorthodox in afternoon, and he patiently waits. He never would malinger at the bar. In and out. That's the way it's done. Then back on the road, with the fully leaded espresso zinging through him, the speedometer climbing to cruising speed. *Paradiso!*

At a more fundamental level, he has been changed by the land. At first we thought we wanted twenty or thirty acres. Five seemed small, until we started clearing it of jungle, until we started maintaining it. The *limonaia* is full of tools. At home we have our tools in a shiny red metal toolbox—the small size. We did not expect to have pole digger, chain saw, hedge clippers, weed machine, a whole line of hoes, rakes, a corner for stakes, innumerable hand tools that look pre-Industrial Revolution—sickles, grape cutters, and scythe. If we thought, I suppose we thought we'd clear the land, prune the trees, and that was it. An occasional mowing, fertilizing, trimming. What we never knew is the tremendous resurgent power in nature. The land is implausibly regenerative. My experience with gardening led me to think plants must be coaxed along. Ivy, fig, sumac, acacia, blackberry can't be stopped. A vine we call "evil weed" twines and chokes. It must be dug out down to its carrot-sized root; so must nettles. It's a wonder nettles have not taken over the world. Digging them out, even with heavy gloves, it's almost impossible not to get "stung" by their juices. Bamboo, too, has its runners constantly sending shoots into the driveway. Limbs fall. New olives must be restaked after storms. The terraces must be plowed, then disced. The olives must be hoed around, fertilized. The grapes still need weeks of attention. In short, we have a little farm here and we must have a farmer. Without constant work, this place would revert in months to its previous state. We could either feel burdened by this or enjoy it.

"How's Johnny Appleseed?" a friend asks. She, too, has seen Ed up on a high terrace examining each plant, fingering the leaves of a new cherry tree, picking up stones. He has come to know every ilex, boulder, stump, and oak. Perhaps it was the clearing that forged the bond.

Now he walks the terraces daily. He has taken to wearing shorts, boots, and a "muscle shirt," one of those cutaway undershirts my father used to wear. His biceps and chest muscles bulge like "after" pictures on the backs of old comic books. His father was a farmer until the age of forty, when he had to give up and work in town. His ancestors must have come out of the Polish fields. They, I'm certain, would recognize him across a field. Although he never remembers to water the houseplants in San Francisco, he hauls buckets up to the new fruit trees in dry spells, babies a special lavender with scented foliage, reads into the night about compost and pruning.

*

How Italian will we ever be? Not very, I'm afraid. Too pale. Too unable to gesture as a natural accompaniment to talking. I saw a man step outside the confining telephone booth so he could wave his hands while talking. Many people pull over to the side of the road to talk on their car phones because they simply cannot keep a hand on the wheel, one on the telephone, and talk at the same time. We never will master the art of everyone talking at once. Often from the window, I see groups of three or four strolling down our road. All are talking simultaneously. Who's listening? Talking can be about talking. After a soccer game, we'll never gun through the streets blowing the horn or drive a scooter around and around in circles in the piazza. Politics always will passeth understanding.

Ferragosto, at first, baffled us as a holiday until we began to understand it as a state of mind. We, gradually, have entered this state of mind ourselves. Simply put, *ferragosto*, August 15, marks the ascension of the corporeal body and soul of the Virgin Mary into heaven. Why August 15? Perhaps it was too hot to remain on earth another day. The domed ceiling of the cathedral in Parma depicts her glorious skyward rise, accompanied by many others. From the perspective below, you're looking up their billowing skirts as they balloon above the cathedral floor. This is a triumph of art—no one's underwear shows. But the day itself is only a marker in the month, for the broader meaning of the word is August holidays and a period of intense *laissez-faire*. We're coming to understand that everyday work life is suspended for *all* of August. Even though throngs of tourists descend on a town, the best *trattoria* may have tacked up a *chiuso per ferie* sign, closed for vacation, and the owners have packed and taken off for Viareggio. American business logic does not bear up; they do not necessarily rake in money during tourist season and take their holiday during April or November when tourists are gone. Why not? Because it is August. The accident rates soar on the highways. The beach towns are mobbed. We have learned to forget all projects more complicated than putting up jam. Or to abandon even that—I fill my hat with plums then sit down under the tree, suck the juice, and toss skin and seed over the wall. All over Italy, the feast of the Assumption calls for a celebration. Cortona throws a grand party: the *Sagra della bistecca*, a *festa* for the great beef-steaks of the area.

Sagra is a wonderful word to look for in Tuscany. Foods coming into season often cause a celebration. All over the small towns, signs go up announcing a *sagra* for cherries, chestnuts, wine, *vin santo,* apricots, frog legs, wild boar, olive oil, or lake trout. Earlier this summer, we went to the *sagra della lumaca*, the snail, in the upper part of town. About eight tables were set up along the street and music blared over them, but because of no rain the snails had disappeared and a veal stew was served instead. At the *sagra* in a mountain *borgo*, I came within one number of winning a donkey in the raffle. We ate pasta with *ragù,* grilled lamb, and watched a dignified old couple, him in a starched collar and her in black to her ankles, dance elegantly to the accordion.

Preparations for Cortona's two-day feast start several days in advance. Town employees construct an enormous grill in the park—a knee-high brick foundation about six by twenty feet and a foot high, with iron grills placed over the top, somewhat like the barbecue pits I remember from home. On the same spot, the grill is used later in the year for the town's *festa* for the autumn *porcini*. (Cortona claims to use the largest frying pan in the world for the mushrooms. I've never been here for that *festa* but can imagine the savory aroma of *porcini* filling the whole park.) The men arrange tables for four, six, eight, twelve under the trees and decorate with lanterns. Little booths for serving go up near the grill, then the ticket booth is taken out of a shed, dusted off, and set up at the entrance to the park. Walking through, I glimpse stacks of charcoal in the shed.

The park, normally closed to cars, is opened these two days of the year to accommodate all the people arriving for the *sagra*. Bad news for our road, which links to the park. Traffic pours by starting at around seven, then pours by again from eleven on. We decide to walk in over the Roman road to avoid clouds of white dust. Our neighbor, one of the grill volunteers, waves.

Big steaks sizzle over the huge bed of red coals. We join the long line and pick up our *crostini*, our plates and salad and vegetables. At the grill, our neighbor spears two enormous steaks for us and we lurch to a table already almost full. Pitchers of wine pass round and round. The whole town comes out for the *sagra* and, oddly, there seem to be no tourists here, except for a long table of English people. We don't know the people we're with. They're from Acquaviva. Two couples and three children. The baby girl is gnawing on a bone and looks delighted. The two boys, in the well-behaved way of Italian children, focus on sawing their steaks. The adults toast us and we toast back. When we say we're Americans, one man wants to know if we know his aunt and uncle in Chicago.

After dinner, we walk through town, along with throngs of people. The Rugapiana is jammed. The bars are jammed. We manage to obtain hazelnut ice cream cones. A bunch of teenagers is singing on the steps of the town hall. Three small boys toss firecrackers, then try to look innocent of the act without succeeding. They double over with laughter. I wait outside listening to them while Ed goes in a bar for a shot of the black elixir he loves. On the way home, we pass back through the park. It's almost ten-thirty and still the grill is smoking. We see our neighbor dining with his gorgeous wife and daughter and a dozen friends. "How long has the town had this *sagra*?" Ed asks them.

"Always, always," Placido answers. Scholars think the first commemoration of Mary's feast day was celebrated in Antioch back in 370 A.D. That makes this year's the 1,624th event for her. Old as Cortona is, perhaps killing the white cow and serving it forth in honor of some deity goes back even farther than that.

❋

After *ferragosto*, Cortona is unusually quiet for a few days. Everyone who was coming to town has been. The shopkeepers sit outside reading the paper or looking absently down the street. If you've ordered something, it won't be coming until September.

❋

Our neighbor, the grill master, is also the tax collector. We know the time by when he passes our house on his Vespa in the morning, at lunch, after siesta, and as he comes home at night. I have begun to idealize his life. It is easy for foreigners to idealize, romanticize, stereotype, and oversimplify local people. The drunk who staggers down the road after unloading boxes at the market in the mornings easily falls into the Town Drunk character from central casting. The hunched woman with blue-black hair is known as The Abortionist. The red and white terrier who visits three butchers to beg for scraps each morning turns into Town Dog. There's the Mad Artist, the Fascist, the Renaissance Beauty, the Prophet. Once the person is really known, of course, the characterization blessedly fades. Placido, the neighbor, however, owns two white horses. He sings as he rides by on his Vespa. We hear him clearly because he coasts by our house on his way in. Starts the motor down the road where the hill levels out. He keeps peacocks and geese and white doves. In early middle age, he wears his light hair long, sometimes tied with a bandanna. On horseback, he looks totally at home, a born rider. His wife and daughter are unusually pretty. His mother leaves flowers in our shrine and his sister refers to Ed as that handsome American. All this—but what I idealize is that Placido seems utterly happy. Everyone in town likes him. "Ah, Placi," they say, "you have Placi for a neighbor." He walks through town to greetings from every door. I have the feeling that he could have lived in any era; he is independent of time there in his stone house on the olive terraces with his peaceable kingdom. To reinforce my instinct, he has appeared, my Rousseau paradigm neighbor, at our door with a hooded falcon on his wrist.

    With my bird phobia, left from some forgotten childhood transference, the last thing I want to see at the door is a predatory bird.

Placido has a friend with him and they are beginning to train the falcon. He asks if they can go out on our land to practice. I try not to show the extent of my fear. *"Ho paura,"* I admit, thinking how accurate the Italian is: I *have* fear. Mistake. He steps forward with the twitchy bird, inviting me to take it on my arm; surely I won't be afraid if I see the magnificence of this creature. Ed comes downstairs and steps between us. Even he is somewhat alarmed. My phobia gradually has rubbed off on him. But we are happy that our Placido feels neighborly enough toward the *stranieri* to come over, and we walk out to the far point of land with him. His friend takes the bird and stands about fifty feet away. Placido removes something from his pocket. The falcon extends its wings—a formidable span—and flaps madly, rising up on his talons.

"A live quail. Soon I'll take pigeons from the piazza," he laughs. The friend unfastens the cunning little leather hood and the bird shoots like an arrow to Placido. Feathers start to fly. The falcon devours quickly, making bloody work of the former quail. The friend signals with a whistle and the falcon flies back to his wrist and takes the hood. A chilling performance. Placido says there are five hundred falconers in Italy. He has bought his bird in Germany, the little hood in Canada. He must train it every day. He praises the bird, now immovable on his wrist.

This sport certainly does nothing to subtract from my impression that Placido lives across time. I see him on the white horse, falcon on his wrist, and he is en route to some medieval joust or fair. Walking by his house, I see the bird in its pen. The stern profile reminds me of Mrs. Hattaway, my seventh-grade teacher. The sudden swivel of its head brings back her infallible ability to sense when notes were tossed across the room.

✻

I'm packing for my flight home from Rome when a stranger calls me from the United States. "What's the downside?" a voice asks on the telephone. She's read an article I wrote in a magazine about buying and restoring the house. "I'm sorry to bother you but I don't have anyone to discuss this with. I want to do *something* but I don't know exactly what. I'm a lawyer in Baltimore. My mother died and . . ."

I recognize the impulse. I recognize the desire to surprise your own life. "You must change your life," as the poet Rilke said. I stack like ingots all I've learned in my first years as a part-time resident of another country. Just the satisfaction of feeling many Italian words become as familiar as English would be pleasure enough: *pompelmo, susino, fragola*—the new names of everything. What I feared was that with the end of my marriage, life would narrow. A family history, I suppose, of resigned disappointed ancestors, old belles of the county looking at the pressed roses in their world atlases. And, I think, for those of us who came of age with the women's movement, there's always the fear that it's not real, you're not really allowed to determine your own life. It may be pulled back at any moment. I've had the sensation of surfing on a big comber and soon the spilling wave will curl over, sucking me under. But, slow learner, I'm beginning to trust that the gods are not going to snatch my firstborn if I happen to enjoy my life. The woman on the other end of the line has somehow, through the university, obtained my number in Italy.

"What are you thinking of doing?" I ask this total stranger.

"The islands off the coast of Washington, I've always loved them. There's this place for sale, my friends think I'm crazy because it's all the way across the country. But you go by ferry . . ."

"There's no downside," I say firmly. The waterfall of problems with Benito, the financial worries, the language barriers, the hot water in the toilet, the layers of gunk on the beams, the long flights over from California—this is *nothing* compared to the absolute joy of being in possession of this remarkable little hillside on the edge of Tuscany.

I have the impulse to invite her over to visit. Her desire makes her familiar to me so that we would immediately be friends and talk long into the night. But I'm leaving soon. As I speak to her in her high-rise office, the half moon rises above the Medici fortress. Way up, I see the bench Ed made for me under an oak tree. A plank over two stumps. I like to zigzag up the terraces and sit there in late afternoons when the gilded light starts to sift over the valley and shadows stretch between the long ridges. I was never a hippie but I ask her if she ever heard the old motto "Follow your bliss."

"Yes," she replies, "I was at Woodstock twenty-five years ago. But now I handle labor disputes for this transnational conglomerate . . . I'm not sure this makes sense."

"Well, does it seem that you'd be moving into a larger freedom? I've had an incredible amount of fun here." I don't mention the sun, how when I'm away and picture myself here, it's always in full light; I feel *permeable* now. The Tuscan sun has warmed me to the marrow. Flannery O'Connor talked about pursuing pleasure "through gritted teeth." I sometimes must do that at home but here pleasure is natural. The days right themselves one after another, as easily as the boy holding up the jingling scale easily balances the fat melon and the rusty iron discs.

I am waiting to hear if she took the clapboard cottage with its own deep-water pier.

I see her blue bicycle leaning against a pine tree, morning glories climbing up the porch railing.

❋

Brave girl! Placido is walking with his daughter out to the point. She holds up the falcon on her wrist. Her long curls bounce as she walks. Even something to fear is layering into memory; I'm going to dream about this over the winter. Perhaps the falcon will fly through a nightmare. Or perhaps it only will accompany these neighbors in late afternoon as they walk up the cypress drive and out to where they release the bird, allowing it to fly farther each time. So much more to take home at the end of summer. "The Night," by Cesare Pavese, ends:

> *At times it returns,*
> *in the motionless calm of the day, that memory*
> *of living immersed, absorbed, in the stunned light.*

"DON'T PICK TODAY—TOO WET." MARCO OBSERVES US taking down the olive baskets. "And the moon's wrong. Wait until Wednesday." He's hanging the doors, two original chestnut ones he oiled and repaired, and new ones, virtually indistinguishable from the old, that he has made during the fall while we were gone. They replace the hollow-core doors our great improver in the fifties preferred.

We're already late for the olive harvest. All of the mills close before Christmas and we've arrived with a week to spare. Outside, a gray drizzle blurs the intense green grasses that thrived on November rains. I put my hand on the window. Cold. He's right, of course. If we pick today, the wet olives might mildew if we don't finish and get them to the mill. We gather our osier baskets that strap around the waist— so handy for stripping a branch—and the blue sacks the olives are loaded into, the aluminum ladder, our rubber boots. Still jet-lagged and dazed, we're up early, thanks to Marco's arrival at seven-thirty when it barely was light. He tells us to go make an appointment at a mill; maybe it will clear up later. If so, the sun will dry the olives quickly.

"What about the moon?" I ask. He just shrugs. He wouldn't pick now, I know.

We feel like tumbling back into bed, having had no time since arriving last night to get beyond the twenty-hour trip, with storms buffeting the plane most of the way across the ocean. I felt like kissing the ground when we stepped out on the tarmac at Fiumicino. We crazily went into Rome to do a little shopping, then were really beyond thinking as we drove to Cortona in a hilarious rented Twingo, purple with mint green interior. We hit the *autostrada* in a bumper car and in a state of exhaustion. Still, the wet and vibrant landscape filled us with elation—that lit-from-within green and many trees still twirling colored leaves. When we left in August, it was sere and dry; now the freshness has reasserted itself. At dark we finally arrived. In town we picked up bread and a pan of veal *cannelloni*. The air felt charged and invigorating; we no longer wanted to collapse. Laura, the young woman who cleans, had turned up the radiators two days ago and the stone walls had time to lose their chill. She even had brought in wood, so on our first night here, we had a little feast by the fire, then wandered from room to room, checking and touching and greeting each object. And so to bed, until Marco aroused us this morning. "Laura said you arrived. I thought you'd want the doors right away." Always, always when we arrive there is something to haul from A to B. Ed helped him hoist the doors and held them steady while Marco wiggled the hinges onto the metal spurs.

The venerable mill at Sant'Angelo uses the purest methods, Marco tells us, cold-pressing each person's olives individually, rather than requiring small growers to double up with someone else. However, you must have at least a *quintale*, one hundred kilograms. Our trees, not yet recovered from thirty years of neglect, may not give us that bounty yet. Many trees have nothing at all.

The mill smells thickly oleaginous and the damp floor feels slippery, possibly oily. Rooms where grapes and olives are pressed have the odors of time, as surely as the cool stone smell of churches. The permeating ooze and trickle must move into the workers' pores. The man in charge tells us of several mills that press small batches. We never knew there were so many. All his directions involve turning right at the tallest pine or left beyond the hump or right behind the long pig barn.

Before we leave, he extols the virtues of the traditional methods and to prove his point dips two tablespoons into a vat of new oil and hands them to us to taste. It can't be poured onto the floor; there's nothing to do but swallow the whole thing. I can't but I do. First, a tiny taste and the oil is extraordinary, of a meltingly soft fragrance and essential, full olive taste. The whole spoon at once, however, is like taking medicine. *"Splendido,"* I gulp and look at Ed, who still hesitates, pretending to appreciate the greeny beauty. "What happens to that?" I ask, gesturing to troughs of pulp. Our host turns and Ed quickly slips his oil back in the vat, then tastes what's left on the spoon.

"Favoloso," Ed says to him. And it is. After the first cold pressing, the pulp is sent on to another mill and pressed again for regular oils, then pressed last for lubricating oils. The dried-out remains, in a wonderful cycle of return, often are used to fertilize olive trees.

As we start to drive away, we see that the doors of San Michele Arcangelo, a church we've admired, are open today. The threshold is scattered with rice—*arborio*, I notice, the rice for risotto. A wedding has taken place and someone must be coming to take down the pine and cedar boughs. The church is almost a thousand years old. Just across the road from each other, the church and mill have served two of the basic needs—and the grain and the vine are not far away. The beamed and cross-beamed ceilings of these old churches often remind me of ship hulls. I've never mentioned this before but now I do. "The church structures reminded someone else of boats, too. 'Nave' comes from *'navis'* in Latin—ship," Ed tells me.

"And what does 'apse' come from then?" I ask, since the lovely rounded forms remind me of bread ovens standing alone in farm yards.

"I believe that root means a fastening together of things, just practical, no poetry there."

There is poetry in the rhythm of the three naves, the three apses, the classic basilica plan in miniature. The lines rhyme perfectly in their stony movement along such a small space. The only adornment is the scent of evergreens. As much as I love the great frescoed churches, it's these plain ones that touch me most deftly. They seem to be the shape and texture of the human spirit, transformed into stone and light.

Ed swings the car out onto what once was a Roman road. Later it led pilgrims on their way to the Holy Land. San Michele was a place to rest and restore. I wonder if a mill stood here, too. Perhaps the pilgrims rubbed oil into their weary feet. We, however, are just searching for a mill that will transform our sacks of black olives into bottles of oil. Two of the mills already have closed. At the third, a woman in about six layers of sweaters comes down her steps and tells us we're too late, the olives should have been picked and now the moon is wrong. "Yes," we tell her, "we know." Her husband has closed his mill for the season. She points down the road. At a grand stone villa, we turn in. A discreet sign, IL MULINO, directs us to the rear but when we drive around, two workers are hosing off their equipment. Too late. They direct us to the large mill near town.

Whizzing along, I look at the winter gardens. Everyone's growing pale, stalky *cardi*, cardoons—called *gobbi* in the local dialect— and green-black *cavolo nero*, black cabbage, which grows not in a head but in upright plumes. Red and green radicchio star in every garden. Most have a few artichoke plants. Until winter, I never knew there were so many persimmon trees. With the lacquered orange fruit dangling in bare limbs, the trees look composed of quick brush strokes, like Japanese drawings of themselves.

At the mill, everyone is so busy that we're ignored. We walk around watching the process and aren't drawn to having our precious olives pressed here. It's all quite mechanized looking. Where are the big stone wheels? We can't really tell if they use heat, a process that supposedly damages the taste. We watch a customer come in, have his fruit weighed, then see it dumped into a large cart. Maybe the olives are all the same and mixing doesn't matter but somehow, this time, we would love to have the pleasure of oil from the land we've worked on. We exit quickly and drive to our last hope, a small mill near Castiglion Fiorentino. Outside the door, three huge stone wheels lean against the building. Just inside, wooden bins of olives are stacked, each one with a name on it. Yes, they can press ours. We are to come back tomorrow.

The afternoon warms and clears. Marco gives us the O.K. to begin. Moon or no, we start picking. It's fast. We empty our baskets into the laundry basket and, as that fills, pour the olives into the sack. Few have fallen though they yield easily to our fingers. A strong wind could cause a lot of damage unless one had spread nets under the trees. The shiny black olives are plump and firm. Curious about the raw drupe, I bite one and it tastes like an alum stick. How did anyone ever figure out how to cure them? The same people, no doubt, who first had the nerve to taste oysters. Ligurians used to cure them by hanging bags in the sea; inland people smoked them over the winter in their chimneys, something I'd like to try. We peel off jackets, then sweaters as we work, hanging them in the trees. The temperature has climbed to about fifty-five degrees and although our boots are wet, the air feels balmy. Off in the distance, we see the blue swath of Lake Trasimeno under an intense blue sky. By three, we have stripped every single olive off twelve trees. I've put my sweater on again. Days are short here in winter and already the sun is headed for the rim of the hill behind the house. By four, our red fingers are stiff and we quit, hauling the sack and basket down the terraces into the cantina.

Not for the first time in our history here, my body is jarred into awareness. Today: shoulders! Nothing would be nicer than a long soak in a bubble bath and a massage. I have left my body oil to warm on the radiator in anticipation. But with only twenty days here every minute counts. We force ourselves to go into town to stock up on food.

My daughter and her boyfriend Jess arrive in three days. We're planning several major feasts. We drive in just as the stores are reopening after siesta. Strange—it's already dark as the town comes back to life. Swags of white lights strung across the narrow streets swing in the wind. The A & O market, where we shop, has a rather ratty artificial tree (the only tree in town) outside and big baskets of gift foods inside.

From our brief Christmas visit last year, we know that the focus of the season is twofold: food and the *presepio*, the crèche. We're ready to launch into one and are intrigued by the other. The bars display fancy candies and that lighter Italian parallel to our ubiquitous Christmas fruitcake, the *panettone*, in colorful boxes. A few shops have distinctly homemade wreaths. That's it for decoration, except for the crèches in all the churches and in many windows. *"Auguri, auguri,"* everyone says, best wishes. No one is rushing about. There seems to be no gift wrap, no hype, no frantic search.

The window of the *frutta e verdura* is steamed. Outside, where we're used to seeing the fruits of summer, we find baskets of walnuts, chestnuts, and fragrant clementines, those tiny tangerines without seeds. Maria Rita, inside in a big black sweater, is cracking almonds. *"Ah, benissimo!"* she greets us. *"Ben tornato!"* Where there were luscious tomatoes, she has piled stacks of *cardi*, which I've never tasted. "You boil it but first you must take off all the strings." She cracks a stalk and peels back the celerylike filaments. "Throw it in some lemon water quickly or it will turn black. Then boil. Now it's ready for the *parmigiano*, the butter."

"How much?"

"Enough, enough, signora. Then the oven." Soon she's telling us to make *bruschetta* on the grill in the fireplace and pile on it chopped black cabbage cooked with garlic and oil in a frying pan. We buy blood oranges and tiny green lentils from a jar, chestnuts, winter pears, winy little apples, and broccoli, which I've never seen in Italy before. "Lentils for the New Year," she tells us. "I always add mint." She piles in our bags all the ingredients for *ribolitta*, the wintery soup.

At the butcher's, new sausages are in, looped along the front of the meat case. A man with a sausage-shaped nose himself elbows Ed and acts out saying the rosary, then points to the long links of fat sausages. It takes us a moment to make the connection, which he thinks is very funny. Quail and several birds that look as though they should be singing in a tree lie still in their feathers in the case. Color photos on the wall show the butcher's name written on the backsides of several enormous white cows, source of the Val di Chiana steak that Tuscany celebrates. There's Bruno with his hand possessively around the neck of a great beast. He motions for us to follow him. He opens the freezer room and we follow him in. A cow the size of an elephant hangs from ceiling hooks. Bruno slaps a flank affectionately. "The finest *bistecca* in the world. A hot grill, rosemary, and a little lemon at the table." He turns up both hands, a gesture that adds "What else is there in life?" Suddenly, the door slams shut and we are locked inside with this massive body encased in white fat.

"Oh, no!" I flash on the three of us caught as in the child's game of Freeze. I swing around toward the door but Bruno is laughing. He easily opens the door and we rush out. I don't want any steak.

✳

We intended to cook but we have lingered. We deposit all the food in the car and walk back to Dardano, a favorite *trattoria*, for dinner. The son who has waited tables since we came here suddenly looks like a teenager. The whole family sits around a table in the kitchen. Only two other customers are here, local men bent over their bowls of *penne*, each eating as though he were alone. We order pasta with black truffles, a carafe of wine. Afterward we walk around in the quiet, quiet streets. A few boys play soccer in the empty piazza. Their shouts ring in the cold air. The outdoor tables are stored, the bar doors closed tight with everyone inside breathing smoke. No cars. A lone dog on a walk. Totally emptied of foreigners, except us, the town reveals its silences, the long nights when men play cards way past the nine o'clock bells, the deserted streets that look returned to their medieval origins. At the *duomo* wall, we look out over the lights of the valley. A few other people lean on the wall, too. When we're really freezing we walk back up the street and open the bar door to a burst of noise. The cocoa, steamed on the espresso machine, is thick as pudding. One day back and I'm falling in love with winter.

✳

At first light, we are out on the terraces, even though heavy dew is on the olives. We intend to finish today, not leaving them time to mildew. Below us the valley surges with fog as thick as mascarpone. We are above it in clear, frosty air, utterly fresh and sharp to inhale, as if we're looking down from a plane: a disembodied feeling—this hillside is floating. Even the red roof of our neighbor Placido's house has disappeared. The lake gives this landscape some of its mystery. Large mists rise off the water and spread over the valley. Fog billows and rises. As we pick olives, wisps of clouds pass us. Soon the sun asserts itself and begins to burn off the fog, showing us first the white horse in Placido's pen, then his roof and the olive terraces below him. The lake stays hidden in a pearly swirl of clouds. We come to trees with nothing on them, then a laden tree. I take the lower branches; Ed leans the ladder into the center and reaches up. To our joy, Francesco Falco, our caretaker of the olives, joins us. He's the quintessential olive picker in his rough wool pants and tweed cap, basket strapped to his waist. He sets to work like the pro he is, picking more than we're able to. He's not as careful, just lets twigs and leaves fall in, whereas we've fastidiously removed any stray leaf after reading they add tannin to the taste of oil. Now and then he pulls out his machete from the back of his pants (how does he not get poked in the bottom?) and hacks off a sucker sprouting up. We must get the olives in, he tells us, a big freeze may be coming. We pause for a coffee but he keeps picking. All fall he has cut back the dead wood so that new growth is encouraged. By spring he will have hacked off everything except the most promising limbs and cleared around each tree. We ask about bush olives, more experimental techniques of pruning we've read about but he will hear nothing of those. The way to take care of olives is second nature, unquestionable. At seventy-five, he has the stamina of someone half his age. The same stamina, I suppose, that gave him the strength to walk home to Italy from Russia at the end of World War II. We identify him so totally with the land around Cortona that it's hard to imagine him as the young soldier stranded thousands of miles from home when the ugly war ended. He jokes constantly but today he has left his teeth at home and we have a hard time understanding him. Soon he heads for the lower terraces, an area still overgrown, because he has seen from the road that some of the olives there are bearing fruit.

With the olives from below, we do have a *quintale*. After siesta, which we've worked through, we hear Francesco and Beppe coming up the road on a tractor pulling a cart of olives. They've taken the sacks of their friend Gino and are on their way to the mill. They load Gino's olives into Beppe's Ape and help us load ours on, too. We follow them. It's almost dark and the temperature is dropping. Many California winters have dimmed my memory of real cold. It's a presence of its own. My toes are numb and the Twingo heater is sending out a forlorn stream of tepid air. "It's only about twenty-five degrees," Ed says. He seems to radiate warmth. His Minnesota background reawakens anytime I complain that I'm cold.

"Feels like Bruno's freezer to me."

✳

Our sacks are weighed, then the olives are poured into a bin, washed, then crushed by three stone wheels. Once mashed, they're routed to a machine that spreads them on a round hemp mat, stacks on another mat, spreads more until there is a five-foot stack of hemp circles with the crushed olives sandwiched between each. A weight presses out the oil, which oozes down the sides of the hemp into a tank. The oil then goes through a centrifuge to get all the water out. Our oil, poured into a demijohn, is green and cloudy. The yield, the mill owner tells us, was quite high. Our trees have given us 18.6 kilograms of oil from our *quintale*—about a liter for each fully bearing tree. No wonder oil is expensive. "What about the acid?" I ask. I've read that oil must have less than one percent of oleic acid to qualify as extra virgin.

"One percent!" He grinds his cigarette under his heel. *"Signori! Più basso, basso,"* he growls, lower, lower, insulted that his mill would tolerate inferior oil. "These hills are the best in Italy."

At home we pour a little into a bowl and dip in pieces of bread, as people all over Tuscany must be doing. Our oil! I've never tasted better. There's a hint of a watercress taste, faintly peppery but fresh as the stream watercress is pulled from. With this oil, I'll make every *bruschetta* known and some as yet unknown. Perhaps I'll even learn to eat my oranges with oil and salt as I've seen the priest do.

The sediment will settle in the big container over time but we like the murky, fruity oil, too. We fill several pretty bottles I've saved for this moment, then store the rest in the semidarkness of the cantina. Along the marble counter, we line up five bottles with those caps bartenders use to pour drinks. I've found those perfect for pouring slowly or dribbling oil. The little lid flaps down after you pour so the oil stays clean. We'll cook everything this holiday season in our oil. Our friends will have to visit and take bottles home with them; we have more than we can use and no one to give it to, since everyone here has their own, or at least a cousin who supplies them. When our trees yield more, we may sell the extra oil to the local consortium. I've bought the terrific *comune* oil in a gallon jug for about twenty dollars. I once lugged one home and it was worth the long flight with the cold jug balanced between my feet.

Our herbs still thrive, despite the cold. I cut a handful of sage and rosemary sprigs, quarter onions and potatoes, and arrange them around a pork roast and pop it in the oven, after a liberal sprinkling of our first season's oil baptizes the pan.

The next afternoon, we find an olive oil tasting in progress, the town's first *festa* for *olio extravergine del colle Cortonese*, the extra virgin oil of the Cortona hills. I remember my tablespoon at the *mulino*, but this time there's bread from the local bakery. Nine growers' oils are lined up along a table in the piazza, with pots of olive trees around for ambiance. "I couldn't have imagined this, could you?" Ed asks me as we try the fourth or fifth oil. I couldn't. The oils, like ours, are profoundly fresh with a vigorous element to the taste that makes me want to smack my lips. The shades of difference among the oils are subtle. I think I taste that hot wind of summer in one, the first rain of autumn in another, then the history of a Roman road, sunlight on leaves. They taste green and full of life.

FLOATING WORLD: A WINTER SEASON

THERE IS SOMETHING AS INEVITABLE AS LABOR THAT takes over around Christmas. I feel impelled to the kitchen. I feel deep hungers for star-shaped cookies and tangerine ices and caramel cakes, things I never think of during the rest of the year. Even when I have vowed to keep it simple, I have found myself making the deadly Martha Washington Jetties my mother made every year on the cold back porch. You have to make them in the cold because the sinful cream, sugar, and pecan fondant balls are dipped by toothpick into chocolate and held up to set before being placed on the chilled wax-papered tray. The chocolate dip, of course, constantly turns hard and must be taken into the kitchen and heated. My mother made Jetties endlessly because her friends expected them. We professed to find them too rich but ate them until our teeth ached. I still have the cut-glass candy jar they spent their brief tenures in.

The other absolute was roasted pecans. Nuts roasted in butter and salt; the arteries tense even to read this—we ate them by the pound. I cannot get through a Christmas without them, although now I usually give most to friends and save only a small tin for the house. For guests, of course.

This year, no Jetties. But our almond crop must be used so roasted almonds seem inevitable. This weather demands the red soup pot. In preparation for Ashley and Jess's arrival, I'm making the big pot of *ribollita,* a soup for ending a day of fieldwork, or, as I think of it, for arriving from New York. Reboiled is the unappetizing translation and, naturally, it is, like so many peasant dishes, a soup of necessity: beans, vegetables, and hunks of bread.

Winter food makes me understand Tuscan cooking at a deeper level. French cooking, my first love, seems light years away: the evolution of a bourgeois tradition as opposed to the evolution of a peasant tradition. A local cookbook talks about *la cucina povera,* the poor kitchen, as the source of the now-abundant Tuscan cuisine. *Tortellone in brodo,* a Christmas tradition here, seems like a sophisticated concept. Three half moons of stuffed pasta steaming in a bowl of clear broth—but, really, what is more frugal than to combine a few leftover *tortellone* with extra broth? More than pasta, bread is the basic ingredient of the repertoire. Bread soups, bread salads, which seem rich and imaginative in California restaurants, were simply someone's good use of leftovers, possibly when there was little in the house except a little stock or oil to work with. The clearest example of the poor kitchen must be *acqua-cotta,* cooked water—probably a cousin of stone soup. This varies all over Tuscany but always involves invention around a base of water and bread. Fortunately, wild edibles always abound along the roadsides. A handful of mint, mushrooms, a little sweet burnet, or various greens might flavor cooked water. If an egg was handy, it was broken into the soup at the last moment. That Tuscan cooking has remained so simple is a long tribute to the abilities of those peasant women who cooked so well that no one, even now, wants to veer into new directions.

❋

Ashley and Jess arrive within an hour of each other, a miracle of scheduling since she is coming to Chiusi from the Rome train and he is coming into Camucia from Pisa and Florence after landing from London. We pick her up, then speed the forty minutes back and arrive just as he steps off the train.

The people one's children bring home are problematic. One came to visit when we were renting a house in the Mugello north of Florence. He was deeply into Thomas Wolfe and sat in the backseat engrossed in *Look Homeward Angel*. We madly drove all over Tuscany to show them (both artists) the Piero della Francescas but he only turned pages and sighed now and then. Once he looked up and saw the round gold bales of hay in the lovely fields and said, "Cool, those look like Richard Serra sculptures." We never were sure anything else penetrated. A young woman Ashley brought over suffered from dire toothache except when shopping was mentioned. She miraculously recovered long enough to buy everything in sight—she had an excellent eye for design—then relapsed in her room, requiring meals on trays. Nothing was wrong with her appetite. When she returned to New York, she had to have extensive root canal work on three teeth, so her forays into the shops *were* remarkable mental triumphs over pain. Another never paid me for his round-trip New York–Rome ticket, which was charged to my AmEx because Ashley picked up their tickets. Naturally, we have been wondering about the person who will be spending a couple of weeks.

If I'd had a boy, I'd have wanted him to be like Jess. We both fall right away for Jess's humor, intellectual curiosity, and warmth. He arrives with a wicker hamper of smoked salmon, Stilton, oat biscuits, honeys, and jams. He spent his last two days in London buying beautifully wrapped gifts for everyone. Best of all, we don't seem like capital P parents to him but potential friends. Relieved that this will be effortless, I'm buoyed, too, by that expansion I feel when someone new is admitted into my life. My Iranian friend maintains that attractions among people are based on smell, which seems logical enough to me. Most of those most important to me I've liked instantaneously and have known I wanted a permanent friendship. (The times the connection has not lasted still sting.) Jess knows all the words to every rock song. Ashley is laughing. We're already singing in the car. What luck.

It's midday and too warm for *ribollita*. We stop in town and have sandwiches at a bar and Jess tells us about the wedding he was just in at Westminster Abbey. Ashley has had the longer trip and wants to fade. Ed and I take a walk, then, because the day is warm and the force of habit strong, we start to work in the garden. I pull weeds away from herbs and lift geraniums out of pots, shake off dirt from the roots and wrap them in newspaper to store over the winter. Ed mows the long grass and rakes. Everything is drenched, sweet, lush; even the weeds are beautiful. I decorate the shrine with boughs of spruce and its nuts, olive branches and a gold star over Mary's head. Ed tries to burn a pile of leaves we never were able to burn last summer because of the dryness. They're so wet now that they just smoke. When Ashley and Jess reappear, we drive to the nursery and buy a living tree and a big pot to plant it in. Small as it is, it dominates the living room. Since we have nothing for decoration except a string of white lights, we decide to go to Florence tomorrow and buy a few ornaments. I've brought over some candles shaped like stars and some distinctly non-Tuscan *farolitos*, a Santa Fe custom I've kept since spending a Christmas there once and loving the candles in paper bags outlining the adobe houses. These are glazed bags with cut-out stars. We line the front stone wall with a dozen of them and they look magical with their glowing stars. We fill the fireplace overhang with pine cones and branches of cypress Ed cut this afternoon. How easy everything seems and what a pleasure to recover the fun of Christmas. The bowls of *ribollita* and a fire act as knock-out drops. In the big armchairs, we're wrapped in mohair blankets, listening to Elvis singing blue, blue, blue Christmas on the CD.

*

At the outdoor market in Florence, we find papier-mâché balls and bells with decoupage angels. A wagon off to the side serves bowls of

208

trippa, tripe, a special love of the Florentines. Business looks brisk. If I thought yesterday that I was falling in love with winter, today it's certain. Florence is redeemed and magnificent on a cold December morning. As in all the towns, the decorations are sweet—lights strung across the narrow streets at short intervals, necklaces of light with dangling pendants. Obviously the women of this city have not heard of cruelty to wildlife; I never have seen so many long, lavish fur coats. We look in vain for fake fur. The men are dressed in fine wool overcoats and elegant scarves. Gilli, one of my favorite bars, is crowded with noisy voices and clinks of cups and constant rushes of steam from the espresso machine. In the middle of the street, Ed pauses and holds up his hands. "Listen!"

"What is it?" We all stop.

"Nothing! How could we not have noticed? No motorcycles. It must be too cold for them."

Ashley wants boots for Christmas. Obviously, this is the place. She finds black boots and brown suede ones. I see a black bag I really admire, don't need, and manage to resist. Just before everything closes, we dash over to San Marco, the serene monastery with Fra Angelico frescoes in the cells. Jess never has seen it and the twelve angel musicians seem good to look at during this season. Siesta catches up with us, so we settle into a long lunch at Antolino's, a righteous *trattoria* with a potbellied stove in the middle of the room. The menu lists pastas with hare and boar *ragù*, duck, polentas and risottos. The waiters rush by with platters of big roasts.

There's plenty of time for a long walk before the town reopens. Florence! The tourists are gone, or if they're here, the fine misty rain must keep them inside. We pass the apartment we rented five years ago, when I swore off Florence. In summer, wads of tourists clog the city as if it's a Renaissance theme park. Everyone seems to be eating. That year, a garbage strike persisted for over a week and I began to have thoughts of plague when I passed heaps of rot spilling out of bins. I was amazed that long July when waiters and shopkeepers remained as nice as they did, given what they had to put up with. Everywhere I stepped I was in the way. Humanity seemed ugly—the international young in torn T-shirts and backpacks lounging on steps, bewildered bus tourists dropping ice cream napkins in the street and asking, "How much is that in dollars?" Germans in too-short shorts letting their children terrorize restaurants. The English mother and daughter ordering *lasagne verde* and Coke, then complaining because the spinach pasta was *green*. My own reflection in the window, carrying home all my shoe purchases, the sundress not so flattering. Bad wonderland. Henry James in Florence referred to "one's detested fellow-pilgrim." Yes, indeed, and it's definitely time to leave when one's own reflection is included. Sad that our century has added no glory to Florence—only mobs and lead hanging in the air.

In early morning, though, we'd walk to Marino's for warm brioche, take them to the middle of the bridge and watch the silvery celadon light on the Arno. Most afternoons we sat in a café at Piazza Santo Spirito, where a sense of neighborhood still exists even in summer. The sun angling through the trees hit that grand undecorated sculptural facade of Brunelleschi's, with the boys playing ball beneath it. Somehow it must make a difference to grow up bouncing your ball against the wall of Santo Spirito. Perhaps many who come to Florence in summer are able to find moments and places like this, times when the city gives itself over by returning to itself.

Today, the stony streets take a shine from the mist. We walk right in the Brancacci chapel. No line; in fact, only a half dozen young priests in long black gowns, following an older priest as he points and lectures about the Masaccio frescoes. I haven't seen Adam and Eve leaving Eden since the vines over their genitals, painted during some fit of papal modesty, were removed and the frescoes cleaned and restored. Shocking to see them lifted out of the film of centuries of candle smoke: all these distinct faces and the chalky rose and saffron robes.

Every face, isolated and examined, reveals character. "I wanted to see what made each one that one," Gertrude Stein said about her desire to write about many lives. Masaccio had a powerful sense of character and narrative and a sharp eye for placing the human in space. A neophyte kneels in a stream to be baptized. Through the transparent water we see his knees and feet. San Pietro flings the basin, showering his head and back with water. All the symbolism of earlier art is abandoned for the cold splash on the boy. Another pleasure is Masaccio's (and Masolino's and Lippi's, whose hands are apparent) attention to architecture, light, and shadow. Here's Florence as he saw, or idealized it, with the sun falling logically—not the sourceless light of his predecessors—on this cast of characters who surely walked the streets of this city.

211

We hurry to the six-nineteen train and miss it. As we wait, I mention the black bag I didn't buy and Ed decides it would be a terrific Christmas present, although we have said we only are buying things for the house. He and Jess literally *run* back to the shop, halfway across town from the train station. Ashley and I are uneasy when it's five minutes until departure but here they come, smiling and panting, waving the shopping bag just as the train is announced.

On Christmas Eve eve, we take off on a quest in Umbria. Ed thinks we must have one of his favorite reds for Christmas dinner, the Sagrantino, impossible to find this far from its origins. I am after the ultimate *panettone*. I called Donatella, an Italian friend who's a wonderful cook, and asked if we could make one together, thinking the homemade would be better than the commercial ones stacked in colorful boxes in every grocery and bar. "It takes twenty hours of rising," she says. "It must rise four times." I remember how many times I've killed the yeast when making simple bread. When her mother was small, she tells me, *panettone* was just ordinary bread with some nuts and dried fruits tucked into the dough. *La cucina povera* again. "It's really best to buy it." She gave me several brands and I picked out one for Francesco's family. As I was about to take another, a woman buying at the same time told me that the very best are made in Perugia. She wrote the name of a shop, Ceccarani, on a piece of paper. So we are off to Perugia.

Ceccarani's window display is a full crèche intricately executed in glazed bread dough. Dough must be a good medium; the figures have expressive faces, sheep look woolly, fronds on the palm trees are finely detailed. The nativity scene is surrounded by marzipan mushrooms and *panettoni* hollowed out on the side. Inside each—what else but a miniature crèche? Incredible!

Throngs of women fill the shop. I push to the back and select a *panettone* as tall as a top hat.

Deeper into Umbria, we come to Spello and walk all over the steeply terraced town. Coming down from Spello, we see the early moon hoisting itself over the hills. We keep losing it as we turn then face it again, the largest, whitest, spookiest moon I've ever seen. All the way to Montefalco, home of the Sagrantino, we dodge the moon. Two or three times we see it rise again, over a different hill. Jess has taken to calling Ed "Montefalco" for his black leather jacket and tendency to speed. He makes up Montefalco adventures as we take several wrong turns. In the piazza, the wine store is open but the proprietor is missing. We look around, look outside, come back—no sign of him. We take a walk around the piazza. The store stands wide open but still the owner is gone. Finally, we ask at the bar and the bartender points to a man playing cards. We buy our four bottles and head home, chasing the moon across Umbria.

On Christmas Eve, Ashley and I launch into cooking. Jess, a novice, is given tasks and entertains us with rock lyrics. Ed dedicates the morning to squeezing silicone around the windows. He runs into town to pick up tonight's first course, *crespelle*, from the fresh pasta shop. The delicate crêpes are filled with truffles and cream. Our menu after the *crespelle*: a warm salad of *porcini*, roasted red peppers, and field lettuces, grilled veal chops, the local cardoons with béchamel and toasted hazelnuts. For dessert, a family cake I know by heart and *castagnaccio,* the classic Tuscan chestnut flour cake. My neighbor says not to try it. Her grandmother used to make it when they were very poor. "All it takes is chestnut flour, olive oil, and water," she says, grimacing. "My grandmother said that they always had those. They flavored it with rosemary and some pine nuts, fennel seeds, and raisins if they had some." I've never worked with chestnut flour, an ingredient I'd considered esoteric until I learned that it was a staple of *la cucina povera.* This recipe is decidedly weird. As my neighbor indicates, it must be one of those acquired tastes.

213

"But where are the sugar and eggs—can this really turn into a cake? And how much water to use? The recipe only says to use enough for the batter to pour easily." My neighbor just shakes her head. I'm intrigued. This cake will send us back to the roots of Tuscan cooking. Ashley and Jess are not so sure they want to be transported that far.

Before siesta, we walk over the Roman road into town for last-minute lettuces and bread. Where is our "angel"? In winter, he does not seem to come to the shrine. I watch for his slow approach, his eyes on the house, then his long pause while he places his flowers. Would he bring a twig of bright rose hips, a shriveled bunch of dried grapes, a spiny chestnut casing split to reveal three brown nuts? Perhaps he walks elsewhere in winter, or stays in his medieval apartment, feeding logs into the woodstove.

Cortona is hopping. Everyone carries at least one *panettone* and one basket of cellophane-wrapped gift foods. No shop plays that canned, generic Christmas music I find so dispiriting at home. People crowd the bars, stoking themselves with coffee and hot chocolate because the sharp *tramontana* has started to blow in from the north, bringing frigid air from the Alps and northern Apennines.

Peaceful eve, bountiful feast, dessert by the fire. We all hate the chestnut cake. Flat and gummy, it probably has the exact taste of a

Christmas dessert during the last war, when chestnuts could be foraged in the forest. We trade it for a platter of walnuts, winter pears, and Gorgonzola, a dessert for the gods. Long before midnight mass, which we'd hoped to experience in one of the small churches, we fade.

*

Ed calls up from downstairs, "Look out the window." Snow fell in the night, just enough to dust the fronds of the palm tree and glaze the terraces with a sheen of white.

"Beautiful! Turn up the heat." My bare feet feel icy. I pull on a sweatshirt, jeans, and shoes and run downstairs. The front doors are wide open, the frosty light pouring in. Ed scrapes a snowball off the outdoor table. I jump aside and it lands in the hall. The sleeping beauties have not yet emerged. We take our coffee to the wall, brush it off, and watch the fog below us moving like an opalescent sea. Snow on Christmas!

Is this much happiness allowed? I secretly ask myself. Will the gods not come down and confiscate this health, abundance of cheer, these bright expectations? Is this the old scar, this rippling of want and fear? My father died on the eve of Christmas Eve when I was fourteen. The funeral day was rainy, so rainy that the coffin floated for a moment before it settled into the earth. My pink tulle Christmas dance dress hung on the back of my closet door. Or is this unrest just part of the great collective holiday blues all the newspapers focus on every year? Many Christmases in my adult life have been exquisite, especially when my daughter was a child. A few have been lonely. One was very rocky. Either way, the season of joy comes with a primitive urge that runs deep into the psyche.

After breakfast, we build up the fire and open presents. We brought over a few and slowly have accumulated the usual pile around the tree. We hadn't intended to have so many but the day in Florence inspired us to pick out soaps, notebooks, sweaters, and a surprisingly huge quantity of chocolate. One of our gifts is a chestnut roasting pan, which we put to immediate use. We're gathering at four at Fenella and Peter's and one of our contributions will be roasted chestnuts in red wine. We cut a thin slit on each, shake them over the coals for less than ten minutes, then prepare to ruin our nails peeling them. Perhaps because they are fresh, the shells come right off, revealing the plump toasted nut. Everyone takes a job and we fly through the preparation of two *faraone,* guinea hens, and a rustic apple tart made by rolling a large round of pastry on a cookie sheet, piling the buttered and sugared fruit and toasted hazelnuts in the center, then flapping the pastry irregularly around it. Our cook, Willie Bell, would be proud of my variation on her cream gravy. To the *faraone* pan juices, I add béchamel and chopped roasted chestnuts. I want chestnuts in everything. Fenella is preparing a pork roast and polenta, Elizabeth will bring salad, and Max is in charge of another vegetable and dessert. We could fast before such a feast but we have a light lunch of wild mushroom lasagne. A Christmas walk is a long tradition, for Ashley and me at least. Ed and I haven't told them yet where we are going.

We drive to the end of a road near our house and get out. We discovered this walk purely by chance one day when we walked this road and spotted a path at the end of it. We kept walking and made a fantastic discovery. It was one of the great walks I've ever had and we decided then to come back at Christmas. Water is flowing where I've never seen it in summer. Sudden streams gush out of crevices and wash over the road. We come to a waterfall and several torrents. Soon we're in a chestnut and pine forest of huge ancient trees. We see a few patches of snow in the woods and more snow higher up in the distance. The air, deeply moist, smells of wet pine needles. We come to paving stones laid end to end. "Look, a path," Ashley says. "What is this? It's wider up ahead." Out here in nowhere, we're on a Roman road in incredibly good condition for long stretches. We never have reached the end but Beppe, who knows it from childhood, told us it goes to the top of Monte Sant'Egidio, twenty kilometers away. Instead of winding and skirting, Roman roads tend to go straight to the top. The chariots were light and the shortest distance between two points seemed to have governed their surveyors. I've read that some of their roadbeds go down twelve feet. We're on the lookout for the distance markers but they have disappeared. Cortona lies below us, and below the town the valley and the horizon look polished and gleaming. We see mountains in the distance we've never seen, and the hilltowns of Sinalunga, Montepulciano, and Monte San Savino rise sharply like three ships sailing against the sky. The last knot of my unrest unravels. I start to hum "I saw three ships come sailing in on Christmas Day, on Christmas Day in the morning." A red fox leaps down onto the path ahead of us. He sweeps his plumy tail back and forth, regards us for a moment, then darts into the woods.

✳

The road to Fenella and Peter's noble farmhouse is rough enough in summer. Now we're holding on to pots and trays and trying not to empty them into one another's laps. The poor Twingo's axle! We ford several impromptu streams and almost get stuck in a washout of near-ditch proportions. When we arrive everyone is gathered by the gigantic fireplace, already into the red wine. This is one of the most magnificent houses in the local vernacular. The living room, formerly a granary, soars two stories high with rows of dark beams. The immense room is filled with a lifetime collection of antiques, rugs, and treasures. The space is too large to heat, however, so we settle into big sofas in the former kitchen, with its fireplace large enough for the original cooks to set their chairs inside it and tend their pots. Downstairs the thirty-foot-long table is laid with pine boughs and red candles. Ghosts of Christmases past join us in everyone's stories of other holidays. Fenella pours the hot polenta onto a cutting board. Ed carves the *faraone* while Peter slices the succulent roast. We pile our plates. Fenella has journeyed to Montepulciano for a stash of her favorite *vino nobile*, which travels around the table. "To absent friends," Fenella toasts. "To the polenta!" Ed rejoins. Our little expatriate band is merry, merry.

En route home, we stop in town for a coffee. We expect the streets to be deserted on Christmas night at nine o'clock, but *everyone* is out, every baby and grandmother and everyone in between. Walking and talking, always talking. "Well, Jess, you're objective," I say. "You're new here so you must tell me if I'm under an illusion—or is this the most divine town on the planet."

Without a pause, he says, "I'd say so. Yes. Extra *primo* good."

The *passeggiata* activity is to stroll from church to church, viewing the scenes of Christ's birth. The reminder of birth is everywhere, is still the major focus of Christmas here. Pagan, I suppose I am, but I think what a glorious *metaphor* the birth is at year's end, the dark and dead end of the year. The one cry of the baby in the damp straw and death is denied. The baby in every scene has a nimbus of light around his head. The sun is crossing the celestial equator, bringing back the days I love. One foot over and we're on a swing toward light. That restless urge at this season, maybe it's the desire to find the light of one's own again. I've read that the body contains minerals in the exact proportions that the earth does; the percentages of zinc and potassium in the earth are the same amounts we have in our bodies. Could the body have an innate desire to imitate the earth's push toward rebirth?

All the Cortona churches display their *presepi*, nativity scenes. Some are elaborate reproductions of paintings in wax and wood models with elaborate architecture and costume; some are terra-cotta. One crib is made of ice cream sticks. At the middle school's exhibit of students' *presepi*, we're touched to see the children's less ornate versions. Most are traditional, with small dolls, twig trees, and hand-mirror ponds, but one astonishes us. Paolo Alunni, aged perhaps ten, is a true heir of the Futurists and their love for the mechanical and its energy. His crèche—stable, people and animals—is constructed entirely of keys. The animal keys are horizontal and it's clear which are sheep, which are cows. The humans are upright except for the cunning little diary-sized key that is the baby Jesus. He's made the stable roof from a hinge. Eerie and effective—a stunning piece of art among all the earnest projects.

✳

Every morning I look out the window at the valley filled with fog, pink tinted at dawn on clear days, a roiling gray when high clouds blow across from the north. These are seamless days of walks and books, of taking trips to Anghiari, Siena, Assisi, and nearby Lucignano, whose town walls describe a graceful ellipse. At night, we grill in the fireplace—*bruschetta* with melted *pecorino* and walnuts, slices of fresh *pecorino* with *prosciutto*, and sausages. *Scamorza*, more native to the Abruzzo but growing popular in Tuscany, is a hard rind cheese shaped like an 8. It melts to almost a fondue and we spread it on bread. I learn to use the hearth to warm plates and keep food hot, just as my imagined *nonna* must have done. Our favorite pasta becomes *pici con funghi e salsiccie*, pencil-thick pasta with wild mushrooms and the grilled sausages. A seven-mile walk along the fire road cancels the effects of one evening of grilling.

On New Year's Eve, I am coming home from town with a carload of groceries. We're cooking the traditional lentils (tiny coin shapes are the symbol of prosperity) and *zampone*, sausage in the shape of a pig's foot. As I climb the road toward home, I pass the dome of Santa Maria Nuova below me. Fog completely surrounds the church and the dome floats above the clouds. Five intersecting rainbows dive and arch around the dome. I almost run off the road. At the curve, I stop and get out, wishing everyone were with me. This is staggering. If it were the Middle Ages, I'd claim a miracle. Another car stops and a man dressed in fancy hunting clothes jumps out. Probably he is one of the murderers of song birds but he, too, looks stunned. We both just stare.

As the clouds shift, the rainbows disappear one by one but the dome still drifts, ready for any sign that might be about to happen. I wave to the hunter. *"Auguri,"* he calls.

✸

Before Ashley and Jess go back to New York, where serious winter waits to kick in, and before we go back to San Francisco, where paperwhite narcissi already are blooming in Golden Gate Park, we plant the Christmas tree. I expect the ground to be hard but it is not. Loamy and rich, it yields to the shovel. As Jess shovels dirt, the white skull of a hedgehog turns up with its perfectly articulated jaw and teeth still attached by a string of ligament. *Memento mori,* a useful thought as the end of one year folds into the new. The sturdy tree looks immediately at home on the lower terrace. As it grows it will tower over the road below. From the upstairs, we'll see its peak growing higher and higher each year. If the rains these first few years are plentiful, in fifty years it may be the giant tree of the hillside. Ashley, old by then, may remember planting it. Because she is flush with beauty, I can't imagine her old. She will come with her friends or family, all of whom will marvel. Or strangers who own the house may take its lower limbs for firewood. Surely Bramasole will still be here, with the olives we've planted thriving on the terraces.

CIBO, FOOD, A BASIC WORD. I'M GATHERING A BAG OF *cibo* to take back to California with me. I'm not sure exactly when my carry-on bag became a grocery bag in disguise. Besides olive oil (each of us carries back two liters), I take tubes of those pastes that are marvelous for quick hors d'oeuvres: white truffle, caper, olive, and garlic. They're very inexpensive here and easy to transport. I take boxes of *funghi porcini* bouillon cubes, which I can't get at home, and a pound or so of dried *porcini*. The bright boxes and foil bags of Perugina chocolates make handy gifts. I would like to take a wheel of *parmigiano* but my bag is not that accommodating. This time I'm stuffing in a truffle-flavored vinegar and a good *aceto balsamico*. I notice that Ed has added a bottle of *grappa* to the bag, as well as a jar of chestnut honey.

To the question "Are you carrying any food items?" on the customs form, I must answer yes. As long as products are sealed, no one seems to care. A friend who had special sausages from his hometown of Ferrara stuffed in his raincoat pockets was sniffed by airport beagles and stripped of his heirlooms.

The only kitchen item I usually bring with me *to* Italy is plastic wrap; the Italian kind always gets off to a bad start, leaving me untangling a two-inch strip. This time, however, I have brought one bag of Georgia pecans and a can of cane syrup, pecan pie being a necessary ingredient of Christmas. All the other ingredients of Christmas in Tuscany seem new. One pleasure of the cook is that now and then you learn all over again.

Winter food here recalls the hunter stepping in the door with his jacket pockets filled with birds, the farmer bringing in the olive harvest and beginning the cold-weather work of clearing and preparing the trees, trimming back vines for spring. Tuscan food of this season calls for massive appetites. For us, long walks build us up to the hefty dishes that we order in *trattorie:* pasta with wild boar *ragù*, *lepre*, hare, fried mushrooms, and polenta. The rich smells drifting from our kitchen are different in winter. The light summer fragrances of basil, lemon balm, and tomatoes are replaced by aromas of succulent pork roast glazed with honey, guinea hens roasting under a layer of *pancetta*, and *ribollita*, that heartiest of soups. Subtle and earthy, the fine shavings of Umbrian truffle over a bowl of pasta prick the senses. At breakfast, the perfumed melons of summer are forgotten and we use leftover bread for slabs of French toast spread with plum jam I made last summer from the delicate *coscia di monaca*, nun's thigh, variety that grows along the back of the house. The eggs always startle me; they're so *yellow*. The freshness does make a tremendous difference, so that a platter of eggs scrambled with a big dollop of mascarpone becomes a very special treat.

I didn't anticipate the extent of the excitement of cooking in winter: The entire shopping list is changed by the cold season. In winter here, there are no asparagus from Peru, no grapes from Chile. What's available, primarily, is what grows, though citrus comes up from the south and Sicily. A mound of tiny orange clementines, bright as ornaments, shines in a blue bowl on the windowsill. Ed eats two or three at a time, tossing the peels into the fire, where they blacken and shrivel, sending out the pungent scent of their burning oil. Because the days are so short, the evening dinners are long, and long prepared for.

ANTIPASTI

✼

Winter Bruschette

Crostini, the *antipasti* that appear on every menu in Tuscany, and *bruschette* are both pieces of bread onto which various topping are piled or spread. The *crostini* are rounds of bread; the baguette-shaped loaves are sold at the *forno*. A typical platter of *crostini* includes several choices; *crostini di fegatini*, chicken liver spread, is the most popular. I often serve *crostini* with garlic paste and a grilled shrimp on each. *Bruschette* are made from regular bread, sliced, dipped quickly in olive oil, grilled or broiled, then rubbed with a clove of garlic. In summer, topped with chopped tomatoes and basil, it appears frequently as a first course or snack. Winter's robust *bruschette* are fun to prepare at the fireplace. When friends stop in, we open a hefty *vino nobile*.

Bruschette with Pecorino and Nuts

Prepare bruschette *as described above. For each* bruschetta, *slowly melt a slice of* pecorino *(or fontina) in a pan on hot coals or on the stove. When slightly melted, sprinkle chopped walnuts over the cheese. With a spatula, slide the cheese onto the grilled bread.*

Bruschette with Pecorino and Prosciutto

Prepare bruschette. *In an iron skillet over the coals or in a nonstick pan on the stove, slightly melt slices of* pecorino, *top with* prosciutto, *then another slice of* pecorino. *Flip over so that both sides melt and are crisp around the edges. Slide onto bread.*

Bruschette with Greens

Chop cavolo nero, *black cabbage (or Swiss chard). Season and sauté in olive oil with 2 cloves of minced garlic. Spread 1 or 2 tablespoons on each* bruschetta.

Bruschette con Pesto di Rucola

This variation on the standard pesto is equally good with pasta. Arugula is satisfying to grow. It sprouts quickly and the young peppery leaves are best. By the time the leaves are large, the taste usually turns bitter.

Prepare bruschette, this time cutting the bread into small pieces. In a food processor or mortar, combine a bunch of arugula, salt and pepper, 2 cloves of garlic, and 1/4 cup of pine nuts. Blend together, then slowly incorporate enough olive oil to make a thick paste. Add 1/2 cup of grated parmigiano. Spread on grilled bread. Makes about 1-1/2 cups.

Bruschette with Grilled Eggplant

I've often burned eggplant on the grill—by the time it's done it's black—so now I bake the whole eggplant in the oven for about 20 minutes, then slice it and, for taste, just finish it off on the grill.

Bake an eggplant on a piece of foil in a moderate oven until it is almost done. Slice and salt. Let rest on paper towels for a few minutes. Brush each slice lightly with olive oil, sprinkle with pepper, and grill. Chop 1/2 cup of fresh parsley, mix with some chopped fresh thyme and marjoram. Lightly brush the eggplant with oil again if it looks dry. Place a slice on a piece of pre-pared bruschetta, sprinkle with some of the herb mixture and a little grated pecorino or parmigiano. Heat briefly in the broiler to melt cheese slightly.

PRIMI PIATTI

❋

Wild Mushroom Lasagna

Dried lasagna in boxes leaves me cold—those wavy edges like tractor tires, the gummy pasta. Thin sheets of fresh pasta create a light, light lasagna. I watched a real pro with pasta in a local shop. Hers is thin as a bedsheet and supple. In summer, this recipe works well with vegetables instead of mushrooms: sliced zucchini, tomatoes, onions, and eggplant, seasoned with fresh herbs. Both recipes can be used as a filling for long, rolled *crespelle*, crêpes, as well.

Cut sheets of pasta to fit 6 layers in a large baking dish. (Some of the middle layers can be in more than 1 piece.) Prepare a béchamel sauce: Melt 4 tablespoons of butter. Stir in 4 tablespoons of flour, and cook but do not brown. After 3 or 4 minutes, remove from heat and whisk in 2 cups of milk all at once. Return to heat, stir and simmer until the sauce thickens. Mince 3 cloves of garlic and add it to the sauce, along with 1 tablespoon of chopped thyme, salt and pepper. Grate 1-1/2 cups of parmigiano. *In a large pan, heat 2 tablespoons of olive oil or butter and sauté 3 cups of sliced fresh mushrooms—preferably* porcini *or* portobello. *If you don't have wild mushrooms, use a mixture of button mushrooms and dried* porcini *that have been revived by soaking them for 30 minutes in stock, water, wine, or cognac.*

Assembly: Cook 1 sheet of pasta until it is barely done, remove it from the boiling water, and let it briefly drain on a cloth towel spread on the counter. Place the semidry pasta sheet in the lightly oiled baking dish and cover it with a layer of béchamel sauce, a layer of sautéed mushrooms, and a sprinkling of the cheese. Continue cooking the next pasta sheet as you prepare each layer. Add a spoonful or two of the pasta water to the sauce if you've used too much on the first layers. Tuscan cooks usually use some of the pasta water in their sauces. Top the dish with buttered bread crumbs and more parmigiano. *Bake, uncovered, at 350° for 30 minutes. Serves 8.*

❋

Ribollita

A thick, soul-stirring soup with white beans, the ubiquitous bread, and vegetables. As the translation "reboiled" indicates, this is a soup that is easily made using leftovers, probably from a big Sunday dinner. The classic recipe calls for hunks of bread to be added to the pot at the end. Tuscans pour oil into each bowl at the table. The soup, with a salad, is a complete meal—unless you've been out plowing. Almost any vegetable can be used. If I say "zuppa" to Maria Rita, she piles in everything I'll need, plus handfuls of fresh parsley, basil, and garlic. I take her advice to include the heel of the *parmigiano*. Once cooked, the softened heel is the cook's treat.

Prepare a pound of white beans by washing them well. Cover with water in a stock pot and bring them to a boil. Take them off the heat and let them sit in the water for a couple of hours. Add more water to cover, add seasonings, and simmer until barely done. They should be watched because they tend to become mushy soon after they're done. Clean and cut into medium dice: 2 onions, 6 carrots, 4 ribs of celery, a bunch of curly cabbage or chard, 4 or 5 cloves of garlic, and 5 large tomatoes (or a box of chopped tomatoes in winter). Mince a bunch of parsley. Sauté the onions and carrots in olive oil. After a few minutes, add the celery, then the chard and the garlic, adding more oil as needed. Cook 10 minutes, then add the tomatoes, a heel of parmigiano, *and the beans. Add enough stock (vegetable, chicken, or meat) to cover. Bring to a boil, then simmer 1 hour to blend flavors. Add the cubes of bread. Allow to rest for several hours. Add the parsley, reheat, and serve with grated* parmigiano *on top and olive oil to pass around the table. Leftover pasta, green beans, peas, pancetta, and potatoes all can be added to the pot the next day. At least 15 servings, depending on the amount of stock used.*

❋

Pici with Quick Tomato-Cream Sauce

Hearty sauces of hare and boar adhere especially well to the long, thick strands of this local pasta, which is almost as thick as a pencil. I use this sauce on *fusilli* and *pappardelle* or any broad pasta. This is a favorite.

Cook 4 or 5 slices of pancetta, drain on paper towels, then crumble and set aside. Chop 2 medium onions and 2 or 3 cloves of garlic and sauté in olive oil for 5 minutes. Chop and add 1 large red pepper and 4 or 5 tomatoes. Season and cook 5 minutes more. Season with chopped thyme, oregano, and basil. Stir in 1/2 cup of light cream and 3/4 cup of puréed tomatoes. Add a spoonful or so of the pasta water to the sauce. Stir the pancetta into the sauce at the last minute to retain crispness. Cook and drain enough pasta for 4. Mix the pasta with half the sauce; serve the rest of the sauce over the pasta. Pass the parmigiano! Serves 4.

SECONDI

✸

Quail, Slowly Braised with Juniper Berries and Pancetta

My father was a hunter and our cook, Willie Bell, often was lost in a cloud of tiny feathers as she plucked a mound of quail. The drooping little heads all fell in the same direction. I wouldn't eat them, even after she smothered them with cream and pepper in the huge covered frying pan on the outdoor fireplace. With more equanimity, I've met them in a new guise. The balsamic vinegar should come from Modena. Those that are labeled *Aceto Balsamico Tradizionale di Modena* and are marked *API MO* are the real thing, aged for at least twelve years. Some of the ancient balsamics are so fine that they're sipped like liqueur. I think Willie Bell would approve of these quail.

Flour and quickly brown 12 quail (2 per person) in hot olive oil. Arrange the quail in a heavy casserole with a tight-fitting lid and pour in 1/4 cup of balsamic vinegar. Cover quail with strips of pancetta and 2 minced shallots. Sprinkle with sprigs of thyme, crushed peppercorns, and juniper berries. Braise in a slow oven (275°) for 3 hours. Turn the quail over after about an hour and a half. Moisten with a little red wine or more balsamic vinegar if they look dry. They are excellent served with polenta. Serves 6.

✺

Roast Chickens Stuffed with Polenta

In Georgia when I was growing up, the Christmas turkey always was stuffed with a cornmeal dressing. This adaptation of my mother's recipe uses Italian ingredients.

Soak 2 cups of polenta in 2 cups of cold water for 10 minutes, then add it to 2 cups of boiling water in a stock pot. Bring to a boil, then lower the heat and cook, stirring constantly, for 10 minutes. Stir in 1 cup of butter. Remove from the heat and beat in 2 eggs. Add 2 cups of fresh croutons, 2 chopped onions, 3 ribs of chopped celery, and season generously with salt, pepper, sage, thyme, and marjoram. Stuff 2 chickens (or 1 turkey) loosely, tie the legs together, and scatter sprigs of thyme over the birds. Roast on oiled racks in a large pan. 25 minutes a pound at 350° is a rough estimate for the perfectly roasted bird—but start testing sooner. Leftover stuffing can be baked separately in a buttered dish. Serves 8.

✺

Faraone (Guinea Hens) with Fennel

Delicate and flavorful, guinea hens are always available at the butcher. For Christmas, we roasted two and presented them on a large platter, surrounded by grilled local sausages and a wreath of herbs. The bones made a rich stock for soup the next day. Oven-roasted potatoes with rosemary and garlic are a natural companion.

I'm afraid the faraone must first be approached with tweezers to remove remaining pin feathers. Wash and dry 2 birds well. Simplest preparation is best—the flavor of the bird is emphasized. Lay rosemary branches on an oiled roasting pan and place the birds on top. Rub with a mixture of chopped rosemary, basil, and thyme, then lard with strips of pancetta. Remove the tough outer portions of 2 fennel bulbs. Cut in half-inch crescents, drizzle with olive oil, and scatter them around the birds, along with a couple of quartered onions.

*Roast at 350° at 20 minutes per pound. These birds are leaner than chickens;
be careful not to overcook. For a rich sauce, add béchamel sauce and roasted
chestnuts to the pan juices. Serves 4.*

❋

Rabbit with Tomatoes and Balsamic Vinegar

Coniglio, rabbit, is a staple of the Tuscan diet. At the Saturday market,
a farm woman usually has three or four fluffy bunnies looking up at
you from an old Alitalia flight bag. In the butcher's case, they're more
remote, clean and lean, ruddy pink, sometimes with a bit of fur left on
the tail to prove it's not cat. Unappetizing as this note is, the rabbit,
simmered in thick tomato sauce with herbs, is delightful. Just call it
coniglio for the children's sake.

*Have the rabbit cut into pieces. Flour them and quickly brown in olive
oil. Arrange in a baking dish and cover with the following tomato-balsamic
sauce. Sauté 1 large chopped onion and 3 or 4 cloves of minced garlic until
translucent. Chop 4 or 5 tomatoes and add them to the pan. Season with
1/2 teaspoon of turmeric, rosemary, salt, pepper, and toasted fennel seeds. Stir
in 4 tablespoons of balsamic vinegar and simmer until sauce is thick and
reduced. Roast the rabbit, uncovered, for about 40 minutes in a 350° oven.
Midway, baste with 2 to 3 tablespoons of additional balsamic vinegar.
Serves 4.*

❋

Polenta with Sausage and Fontina

In winter, the local fresh pasta shop sells polenta with chopped walnuts, a simple but interesting accompaniment to roasts or chicken. The
polenta and sausages, with a grand salad, is a robust meal in itself.

*Prepare classic polenta (page 131). Pour half of the polenta
into an oiled baking dish. Thinly slice or grate 1-1/2 cups of Fontina and
spread over the layer of polenta. Season with salt and pepper. Pour on the rest*

of the polenta. Slice 6 sautéed Italian sausages over the top and pour on the pan juices. Bake for 15 minutes at 300°. Serves 6.

✼

Honey-Glazed Pork Tenderloin with Fennel

The tenderest, leanest pork is the tenderloin. One tenderloin serves two hungry people and the fennel pairs well with the pork. Wild fennel grows all over our land. Whether its local popularity first came from its aphrodisiacal powers or its curative uses for eye problems, I don't know. I like its feathery foliage and its mythic connections. Prometheus is said to have brought the first fire to humans inside the thick, hollow stalk.

Brush 2 tenderloins lightly with honey. In a mortar or food processor, crush 1 tablespoon of fennel seeds. Add them to 1 tablespoon of finely chopped rosemary, salt, pepper, and 2 cloves of minced garlic. Spread this mixture on the pork. Place in a shallow, oiled pan. Roast in the oven at 400° until the pork is faintly pink in the middle, about 30 minutes. Meanwhile, cut 2 fennel bulbs in 1/2-inch slices. Toss out the tough root end. Steam for about 10 minutes, until cooked but not soft. Purée until smooth, then add 1/4 cup of white wine, 1/2 cup of grated parmigiano, and 1/2 cup of mascarpone (or sour cream). Place tenderloins into a buttered dish and pour sauce over; top with buttered bread crumbs. Cook at 350° for about 10 minutes. Garnish tenderloins with fennel leaves, if available, or with wands of fresh rosemary. Serves 4.

CONTORNI

✼

Chestnuts in Red Wine

Even though I'm living near a chestnut forest, chestnuts still seem luxurious. We roast a few every night to enjoy with a glass of *amaro, grappa,* or a last coffee. Just a short gash or x in the shell before they're put in the pan and they open easily while still hot. Many cookbooks advise roasting chestnuts for up to an hour! In the fireplace, they're ready quickly—15 minutes at the most, depending on how hot the coals are. Jiggle the pan often and remove them at the first sign of charring. Chestnuts taste good with all the flavorful winter meats, especially with guinea hens.

> *Roast and peel 30 or 40 chestnuts. Simmer the chesnuts in just enough red wine to cover for half an hour, long enough for the two flavors to intertwine. Pour off most of the wine. Serves 6.*

✳

Garlic Flan

Excellent with any roast.

> *Separate the cloves from a large head of garlic. Without peeling, place the cloves in boiling water for 5 minutes. Cool, and squeeze out the garlic. Mince and crush the cloves with a fork, then stir into 2 cups of cream. Bring cream and garlic just to a simmer in a saucepan. Add a little ground nutmeg, salt, and pepper. Remove from the flame and beat in 4 egg yolks. Pour into 6 individual molds, well-oiled, or into a shallow baking pan. Bake in a bains-marie at 350° for 20 minutes or until set. Cool for 10 minutes before unmolding.*

✳

Cardoons

As long as your arm, prickly, and pale green, cardoons are trouble but worth it. This vegetable was new to me. I learned to strip the tough, stringy exterior from the stalks—the stalks are somewhat like celery—and quickly place the cardoon pieces in water and lemon juice because they otherwise turn dark in a hurry. At first I steamed them but they never seemed to get done. I found that boiling them is best, just to the point of fork tenderness. They have a taste and texture similar to heart of artichoke—not surprising since they come from the same family.

After stripping a large bunch of cardoons and bathing them in acidulated water, cut in two-inch pieces and boil until just done. Drain and arrange in a well-buttered baking dish. Season with salt and pepper and lightly cover with a béchamel sauce (see recipe on page 224), dots of butter, and a sprinkling of parmigiano. Bake at 350° for 20 minutes.

231

✳

Warm Porcini (or Portobello) Salad with
Roasted Red and Yellow Peppers

Serve this colorful composed salad as a first or main course.

Grill 2 large mushrooms or sauté them topside down in olive oil (this prevents them from losing their juices). Slice and drizzle lightly with vinaigrette. Grill 2 peppers, one red and one green, and let them cool in a bag, then slide off the charred skin. Slice and drizzle with the vinaigrette. Separate a Bermuda (red) onion into rings. Toast 1/4 cup of pine nuts. Toss greens— radicchio, arugula, and other lettuces of varying textures and colors—with vinaigrette and arrange on each plate. Arrange the warm peppers, rings of onion, and mushroom slices over the greens and top with pine nuts. Serves 6.

DOLCI

✳

Winter Pears in Vino Nobile

Steeped pears are pretty to serve. Their taste seems heightened when served along with some Gorgonzola, toasted bread, and walnuts roasted with butter and salt.

Peel 6 firm pears and stand them upright in a saucepan. Leave stems on, if they still have them. Squeeze lemon juice over each. Pour 1 cup of red wine over them and sprinkle 1/4 cup of sugar over the tops. Add 1/4 cup of currants, a vanilla bean, and a few cloves to the wine. Cover and simmer for 20 minutes (or longer, depending on the size and ripeness of the pears); don't allow them to become soft. Midway, turn pears on their sides and baste several times with the wine sauce. Transfer to serving dishes, pour the currents and some of the wine over each, and garnish with thin strips of lemon peel. Serves 6.

✳

Rustic Apple Bread Pudding

I'm surprised that the gnarly apples I find at the Saturday market have intense flavor. Even our long-neglected apple trees bravely put forth their scrawny crop. Too tiny to slice, they at least make a respectable apple butter. For this husky dessert, cut the apples in chunky slices.

Peel, core, and cut 4 or 5 crisp baking apples in large slices. Squeeze lemon juice over them, then dust with nutmeg. Toast 1 cup of sliced almonds. Remove any hard crust from a loaf of leftover bread (fresh bread would be too soft for this recipe). Cut the bread into slices and lay some of them on the bottom of a buttered rectangular pan, 9 by 12 inches or so. In a sauté pan, melt 6 tablespoons of butter and 6 tablespoons of sugar. Add 3/4 cup of the toasted almonds, 2 tablespoons of lemon juice and 1/4 cup of cider or water. Toss the apple chunks in this. Layer the apple mixture and bread in the pan, ending with a layer of bread. Beat together 6 tablespoons of softened butter and 4 tablespoons of sugar. Beat in 4 eggs, then 1-1/4 cups of milk and 3/4 cup of light cream. Pour evenly over the bread. Sprinkle the top with a little sugar, nutmeg, and the remaining toasted almonds. Bake at 350° for an hour. Allow to rest for 15 or 20 minutes. Serve with sweetened mascarpone or whipped cream. Serves 8.

✳

Tangerine Sorbet

If I'd grown up here, I'm sure the fragrance of citrus would be indelibly associated with Christmas. The holiday decorations in Assisi are big lemon boughs on all the stores. Against the pale stones, the fruit glows like lighted ornaments and the scent of lemons infuses the cold air. Outside the groceries all over Cortona, baskets of clementines brighten the streets. Bars are squeezing that most opulent of juices, the dark blood orange. The first taste, tart as grapefruit, quickly turns to a deep aftertaste of sweetness. This sorbet, which works wonders as a pause in a winter dinner, can be made with other juices. Equally good as a light dessert, the sorbet is delectable served with thin chocolate butter cookies.

> Make a sugar syrup from 1 cup of water and 1 cup of sugar by bringing them to a boil, then simmering for about 5 minutes. Stir in 1-1/4 cups of fresh tangerine juice, 1 cup of water, 1 tablespoon of lemon juice, plus the zest of the tangerines you've used. Chill thoroughly in the fridge—until cold to the touch. Process in an ice cream machine, according to manufacturer's instructions. Serves 6.

❋

Lemon Cake

A family import, this Southern cake is one I've made a hundred times. Thin slices seem at home here with summer strawberries and cherries or winter pears—or simply with a small glass of one of the many fantastic Italian dessert wines, such as Banfi's B.

> Cream together 1 cup of sweet butter and 2 cups of sugar. Beat in 3 eggs, one at a time. The mixture should be light. Mix together 3 cups of flour, 1 teaspoon of baking powder, 1/4 teaspoon of salt, and incorporate this with the butter mixture alternately with 1 cup buttermilk. (In Italy, I use one cup of cream since buttermilk is not available.) Begin and end with the flour mixture. Add 3 tablespoons of lemon juice and the grated zest of the lemon. Bake in a nonstick tube pan at 300° for 50 minutes. Test for doneness with a toothpick. The cake can be glazed with 1/4 cup of soft butter into which 1-1/2 cups of powdered sugar and 3 tablespoons of lemon juice have been beaten. Decorate with tiny curls of lemon rind.

IN THE TEN HOURS UPRIGHT IN MY AISLE SEAT, HEADED toward Paris, I read with intense concentration a history of experimental French poetry, the flight magazine, even the emergency instruction card. So many crises happened at work before I left San Francisco at the end of May that I wanted to be loaded onto the plane on a stretcher, wrapped in white, put in the front aisle of the plane with curtains around me, the flight attendant looking in now and then with a cup of warm milk—or a sapphire gin martini. I left a week before Ed finished his classes, fled, really, on the first plane smoking on the runway the day after graduation.

After a short wait at Charles de Gaulle, I caught an Alitalia flight. The pilot wasted no time in heading straight up. An Italian driver, I guess, is an Italian driver; suddenly I felt a surge of energy. I wondered if he was trying to pass someone. Soon he aimed down, almost straight down, toward the Pisa airport. No one seemed alarmed, so I practiced breathing evenly and holding up the plane by the armrests.

I'm staying overnight. If we had been late, the prospect of changing trains in Florence at night sounded exhausting. I check into a hotel and find I'm ready to walk. It's *passeggiata* hour. Hoards of people mingling, visiting, strolling, running errands. The tower still leans, tourists still take photos of themselves leaning to one side or the other in front of it. The pastel and ocher houses still curve along the river like an aquarelle of themselves. Women with shopping bags crowd into the fragrant bread store. Splendid to arrive alone in a foreign country and feel the assault of difference. Here they are all along, busy with living; they don't talk or look like me. The rhythm of their day is entirely different; I am thoroughly foreign. I have dinner at an outdoor restaurant on a piazza. Ravioli, roast chicken, green beans, salad, a half carafe of local red. Then my elation ebbs and a total, delicious tiredness rushes over me. After a soaking bath with all the hotel's bubble bath, I sleep for ten hours.

The first morning train takes me through fields of red poppies in bloom, olive groves, and by now familiar stony villages. Haystacks, nuns in white four abreast, bed linens flung out the window, sheepfold, oleander, Italy! I stare out the window the whole way. As we approach Florence, I worry about banging my new small computer against something while juggling my bag. Most of my summer clothes are at the house so I can travel lightly. Even so, I feel like a pack animal with my handbag, computer, and carry-on bag hanging on me. But it's fun to get off at the Florence station, which always brings me the fresh memory of my first trip to Italy almost twenty-five years ago, the exotic, smoky sound of the loudspeaker announcing the arrival from Rome on *binario undici* and the departure for Milano on *binario uno*, the oily train smells and everyone going somewhere.

Fortunately, the train is almost empty and I easily stow my bags. Midway home (*home*, I've said to myself), a cart comes through with sandwiches and drinks. The train doesn't stop at Camucia so I get off at Terontola, about ten miles away, and call a taxi.

Fifteen minutes later a taxi pulls up. As soon as I get in, a second taxi pulls alongside us and the driver starts to shout and gesture. I assumed the taxi I got in was the one I called but no, he just happened along. He does not want to give up the fare. I tell him I called a taxi but he starts to take off. The other driver bangs on the door shouting louder, he was having lunch, he drove here especially for the *Americana*, he has to earn his bread, too. Spit gathers in the corners of his lips and I'm afraid he's about to foam at the mouth. "Stop, please, I should go with him. I'm very sorry!" He growls, slams on brakes, jerks my bag out. I get in the other taxi. They face off to each other, both talking at once, jowls and fists shaking, then abruptly come to terms and start shaking hands, smiling. The deserted driver comes around to me, smiles, and wishes me a good trip.

When I arrive, my sister, nephew, and friends of theirs have been at the house for a couple of weeks. My sister has had all the pots planted with white and coral geraniums. The green smell of freshly cut grass tells me Beppe must have mown the lawn this morning. Despite my severe pruning in December, the roses we planted last summer are as tall as I am. They're profuse with bloom—apricot, white, pink, yellow. Hundreds of butterflies flitter among the lavender. The house has vases of gold lilies and daisies and wildflowers. It's clean and full of life. My sister even has a pot of basil going outside the kitchen door.

They are on a day trip to Florence when I arrive so I have the afternoon to pull the duffel out from under the bed and air out my summer clothes. Since five others are here and settled, I will be sleeping in my study for a few days. I make up the narrow bed with yellow sheets, set up the computer on my travertine desk, open the windows, and I'm here.

Late, I find my boots and walk the terraces. Beppe and Francesco have cut the weeds. Again, I've lost the battle of the wildflowers. In their zeal to clear, they have stopped for nothing, not even the wild (what I know as Cherokee) roses. Poppies, wild carnations, some fluffy white flower, and the host of yellow blooming weeds survive only along the terrace edges. The big news is the olives. In March, they planted thirty in the gaps on the terraces, bringing us up to a hundred and fifty trees. Already they're flowering. We ordered larger trees this year than the ten Ed planted last year; at the rate olives grow, we want to be around to collect a little oil. Beppe and Francesco staked each new tree and stuffed a nest of weeds between the stake and the trunk to prevent chaffing. Ed knew to dig a big hole for each tree but he didn't know to dig an enormous, deep one; Beppe explained that the new trees need a big *polmone*, a lung. Around each, they've dug to a circumference of about four feet. They also planted two more cherries, to go with the ones Ed planted last spring.

237

For a week, we cook, run around to Arezzo and Perugia, walk, buy scarves and sheets at the Camucia market, and catch up on family news. Ed arrives in time for a farewell dinner with liberal pourings of several Brunellos my nephew bought in Montalcino, then they pack, pack, pack (so much to buy here) and are gone.

They've had a warm May; now it begins to rain. The run-rampant roses bend and sway in the wind. We run out with shovels and stake them, getting soaked. Ed digs while I clip off the dead blooms, cut back some of the stalky branches, and give them fertilizer, though I'm afraid it will promote even more of the Jack and the Beanstalk mode. I cut an armful of white ones that bloom in ready-made bouquets. Inside, we iron our clothes, rearrange what has been shifted as many people made themselves comfortable to their own tastes. Everything quickly falls into place. Eons ago, it seems, I arrived in June to find ladders, workmen, pipes, wires, rubble, and dust everywhere. Now we just begin living.

A pot of minestrone for the rainy nights. A walk over the Roman road into town for cheese, arugula, coffee. Maria Rita's cherries are the best ever; we eat a kilo every twenty-four hours. All the stump and stone removal and clearing has paid off. Cleaning up the land is easier now. Not as many rocks fly up when the weed machine splits through the weeds. How many stones have we picked up? Enough to build a house? Fireflies flickering on the terraces at night, cuckoos (don't they say *whoocoo* instead?) in the soft blue dawns. A timid bird that sings "Sweet, sweet." Hoopoes all dressed up in their exotic plumage with nothing more to do than peck in the dirt. Long days with birdsongs instead of the sound of the telephone.

We plant more roses. In this area of Tuscany, they bloom spectacularly. Almost every garden spills and flourishes with them. We select a Paul Neyron, with ruffled hot-pink petals like a tutu and an astonishing lemony-rose scent. I must have two of the soft pink ones the size of tennis balls called Donna Marella Agnelli. Their perfume carries me back to the memory of being hugged to the bosom of Delia, one of my grandmother's friends, who wore immense hats and was a kleptomaniac no one ever accused because it would embarrass her husband to death. When he noticed a new object around the house, he would stop into the store he figured it came from and say, "My wife completely forgot to pay for this—just walked right out with it in her hand and remembered last night. How much do I owe you?" Perhaps her powdery rose perfume was stolen.

"Don't plant any Peace roses," a friend and connoisseur of roses advised. "They're such a cliché." But not only are they dazzling, the vanilla cream, peach, and rosy blush colors repeat the colors of the house. They belong in this garden. I plant several. Last year's gold-orange roses open to flagrant size, the rash colors contributing to their beautiful vulgarity. Now we have a line of roses all along the walk up to the house, with lavender planted between each one. I'm coming to believe in aromatherapy. As I walk to the house through waves of scent, it's impossible not to inhale deeply and feel an infusion of happiness.

At the steps up to the front terrace, the old iron pergola remains at the top and bottom, with jasmine we planted two years ago twining around them and down the iron railings of the steps. Now we decide on another long row of roses on the other side of the walk and a pergola at the opposite end of that walk. This restores the impression of the original rose pergola that existed when we first saw the house, but now we want the open feeling to the wide walk instead of reconstructing the continuous pergola. Two roses we choose—one milky pink, one a velvet red—are Queen Elizabeth and Abe Lincoln (pronounced Eh-bay Lin-cónay at the nursery). Nice to think of those two forces side by side. My favorites start as one color and open to another. *Gioia*, Joy, is pearly as a bud and full blown turns straw yellow, with some petals still veined and edged with pink. We plant more of the apricot-dawn roses, one that's traffic-light yellow, a Pompidou, and one named for Pope John XXIII. So many important people just blooming in our garden. I don't resist a decadent, smoked lilac one that looks as if it belongs in the hand of someone in a coffin.

We visit a *fabbro*, blacksmith, just over the river in Camucia. His two boys gather near as we talk to their father, their chance to see weird foreigners up close. One boy, about twelve, has icy, eerie green eyes. He's lithe and tan. I can't help but stare back at him. All he needs is a goatskin and a crude flute. The *fabbro* also has green eyes but of a more direct color. By now, I've visited the workshops of five or six *fabbri*. The craft must attract particularly intense men. This shop is open on one side so it doesn't have the sooty air of most. He shows us his well covers and manhole grids, practical items. I think of the brooding *fabbro* we first met, now dead from stomach cancer, him wandering in his own world in his blackened shop, fingering the serpentine torch holder and the archaic animal-headed staffs. Our gate still leans open; he died before he repaired it and we've grown used to its rust and bends. The green-eyed *fabbro* shows us his garden and nice house. Perhaps his faun son will follow him in the craft.

Some things are so easy. We'll simply dig holes, fix the iron poles, then fill the holes with cement. We choose a pink climbing rose ("What's its name?" "No name, signora, it's just a rose. *Bella, non?*") for either side.

I've had several gardens but never have planted roses. When I was a child, my father landscaped around the cotton mill he managed for my grandfather. With a single-mindedness I can only wonder at, he planted a thousand roses, all the same kind. *L'étoile de Holland*, a vital heart's blood red rose, is the flower of my father. To put it mildly, he was a difficult man and to complicate that, he died at forty-seven. Until he died, our house always was filled with his roses, large vases, crystal bowls, single silver bud vases on every available surface. They never wilted because he had someone cut a fresh armful every day during seasons of bloom. I can see him at noon coming in the back door in his beige linen suit, somehow not rumpled from the heat. He carries, like a baby in his arms, a cone of newspaper around a mass of red, red buds. "Would you look at these?" He hands them to Willie Bell, who already is waiting with scissors and vases. He twirls his Panama hat on the tip of his finger. "Just tell me, who needs to go to heaven?"

In my gardens I have planted herbs, Iceland poppies, fuchsias, pansies, sweet William. Now I am in love with roses. We have enough grass now that I can walk out in the dew barefooted every morning and cut a rose and a bunch of lavender for my desk. Memory cuts and comes again: At the mill, my father kept a single rose on his desk. I realize I have planted only one red one. As the morning sun hits, the double fragrance intensifies.

✻

Now that so much work is finished, we taste the future. A time is coming when we will just garden, maintain (astonishingly, some of the windows inside already need touching up), refine. We have a list of pleasurable projects such as stone walkways, a fresco on the kitchen wall, antique hunting trips to the Marche region, an outdoor bread oven. And a list of less glorious projects: figuring out the septic system, which sends out a frightening turnip smell when lots of people are using the house; cleaning and repointing the stone walls of the cantina; rebuilding sections of stone walls that have collapsed on several terraces; retiling the butterfly bathroom. These would have seemed major once and now just seem like things on a list. Still, days are near when we will work with an Italian tutor, take the wildflower book on long walks, travel to the Veneto, Sardinia and Apulia, even take a boat from Brindisi or Venice to Greece. To embark from Venice, where the first touch of the East is felt!

That time is not yet, however; the last big project looms.

SEMPRE PIETRA (ALWAYS STONE)

PRIMO BIANCHI CHUGS UP THE DRIVEWAY IN HIS APE loaded with bags of cement. He jumps out to direct a large white truck full of sand, steel I-beams, and bricks as it backs up the narrow driveway, scraping its mirror on the pine trees and pulling off one limb of a spruce with a loud crack. Primo was our choice for remodeling three years ago but was unable to work then because of a stomach operation. He looks the same—like an escapee from Santa's workshop. We go over the project. The yard-thick living room wall will be opened to connect with the *contadina* kitchen, which will get a new floor, new plaster, new wiring. He nods. *"Cinque giorni, signori,"* five days. This crude room, totally untouched, serves as a storage room for garden furniture over the winter and as the last bastion for scorpions. Because of earthquake standards, the opening will be only about five feet, not as wide as we wanted. But there will be doors opening to the outside, and the rooms, at last, will be joined.

We tell him about Benito's men running out of the house when they opened the wall between the new kitchen and the dining room. I'm reassured when he laughs. Will they start tomorrow? "No, tomorrow is Tuesday, not a good day for starting work. Work started on Tuesday never ends—an old superstition, not that I believe it but my men do." We agree. We definitely want the project to end.

On evil Tuesday, we take all the furniture and books out of the living room, remove everything from the walls and fireplace. We mark the center of the wall and try to visualize the expanded room. It's the imagination that carries us through the stress of these projects. Soon we will be happy! The rooms will look as though they've always been one! We'll have lawn chairs on that end of the front terrace and can listen to Brahms or Bird wafting out of the *contadina* kitchen door. Soon it will not be called that anymore; it will be the living room.

243

Intercapedine is a word I know only in Italian. My dictionary translates it as "gap, cavity." It's a big word in the lingo of restoring humid stone houses. The *intercapedine* is a brick wall constructed part of the way up a humid wall. A gap *due dita*, two fingers, wide is left between the two so that moisture is stopped by the brick barrier. The *contadina* kitchen has such a wall on the far end of the house. It looks deeper than is usual. Impatient, Ed and I decide to take down some of it, to see if possibly the *intercapedine* could be moved farther back toward the wall, thus enlarging the small room. As the bricks fall, we are stunned to find that there *is* no end wall of the house on the first floor; it was built directly *into*, *onto* the solid stone of the hillside. Behind the *intercapedine* we find Monte Sant'Egidio! Craggy, huge rock! "Well, now we know why this room had a moisture problem." Ed is pulling out fig and sumac roots. Along the edge of the floor, he uncovers the rubble-filled remains of a moisture canal that must have functioned once.

"Great wine cellar," is all I can think of to say. Not knowing what else to do, we take a few photos. This discovery definitely doesn't conform to the transcendent dream of a hundred angels.

Auspicious Wednesday arrives and with it, at seven-thirty, Primo Bianchi with two *muratori*, masons, and a worker to haul stone.

They arrive without any machinery at all. Each man carries a bucket of tools. They unload scaffolding, sawhorses, called *capretti*, little goats, and T-shaped metal ceiling supports called *cristi* (named for the cross Jesus was crucified on). When they see the natural stone wall we uncovered, they stand, hands on hips, and utter a collective *"Madonna mia."* They're incredulous that we took the wall down, especially that I was involved. Immediately, they go to work—first spreading heavy protective plastic on the floor—opening the wall between this room and the living room. Next, they remove a line of stones along what will be the top of the door. We hear the familiar *chink, chink* sound of chisel on stone, the oldest building song there is. Soon, the I-beam goes in. They pack in cement and bricks to hold it in place. Until the cement dries there's nothing more they can do on the door so they begin to take up the ugly tile floor with long crowbars.

They talk and laugh as fast as they work. Because Primo is a little hard of hearing, they've all learned to converse in a near shout. Even when he's not around, they continue. They're thoroughly neat, cleaning up as they go: no buried telephone this time. Franco, who has glistening black, almost animal eyes, is the strongest. Although he's slight, he has that wiry strength that seems to come more from will than from muscle. I watch him lift a square stone that served as a bottom step for the back stairway. When I marvel, he shows off a bit and hoists it to his shoulder. Even Emilio, whose job it is to haul, actually seems to enjoy what he's doing. He looks perpetually amused. Hot as it is, he wears a wool cap pulled down so far that his hair all around sticks out in a ruff. He looks to be around sixty-five, a little old for a *manovale*, manual laborer. I wonder if he was a *muratore* before he lost two fingers. As they lift out the hideous tile and a layer of concrete, they find a stone floor underneath. Then Franco lifts some of these stones and discovers a second layer of stone floor. *"Pietra, sempre pietra,"* he says, stone, always stone.

True. Stone houses, terrace walls, city walls, streets. Plant any rose and you hit four or five big ones. All the Etruscan sarcophagi with likenesses of the dead carved on top in realistic, living poses must have come out of the most natural transference into death they could imagine. After lifetimes of dealing with stone, why not, in death, turn into it?

The next day, they open the same cavity along the top of the door on the living room side. They call us in. Primo pokes the end of a major beam with his chisel. *"È completamente marcia, questa trava."* He pokes the exposed part. *"Dura, qua."* It's completely rotten inside the wall, although the exposed part is sound. *"Pericoloso!"* The heavy beam could have sheared, bringing down part of the floor above. They support the beam with a *cristo* while Primo takes a measurement and goes off to buy a new chestnut beam. By noon the I-beam on that side is in. They take no breaks, go off for lunch for one hour, and are back at work until five.

By the third full day of work they've accomplished an amazing amount. This morning the old beam comes down as easily as pulling a loose tooth. With long boards held up by *cristi* on either side of the beam, they secure the brick ceiling, knock out stones, wiggle the beam a bit, and lower it to the floor. The new one slides right in. What fabulously simple construction. They wedge rocks around it, pack in cement, then pack more cement into the small space between the beam and the ceiling. Meanwhile, two men shovel and dig the floor. Ed, working in the yard just outside the door, hears *"Dio maiale!"* a strange curse meaning God-pig. He looks in and sees underneath the enormous stone Emilio is propping up with his bar a third layer of stone. The first two layers were of smooth, big stones, burdensome to lug out; this layer is rough—suitcase-sized boulders, some jagged and deep in the ground. From the kitchen, I hear alarming groans as they upend them and roll them up a plank and dump them out the door. I'm afraid they're going to strike water soon. Emilio carts the small

245

stones and dirt to the driveway, where a mountain of rubble is grow-ing. We will keep the giant ones. One has elongated glyphic markings. Etruscan? I look at the alphabet in a book but can't correlate these markings with anything. Perhaps they are a farmer's diagram of plant-ing or prehistoric doodling. Ed hoses off the stone and we look at it sideways. The carving then makes perfect sense. The Christian IHS topped by a cross, with another crude cross off to the side. A grave-stone? An early altar? The stone has a flat top and I ask them to drag it aside; we can use it for a small outdoor table. Emilio shows no inter-est. *"Vecchio,"* old, he says. But he insists there always will be a use for such stones. All afternoon, they dig. I hear them muttering *"Etruschi, Etruschi,"* Etruscans, Etruscans. Under the third layer they come to the stone of the mountain. By now they've uncorked a bottle of wine and take gulps now and then.

    "Come Sisyphus," like Sisyphus, I try to joke.

    "Esattamente," Emilio replies. In the third layer, they're uncov-ering lintels and *una soglia,* a threshold in *pietra serena,* the great build-ing stone of the area. Evidently, an earlier house's stones were used in building this house. These they line up along the wall, exclaiming at the fineness of the stone.

❋

Out on one of the terraces, we have a stack of *cotto* for the floor, saved when the new bathroom was built and the upstairs patio was replaced. We hope to salvage enough of them to use in the new room. Ed and I pull the good ones, chip off mortar, wash them in a wheelbarrow, and scrub them with wire brushes. We have a hundred and eighty of them, a few of which are too pitted but may be useful as half bricks. The men are still hauling stones. The floor level is down about two feet now. The white truck maneuvers up the driveway again to deliver long, flat tiles about ten by twenty-five inches, with air channels through them. Regular bricks are laid in ten lines on the dug-out, leveled floor, now mostly bedrock, with some mountain rock locally referred to as *piscia*, piss, for its characteristic dribble of water in crevices. The bricks form drainage channels. Long tiles are cemented over them. They mix cement as though it were pasta dough—they dump sand into a big mound on the ground, then make a hole and start stirring in cement and water, kneading it with a shovel. On top of the tiles, they spread *membrane*, something that looks like tar paper, and a grid of thick iron wire reinforcement. On that, a layer of cement. A day's work, I'd say.

247

We're spared the whining churn of a cement mixer. We laugh to remember Alfiero's mixer in the summer of the great wall. One day he mixed cement, worked awhile, then ran off to another job. When he came back, we saw him beating the mixer with his fists; he forgot the cement, which by afternoon was solid. We laugh now at the other foibles of past workers; these are princes.

Plaster cracks, like the ones in my dining room in San Francisco after the earthquake, have appeared on the second and third floors above where the door is being opened. Some large chunks have fallen. *Could* the whole house simply collapse into a heap? By day, I'm excited by the project. I dream each night the oldest anxiety dreams—I must take the exam, I have no blue book, I don't know what the course is. I have missed the train in a foreign country and it is night. Ed dreams that a busload of students drives up to the house with manuscripts to be critiqued before tomorrow. In the morning, slightly awake at six, I burn the toast twice.

The wall is almost open. They've inserted a third steel beam over the opening, made the brick supporting column on one side, and have worked on the new double-thick brick wall that will separate us from the mountain. Primo looks over the bricks we've cleaned. As he lifts one, a large scorpion scuttles out and he smacks it with his hammer, laughing when I wince.

Later, reading in my study, I see a tiny scorpion crawling up the pale yellow wall. Usually, I trap them in a glass and escort them

outside; this one I just let crawl along the wall. From here, the stone
tapping of three masons takes on a strange, almost Eastern rhythm. It's
hot, so hot I want to run from the sun, as from a rainstorm. I'm reading about Mussolini. He collected wedding rings from the women of
Italy to finance his Ethiopian war, only he never melted them down.

Years later, when he was caught trying to escape, he still had a sack of
gold rings. In one photo, he has popping eyes, distorted hairless skull,
set jaw. He looks demented or like Casper the ghost. The *chink, chink*
sounds like a gamelan. In the last photo, he's hanging upside down. The
caption says a woman kicked him in the face. I'm sleepy and imagining the men in an Indonesian dance with Il Duce downstairs.

※

The mountain of stone on either side of the door grows daunting. We
must get a start on moving it. Stanislao, our Polish worker, comes at
dawn. At six, Francesco Falco's son Giorgio arrives with his new plow,
ready to ply the olive terraces, and Francesco follows shortly on foot.
As usual, he has his cutting tool, a combination machete and sickle,
stuffed into his pants in back. He prepares to help Giorgio by clearing
stones from the path of the tractor, holding aside branches, and
smoothing out the ground. But our pitchfork is wrong. "Look at this."
He holds it out, prongs up, and it quickly turns over, prongs down. He
hammers the metal until it separates from the handle, turns the handle, then reattaches it. He then holds out the pitchfork, which does not
flip over. We've used the pitchfork a hundred times without noticing
but, of course, he's right.

"The old Italians know everything,'" Stanislao says.

Wheelbarrow after wheelbarrow, we haul stone to a pile out
on one of the olive terraces. I lift only the small and medium stones;
Ed and Stanislao wrestle with the giants. Low-impact aerobics video,
eat your heart out. Drink eight glasses of water a day? No problem,
I'm parched. At home, in my burgundy leotard, I lift and lift, and

one and two, and lift . . . but this is work versus workout. Bend and stretch—easy when I'm clearing a hillside. Whatever, I'm worn out by this labor and I also like it tremendously. After three hours, we've moved about one fourth of the stones. *Madonna serpente!* Don't try to calculate how many more hours we're in for—and all the really huge stones are in the other pile. Dirt and sweat run down my arms. The men are bare-chested, smelly. My damp hair is clotted with dust. Ed's leg is bleeding. I hear Francesco above us on a terrace talking to the olive trees. Giorgio's tractor tilts amazingly on one of the narrow terraces but he is too skilled to come tumbling down the mountain. I think of the long, melting bath I will take. Stanislao begins to whistle "Misty." One stone they can't budge is shaped like the enormous head of a Roman horse. I take the chisel and start to work on eyes and mane. The sun wheels in great struts across the valley. Primo hasn't seen us at hard labor. He's shouting at his men about it. He has worked on many restorations. The foreign *padrone*, he says, only stands and watches. He poses with his hands on his hips, a curled lip. As for a woman working like this, he raises his arms to heaven. Late in the afternoon, I hear Stanislao curse, *"Madonna sassi,"* Madonna-stones, but then he goes back to whistling his theme song, "It's cherry pink and apple blossom white when you're in love . . ." The men come down and we drink beer on the wall. Look at what we've done. This is really fun!

*

The white truck is back, delivering sand for plaster—plaster, they are nearing the end—and hauling away a mound of rubble. The three workers shout about the World Cup soccer matches taking place in the United States, about ravioli with butter and sage, about how long it takes to drive to Arezzo. Thirty minutes. You're crazy, twenty.

Claudio, the electrician, arrives to reroute the plait of dangling wires that somehow provides electricity for that section of the house. He has brought his son Roberto, fourteen, who has continuous, glorious eyebrows and almond-shaped Byzantine eyes that follow you. He is interested in languages, his father explains, but since he must have a practical trade, he is trying to train him this summer. The boy leans indolently against the wall, ready to hand tools to his father. When his father goes out to the truck for supplies, he grabs the English newspaper that protects the floor from paint and studies it.

Canals for wire must be dug in the stone walls before the plastering. The plumber must move the radiator we had installed when the central heating went in. I've changed my mind about the location. So much action. If they hadn't had days of excavating those levels of stone floor, the primary work would be finished. The Poles, who were in Italy working the tobacco fields, now have gone home. Only Stanislao stayed. Who will move all those great stones? Before the masons leave, they show us a neatly woven swirl of grass and twig they found in the wall, a *nido di topo*, so much nicer in Italian than rat's nest.

They're slinging the base for the plaster, literally slinging so it sticks to the wall, then smoothing it out. Primo brought old *cotto* for the floor from his supply. Between his and ours, we must have enough. Since the floor is last, surely we're nearing the end. I'm ready for the fun part; it's hard to think of the furniture when the room looks like a gray solitary confinement space. Finally, we're treated to the first machine noise of the project. The electrician's son, with some uncertainty, attacks the walls with a drill, making channels for the new wiring. The electrician himself left, after receiving a shock when he touched one of the frayed wires. These *must* be among the sorriest wires he's ever come across.

The plumber who installed the new bath and the central heating sends out two of his assistants to move the radiator pipes they disconnected last week. They, too, are extremely young. I remember that students not on an academic track finish school at fifteen. Both are plump and silent but with ear-to-ear grins. I hope they know what they're doing. Everyone talks at once, most of them shouting.

Maybe all will come together quickly now. At the end of each day, Ed and I drag in yard chairs and sit in the new room, trying to imagine that soon we will sit there with coffee, perhaps on a blue linen loveseat with an old mirror hanging above it, music playing, discussing our next project . . . .

251

❋

Because the undercoat for the plaster has to dry, Emilio is working alone, scratching off the old plaster in the back stairwell, carting off fuming loads of it to the rubble mountain.

The electrician can't finish until the plaster is on. I can see the boon of the invention of wallboard. Plastering is an arduous business. Still, it's fun to see the process, which hardly has changed since the Egyptians slathered the tombs. The plumber's boys didn't cut off the water line as far back as they should have and we have to call them to come back. To escape, we drive over to Passignano and have an eggplant pizza by the lake. The five-day estimate! I'm longing for days of *dolce far niente*, sweet to do nothing, because in seven weeks, I must go back. I hear the first cicada, the shrill yammering that alerts us that deep summer is here. "Sounds like a duck on speed," Ed says.

Saturday, and a scorcher. Stanislao brings Zeno, who recently arrived from Poland. They dispense with shirts right away. They're used to heat; both are laying pipes for methane during the week. In less than three hours, they've hauled away a ton of stone. We've separated the flat ones for paths and for large squares of stone around each of the four doors along the front to prevent tracking in. They set to work after lunch digging, laying a sand base, chipping and fitting stone, filling in the cracks with dirt. They easily pull up the puny semicircles we laid out last year from stones we found on the land. The stones from the floor they're choosing are as big as pillows.

I'm weeding when I brush my arms against a patch of nettles. Those plants are fierce. They "sting" immediately, the hairy leaves letting out an irritating acid on contact. Odd that the tiny ones are good in risotto. I run in the house and scrub down with a skin disinfectant but my arms feel alive, as though hot electric worms are crawling on me. After lunch, I decide to bathe, put on my pink linen dress, and sit on the patio until the shops open. Enough work. I find a breeze there and pleasantly waste the afternoon looking at a cookbook and watching a lizard, who appears to be watching a parade of ants. It's a magnificent little creature in sparkling green and black with deft and intricate feet, palpitating throat, and an inquisitive head that jerks. I would like for it to crawl on my book so I could see more, but my every move sends it scuttling. It keeps coming back to look over the ants. What the ants watch, I don't know.

In town, I buy a white cotton dress, navy linen pants and shirt, some expensive body cream, pink nail polish, a bottle of great wine. When I get back, Ed is showering inside. The Poles have slung the hose over a tree limb and opened the nozzle to spray. I glimpse them stripping down for a rinse-off before changing their clothes. The four doorways are now protected by well-fitted entrances of stone.

✳

Franco begins the smooth final coat of plaster. The owner of the plumbing company, Santi Cannoni, arrives in blue shorts to inspect the work his boys have done. We have known him since his company installed our central heating—but only fully dressed. He looks as though he simply forgot his pants. His hairless, moon-white legs so far below his pressed shirt, distinguished tanned face, and gray coifed hair keep drawing my eye. That he has on black silky socks and loafers contributes to his obscene look of undress. Since his boys moved the radiator, the one in the next room has begun to leak.

Francesco and Beppe pull up in the Ape with their weed machines, ready to massacre wild roses and weeds. Beppe speaks clearly and we understand him better, mainly because Francesco still refuses to wear his teeth. Since he loves to talk, he gets mad when Beppe interprets for him. Naturally, when Beppe sees that we don't understand, he explains. Francesco starts calling Beppe *maestro*, teacher, with heavy sarcasm. They argue about whether Ed's blades need to be sharpened or turned over. They argue about whether the stakes in the grape stones should be iron or wood. Behind Beppe's back, Francesco shakes his head at us, eyes turned to heaven: Can you believe this old coot? Behind Francesco's back, Beppe does the same.

A load of sand arrives for the floor but Primo says his old bricks are not the same size as ours and that he must locate another fifty before the floor can be laid.

Piano, piano, the watchword of restoration, slowly, slowly.

More plastering. The mixture looks like gray gelato. Franco says he has a tiny old house and it's all he wants; these big houses, always something wrong. He patches the walls upstairs that cracked when the living room stones were removed, and I ask him to break the plaster and look at what holds up the doors Benito reopened. He finds the original long stones. No sign of the steel I-beams he was supposed to install. Franco says not to worry, stone is just as good on a regular-sized door.

The walls look dry to me but not to them. Another day off. We're anxious to get in there, scrub down the walls, stain the beams, scrape and paint the brick ceiling. We're ready, past ready, to move in. Four chairs have gone to the upholsterer with yards of blue and white checked linen my sister sent for two, and a blue and yellow striped cotton I found in Anghiari for the others. We have ordered the blue loveseat and two other comfortable chairs. The CD player has been in a pile of boxes and books, the chairs and bookcase stuffed into other rooms. Will this go on forever?

During the Renaissance, it was a custom to open Vergil at random and place a finger on a line that would foretell the future or answer a burning question. In the South, we used to do this with the Bible. People always have had ways to grasp for revelation: The Etruscans' haruspication, reading omens from sacrificed animals' livers, is no stranger than the Greeks' finding significance in the flight patterns of birds and the droppings of animals. I open Vergil and put my finger down on "The years take all, one's wits included." Not very encouraging.

254

＊

Tuscany is a xeric land in summer but this year it is deeply green. From the patio the terraces seem to ripple down the hill. No use moving today. Under the barbed sun, I'm reading about saints, admiring especially Giuliana Falconieri, who asked, when dying, to have the host placed on her breast. It dissolved into her heart and disappeared. A pheasant is pecking away at my plot of lettuces. I read on about Colomba, who ate only hosts, then vomited them into a basket, which she stored under her bed. I'm enchanted with Veronica, who chewed five orange seeds in memory of Christ's five wounds. Ed brings up enormous sandwiches and iced tea with a little peach juice in it. I'm progressively more fascinated with the women saints, their politics of denial. Perhaps it's a corrective for the voluptuousness of Italian life. There's always a mystery within a sudden attraction to a subject. Why is one suddenly lugging home four books on hurricanes or all the operas of Mozart? Later, much later sometimes, the reason for the quest emerges. What will I come to realize from these quirky women?

Primo arrives with still more old bricks and Fabio starts cleaning them. He's working in spite of toothache and shows us the rotting lower left area of his mouth. I bite my lip to keep from looking startled. He's having four pulled next week, all at once.

Primo's tools for laying out the floor are some string and a long level. His skill is sure and quick; he knows instinctively where to tap, what fits where. After all the stone is hauled out, the floors between the two rooms are almost even; he builds in a slight rise, barely noticeable, in the doorway. They begin tamping down and leveling. Fabio cuts through bricks with a high wheezing machine that sends up a cloud of red dust. His arms are brick-colored up to his elbows. Laying brick looks fun. Soon the floor is down, matched to the interlocking L pattern of the adjoining room.

Houseguests arrive, despite the plastic-covered piles of lamps, baskets, books in the hallways, the living room furniture scattered around the house. Simone, a colleague of Ed's, is celebrating her Ph.D. with a trip to Greece, and Barbara, a former student, who is just finishing a two-year stint in Poland with the Peace Corps, is en route to Africa. I suppose Italy always has been a crossroads. Pilgrims to the Holy Land skirted Lake Trasimeno in the Middle Ages. Latter pilgrims of all sorts traverse Italy; our house is a good spot to rest for a few days. Madeline, an Italian friend, and her husband, John, from San Francisco are coming for lunch.

We're running back and forth between guests and decisions that need to be made. The workers are finishing today! The well-timed lunch is a double celebration. We've ordered *crespelle* from Vittorio, who makes fresh pasta in town. His crêpes are air. Though we are only six, we've ordered a dozen each of the *tartufo* (truffle), the pesto, and, our favorite, *piselli e prosciutto* (peas and cured ham). Before that, *caprese* (tomato, mozzarella, and basil salad dribbled with oil) and a platter of olives, cheeses, breads, and slices of various local salami. We're able to make the salad from the arugula in our garden. The wine we bought at Trerose, a chardonnay called Salterio, may be the best white I've tried in Italy. Many chardonnays, especially California ones, are too oaky and syrupy for my taste. This one has a peach-tinged, flinty taste with just a faint hint of oak.

The long table under the trees is set with yellow checked linen and a basket of sun-colored broom. We offer wine to the workmen but no, they're pressing into the final hours. They've spread cement over the floor to fill in the narrow cracks between bricks. To clean up, they wash down the floor, then sprinkle sawdust and sweep. They build two columns against the outside of the house for the stone sink we discovered in the dirt. It has rested these two years in the old kitchen. Primo calls to Ed to help move the monstrous stone. Two men "walk" it across the front terrace and up the three steps into the shady area where we are having lunch. Our guest, John, jumps up to help. Five men lift. *"Novanta chili, forse cento,"* Primo says. The sink weighs around two hundred pounds. After that, they load their *cristi*, their tools, and that's it—the room is finished. Primo stays to make a few repairs. He takes a bucket of cement and patches minor cracks in the stone wall, then goes upstairs to secure a few loose floor tiles.

Doesn't everything reduce in the end to a poetic image—one that encapsulates an entire experience in one stroke?

Not only this project but the whole major restoration that has stretched over three years is ending today. We're entertaining friends in the sun-dappled bower, just as I envisioned. I go into the kitchen and begin arranging a selection of local cheeses on grape leaves. I'm flushed and excited in my white linen dress with short sleeves that stand out like little wings. Above me, Primo is scraping the floor. I look up. He has removed two tiles and there is a hole in the ceiling. Just as I look back at my cheese platter, Primo accidentally kicks over his bucket and cement pours onto my head! My hair, my dress, the cheese, my arms, the floor! I look up and see his startled face peering down like a cherub in a fresco.

The humor is not entirely lost on me. I walk out to the table, dribbling cement. After dropped jaws and stunned looks, everyone laughs. Primo runs out, hitting the heel of his hand to his forehead.

The guests clear up while I shower. With Primo, they're all sitting along the sun-warmed wall when I come down. Ed is asking about Fabio's dental surgery. He only missed two days of work and will get new teeth in a month. Now Primo *will* join us in a toast. The guests are toasting an amusing day and the end of the project. Ed and I, having been literally doused in this restoration, raise our glasses, too. Primo just enjoys himself. He launches into a history of his own teeth and shows us big gaps in his mouth. Five years ago he had such a toothache—he holds his head and leans over moaning—that he pulled out his own tooth with the pliers. *"Via, via,"* he shouts, motioning the tooth out of his jaw. *Via* somehow sounds more emphatic than "go."

✳

I don't want him to go. He has been such a charmer and so careful as a *muratore*. The work is impeccable as well as miraculously reasonable. Yes, I do want him to go! This project was estimated to last five working days; this is day number twenty-one. No way, of course, to predict three levels of stone floor and a rotten beam. He'll be back next summer—he will retile the butterfly bathroom and repoint the stones in the cantina. He hoists his wheelbarrow into the Ape. Those are small projects, *cinque giorni, signori*, five days . . . .

THE FONTS IN ALL THE CHURCHES ARE DRY. I RUN MY fingers through the dusty scallops of marble: not a drop for my hot forehead. The Tuscan July heat is invasive to the body but not to the stone churches that hold on to the dampness of winter, releasing a gray coolness slowly throughout the summer. I have a feeling, walking into one, then another, that I walk into palpable silence. A lid seems to descend on our voices, or a large damp hand. In the vast church of San Biago below Montepulciano, there is an airy quiet as you enter. Right under the dome, you can stand in one spot and speak or clap your hands and far up against the inner cup of the dome an eerie echo sends the sound rapidly back. The quality of the sound is not like the hello across a lake but a sharp, repeated return. Your voice flattened, other-worldly. It is hard to think a mocking angel isn't hovering against the frescoes, though more likely a pigeon rests there.

Since I have been spending summers in Cortona, the major shock and joy is how at home I feel. But not just at home, *returned* to that primal first awareness of home. I feel at home because dusty trucks park at intersections and sell watermelons. The same thump to test for ripeness. The boy holds up a rusty iron scale with discs of different sizes for counterweight. His arm muscle jumps up like Popeye's and the breeze brings me a whiff of his scent of dry grasses, onions, and dirt. In big storms, lightning drives a jagged stake into the ground and hailstones bounce in the yard, bringing back the smell of ozone to me from Georgia days when I'd gather a bowlful the size of Ping-Pong balls and put them in the freezer.

Sunday is cemetery day here, and though our small-town Southern plots are austere compared to these lavish displays of flowers on almost every grave, we, too, made Sunday pilgrimages to Evergreen with glads or zinnias. I sat in the backseat, balancing the cool teal vase between my knees while my mother complained that Hazel never turned her hand to pick one stem and it was *her* own mother lying there, not just a mother-in-law. Gathered around Anselmo Arnaldo, 1904-1982, perhaps these families are saying, as mine did, Thank God the old goat's lying here rather than still driving us crazy.

Sweltering nights, the air comes close to body temp, and shifting constellations of fireflies compete with stars. Mosquito nights, grabbing at air, the mosquito caught in my hair. Long days when I can taste the sun. I move through this foreign house I've acquired as though my real ancestors left their presences in these rooms. As though this were the place I always came home to.

Living near a small town again certainly is part of it. And living again with nature. (A student of mine from Los Angeles visited. When I walked him out to the end of the point for the wide-angle view of lake, chestnut forests, Apennines, olive groves, and valleys, he was unprepared. He stood silently, the first time I'd known he could, and finally said, "It's, uh, like nature.") Right, nature: Clouds swarm in from over the lake and thunder cracks along my backbone, booms like waves boom far out at sea. I write in my notebook: "The dishwasher was struck. We heard the sizzle. But isn't it good, the gigantic storm, the flood of terror they felt beside fires in the cave? The thunder shakes me like a kitten the big cat has picked up by the neck. I ricochet home, heat lightning; I'm lying on the ground four thousand miles from here, letting rain soak through me."

Rain flays the grapes. Nature: What's ripe, will the driveway wash away, when to dig potatoes, how much water is in the irrigation well? Early life reconnects. I go out to get wood; a black scorpion scuttles over my hand and suddenly I remember the furry tarantulas in the shower at Lakemont, the shriek when my barefooted mother stepped on one and felt it crunch, then squash up soft as a banana between her toes.

Is it the spill of free days? I dream my mother rinses my tangle of hair with a bowl of rainwater.

Sweet time, exaggerated days, getting up at dawn because when the midsummer sun tops the crests across the valley, the first rays hit me in the face like they strike some rock at Stonehenge on the solstice. To be fully awake when the sky turns rose-streaked coral and scarves of fog drift across the valley and the wild canaries sing. In Georgia, my father and I used to get up to walk the beach at sunrise. At home in San Francisco what wakes me is the alarm at seven, or the car pool horn blowing for the child downstairs, or the recycle truck with its crashing cascade of glass. I love the city and never have felt really at home there.

I was drawn to the surface of Italy for its perched towns, the food, language, and art. I was pulled also to its sense of lived life, the coexistence of times that somehow gives an aura of timelessness—I toast the Etruscan wall above us with my coffee every morning—all the big abstracts that act out in everything from the aggression on the *autostrada* to the afternoon stroll through the piazza. I cast my lot here for a few short months a year because my curiosity for the layered culture of the country is inexhaustible. But the umbilical that is totally unexpected and elides logic reaches to me through the church.

To my surprise I have bought a ceramic Mary with a small cup for home use of holy water. As a fallen-away Methodist, then a fallen-away Episcopalian, I suppose my holy water is a sham. However, I have taken it from the spring I discovered near the house, the artesian spring where clear water rises in a declivity of white stone. This looks like holy water to me. It must have been the house's original source. Or it's older than the house—medieval, Roman, Etruscan. Though some interior juggling is going on, I do not expect to emerge as a Catholic, or even as a believer. I am essentially pagan by birth. Southern populism was boiled into my blood early; the idea of a pope with the last word gives me hives. "Idolatrous," our minister called the worship of Mary and the saints. "Mackerel snapper," my classmates teased Andy Evans, the lone Catholic in our school. Briefly, in college, I was drawn to the romance of the Mass, especially the three A.M. fishermen's Mass in St. Louis's Cathedral in New Orleans. I lost interest in the whole show when my good friend, a New Orleans Catholic, told me in complete seriousness that mortal sin began if you kissed longer than ten seconds. A ten-second French kiss was O.K., but a dry twenty-second kiss would land you in trouble. Though I still like rituals, even empty ones, what magnetizes me here feels more radical.

Now I love the quick Mass in tiny upper Cortona churches, where the same sounds have provided a still point for the residents for almost eight hundred years. When a black Labrador wandered in, the priest interrupted his holy spiel to shout, "For the love of God, somebody get that dog out of here." If I stop in on a weekday morning, I sit there alone, enjoying the country Baroque. I think: *Here I am*. I love the parade of relics through the streets, with gold-robed priests travelling along in a billow of incense, their way prepared by children in white, scattering the streets with petals of broom, rose, daisy. In the noon heat, I almost hallucinate. What's in the gold box held aloft with banners—a splinter from the cradle? Never mind we thought Jesus was born in a lowly manger; this is the splinter of the true cradle. Or am I confused? It's a splinter of the true cross. It is on its way through the streets, brought out into the air one day a year. And suddenly I think,

What did that hymn mean, *cleft for me*, rising years ago, perpendicular from the white board church in Georgia?

✳

In my South, there were signs on trees that said "Repent." Halfway up a skinny pine, up beyond the tin trough that caught the resin, hung a warning, "Jesus is coming." Here, when I turn on the car radio, a lulling voice implores Mary to intercede for us in purgatory. In a nearby town, one church has as its relic a phial of Holy Milk. As my student would say, that's from, like, Mary.

On the terrace at noon, I'm tanning my legs as I read about early martyrs and medieval saints. I'm drawn to the martyred San Lorenzo, who was put on a grill for his troublesome faith and seared until he reportedly said, "Turn me over, I'm done on this side," and thereby became the favorite saint of chefs. The virginal young women martyrs all were raped, stabbed, tortured or locked away because of their devotion to Christ. Sometimes the hand of God reached down and swept one away, like Ursula, who did not wish to marry the barbarian Conan. With her ten thousand virgins (all avoiding men?) loaded into boats, she was lifted miraculously by God and sailed across the unfriendly skies, then deposited in Rome, where they all bathed in lime-scented water and formed a sacred order. Stunning, the prevalence of the miracle. In the Middle Ages, some of the venerated women found the foreskin of Jesus materialized in their mouths. I don't know if there exists a relic of that. (Would it look like a chewed rubber band? A dried wad of bubble gum?) The foreskin stops me for a good ten minutes and I stare out at the bees swarming the *tigli* trees, trying to imagine that event happening, and not just once. The moment of recognition, what she said, what the reaction was—a boggling speculation. Somehow, I'd never heard of these kinkier saints in America, although someone once sent me a box of new books, each one about a saint's life. When I called the bookstore, they told me my benefactor wished to remain anonymous. Now I read on and find that some had "holy anorexia" and lived on the wafer alone. If a saint's bones were dug up, a flowery fragrance filled the town. After Saint Francis preached to the birds, they flew up into the shape of a cross then separated into the four directions. The saints would eat the pus and lice of the poor to show their humility; in turn, the faithful liked to drink the bathwater of a holy person. If, after death, a saint's heart was cut out, perhaps an image of the Holy Family carved in a ruby would be found inside. *Oh, I realize, here's where they put their awe. I understand that.*

I understand because this everyday wildness and wonder come back so naturally from the miracle-hungry South. They almost seem like memories somehow, the vertebrae of the Virgin, the toenail of San Marco. My favorite, the breath of San Giuseppe, foster father of Christ. I imagine an opaque green glass bottle with a ground stopper, the swift exhaling of air as it opened. At home when I was small, our seamstress kept her jar of gallstones on the windowsill above her Singer. Marking my hem, her mouth full of pins, she'd say, "Lord, I don't want to go through nothing like that again. Now you turn round. Those things won't even dissolve in gasoline." Her talisman against sickness. Emblems and omens.

Santa Dorotea immured in her cell for two years, against a high-walled pit in the dank cathedral. Communion through a grate and a diet of bread and gruel. I hated visiting Miss Tibby, who treated the corns on my mother's little toes, shaving yellow curls of skin off with a vegetable peeler, then rubbing her feet with thick lotion that smelled like crank case oil and Ovaltine. The bare bulb lit not only my mother's foot on a cushion but also a coffin where Miss Tibby slept at night so there would be no surprises later.

In high school my friends and I parked a block away and secretly peered in the windows of the Holy Rollers, who spoke in tongues, sometimes screaming with a frightening ecstatic look on their faces and falling to the floor writhing and jerking. We were profane, smothering our laughter at the surely sexual fervor and the contorted postures. Later we'd sit in the car, Jeff smoking, and watch them file out of the peeling church, looking as normal as anyone. In Naples, the phial of San Gennaro's congealed blood liquifies once a year. There's also a crucifix that used to grow one long hair of Jesus that would have to be barbered once a year. That one seems particularly close to Southern sensibilities.

In the United States, I think there is no *sanctioned* place to put such fixated strangeness so it just jumps out when it has to. Driving through the South recently, I stopped near Metter, Georgia, for a barbecue sandwich. After the sweet salty pork and iced tea, I was directed out back to the bathroom by the owner; pork-bellied, sweating over his pit, he merely nodded toward the rear. No sign at all that as I opened the screen door I would encounter two molting ostriches. How they came to be in that remote town in South Georgia and what iconographical necessity led the family to gaze on and house these dusty creatures is a philosophical gift I've been given to ponder in nights of insomnia.

Growing up in the God-fearing, faith-healing, end-of-the-world-is-at-hand South gave me many chances to visit snake collections beside gas stations when my parents stopped to fill up; to drive past roadside religious ceremonies in which snakes were ecstatically "handled"; to see shabby wonders-of-the-world exhibits—reliquaries of sorts—in the towns bordering the swamps. I know a box of black cat's bones makes a powerful conjure. And that a bracelet of dimes can ward it off. I was used to cages of baby alligators crawling on the back of the mother of all, a fourteen-foot beauty who opened her jaws wide enough that I could have stood in them. The sagging chicken-wire fences couldn't save you if those sleeping logs rose up and decided to take off after you—alligators can run seventy miles an hour. Albino deer covered with ticks that leapt on my hand when I petted their mossy noses, a stuffed painter (panther) with green marbles for eyes, a thirty-foot tapeworm in a jar. The owner explains that it was taken from the throat of his seventeen-year-old niece when the doctor lured it out of her stomach with a clove of garlic on a toothpick. They waited until it showed its head, lured it out further, then grabbed, chopped off its head with a straight razor while hauling the thing out of Darleen's stomach like a rope out of the river.

Wonders. Miracles. In cities, we're less and less capable of the imagination for the super real, ground down as we are by reality. In rural areas, close to the stars and groves, we're still willing to give it a whirl. So I recover the cobra, too, so much more impressive with his flattened head than rattlesnakes, whose skins paper the office of the owner of the Eighth Wonder of the World, where we have stopped for gas at the Georgia border. We are close to Jasper, Florida, where my mother and father were married in the middle of the night. I am amazed, despite my mother's warning that the owners are carnival people and it is not worth seeing and I have exactly ten minutes or they will go on to White Springs without me. The slight thrill at the possibility of being left behind on this curve of road lined with moss-draped oaks, the silver-bullet trailer set up on concrete blocks, a woman glimpsed inside, washing her hair over a tin bowl and the radio blaring "I'm So Lonesome I Could Cry." I knew then and still know that the man with the phosphorescent glow-in-the-dark torch tattooed on his back and the full-blown roses tattooed on his biceps believed his wonders were real. I follow him to the bamboo hut, where the cobra from darkest Calcutta rises to the song made by blowing on a comb covered with cellophane. The cobra mesmerizes the mangy dog thumping his tail in the doorway. The peacock gives a powerful he-haw, shakes himself into full regalia, the blues in his fan of feathers more intense than my own or my mother's eyes, and, as everyone knows, we have the purest sky-blue eyes. The peacock's eyes look exactly like the snake's. The owner's wife comes out of the trailer with a boa constrictor casually draped around her neck. She checks on another snake, to whom she has fed a large rat without even cutting it up. The rat is simply disappearing, like a fist into a sweater sleeve. I buy a Nehi and an oatmeal cookie sandwich, run out to the Oldsmobile vibrating in the heat. My father scratches off; gravel spumes behind us. "What have you got?" My mother turns around.

"Just a cold drink and this." I hold up the large cookie.

"Those things have lard in the middle. That's not icing—that's pure-T lard with enough powdered sugar to make your teeth crack."

I don't believe her but when I break open the cookie, it is crawling with maggots. I quickly throw it out the window.

"What did you see in that awful gyp joint?"

"Nothing," I answer.

Growing up, I absorbed the Southern obsession with place, and place can seem to me somehow an extension of the self. If I am made of red clay and black river water and white sand and moss, that seems natural to me.

However, living as a grown woman in San Francisco, I never have that belonging sensation. The white city with its clean light on the water, the pure, heart-stopping coast, and the Marin hills with the soft contours of sleeping giants under blankets of green—I am the awed tourist, delighted to have made this brief escape, which is my adult life. My house is just one of thousands; my life could be just another story in the naked city. My eye looks with insouciance at the scissors point of the Transamerica pyramid and jagged skyline I can see from my dining room window. Everyone seems to have cracked the door two inches to see who's there. I see you through my two inches; you see me through yours. We are monumentally self-reliant.

✳

I never tire of going into Italian churches. The vaulted arches and triptychs, yes. But each one also has its characteristic blue dust smell, the smell of time. The codified Annunciations, Nativities, and Crucifixions dominate all churches. At the core, these all struggle with the mystery of the two elementals—birth and death. We are frangible. In the side altars, the high arches, the glass manuscript cases in the crypts, the shadowed curves of the apse, these archetypal concerns and the dreamland of religious fervor lock horns with the painterly subject matter in individualized ways. I'm drawn to a bizarre painting that practically leaps off the wall. In a dark, high panel close to the ceiling in San Gimignano, there's Eve rising boldly out of supine Adam's open side. Not the *whoosh* of instantaneous creation I've imagined from reading Genesis, when she appeared as easily as "Let there be Light." This is graphic, someone's passion to be *present* at the miracle. As graphic as the wondrous cobra of Calcutta spiraling up in the humid air of South Georgia before my very eyes. Adam is meat. The vision grabs the viewer like the glow-in-the-dark torch. Now hear this, loud and clear. In Orvieto's Duomo, Signorelli's humans, just restored to their flesh on Judgment Day, stand grandly and luxuriously beside the grinning skeletons they were just moments before. Parts of the body still glow with the aura of the bare bone, a gauzy white light emanating from the firm, new flesh in its glory. A strange turn—we're used to thinking of the decay of the flesh; here's the dream of rejuvenation. Flitting around in the same arena of that cathedral are depictions of hell, green-headed devils with snaky genitals. The damned are twisted, poked, jabbed, while one voluptuous blonde (no doubt what *her* sins were) flies away on the back of a devil with stunted, unaerodynamic wings. Clearly we are in someone's head, midnight imaginings of the descent, the fall, the upward turn. The paintings can be sublime but there is a comic book aspect to much church painting, a wordless progression of blunt narrative very close to those of fire-and-brimstone fundamentalists who still hold forth in the South. If there was more than one word, Repent, hanging on those Southern pines, it was bound to be Doomsday.

Wandering around in churches, I see over and over San Sebastiano pierced with arrows, martyred Agata holding out her breasts on a plate like two over-easy eggs, Sant'Agnes kneeling piously while a lovely youth stabs her in the neck. Almost every church has its locked relic box like a miniature mausoleum, and what does this mean? Thorn from the crown. Finger digits of San Lorenzo. The talismans that say to the viewers, "Hold on; like these, have faith." Standing in the dim crypt in a country church where a handful of dust has been venerated for several hundred years, I see that even today, toward the end of the century, the case is remembered with fresh carnations. I uncover my second realization: *This is where they put their memories and wants.* Besides functioning as vast cultural repositories, these churches map intimate human needs. How familial they begin to seem (and how far away from the historical church, the bloody history of the Papacy): the coarse robe of St. Francis, another phial of Mary's, this one filled with tears. I see them like the locket I had, with a curl of light brown hair, no one remembered whose, the box of rose petals on the closet shelf behind the blue Milk of Magnesia bottle and the letters tied with frayed ribbon, the translucent white rock from Half Moon Bay. *Never forget.* As I wax the floor tiles and wring out the mop, I can think of Santa Zita of Lucca, saint of housekeeping, as was Willie Bell Smith in my family's house. Basketmaker, beggar, funeral director, dysentery sufferer, notary, speleologist—everyone has a paradigm. *I once was lost but now I'm found.* The medieval notion that the world reflects the mind of God has tilted in my mind. Instead, the church I perceive is a relief map of the *human* mind. A thoroughly secular interpretation: that *we* have created the church out of our longing, memory, out of craving, and out of the folds of our private wonders.

If I have a sore throat from drinking orange juice when I know I'm allergic to it, the saint is there in his monumental church at Montepulciano, that town whose syllables sound like plucked strings on the cello. San Biago is a transubstantiated metaphor and a handful of dust in a wrought box. Its small keyhole reminds us of what we most want to be reminded of, *you are not out there alone.* San Biago focuses my thoughts and throws me beyond the scratchy rawness of my own throat. *Pray for me, Biago, you are taking me farther than I go.* When the TV is out of whack and the buttons won't improve the picture, nor will slapping the side soundly, Santa Chiara is out here somewhere in saintland. *Chiara*, clear. She was clairvoyant and from there is only a skip and jump to *receiver*, to patron saint of telecommunications. So practical for such a transcendent girl. A statue of her on top of the TV won't hurt a thing. Next year on July 31, the wedding ring of Mary will be displayed in the Duomo in Perugia. The history says it was "piously stolen"—isn't that an oxymoron—from a church in Chiusi. Without a shred of literal belief, I, for one, will be there.

✳

At the top of the stairs, I touch the spring water in my ceramic Mary with my fingertip and make a circle on my forehead. When I was baptized, the Methodist minister dipped a rose in a silver bowl of water and sprinkled my hair. I always wished I'd been baptized standing knee deep in the muddy Alapaha, held under until the last moment of breath then raised to the singing congregation. My spring water in Mary's cup is not transformed to wash away my sins or those of the world. She always seems like *Mary*, the name of my favorite aunt, rather than Santa Maria. Mary simply became a friend, friend of mothers who suffered their children's pain, friend of children who watched their mothers suffer. She's hanging over almost every cash register, bank teller, shot giver, bread baker in this town, and I've grown used to her presence. The English writer Tim Parks says that without her ubiquitous image to remind you that all will go on as before, "you might imagine that what was happening to you here and now was unique and desperately important . . . I find myself wondering if the Madonna doesn't have some quality in common with the moon." Yes. My unblessed water soothes. I pause at the top of the stairs and repeat the lovely word *acqua*. Years ago, the baby learned to say *acqua* on the lake shore at Princeton, under a canopy of trees blooming madly with pink pompons. *Acqua,*

acqua, she shouted, scooping up water and letting it rain on her head. *Acqua* sounds closer to the sparkle and fall, closer to wetness and discovery. Her voice still reverberates but now I touch my little finger as I remember. The gold signet ring, a family treasure, slipped off in the grass that day and was not to be found. *Water of life. Intimacy of memory.*

      Intimacy. The feeling of touching the earth as Eve touched it, when nothing separated her.

      In paintings, the hilltop town rests in the palm of Mary's hand or under the shelter of her blue cloak. I can walk every street of my Georgia town in my mind. I know the forks in the pecan trees, the glut of water in the culverts, the hog pear in the alley. Often the Tuscan perched villages seem like large castles—extended homes with streets narrow as corridors, and the *piazze*, like public receptions rooms, teeming with visitors. The village churches have an attitude of privacy; the pressed linen and lace altar cloths and scarlet dahlias in a jar could be in family chapels; the individual houses, just suites in the big house. I expand, as when my grandparents' house, my aunt's, my friends', the walls of home were as familiar to me as the lines in my own palm. I like the twisted streets up to the convent where I may leave a bit of lace to be mended on a Catherine wheel, spin it in to the invisible nun, whose sisters have tatted in this great arm of the castle for four hundred years. I do not glimpse even the half moons of her nails or the shadow of her habit. Outside two women who must have known each other all their lives sit in old wooden chairs between their doorways and knit. The stony street slopes abruptly down to the town wall. Beyond that stretches the broad valley floor. Here comes a miniature Fiat up this ridiculously steep street no car should climb. Crazy. My father would drive through swollen streams that flooded sudden dips in the dirt roads. I was thrilled. While he laughed and blew the horn, water rose around the car windows. Or was the water really that high?

      We can return to live in these great houses, unbar the gates, simply turn an immense iron key in the lock and push open the door.

SOLLEONE. HOW USEFUL THE -ONE SUFFIX IN ITALIAN; the noun expands. *Porta*, door, becomes *portone*, and there's no doubt which is the main door. *Torre* becomes *torreone*, the name of our part of Cortona, where a great tower must have stood once. *Minestrone*, then, always is a big soup. Days of high summer: *Solleone*—big sun. Dog days we called them in the South. Our cook told me the name was because it was so hot that dogs went mad and bit people and I would be bitten if I didn't mind her. Eventually, I was disappointed to find the name only meant that Sirius, the dog star, was rising and setting with the sun. The science teacher said Sirius was twice the size of the sun and I thought, secretly, that somehow the heat was augmented by that fact. Here, the expanded sun fills the sky, as in the archetypal child's drawing of house, tree, and sun. The cicadas are in the know—they provide the perfect accompaniment to this heating up. By dawn they're hitting their horizon note of high screech. How a finger-sized insect can make such a racket only by vibrating its thorax, I don't know. As they tune up to their highest pitch, it sounds as though someone is shaking tambourines made from the small bones of the ear. By noon, they've switched to sitars, that most irritating of instruments. Only the wind quiets them; perhaps they must hang on to a limb and can't clutch and vibrate at the same time. But the wind seldom blows, except for the evil appearance now and then of the *scirocco*, which gusts but doesn't cool, while the sun roars. If I were a cat, I would arch my back. This hot wind brings particles of dust from the African deserts and deposits them in your throat. I hang out the clothes and they're dry in minutes. The papers in my study fly around like released white doves, then settle in the four corners of the room. The *tigli* are dropping a few dry leaves and the flowers suddenly seem leached of color, although we have had enough rain this summer that we have been able to water faithfully every day. The hose pulls water directly from the old well and they must feel blasted at the end of the hot day by the rush of icy water. Perhaps this has exhausted them. The pear tree on the front terrace has the look of a woman two weeks overdue. We should have thinned the fruit. Branches are breaking under the weight of golden pears just turning ruddy. I can't decide whether to read metaphysics or to cook. The ultimate nature of being or cold garlic soup. They are not so far apart after all. Or if they are, it doesn't matter; it's too hot to think about it.

The hotter the day, the earlier I walk. Eight, seven, six o'clock, and even then I rub my face with number thirty sunblock. The coolest walks start at Torreone. A downhill road leads to Le Celle, a twelfth-century monastery where Saint Francis's minute cell still opens onto a seasonal torrential stream. Many of the first Franciscan monks who lived as hermits on Monte Sant'Egidio started Le Celle in 1211. The architecture, a stacked stone honeycomb up against the hillside, recalls their caves. When I walk there, peace and solitude are palpable. In early summer, the rush of water down the steep canyon makes its own music and sometimes, above that, I hear singing. By now the stream is almost dry. Their vegetable garden looks like a model. One of the Capuchin friars who lives there now trudges uphill barefooted toward town. He's wearing his scratchy brown robe and strange pointed white hat (hence cappuccino), using two sticks to pull himself along. With his white beard and fierce brown eyes, he looks like an apparition from the Middle Ages. When I pass him he smiles and says, *"Buon giorno, signora. Bene qua,"* nice here, indicating the landscape with a rotation of his beard. He glides by, Father Time on cross-country skis.

But I take the slightly uphill road this morning, passing a few new houses, then a kennel, where dogs go into an uproar until I am about five feet beyond their pen; the road is then just a white track through pine and chestnut forests, no cars, no people. The shoulders look as though someone scattered one of those cans of native wild-flowers seeds and they all took root, then flourished. I climb a hill to look at an abandoned house so old that it still has a thick slate roof. Brambles surround the doors and windows. I glimpse dark rooms with stone walls. In front, I look down on a 180-degree view of Cortona in profile and on the entire length of the Val di Chiana, a yellow and green patchwork of sunflower and vegetable fields. The upstairs must have a low ceiling, right for a crude bed made of chestnut limbs, a white goose-down quilt. The terrace should go there—in front of the lilac bushes. A pink rose still blooms its heart out without any care at all. Whose was it? The wife of a silent woodcutter who smoked his pipe and drank *grappa* in the winter evenings when the *tramontagna* shook the windows on the back of the house? Perhaps she growled at him for sticking her so far in the country. No, she was content with her work embroidering the linens for the *contessa*.

The house is small—but who would stay inside when there's a broad terrace overlooking the world? The waiting house: all poten-tial. To see one and start dreaming is to imagine being extant in another version. Someone eventually will buy it and perhaps will run all over Tuscany looking for old slate to restore the roof authentically. Or the new owner might rip off the roof and put on flat new tiles. Whatever the predilections, the owner will respond to the aerie's isolation, that and the magnetic pull of the panorama, a place to linger and soothe the restless beast every day.

At the end of the road, a path through the woods leads to our favorite Roman road. I suppose it was laid by slaves. When I first heard about the Roman road near our house, I assumed it was unique. Not long after that I saw a rather thick book on the many Roman roads of this area. Walking alone, I try to think of chariots tearing down the hill, though the only thing I'm likely to meet is a *cinghiale*, a wild boar, roaming around. One stream still has a trickle of water. Maybe a Roman messenger verging on heat stroke paused here and cooled his feet, as I do, when running south with news of how Hadrian's wall was coming along. There have been more recent visitors; on the grassy bank, I see a condom and a wad of tissue.

When I walk into town, I see a shriveled, pasty man who, clearly, is dying. He has been propped in the doorway with the sun fully on him, his last chance for revival. He spreads out his fingers on his chest, warming everything he can. He has enormous hands. Yesterday I received a shock so hard my thumb went numb for half an hour. I was trying to pull the cord that turns on the overhead light in my study from the inside of the radiator, where it somehow had fallen. The clicker I had hold of split, leaving me with my thumb on the hot wires, my other hand on the metal radiator. I screamed and jumped back. That mindless, animal feeling of shock—I wonder if the man in the doorway feels that way in the sun. His life force siphoning off, the great solar energy coming at him, filling him up. His wife sits beside him and appears to be waiting. She's not mending or pinching back her flowers. She's his guard for his trip to the underworld. Perhaps she'll dry his dead body, then anoint his bones with olive oil and wine. Or maybe the heat is getting to me, too, and he's just recovering from an appendectomy.

✸

We must go to Arezzo, about half an hour away, to pay our insurance for next year. They seem to expect us to turn up rather than send a check. We park in the broiling train station lot. The station's full-sun digital thermometer-clock says it is 36° (103°F). After our pleasant interview with Signor Donati, an ice cream, a stop for Ed to buy a shirt at his favorite store, Sugar, and one for me to buy hand towels at my favorite shop, Busatti, we come back to the car and find the big 40 (111°) flashing over the car. The door handles appear to be on fire. The heat inside slams into us. We air out the car and finally get in. My eyelids and earrings are hot. Ed touches the steering wheel with his thumbs and index fingers. My hair seems to be steaming. Stores are closing; it's the hottest part of the hottest day of the year. At home, I lower myself into a cool bath, wet washcloth over my face, and just lie there until my body takes on the temperature of the water.

275

Siesta becomes a ritual. We pull in the shutters, leaving the windows open. All over the house, ladders of light fall across the floor. If I am mad enough to take a walk after one-thirty, no one is out, not even a dog. The word *torpor* comes to mind. All shops close during the sacred three hours. If you need something for bee sting or allergy, too bad. Siesta is prime time for TV in Italy. It's prime time for sex, too. Maybe this accounts for the Mediterranean temperament versus the northern: children conceived in the light and children conceived in the dark. Ovid has a poem about siesta, written before the first millennium turned. He's lying relaxed in sultry summer, one shutter closed, the other ajar, "the half-light shy girls need," he wrote, "to hide their hesitation." He goes on to grab the dress, which didn't hide much. Well, everything is always new under the sun. Then, as now, a quick wash in the bidet and back to work.

What a marvelous concept. For three hours in the middle of the day, you are invited to your own interests and desires. In the good part of the day, too, not just the evening after an eight- or nine-hour day slogging away.

Inside the high-roomed, shuttered house, it's completely silent. Even the cicadas have quit. Peaceful, dreamy afternoon. Partly for the pleasure of my feet sliding on soothing *cotto* floors, I walk from room to room. The classic look—I've seen it eleven times before and now I see it again in the new living room: dark beams, white brick ceiling, white walls, waxy brick floors. To my eye, the rugged textures and the strong color contrasts of the typical Tuscan house create the most welcoming rooms of any architectural style I know. Fresh and serene in summer, they look secure and cozy in winter. Tropical houses with bamboo ceilings and shuttered walls that open to catch every breeze, and the adobe houses of the Southwest, with their banquettes and fireplaces that are rounded like the curves of the human body, impart the same connected sense: *I could live here.* The architecture seems natural, as if these houses grew out of the land and were easily shaped by the human hand. In Italian, a coat of paint or wax is a *mano*, a hand of that substance. Before the plastering started, I noticed Fabio's initials scratched in a patch of wet cement. The Poles, I remembered, wrote POLONIA at the base of the stone wall. I wonder if archaeologists find many reminders of the anonymous hands behind enduring work. On the wall of the prehistoric Pech Merle cave in France, I was stunned to see handprints, like ones children make in kindergarten, above the spotted horses. The actual "signature" of the preliterate artist outlined in blood, soot, ashes! When the great tombs of Egypt were opened, the footprints of the last person out before the entrances were sealed remained in the sand: the last work finished, a day's work over.

A butterfly, trapped inside, bats and bats the shutter but does not find the way out. As I fall asleep, the fan drones, a shimmering head looking left and right.

✳

I love the heat. I love the excessive insistence. Something in me says yes. Maybe it's only that I grew up in the South, but it feels like a basic yes, devolving back to those old fossil heads of the first people who came into being under a big sun.

The landscape appears cool although it's cooking. The terraces aren't bleached this year, as they sometimes are. Our view to the Apennines is green and forested. In someone's swimming pool at the bottom of the valley, I see a little stick figure jump in.

Since we're up high, nights cool off to a lovely softness. In late afternoon, heaps and piles of clouds cross over, their shadows roving across the green hills. Tonight the Perseids shower, it's San Lorenzo's night of the shooting stars—cause for a celebratory dinner. We've seen them before and we know the gasps, our quick pointing a second too late, the bright cascade of a meteor, so momentary, so long expired. The garlic soup, chosen over Boethius, is chilling in the fridge. Lemon and Basil Chicken, an accidental discovery, and a terra-cotta dish of Gratin Dauphinois, an old Julia Child potato favorite I've made for years, are ready to cook. I have enough ripe pears to peel and slice and improvise a mascarpone custard for them to bake into. I scrub the bird droppings off the yellow table, spread the cloth I made over the winter from leftover fabric I used for the wicker on my Palo Alto patio fifteen years ago. I spent days on the double welting around the cushion for the chaise longue. I could walk out of that dining room door right now, fluff those cushions, tell the dog "Down," walk into the yard filled with kumquat and loquat, mock orange and olive. Or could I? Everything stays. What chance, when I bought that yellow-flowered bolt at Calico Corners, to think it would end up on a table in Italy, with me in a new life.

Like fanning through a deck of cards, my mind flashes on the thousand chances, trivial to profound, that converged to re-create this place. Any arbitrary turning along the way and I would be elsewhere; I would be different. Where did the expression "a place in the sun" first come from? My rational thought processes cling always to the idea of free will, random event; my blood, however, streams easily along a current of fate. I'm here because I climbed out the window at night when I was four.

❋

All the summer fruits of the great Mediterranean sun have ripened. Beginning with cherries when I arrive, the summer progresses to yellow peaches. Along the Roman road up Sant'Egidio, we pick handfuls of the most divine fruit of all, the minute wild strawberries that dangle like jewels under their jagged leaves. Then come the white peaches with pale and fragrant flesh. Gelato made of these makes you want to dance. Then the plums, all the varieties—the small round gold, the dusky purple-blue, and the pale green ones larger than golf balls. Grapes start to arrive from farther south. A few ruddy apples, then the first pears ripen. The small green ones couldn't be ripe but they are, then the globular speckled yellows. In August, the figs just start to plump up, not reaching their peak until September. But, finally, the blackberries, that heart-of-summer fruit, are ripe.

Days before I go home, at the end of August, I can take out my colander and pick enough for breakfast. Every morning the birds are wild for them but can't manage to eat quite all. Picking blackberries—a back-to-basics pleasure—passing over the ones still touched with a hint of red and those that squish to the touch, pulling off only the perfectly ripe ones until my fingers are rosy. The taste of sun-warmed berries brings me the memory of filling my jar with them in an abandoned cemetery. As a child, I sat down on a heaped mound of dirt, unconsciously eating luscious berries from a plant whose roots intertwined with old bones.

Bees burrow in the pears. Where they've fallen, thrushes feast. Who knows how the wants of our ancestors act out in us? The mellow scents somehow remind me of my mean Grandmother Davis. My father privately called her The Snake. She was blind, with Greek-statue eyes, but I always believed she could see. Her charming husband had lost all the land she inherited from her parents, who owned a big corner of South Georgia. On Sunday rides, she'd always want Mother to drive her by the property she'd lost. She couldn't see when we got there but she could smell peanut and cotton crops in the humid air. "All this," she'd mutter, "all *this*." I'd look up from my book. The brown earth on either side of the car spread flat to the horizon. From there, who could believe the world is round? I first thought of her when we had the terraces plowed and the upturned earth was ready for planting. Fertile earth, rich as chocolate cake. Big Mama, I thought, biscuit-face, old snake, just look at this dirt, all *this*.

     The heat breaks with a fast rain, a pelting determined rain that soaks the ground then quits—gone, finished. The green landscape smears across the windows. The sun bounces back out but robbed of its terror now. Here, the edge of autumn. What is it? The smell of leaves drying. A sudden shift in the air, a slightly amber cast to the light, then a blue haze hanging over the valley at evening. I would love to see the leaves turn, pick up the hazelnuts and almonds, feel the first frost and build a little olive wood fire to take the chill off the morning. My summer clothes go in the duffle under the bed. I make a few wreathes of grape vine and twine them with sage, thyme, and oregano, herbs I can use in December. The fennel flowers I've been drying on a screen go in a painted tin I found in the house. Perhaps the *nonna* I've grown fond of kept hers here, too.

     The man with his coat over his shoulders stops in front of the shrine with his handful of dried yarrow. He brushes out the shrine with the side of his hand. All fall, when I am busy with students, he will walk the white road, perhaps wearing an old knitted sweater, later a scarf around his neck. The man is walking away. I see him stop in the road and look back at the house. I wonder, for the thousandth time, what he is thinking. He sees me at the window, adjusts his coat over his shoulders, and turns toward home.

Scattered books go back to their proper shelves: my house in order. One final blackberry cobbler and I'm gone. A lizard darts in, panics, flees out the door. The thought of the future spins through me. What magnet out there is pulling now? I stack pressed sheets on the *armadio* shelves. Clearing my desk, I find a list: copper polish, string, call Donatella, plant sunflowers, double hollyhocks. The sun hits the Etruscan wall, turning the locust trees to lace. Two white butterflies are mating in midair. I walk from window to window, taking in the view.

Bella Tuscany

The Sweet Life in Italy

FRANCES MAYES

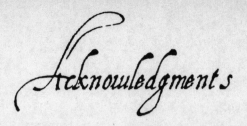

Acknowledgments

My great thanks to Peter Ginsberg, my agent, and Charles Conrad, my editor at Broadway Books. Special thanks to Dave Barbor and Fiona Inglis, both of Curtis Brown Ltd. At Transworld in Australia, my gratitude to Shona Martyn. To Karen Reid and Sandra Noakes—*grazie.*

Many friends were important to me while I was writing this book: Josephine Carson, Susan MacDonald and Cole Dalton, Ann and Walter Dellinger, Robin and John Heyeck, Kate Abbe, Rena Williams and Steve Harrison, Todd Alden, Toni Mirosevich and Shotsy Faust—you're welcome to pull up a chair at my table any time. All thanks to my family and to Ed's—Bramasole's *portone* always will swing open to greet you.

The people who live in Cortona have given me this book; all I had to do is write. Special thanks to Donatella di Palme and Rupert Palmer, Giuseppina Paolelli, Serena Caressi, Giorgio Zappini, Guiseppe Agnolucci, Riccardo and Amy Bertocci, Nella Gawronska, the Molesini family, Riccardo and Sylvia Baracchi, Guilio Nocentini, Antonio Giornelli, Lucio Ricci, Edo Perugini, and to our great neighbours, the Cardinali family: Placido, Fiorella and Chiara. We are fortunate to have landed in their midst. With tremendous gratitude, I thank il Sindaco, Ilio Pasqui, and il Consiglio Comunale di Cortona for conferring on me *la cittadinanza onoraria,* honorary citizenship.

My thanks to the editors of *National Geographic Traveler, Attche, San Francisco Magazine, The San Francisco Examiner,* the *Land's End* catalogue, and *Within Borders* for publishing portions of this book in their pages.

FOR EDWARD

Contents

6

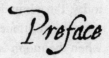

Preface

STEPPING INSIDE THE *FORNO*, I'M SUDDENLY SUR-
rounded by the warm aromas of just-baked bread. "Welcome back," a Cortona woman greets me. Maybe I look
dazed, having arrived last night from California, a
twenty-hour ordeal, because she asks, "What do you do for jet
lag?"

"I usually just wait it out. I'm so happy to be here that I don't
notice it very much—just get up at four in the morning for a
few days. What do you do?"

"I stare at the sunset. Then the body knows."

I merely smile, but mentally I make a little bow to her. Maybe
it's a small world, maybe we're in a global economy, and maybe
we're slowly melting into one pot, but everyday life is still radically particular in rural Italy. Cut a slice anywhere: It remains
purely *Italian*.

When Beppe, who helps in our garden, tells me, *"La luna è
dura,"* the moon is hard, and that we must harvest the onions

today, I'm reminded that the moon holds sway. "But we must wait," he continues, "and plant lettuces *quando la luna è tenera,*" when the moon is tender.

Walking down into town for coffee, I see a waiter bring out a bowl of water for a customer's dog. Overhead I hear, "*Buon giorno, una bella giornata,*" good morning, a beautiful day. An ancient man, who has slipped into a happy dementia, leans from his second-storey window, waving and shouting. Everyone greets him with equal enthusiasm. Shop owners are sprinkling water around their entrances with watering cans, nipping into the bars for a quick coffee, their shops untended, the doors open. After a leisurely half-hour with a cappuccino and a novel, I start to pay and am told that Simonetta has paid. Simonetta? The very quiet woman who owns a profumeria where I sometimes buy soap and lotion. This gentle courtesy happens frequently.

At Matteo and Gabriella's *frutta e verdura,* I see the first basket of hazelnuts still in their ruffs. The season is changing and soon all the luscious peaches and peppers of summer will give over to citrus and cauliflower, an entirely different selection. "Look," Matteo says, "the green walnut." He cracks it, carefully peels the skin, and hands me a smooth piece, the color of ivory. "You must eat them in three or four days. After that they are too dry." The taste of green walnuts is not unknown to me. When I was a child, our cook Willie Bell used to squeeze the juice and rub it into my hands if I got ringworm or poison ivy. The new walnuts are gold balls, slightly damp. "Very good for low blood pressure," Matteo continues, "but don't eat too many or you'll have a rise in temperature."

And so another day begins in this Tuscan hilltown. I came to Italy expecting adventure. What I never anticipated is the absolute sweet joy of everyday life—*la dolce vita.*

Under the Tuscan Sun, my first memoir, chronicled the discovery of Bramasole, an abandoned house situated beneath an eighth-century B.C. Etruscan wall. Getting to know the superb hilltown of Cortona, the excitement of cooking in a foreign country, the intense labor of rescuing a house from ruin and the land from brambles, and meeting the people here—these pleasures paralleled the deeper pleasure of learning how to live a new life. Even the name of the house drew me here: *Bramasole,* something that yearns for the sun, and, yes, I did.

I walk from window to window, taking in the view: When I wrote the last line of *Under the Tuscan Sun,* I wrote the first line of *Bella Tuscany.* I knew I was at the beginning of my experience of Italy, the inner experience as well as the outer. Views—they are so various. From my upstairs window, I see a green sweep of the Apennines. As the wooded slopes angle toward the valley, olive orchards begin, and mellow stone farmhouses with tile roofs anchor each farm to the land. There is no entrance of time into this view, except for a turquoise postage stamp far below, the swimming pool of friends. Looking out—looking into Italy! North, south, east, west is the allure of the whole country. I know more now, after several seasons of travels. I've been to the heel, to Sicily, to the watery reaches of the Veneto, those reveaing extremes of this country. I've fallen in love with Verona, the Basilicata and Marche regions, Bellagio, Asolo, Bologna, and more and more with the castle towns around Lago Trasimeno, which I can see from my land.

Travelling the circles, concentric from Bramasole, enlarges my perception of the endless complexity and richness of this country. At the same time, my travels bring me back to this rose and apricot house facing the valley. Because it seems like paradise, I continue to work to make it so. Gardening is something I always enjoyed on a capricious level. I was interested not so much in gardening as in the effects of gardening—the flower beds that bloomed on cue and the design of the yard—where to place big pots and how to see a fine range of colors from the windows. I bought flats of just-about-to-bloom flowers, and plopped them in the ground. Now I am a convert. I've fallen into the sustained rhythm of the garden. I compost the coffee grounds and the potato peels. I've learned to double-dig.

With two men who know everything about the land, Ed and I have created extensive herb and vegetable plots. We acknowledge the distant future by planting chestnut, cypress, and evergreens—trees for the long haul—as well as the more winsome and immediate pomegranate, cherry, and pear trees. No trip to a nursery ends without the purchase of still another fragrant rose. Rain reactivates another fragrance, the acrid, steamy smell of sheep dung, delivered by a canny Sardinian shepherd to the second terrace just above the living room. We can't move the stuffed bags, so when it rains, *we* move to the other side of the house.

Buying a house seven thousand miles from home once felt like an enormous risk. Now we just live here. How to quantify happiness? Any loved house you've personally slaved over feels like an extension of yourself. Many people have told me that when they arrived in Italy, they've surprised themselves by thinking, *I'm home*. I, too, had that sensation when I first came here. By now, that feeling has magnified. And, as for a loved one, I have that scarier feeling, *I can't be without you*. Meanwhile, the house just stands here, indifferent, facing the changing light and weather.

Cortona
1 September 1998

FORTUNATE THAT CYPRESS SHADOWS FALL IN wide bands across the sunlit road; fortunate that on the first day back in Cortona I see a carpenter carrying boards, his tabby cat balanced on his shoulders, tail straight up, riding like a surfer. The carpenter tosses the wood on sawhorses and begins to whistle. The cat bends and leans as he moves—a working cat. I watch for a few moments then walk on into town for a cappuccino. *Thank you,* I think. Fortunate that yellow blazes of forsythia light the hills. After seven summers on this terraced land, Ed and I feel a rush of happiness on turning the front-door key. I'm enchanted by the rounded Apennines, this quirky house that takes in the sun, and the daily rhythms of life in a Tuscan hilltown. He's far in love with the land. By now he knows the habits of every olive tree.

Fortunate. Otherwise, we might want to post a For Sale sign on the gate ten minutes after arrival because neither well pump is working: a grinding noise in the switch for the old well, a buzz for the new well. We peer into the cistern—at least there's enough water for a few days.

When the pump went down into the new well six years ago, I never expected to see it again. Now, on our first morning, three plumbers are hauling up ropes, their heads down the well. It's a beast. Then Giacomo stands on the well wall, the others beside him. They're counting, *uno, due, tre,* giving the heave-ho. Soon they're stripped to their pants, cursing and laughing. Up it comes, and Giacomo almost falls backward. They carry it to the truck.

The old well's pump—replaced just last year—they yank out easily. The contraption comes up with fig roots dangling and is pronounced dead on arrival. Why? They begin to dig for wires. By noon, the walkway is torn up, the lawn is carved into ditches and the mystery is solved. Mice have eaten the insulation around the wires. Why would they eat plastic when they can eat hazelnuts and almonds? The pumps have shorted out.

The new well's pump, it turns out, is also dead. Fizzled. Kaput. By the third day, we have new pumps, new wires sealed with silicone, which the original electrician neglected to do, lots of water, a patched walkway, and a depleted bank account. If mice eat plastic, what's to keep them from eating silicone?

Fortunate that we are served pheasant with roasted potatoes for dinner at the *trattoria* up the mountain, and that the early March dark spills forth a million twirling stars, because otherwise Ed's scrawled list might seem daunting: new grass, prune trees, build a shed for tools, remodel two old bathrooms, new septic system, paint shutters, buy desk and something with space to hang clothes, plant trees, extend garden.

~

Primo Bianchi, a stonemason who has done extensive work here during our restoration, arrives to discuss the projects. He can start in July. "I was on your roof in January," he tells us.

"Your friend Donatella called and said there was a leak." We've seen the dripping stain on the yellow wall of my study. "It was the wind. You lost some tiles. When I was working in the afternoon, the wind came again and blew down my ladder."

"Oh, no!"

He laughs, pointing both forefingers at the ground, that gesture meaning *Let it not happen here*. Dark comes early in winter. I imagine him, his back against the chimney, sitting on the cold tiles, his pale blue eyes squinting at the road below, the wind standing his hair on end. "I waited. No one came by. Then a car but he did not hear me. After perhaps two hours a woman walked by and I called for help. This house was empty so long— she thought I was a spirit and let out a scream when she saw me waving on the roof. You need to think of a new roof soon."

He walks off a measurement of pipes we'll need for the new drainage system. It looks like a plan for trench warfare. "Hurry and order the furnishings for the bathrooms if you want everything here by July."

Fortunate that the place is restored—central heating, new doors, finished kitchen, one lovely bath, refinished beams, barrels of new paint, rebuilt stone walls, refitted *cantina* for oil and wine. Otherwise, these new projects might seem like restoration itself. "You may think you're through with old houses," Primo tells us, "but they are never through with you."

Soft spring air, an elixir of joy simply to breathe in and out. Quick streams are opening on the terraces. I take off my shoes and let the cold, cold water bathe my feet. The rocky hillsides sprout ferns, glossy green. A new lizard runs across my toes and I feel the clutch of the tiny feet.

⌒

Primavera, first green, and the wet grasses shine. A European spring, my first. I only have read of Proust's chestnuts flowering,

Nabokov's linden lanes, Colette's double-red violets. But no one ever told me about quince, their sudden pink flares against stone walls. No one said the spring winds can turn murderous. No one mentioned lilac, and somehow during my summers in Italy, I never noticed the heart-shaped leaves. Now I see the Tuscan hills spattered with enormous white or smoky-lavender bushes. Near our house, a hedge of lilac leads to an abandoned farm, and in the rain I cut wet armfuls to fill all my pitchers and vases. More than any flower, the mesmerizing perfume seems to be the very scent of memory, hauling me back to college in Virginia and my first breath of lilac, which didn't grow in the warm latitude of my childhood home in Georgia. I remember thinking, *How could I have lived eighteen years without knowing this?* I had a terrible crush on my philosophy professor, married with three children, and over and over I played Harry Bellafonte, *Green grow the lilacs all sparkling with dew.* My dorm window overlooked the James River through a tangle of brush. *Springtime is here and it's here without you.* That my professor wore drip-dry shirts I crassly blamed on his wife; that he combed a long strand of hair over his pate I tried to ignore.

Violets, the suffocatingly sweet-scented ones, bloom along the spontaneous springs. Naturalized double daffodils, *tromboni* in Italian, mass along the terrace edges. The faint mists of hawthorn (*biancospino,* white thorn, or, locally, *topospino,* mouse-pricker) drift along the upper terraces and, below, the fruit trees continue to outdo themselves. We won't mow—the luxurious grass is overtaken by white camomile and marguerites.

What is this happiness that keeps coming in waves? Time, the gift of time, the free running of time—and Italy owns so much of it. Being from the South, I'm used to people talking about The War Between the States as though it were a decade ago. In the South the long dead and buried are talked about, too. Sometimes I thought Mother Mayes would come walking in the door again, bringing back her powdery lavender scent, her spongy body I could feel beneath the voile print dress. Here, it's Hannibal. Hannibal, who passed this way and fought the Roman Flaminio in 217 B.C. All the hilltowns celebrate jousts or weddings or battles which occurred hundreds of years ago. Maybe having so much time behind them contributes to the different sense I absorb in Italy. Gradually, I fall into time. At home in California, I operate *against* time. My agenda, stuffed with notes and business cards, is always with me, each day scribbled with appointments. Sometimes when I look at the week coming up, I know that I simply have to walk through it. To be that booked-up, blocked-in feels depleting. When I make the weekly list of what needs to be accomplished, I know I'll be running double-time to catch up. I don't have time to see my friends and sometimes when I do, I'm hoping to cut it short because I need to get back to work. I read about an American doctor who pumps her breasts in freeway traffic so she can continue to breast-feed her baby and still keep up with her medical practice. An ad in *The Wall Street Journal* offered engagement rings by telephone for couples who don't have time to shop. Am I that bad?

Sabbatical, what a civilized idea. All jobs should have them. This year both Ed and I have this blessed time-out, which, combined with summer vacation, gives us the chance to spend six months in Italy. Since this is my first leave in twenty years of teaching, I want to bask in every day. To wake up—without having to go anywhere—and wander the terraces to see what is coming into bloom seems like *paradiso.* Soon the wild irises will open. Their pointy, bruise-blue heads seem to push up taller as I watch. Narcissi, just on the verge of glory, run rampant. Already, yellow light emanates from the buds.

I am, every day, shocked by something new and shocked that this house and land, which I thought I knew from my summers and Decembers, continue to astound me. We stepped off the plane in Florence on March 15 to seventy-degree weather and it has held, except for occasional blasts of wind. Now, the pears

are turning from flower to leaf. As white petals drop or flurry—
I remember hearing "peach-blow" as a child—new leaves shoot
out with force. That energy has swollen the limbs of all the old
fig trees and the branches of the spindly pomegranate we have
just planted.

Happiness? The color of it must be spring green, impossible to
describe until I see a just-hatched lizard sunning on a stone. That
color, the glowing green lizard skin, repeats in every new leaf.
"The force that through the green fuse drives the flower . . ."
Dylan Thomas wrote. "Fuse" and "force" are excellent word
choices—the regenerative power of nature explodes in every
weed, stalk, branch. Working in the mild sun, I feel the green fuse
of my body, too. Surges of energy, kaleidoscopic sunlight through
the leaves, the soft breeze that makes me want to say the word
"zephyr"—this mindless simplicity can be called happiness.

~

A momentous change has occurred at Bramasole. "Can you
find someone to take care of the place?" I asked signor Martini
at the end of last summer. We were leaving and had no one to
keep the rampant forces of nature at bay in our garden.
Francesco and Beppe, who've worked this land for several years,
only want to care for fruit trees, grapes, and olives. Once we
asked Beppe to cut the grass. He wielded his weed machine as
though clearing brambles, leaving the yard looking like a dust
bowl. When he and Francesco saw the lawn mower Ed bought,
they took a couple of steps back and said, *"No, no, professore, grazie."* They, men of the fields, did not see themselves pushing the
little humming mower across some lawn.

Signor Martini, who sold us the house, knows everyone. Perhaps some friend would like a part-time job.

He pushed back from his desk and pointed to his chest. *"Io,"*
he pronounced. "I will make the garden." He took down some-

thing framed above his desk, blew off the dust on top, and held out his agricultural diploma. A small photo stuck in the corner of the frame showed him at twenty with his hand on the rump of a cow. He grew up on a farm and always missed the country life he'd known as a boy. After World War II, he sold pigs before moving to town and taking up real estate. Because he is eligible for a pension, he planned to close his office at the end of the year, he explained, and was moving to a large estate as caretaker. Because so many Italians start work in their teens, they become *pensionati,* pensioners, while still relatively young. He wanted to make a mid-course correction.

Usually we arrive at the end of May, when it's too late to plant vegetables. By the time we've cleared a space, turned the soil, and bought seeds, the planting season has left us behind. We look longingly at the *fagiolini,* string beans, climbing tepees of bamboo in our neighbors' gardens. If a few tomato plants happen to survive our ineptitude and lateness, we sit staring at the runty green blobs the morning of our leaving for San Francisco, shaking our heads at the unfulfilled dream of snapping luscious tomatoes from our own labor.

Now, signor Martini has metamorphosed into a gardener. A couple of times a week, he comes here to work, often bringing his sister-in-law as well.

~

Every day involves a trip to a nursery—we've visited every one within twenty miles—or a walk around the terraces and yard sketching possible gardens. Winter rains have softened the soil so that I sink slightly as I walk. Since we're here in time, I aim to have the most riotous, flamboyant, flourishing garden this side of the Boboli in Florence. I want every bird, butterfly, and bee in Tuscany to feel drawn to my lilies, surfinias, jasmine, roses, honeysuckle, lavender, anemones, and to the hundred scents

7

drifting from them. Even though the risk of freeze is still a consideration, I barely can restrain myself from planting. In the nursery greenhouses, the humid air and the narcotizing effect of bright geraniums, hydrangeas, petunias, impatiens, begonias, and dozens of other rosy pinks and corals, entice me to load the car immediately.

"Whoa, slow down," Ed says. "We should buy only what we can plant now, the lavender, rosemary, and sage." These replace what was damaged by the paralyzing winter storm, when it snowed, melted, then froze all in one day. "And more trees can be planted immediately. There's plenty of time."

Plenty of time. What a musical phrase.

Five cypresses, two pears, a cherry, a peach, and two apricots delivered from the nursery line the driveway, awaiting Francesco and Beppe, who already have argued over where each will receive the right amount of sun. They have pruned the olives, which also suffered in the hard freeze. They whipped around the terraces with a ladder, ruthlessly cutting off freeze-burned limbs, then took us on an inspection tour, examining each tree for damage. We stand before a scrawny olive on the first terrace. They shake their heads sadly, as over the deceased body of a friend. Ed grieves, too, since the casualties are his three-year-olds. On the surviving young ones, the usually glistening leaves are dry. The worst sign is split bark; the farther down the tree a split occurs, the more damage. Those split at the base cause the men to shake their heads and say in low tones, *"Buttare via."* Get it out. We will have to dig out at least ten; others they're iffy about—wait and see. A few scraggly leaves on one, shoots at the bottom of another offer just enough hope to leave it. On the lower slopes of town and in the valley, many groves look dead, and grim-faced men are sawing off thick branches. Hard as it is, the lesson from the record-low 1985 freeze was to prune severely and the trees will regenerate in time.

Nothing is more sacred than the olive. Francesco eyes two

oaks on the olive terraces and shakes his head. "Good for the fireplace. Too much shade for the olives." Ed is careful not to disagree but also to point out emphatically that because of me, the trees have to stay. I have a log bench under one and like to read there. Otherwise, we might come home one day to find the trees cut, Francesco having assumed we agreed. I'm blamed for all deviations of the weed machine around flowers and for any decision that interferes with the self-evident rights of olives and grapes. Ed certainly would lose face if they suspected that he will transplant a wildflower in the tractor path. The men prune and fertilize all morning. Beppe and Francesco tie each new cypress to a giant stake. Between the stake and the tree they stuff a handful of grasses to keep the stake from sawing into the slender trunk.

Although the December freeze totally killed my hedge of herbs and the floppy blue plumbago by the cistern, the balmy, delicious early spring compensates. The laurel hedge Ed doesn't like but doesn't have the heart to eliminate, has, of course, thrived. We work all morning, chopping, digging out, and clearing the dried plants. I feel my neck and arms start to turn red. Is the breeze balmy? Or do I feel its sharp origins in the Swiss Alps?

The worst loss by far is one of the two palm trees on either side of the front door. One looks better than ever. The other is now a tall trunk with a fan of brown, drooping forlornly. From my third-floor study window, I can see a green frond emerging. A hand-span wide, it does not look promising.

Signor Martini is now Anselmo to us. He arrives in his real estate clothes, driving his big Alfa and shouting into his *telefonino,* but soon he reappears from the *limonaia* transformed into a farmer—tall rubber boots, flannel shirt, and a beret. What I did not expect is how completely he would take over. "Don't touch!" he warns. "If you touch while the dew is wet on the leaves, the plants will die." I'm startled; he's so emphatic.

"Why?"

He repeats himself. No reason. Usually, these pronouncements have some basis. Perhaps certain funguses are transmitted more easily—or something logical.

"What is that?" I ask him, gesturing to the thriving, knee-high plants he has put in on the third terrace. "There are so many of them." I scan the rows; eight rows of ten—eighty plants. He has neglected to consult with me about expanding the garden exponentially. Formerly, we had potatoes, lettuces, basil.

"*Baccelli*," he answers. "To eat with fresh pecorino."

"What are *baccelli?*"

He is uncharacteristically silent. "*Baccelli sono baccelli.*" They are what they are. He keeps chopping weeds, shrugs.

I look up the word in the dictionary but it says only "pods," so I call my friend, Donatella. "Ah, *sì, i baccelli,* as we call them— they are the *fave* he has planted, but in the local dialect, *'fava'* means penis so I am sure he would not say the word to you."

The *baccelli* flowers are tender white wings with a second pair of petals inside, each marked with a purple-black dot. I examine the leaves, looking for the dark veins forming the letter Θ, which made the Greeks consider the fava dangerous and unlucky because *thanatos* (death) also starts with theta. So far, these are simply green and vigorous.

In our absence, Anselmo has planted enough vegetables for several families. He has converted two terraces to an enormous garden. A Sardinian shepherd sold him fifteen great bags of sheep manure, which he works into the soil. So far, I've counted, besides the eighty fava plants, forty potato plants, twenty artichokes, four rows of chard, a patch of carrots, a large bed of onions, enough garlic for all the *ragù* in Cortona, and a beautiful triangle of lettuces. He has put in asparagus, too, but he says not to pick the scraggly spears coming up. Asparagus is ready after two years. Zucchini, melon, and eggplant are germinating in the *limonaia,* and sharpened bamboo stakes for tomatoes—quite a few stakes—he has stacked at the end of the garden until the weather stabilizes. I may have to set up a stand and sell zucchini flowers at the Saturday market. Since he is paid by the hour, we dread to know how many he already has spent.

He also has pruned the roses, cut down three of my favorite wild plum trees that were in the way of the garden, and has begun to espalier a line of plums along the edge of the terrace. They look tortured. When he sees me looking at them, he shakes his finger, as though to a child contemplating a dash into the street. "Wild trees," he says contemptuously. Whose land is this, I suddenly wonder. Like Beppe and Francesco, he considers anything that interferes with his domain to be a nuisance. And like them, he knows everything, so we do as he says.

"But the best yellow plums. . . ." I will have to keep my eye on these trees. One morning I may wake to find them stacked in the woodpile, along with the oaks Francesco would like to attack.

⟿

Even the spring night is shocking. The silence of the country sounds loud. I'm not yet accustomed to the shrieks of owls tearing apart the stillness. We're coming from burrito-and-a-movie nights, order-out-for-Chinese nights, seventeen-messages-on-the-answering-machine nights. I wake up at three or four and wander from room to room, looking out the windows. What is this quiet, the big, moony night with a comet ball smearing my study window and the dark valley below? Why can't I erase the image my student wrote: *the comet, like a big Q-tip swabbing the sky?* A nightingale practices some nightingale version of scales, lingering on each note. This seems to be a lone bird; no answer comes to the plaintive song.

~

Late every afternoon, Ed hauls in olive wood. We have supper on trays in front of the fire. "Now, we're back," he says, raising his glass to the flames, perhaps to the humble god of the hearth. Happiness, divine and banal word, a complex proposition which shifts its boundaries constantly, and sometimes feels so very easy. I pull a blanket around me and doze over Italian idioms. A wind comes up. Which one? The *tramontana,* tinged with frigid air from the Alps, the *ponente,* bringing rain, or the *levante,* blowing hard and fast from the east? The cypresses outlined by moonlight seem to swirl their pointed tops in all directions. Certainly it is not the *libeccio,* the warm, dry wind from the south, or the summery *grecale* or *maestrale.* These winds in the chimney are serious, reminding me that in March, spring is only an idea.

Bitter Greens of Tuscan Spring

SHEER EXCITEMENT WAKES ME UP EARLY. THIS IS the first market day since I arrived. As I dress, I catch a glimpse from the back window of someone moving along one of the upper terraces. A fox? No, someone leaning down, gathering something. A woman, I think, making out through the milky fog a rounded form and dark scarf. Then she's gone, hidden by the *ginestre* and wild rose bushes. "Probably someone looking for mushrooms," Ed guesses. As I drive away, I think I see a movement in the hawthorn above the road.

Three closed trucks from way south in Puglia and Basilicata have arrived at the Thursday market in Camucia. They're open at the back and sides to reveal their bounty—artichokes, still attached to stalks. The drivers pull out enormous mounds and stack them under signs that say twenty-five for 8000 *lire,* about eighteen cents apiece. Women cluster around, buying in quantity. Most favored are the purple-streaked smallest ones. These artichokes, even the peeled stalks, are greatly tender. Too small for a choke, the whole thing is edible, except for a few outer leaves. They're sold on foot-long stalks, tied in a cumbrous bundle so heavy that my market tour must end right here. I struggle home, trying to decide how I will use the twenty-five artichokes I have somehow hoisted under my arm. As I haul them into the kitchen, I see another huge bundle of tiny purple artichokes on the counter. "Oh no! Where did you get these?"

Ed grabs some of my bags. "I was up at Torreone and a pickup packed with artichokes pulled up to the bar. Everyone ran out to buy from this guy, so I bought some, too." Fifty artichokes. Two people.

All the restaurants and *trattorie* have fried artichokes on the menu. In homes, they're often eaten raw, with seasoned olive oil, or quartered and cooked with potatoes, spring onions, lemon juice, and parsley. The textures and flavors complement each other. Steamed briefly and drizzled with olive oil, their astringent taste seems just right on any spring day.

The winter *rape* is at the end of its tenure but one farmer still shouted out *"Polezze,"* the dialect word. I've seen it already, flowering in home gardens, at first mistaking it for mustard, which is waving its yellow blooms at home in California wine country right now. By the time the *rape* flowers, it's too late to savor its particular flavor. Picked early, cleaned of stems, steamed, then sautéed with garlic, the buds and leaves taste like an untamed cousin of broccoli, somewhat bitter and distinct. *Rape* (both syllables are pronounced) tastes good for you; it must be packed with iron and nitrogen. When I eat it, I feel that I rise from the table a stronger person.

Bitter is a popular taste in Italy. All those herbal after-dinner drinks and *aperitivi,* collectively known as *amari,* bitters, that the Italians knock back are definitely an acquired taste. "Italians seem to have *acquired* more tastes than many of us," Ed observes. The first time I tried Cynar, based on artichoke flavor, I remembered my mother chasing me around the house trying to get me to take cough medicine. Even an orange soda is labeled "*amara.*" At the *pasta fresca* shop, they're making ravioli with ricotta and *borragine,* wild borage. Ravioli stuffed with anything and ricotta is usually mellow. With borage, the little pillows prod the taste buds. Dandelion, turnip, and beet greens—all are savored in this season. Even the hated nettles, which we battle on a hillside all summer, have a snappy taste when picked as soon the leaves unfurl, blanched, then stirred into risotto or pasta and topped with toasted pine nuts.

The green that looks strange and new to me is *agretti.* It must exist somewhere in America but I've never seen it. Tied with a weed, a bunch of it looks like wild grasses, something to hand-feed a horse. Thrown onto a hard and fast boil for a few moments, it then gets a turn in the sauté pan with oil, salt, and pepper. When I first saw *agretti,* I thought, uh oh, one of those acquired tastes. While cooking, it had the smell of dirt—that earthiness you recognize when beets are cooking, but with a verdant freshness, too. An Italian friend recommends lemon juice but as soon as I smelled it, I wanted to taste it unadorned. Because the "grass" is about the same thickness as *vermicelli,* I later tried it tossed with that pasta and slivers of *parmigiano.* Spinach is the closest taste, but while *agretti* has the mineral sharpness of spinach, it tastes livelier, full of the energy of spring.

I am surprised to find that the legendary wild asparagus also is extremely bitter. Chiara, a neighbor, is out on her land with a handful of the weedy little spears. She pushes back spiny strands to reveal the plant, which looks like a coarser, meaner asparagus fern. She is eloquent on the subject of frittata with chopped wild asparagus. Eloquent, that is, in gesture. Her quick motion, like pulling a zipper in front of her mouth, means something is extra-delicious. Had she placed her thumb against her cheek and rotated her fist back and forth, we would have seen how words fail to describe just how good something to eat can be.

The early riser I saw up on the terraces must have been after the asparagus. Now someone has raided the daffodils, too. After a morning of looking at toilets and tile for the remodeling project this summer, we come home to find about two hundred *tromboni* gone from the hillside. Only a few, drooping and past their prime, are left for us.

All along the road in late afternoons, women walk with their sticks and plastic bags, gathering both asparagus and *mescolanza,* wild greens, most of which are bitter, for their dinner salads. I'm just learning about this *insalata mista* for the taking. They look for *tarassaco,* which resembles dandelion, several kinds of *radicchio,* chicory, borage, *barbe dei frati*—friars' beards—and many others.

What else is bulging in those bags? Why do they suddenly stop and study a piece of ground for a few minutes, poking at it with a stick? They bend over and dig with a penknife—some roots, a few leaves, mushrooms—and move on. We've even seen the well-dressed stop their cars, scamper up a hill, and come down waving two or three bunches of mint or fennel for roasting meat, or some medicinal plant, dirt falling off the roots.

I, too, go out hunting for asparagus. Ed cuts what we think will be the perfect stick for me, a magic stick, as if I will be divining water. Odd how something can be invisible to you, then when it's pointed out, you find it everywhere. The upper terraces flourish with prickly wands. They seem to like growing under a tree or next to a hillside. Right away, I learn to look in hidden places, although sometimes there's a feathery renegade just growing out in the open. Usually a tangle of weeds is between my hand and the dark spears poking out of the dirt. A spear here, one there. Asparagus must have appeared early in the food chain. Cultivated asparagus, despite its many elegant preparations, looks primitive; the wild form is even more so. Some stalks are as thin as yarn and the color ranges from viridian to purple. Those thorns your hand must find its way among are needle-sharp. This is slow work, but good.

I cook my thirty spears to go with roast chicken and neither of us likes the wry, almost medicinal taste. Then, at the market, a strange woman barely four feet tall holds out a newspaper cone full of wild asparagus. She looks as if she just materialized out of a fairy tale and might say, "Come to the woods, children." But *"Genuino, genuino,"* she repeats. The real thing. "Fifteen thousand *lire"* (about nine dollars). Because I have the feeling that I will not be seeing her kind at the market many more times, I hand over the money. Just to be in her presence a little longer, I ask her how to prepare it. Like my neighbor, she likes it cut finely into a frittata.

Ed tries the frittata, bolstering it with spring garlic, but the asparagus taste almost disappears, just a crackle of the bony stem to remind us it is there.

On the street in Arezzo, I see another of these woodsy women. The word *strega,* witch, comes to mind, or that old source of wisdom in the South, a conjure-woman. Who could resist? I buy some from her basket, too. A crescent-shaped knife lies in the bottom, its blade worn thin. She is almost toothless, bundled in sweaters with bits of straw sticking out of the wool. "Where did you find so much?" I ask. But she just raises her finger to her lips; her mouth is sealed on that subject. She limps away and I notice she is wearing bright white running shoes. She hoists herself up to the arcade level on the Corso, where sophisticated businessmen at a *caffè* table madly buy her asparagus.

Usually I roast asparagus in the oven—arrange the stalks on a baking sheet, drizzle with oil and salt and pepper and run them in the oven. That's the best asparagus can taste. Without contact with water, even steam, the asparagus retains all succulence and texture without absorbing a watery taste, or worse, going limp. But wild asparagus turned tough as string in the oven, so I learn to steam them very slightly, then roll them around in olive oil. The quality of the oil is crucial; without the best, I'd use butter. With each bite, I imagine the woman foraging in the countryside, her secret hillsides above the vineyards, the years she has attended to this ritual, the surety of her thumb against the curved knife.

When I show Beppe, master grape pruner, the patches of asparagus on the land, he's pleased. He cuts off the dry arching branches. "Like this, cut low under the dirt and more will come next year," he explains. When he leans to show me, he discovers that someone already has begun this pruning process. Old wands have been cut on the diagonal, not snapped off. The mysterious forager. Or some spirit who lived here a century ago and revisits in spring? Or some canny soul who sells both flowers and asparagus at the market? A woman with a curved knife? Beppe starts to eat a raw asparagus and hands me one: a taste to sharpen the teeth. I'm beginning to like this spring treat.

I've been surprised during winter visits to find the food so truly different from what I'm used to in summer, the season I'm usually here. Now, as spring continues to unroll, almost every day brings some new taste. At Matteo and Gabriella's *frutta e verdura,* I see a basket holding something I've never seen before. Gnarly dwarf kiwi? Moldy walnuts? No, *mandorline,* Matteo tells me, a special treat in the Val di Chiana, the expansive valley below Cortona. Matteo bites one then holds out the basket to me. Ah, bitter *and* sour, not like anything I've ever tasted. I know immediately that I will like this new almond in its casing. He eats the whole thing slowly, fuzzed skin and all, relishing the crunch. Beneath the sage-green exterior, there's a neon-green layer, then a yellow layer, then the tender, embryonic nut, still soft and delicately touched with the taste of almond.

At home I go out on my own land where wild almonds grow, but none seems to be the right variety of the *mandorline.* The shells are hardening. I crack one with a rock and taste the nut: hint of rose, hint of peach, and the aftertaste which reminds me that prussic acid also comes from almonds. When ripe, these almonds retain their intense perfume but the acid tamps down to a twist of bitterness.

The land is a mystery to me. After seven years, I think I know it and then, suddenly, I don't. I am watching the season's benefactions. Rivers of wild irises are about to debut along the terraces. These we share with the forager, too, and with the porcupines, who feast on the rhizomes. Symbol of Florence, the iris used to be widely cultivated in Tuscany for the use of its dried root (orris) for the sensuous, deep violet-grape scent in perfumes. Such an unlikely wildflower. In San Francisco, I buy tight bunches of five at the grocery store, the attenuated buds barely able to open. Now I'm almost alarmed to see so many just volunteering and blooming with blowsy abandon.

As we walk back toward the house after the asparagus expedition, Beppe pulls up a slick, thick-leaved plant. "Boil this. It's good for the liver."

"What's its name?"

"In this moment, I do not recall. Look." Beppe points to a spreading ferny plant with tiny fan-shaped leaves. *"Morroncello."* I have no idea what this is. The dictionary does not tell me. I'll try it—another new greeny green of spring.

⁓

Very early, I hear voices in the road below the house and look out to see three women, hunter-gatherers, gesturing up to our land. They must see some new plant, I think. They're down there a long time and I don't see any movement toward the side of the hill. Finally, they walk on.

While dressing, I hear a skid of brakes, and two beeps of a horn, but when I look out, a blue Fiat is speeding on down the road. We're going to Petroio today, the home of handmade terra-cotta pots. As we start down the driveway, I sense something. Coming closer, we see the road littered with large stones. We look up. The tall stone wall which supports the shady part of our garden has collapsed in the night, leaving a fifteen-by-fifteen-foot gap, uglier than missing front teeth. We push the stones off the road and go up to look. The lovely clear springs surging forth from the hills saturated the ground, undermining the wall. Sins come back to haunt. The fey builder we hired to reconstruct the major terrace walls six years ago did not leave enough drainage holes. Our long yellow picnic table leans precariously where the wall tumbled.

We call our trusted Primo and he comes immediately. *"Mah,"* he shrugs. "Walls fall." He comes in the house and calls his crew.

We don't know what else to do, so we take off for Petroio, over in the Siena province. We want to buy large terra-cotta flower pots for the walls—those still standing. We go into the perched, medieval town first for something to drink but everything is closed and the car barely can squeeze through the narrowest street we've yet encountered. Just outside town are several *fabbricanti,* manufacturers, with hundreds of pots of all sizes. One is as large as a California hot tub. The place we choose makes theirs by hand. We've bought the mass-produced ones before and they're attractive too. A ruddy, actually terra-cotta—colored man comes out looking puzzled. We ask if we may look and he explains that he sells only wholesale. Fortunately, he likes to talk about pots. We're taken in a warehouse above the kilns, hot as a sweat lodge. The jars for olive oil, glazed on the inside, come in many sizes. They make herb pots, garden columns, sundials, classic urns and amphoras. Flower pots of every shape known and others unknown are stacked in rows. These handmade ones have rounded edges, a touch of honey color that looks warm and alive, and an occasional thumb print. He shows us the initials or signs of the maker on the bottom.

When he leans over to move a pot, his glasses slip from his pocket and fall out on the floor. One lens breaks out of the frame but does not shatter. We all kneel in the fine clay dust to look for the tiny screw. After the owner and I give up, Ed continues to search until he spots it in the shadows. Twisting the screw with his little fingernail, he repairs the glasses. We thank the owner for his time and start to leave.

"Wait, how many did you want?" he asks.

"Oh, a few—just for flowers at our house."

"Not for resale?"

"No. Three or four."

"Well, you see, I'm not allowed, but three or four, what's the harm?" He gives us a price list and says to deduct forty percent. We select an urn to go with three along our wall and three large pots, all with garlands and swags. When we start to pay, we find that we don't have nearly enough money. He says there's a Bancomat in town so we head back toward the twisted streets, this time parking outside and walking in. Petroio means "large villa," and the town is hardly larger than a huge castle. No one is about. We walk all over the tiny town and see no bank. The oldest church, San Giorgio, is closed tight. We spot a man walking his dog and he leads us to a doorway we wouldn't have found. No sign at all and the Bancomat is hidden away in a little closet opening.

Back we go to the shop, where the owner helps up pack the pots in the car. We take off and I fish the map from under the seat. "We're near the Abbadia a Sicille, supposed to be a refuge and inn for pilgrims on their way to the Holy Land. Embedded in the wall is a Maltese Cross and an emblem of the Knights Templar—"

"Are we avoiding the wall?" Ed interrupts. No need to answer.

Primo's men are loading the Ape (pronounced AH-pay, which means "bee," and is a useful small vehicle, something like a covered scooter with a pick-up bed behind it). They've neatly stacked the fallen stones along with bags of cement. A new bottom row already is in place, boulders with cuneal openings for water to escape. Up top, we find they've dug trenches and laid pipes from the hillside to the terrace edge. I point my two forefingers to the ground. "Let it not happen here. Again." Such a useful gesture.

The streams now have channels, creating several waterfalls over the edge. We squish up to our ankles. *"Tutto bagnato,"* Primo says, all wet. Everyone passing stops to view the disaster. A woman tells us that many years ago a small child fell in a well here and drowned, that her cries can be heard at night in the house. This news is unsettling. "That's why the house was abandoned for thirty years. I was afraid to walk by at night when I was a girl."

"We've never heard cries," Ed tells her. I wish she hadn't told us. Now when I'm alone, I'm sure I'll be listening.

When she walks on, Primo says, "All old houses are haunted." He shrugs, turns out both hands. "Spooks do nothing. Water is what to worry about."

In the night I wake up but all's quiet except for the little Niagaras plummeting into the ditch.

Sfuso: Loose Wine

GITA, ONE OF MY FAVORITE WORDS, A LITTLE trip. This morning, I expected Ed to head to the olive terraces with his hoe but instead, he looked up from Burton Anderson's *The Wine Atlas of Italy*, which he often reads at breakfast, and said, "Let's go to Montepulciano. Our wine supply is getting low."

"Great. I want to go to the garden center there to buy plumbago to plant under the hazelnut tree. And we can pick up fresh ricotta at a farm."

Isn't this what we came to Italy for? Sometimes, in the long restoration, I've thought that I came to Italy only to rip ivy from walls and refinish floors. But now that the main projects are over, the house is—well, not finished, but at least looking more like home.

We will restock our *sfuso,* loose wine. Many vineyards produce a house wine for themselves, their friends, and local customers. Most Tuscans don't drink bottled wine on an everyday basis; either they make their own, they know someone who does, or they buy *sfuso.* In preparation, Ed washes out our enormous green glass demijohn and also our shiny, stainless steel container with a red spigot, an innovation that threatens to replace the traditional demijohns.

To protect wine from air after the demijohn is filled, we learned to pour a splash of olive oil on top, forming a seal, then jam in a fist-sized cork. The new canister has a flat lid which floats on top of the wine. A drizzle of neutral oil is poured around the tiny space between the lid and the side of the canister. A second tight lid then goes on top. As you open the spigot at the bottom and pour your wine into a pitcher, the lid and sealing oil lower too, keeping the seal intact.

When families have seven or eight demijohns, they usually store them in a special cool room, a *cantina,* then uncork each demijohn as they need wine. We've done that, hoisted the demijohn to a table and tipped it, filling old wine bottles through a funnel, then sealed our twenty or so bottles with olive oil. We became adept at tossing off the oil with a jerk when we opened a bottle. But always a few drops floated on the surface. Already, I've consigned two demijohns to decorative functions in corners of rooms. We found our three abandoned by the recycle bin; someone else had given up. But how could they throw the bottles away? I love the curvaceous, globular, pregnant shape and the green glass with bubbles trapped inside. We scrubbed them with bottle brushes made for the job and bought new corks. "Do we really want to use the demijohn again?" I venture.

"You're right. But don't tell the men." He means, of course, Anselmo, Beppe, and Francesco, who scorn any change regarding olives or wine. We load two twenty-liter plastic jugs into the trunk—handy for transporting, but we must transfer the wine into the canister as soon as we come home. A plastic taste can seep quickly into wine.

It's great being a tourist. Guidebook and camera in my bag, a bottle of water in the car, the map spread out on my knees—what could be finer?

The road from Cortona to Montepulciano, one of my favorites, levels from terraced olive groves to luxive, undulating hills, brilliant with golden wheels of wheat in summer, and now in spring, bright green with cover crops and long grasses. I can almost see the July fields in bloom with *girasoli,* giant sunflowers, the hallelujah chorus of crops. Today, lambs are out. The new ones look whiffey on their faltering legs, while those just older cavort about the mothers' udders. This is the sweetest countryside I know. Only occasional blasts of pig barn odors remind me that this is not paradise. In shadowed dips of the hills, shaggy flocks sleep in big white clumps. Wheat fields, fruit orchards, and olives, perfectly cared for inch by inch—all gradually give way to the vineyards of Vino Nobile of Montepulciano.

Chianti, Brunello, and Vino Nobile, the three greatest wines of Tuscany, share a characteristic full-bodied, essential grape taste. Beyond that, Tuscans can discuss endless shades of difference far into the night. Since production of Vino Nobile began in the 1300s, they've had a long time to get it just right. The name of the Tuscan grape, Sangiovese, suggests much older wine production; the etymology is from *sanguis,* Latin for "blood," and from Jove—blood of Jove. The local strain of Sangiovese is called "Prugnolo Gentile," nice little plums.

We turn into a long alley of lofty cypresses lining a *strada bianca,* a white road tunneling under the trees. We drive through bolts of pale green light angling down through gaps between trees. Ed only nods when I remember a line from Octavio Paz, "Light is time thinking about itself." It seems true to me on one level and not on another. The Avignonesi vineyards surround one of those sublime properties that set me to dreaming of living another life in an earlier time. The villa, the family chapel, the noble outbuildings—I'm in a heavy linen dress in 1780, sweeping across the courtyard, a white pitcher and a ring of iron keys in my hands. Whether I'm the contessa of this *fattoria* or the maid, I don't know but I have a flash of my steps years ago, the outline of my shadow on the stones.

Avignonesi's winemaker, Paolo Trappolini, a startlingly good-looking man who looks like a Raphael portrait of himself, tells us about the experiments at the vineyard. "I've been searching out almost-extinct rootstock around Tuscany and saving old strains." We walk out in the vineyard and he shows us new bushy vines planted in the *"settonce"* pattern, a Latin way of placing one vine in the center of a hexagon of other plants. He points uphill at a spiraling planting pattern, *la vigna tonda,* the round vineyard. "This also is an experiment in using different densities to see the effect on wine quantity and quality." He shows us the aging rooms, some of which are covered in thick, gray mold, and the *vin santo* room, deliriously perfumed with smoky, woody scents.

Avignonesi makes many fine wines, which can be tasted here or in their Palazzo Avignonesi in the center of Montepulciano. Ed is especially interested in their *vin santo,* the smooth, nutty wine sipped with *biscotti* after dinner. In homes, at all hours, we've been offered *vin santo,* have had *vin santo* forced on us. It's ready, in every cupboard, and you must try it because it's home-made. Avignonesi's is special, one of Italy's finest. We are able to buy only one bottle; their limited quantity has been sold. Someone has given us two venerable bottles of *vin santo,* a 1953 and a 1962 Ricasoli, bought in New York and now transported back to their place of origin. Anselmo also has given us a bottle of his own. With the precious Avignonesi, we'll invite friends for a tasting after a big feast one summer night.

Next is Tenuta Trerose. Most of their vineyards are planted the usual way, in staked rows, but a large field is planted as a low arbor, the Etruscan style of planting. The offices are in a modern building behind a villa in a cypress grove. A young man, surprised to see visitors, gives us a price list and shows us their wines in a conference room. Ed, having consulted the most recent *Vini d'Italia,* his trusty yearly guide, selects a case of Salterio Chardonnay and a mixed case of reds. We follow the man out onto a catwalk overlooking a warehouse of stainless steel tanks, some oak barrels, and cases and cases of wine. He shouts, and a woman appears from behind boxes. She starts to put together our cases, leaping, as gracefully as a lynx, over and on stacks of boxes.

Inconspicuous yellow signs point the way to vineyards—Fassato, Massimo Romeo, Villa S. Anna (produced by women), Fattoria del Cerro, Terre di Bindella, Podere Il Macchione, Valdipiatta. We know the names, having popped many a cork from their heroic wines. We're headed to Poliziano for our *sfuso.* Ed waves to someone in a field, who meets us in their warehouse. "The best *sfuso* in a decade," he tells us, as he sets out two glasses on a stack of wine boxes. Even at 11 A.M., we're pleased by the hearty red color and the light hint of strawberries in the taste and, what, oh, almost a fragrance of mimosa. We've found our house wine. He fills our jugs from a hose attached to an enormous vat. By law he must seal the jugs and dutifully record our names in his computer. As he pulls up Ed's name, he sees we've been here before. "Americans like our wine, no?" he asks, so we answer yes, for all Americans. Ed wedges the tanks behind the seat, hoping they won't leak as we negotiate the unpaved roads.

~~~

The anguine town of Montepulciano stretches and winds as though it were following a river but it climbs a long ridge instead. Henry James's impression, a view caught between arcades, was of "some big battered, blistered, overladen, over-masted ship, swimming in a violet sea." Tuscan hilltowns often give one the sense of an immense ship sailing above a plain.

On the roof across from Sant'Agostino, an iron *pulcinella* has hit the clock with his hammer to mark all the hours since the 1600s. I stop to buy candles in a small shop. There, among the potholders, key rings, mats, and corkscrews, I find a dim opening into an Etruscan tomb! "Oh yes," the owner says as he flicks on spotlights, "many store owners find these surprises when they renovate." He leads us over to a glass-covered opening in the front of the shop and points. We look down into a deep cistern hollowed from stone. He shrugs. "The roof drained here so they always had water."

"When?" Ed asks.

The owner lights a cigarette and blows smoke against the window. "The middle ages, possibly earlier." We're always amazed by how casually Italians accept their coexistence with such remains of the past.

The street up to the *centro storico,* historic center, jogs off the main shopping street so that the *piazza* is somewhat removed from the bustle of daily shopping. The unfinished front of the massive church adds to the abandoned feeling. A sheepdog on the steps is the most alert being in the *piazza.* We don't go in this time, but, walking by, I imagine inside the polyptych altarpiece by Taddeo di Bartolo, where Mary is dying in one panel, then surrounded by lovely angels while being swooped into heaven, with apostles weeping down on earth. White plastic *caffè* chairs lean onto their tables in one corner of the *piazza.* We have the whole grand, majestic square to ourselves. We look down into the bottomless well, presided over by two stone lions and two griffins. It must have been a pleasure to shoulder your jug and go to the town well to meet your friends and haul up pure water.

In the fine *palazzi,* several vineyards have tasting rooms. Inside Poliziano's, there's a portrait of the Renaissance poet for whom this distinguished vineyard is named. The woman who pours liberal tastes highly recommends two of their *reserve* wines and she is right. Three of their wines are named for poems of Poliziano's: Le Stanze, Ambrae, and Elegia. Stanzas and Elegy we understand but what does the white wine's name, *"ambrae,"* mean? She pauses then shakes her head. Finally she waves her hands, smiles, *"Solo ambrae, ambrae."* She gestures everywhere. Ambiance is my best guess. We buy several *reserve* and the poet's wines.

As a poet, Poliziano made it big in Montepulciano. A bar on the main street is named for him, too, though the decor is strictly nineteenth century instead of the poet's period. Beyond the curved marble bar are two rooms of dark wood and William Morris–style wallpaper with matching upholstered banquettes and proper little round tables, a Victorian tearoom, Italian style. Both rooms open onto the view, framed by flower-filled iron balconies. We have a sandwich and coffee then hurry to the car. The day is slipping away. I stop for a quick look at a church interior I remember, the Chiesa del Gesù, with its small *trompe l'oeil* dome painted to look like an encircling stair rail around another dome. The perspective only makes sense to the eye from the center of the front entrance. From any other, it goes wonky.

The flower nursery takes its name from the massive church, San Biagio, which we skirt quickly in our rush to buy the plumbago before closing. San Biagio is one of my favorite buildings in the world, for its position at the end of a cypress-lined drive, and for its golden stones, which radiate in afternoon sun, casting a soft flush on the faces of those looking up at the austere planes of the building. If you sit on one of the ledges around the base, the light pours over you, while also seeming to seep into your back from the walls. A walk around the building, inside the warm halo surrounding it, gives me a sense of well-being. As we wind around San Biagio on the road going down, we see the church from changing angles.

We find an apricot bougainvillea to replace one that froze, two plumbagos promising soft blue clusters of bloom under the trees, and a new rose, Pierre de Ronsard, a climber for a stone wall. A French poet to join Poliziano in the car.

"Oh, no." Ed hits his fist on the steering wheel.

"What?"

"We forgot to stop for ricotta." The ricotta farms are near Pienza, miles down the road.

The mingled scents of plants and sloshing wine wash through the car, along with the deep grassy smell of spring rain which has begun to fall as we head toward Cortona.

For dinner tonight, we've stopped at the *rosticceria* and picked up some divine *gnocchi* made from semolina flour. I've made a salad. Ed brings out the Ambrae from Montepulciano and holds it up to the light. *Ambrae* is not in my dictionary. It must be Latin, possibly for amber. I take a sip—maybe it *is* ambiance, the way dew on lilacs and oak leaves might taste. *Wine is light, held together by water.* I wish I'd said that, but Galileo did.

Following Spring: The Palms of Sicily

I'M NOT OFF THE PLANE IN PALERMO FIVE
minutes before I have an *arancino* in my hand, ready to
taste *the* signature dish of Sicily. Ed has gone to find the
rental car office and I head to the bar right in the center of the airport. There they are, a line of the deep-fried *risotto*
balls formed into the size and shape of oranges. "What's inside?"
I ask.

A man with those amazing black, Sicilian deep-as-wells eyes
points to the round ones. *"Ragù, signora.* And the oval ones—
besciamella e prosciutto." His eyes fascinate me as much as the
arancini. All through the airport I've seen the same Byzantine,
hidden, historical eyes. At the bar, savoring the crisp creamy texture of the rice, I'm watching a parade of these intensely Italian-
looking Italians. Women with gobs of dark curls cascading and
flowing, slender men who seem to glide instead of walk. Tiny
girls with miniature gobs of the same dark curls, and old men
formed by stoop labor, carrying their hats in their hands.
Crowds surge to meet planes coming in from Rome, which is

only an hour away. They're all waving and shouting greetings to deplaning Sicilians who probably have been gone a few days, judging from their carry-on bags. Ed comes back, bearing keys. He, too, polishes off an *arancino* and orders an espresso. He looks startled when he sees how small it is, barely a spoonful, with rich *crema*. One taste and he's transported.

The waiter sees his surprise. He's about 5'3". He looks up at Ed, almost a foot taller. "The farther south you go, *signore,* the smaller and the stronger."

Ed laughs, *"È fantastico."* He wheels our bag to the green Fiat and zooms out of the garage.

Along the coastal road to Palermo, we glimpse the sea and cubical North African–style houses in a rocky landscape. The instant we enter Palermo, we're in wild traffic, careening traffic, traffic moving too fast for us to locate where we are going. Lanes disappear, avenue names keep changing, we turn and turn in mazes of one-way streets. "That *barista* should have said 'smaller, stronger, and *faster,*'" Ed shouts. At a light, he rolls down the window and calls desperately to a man revving his motorcycle in anticipation of the green, *"Per favore,* which way to Hotel Villa Igiea?"

"Follow me," he shouts back and he's off, spiraling among cars and glancing back now and then to see if we're behind him. Somehow we are. Ed seems to be in his wake, just going. At highway speeds on city streets, cars are neck-and-neck. On all four sides, we are two inches from other bite-sized cars. If someone braked, we'd be in a hundred-car pile-up. But no one brakes. At an intersection, the motorcyclist points to the left then waves. He swerves right so hard his ear almost touches the ground. We're tossed into a roundabout, spun, and emptied suddenly onto a quiet street. And there's the hotel. We creep into the parking lot and stop.

"Let's don't get in this car again until we leave. That was absolutely the worst."

"Suits me," Ed agrees. He's still gripping the wheel. "Let's take taxis. Everywhere. This is more like the running of the bulls than driving." We grab our bag, lock the Fiat, and don't look at the car again until we check out.

~

Because we have ended up with "the most beautiful room in Palermo," according to the manager, I am ready to fill the tub with bubbles, open the minibar for cold water, and recuperate. When the weather turned on us in Tuscany, we decided to follow spring south. The delicious days of early March turned stormy and freezing rain hit the windows. Primo managed to stabilize our sliding hillside wall, and now has moved his men to an indoor job in town until the ground dries. We were toasting in front of the fire when Ed said, "I bet it's already warm in Sicily. Wouldn't it be fun just to take off—go tomorrow?"

I looked up from my book. "Tomorrow?"

"It's close, really. Drive to Florence, quick flight—we'll be there in three hours total, door-to-door. It's no more than going to Seattle from San Francisco."

"I've never been to Seattle."

"That's beside the point. We'll go to Seattle. But the forecast here is for rain all week. Look at the sun all over Sicily." He showed me the weather report in the newspaper, with gray slants covering central Italy and yellow smiley faces dotting Sicily.

"But I have Fear of Palermo. What if we get caught in Mafia crossfire at a funeral and end up on the evening news?"

"We won't be going to any funerals. We don't even know anyone in Sicily. The Mafia is not interested in us."

"Well," I paused for about fifteen seconds, "let's pack."

~

A day later, this corner room has four sets of immense doors opening onto a balcony. Balmy air, palms, and blue, blue, blue

33

water. The twenty-foot ceilings match the grand scale of the Napoleonic furniture. Tile floors, a big sleigh bed—a fabulous room, totally unlike the first one we were shown in another wing of the building. That one was depressingly dark with a carpet I did not want my feet to touch. The bellman opened the shutters to a view of a wall. "No palms," I said.

"Here there is no palm," he agreed.

I loathe complaining and Ed hates it more than I, but after an hour we went downstairs and I asked for the manager. "The room we have is not beautiful. In such a lovely hotel, I expected something more. . . . Is there another available? We'd like to see the palm trees."

He looked up our room number and grimaced. "Come with me," he said. Then he took us miles down marble corridors and came to this one. He flung back the draperies, pushed open the doors, and light off the water bounced into the room. *"Ecco, signori, Palermo!"* He showed us an octagonal sitting room with gilt ballroom chairs, as if we should have a chamber music quartet playing while we slept.

"Now I'm happy," I told him.

~

The taxi arrives quickly and we launch into the bumper-car traffic. Yes, it's always like this, the driver tells us. No, there aren't many accidents. Why? He shrugs, everybody is used to it. We sit back, and he's right, we begin to feel the double-time rhythm of driving here. Drivers look alert, as though engaging in a contact sport. He drops us in the center near an esplanade closed to traffic. Out of the street's chaos, we're greeted by the scent of flowers. Vendors are selling freesias in all the Easter colors, purple, yellow, and white. Instead of the puny bouquets I buy at home, these are sold in armfuls, wrapped in a ruff of brazen pink foil and trailing ribbons.

Not wanting to take time for lunch, we sample *sfincione,* pizza with big bread crumbs on top, then keep going—palms, outdoor tables filled with people, small shops of luxurious bags and shoes, waiters with trays aloft carrying pastries and espresso.

Pastries! Every *pasticceria* displays an astonishing variety. We're used to drier Tuscan pastries; these are mounded with cream. A woman arranges her shop window with realistic marzipan pineapples, bananas, prickly pears, lemons, cherries, and, for the Easter season, lambs complete with curls. Inside, her cases display almond cakes, wild strawberry tarts, *biscotti,* and, of course, *cannoli,* but in all sizes, from thumb-sized to a giant as large as a leg of lamb. Two bakers pause in the kitchen doorway and all the customers step back as they gingerly balance and step. They bring out a three-foot tree made from small *cannoli,* a stiff pyramid like a French *croquembouche* at Christmas. S*fince,* rice fritters filled with ricotta, cinnamon, candied oranges or strawberries, honor San Giuseppe, whose *onomastico,* name day, is March 19, when Italians also celebrate Father's Day.

The freezers glow with *sorbetti*—pistachio, lemon, watermelon, cinnamon, jasmine, almond, as well as the usual fruits. Most children seem to prefer *gelato,* not in a cup or cone, but stuffed inside a brioche. Just looking at the almond cake is almost enough satisfaction, but instead we split one of the crisp *cannoli* lined with chocolate and heavenly, creamy ricotta. No harm done; we're planning to walk for the rest of the afternoon.

On the first day in a new place, it's good to wander, absorb colors, textures, and scents, see who lives here, and find the rhythm of the day. We'll crank into tourist mode later, making sure we don't miss the great sights. Dazed by actually coming to Palermo, by the flight, the espresso, and the day, we just take the appealing street, turning back if it begins to look dicey. Palms are everywhere. I wish I could take one back to Bramasole to replace the one December's freeze probably killed. Not only do I love palms because they mean tropical air, I love the image Wallace Stevens made: "the palm at the end of the mind." To imagine the end of the mind and to see not a blank wall or a roadblock or an abyss but a tall swaying palm seems felicitous to me.

We come upon a botanical park, dusty and empty except for cacti, carob, mulberry, agave, and shrubs with primitive, broad leaves. The palm looks native but was brought by Arabs in the ninth century, along with their fountains, spices, arabesques, ice cream, mosaics, and domes. Palms and domes—gold, pomegranate, aqua, verdigris—characterize Palermo. How bold to color the five domes of San Giovanni degli Eremiti a burnt red. Inside, aromatic citrus blossoms and jasmine suffuse a cloister garden, a secretive respite from the tortured road outside.

On the map, we see that the Palazzo dei Normanni is nearby and decide to go in its famous Cappella Palatina today. The subjects of the mosaics, the guidebook says, seem to have been chosen with reference to the Holy Spirit and the theology of light. I'm intrigued, since these two concepts seem identical in my mind.

Originally built by those busy Arabs in the ninth century, the palace was expanded by the Normans in the twelfth century and established as the residence for their kings. Later residents and royalty left their bits and pieces, and today the styles have so long overlapped that the architecture simply looks like itself. Byzantine Greeks began the mosaic decoration in the twelfth century. Tessera by tessera, it must have taken them forever; every Bible story I ever heard glitters around this room. The floors, too, are mosaic or inlaid marble in designs like Oriental rugs.

The Holy Spirit and the theology of light are only a layer. A lot is going on. It's like Palermo—each square inch occupied with life. I love the word "tesserae." It seems to shower silver and gold on its own. There's the whole Adam and Eve saga, the flood, there's Jacob wrestling with the angel, and in the dome and apse, Christ. In the dome he's surrounded by foreshortened angels, each in intricate clothes. Christ offers a blessing in the apse. In both mosaics, he has long, long fingers. Looking through my opera glasses, I focus for a long time on his right hand, just this one small moment in the entire chapel—the hand held up, the thumb holding down the next-to-last finger, the other three straight, all formed with delicacy and subtle coloration. Late afternoon sun has a weak hold on the walls but still the gold around him sings with burnished amber light.

The rest of the Palazzo is closed. Walking back toward the center of Palermo, we pass rubble-filled lots still unrestored since World War II bombings. We look in open storefronts, where hideous junk is sold, and step off crowded sidewalks with fry-stations selling chickpea fritters. People are out gathering last-minute food for dinner. About their business, the people look contained, silent, often weary, but when they meet an acquaintance their faces break into vibrant expression. In the taxi back to the hotel, we hardly notice the near-death encounters.

The first two restaurants Ed selects for dinner are nixed by the hotel desk clerk. Dangerous areas, he tells us, making the motion of someone slicing a throat. He takes a ballpoint and scribbles out whole areas of our map. "What about this one?" Ed asks, pointing in our Italian restaurant guide to the highly regarded, unpronounceable *N'grasciata*. "And what does that mean?"

"In local dialect that means 'dirty' but don't be alarmed, just a way of speaking."

Speaking of what? I think. Dirty means dirty. "Your highest recommendation?"

"*Sì*. Authentic. They have their own fishing boat. You won't see tourists there. I will call and they will expect you."

We're dropped off at a plain place which is even plainer

inside. No tablecloths, a TV somewhere, no decor, no menu, harsh lighting, and the buzz of bugs hitting the zapper. The waiter starts bringing out the food. I'm crazy about the *panelli,* chickpea fritters, and the platter of fried artichokes. Then comes pasta with *pomarola,* that intense, decocted tomato sauce, and baby octopus. I'm not so sure about this dish. I chew for a long time. The platter comes round again and Ed has more. We're offered another pasta, this one *bucatini* with sardines, currants, and fennel. The next dish is a grilled *orata,* which my dictionary translates as "gilthead," surrounded by fried *frutti di mare*—just various fish. I'm slowing down. I like a little bit of fish, not a lot. Ed loves anything that comes from the sea and is so obviously relishing the food that the waiter starts to hover, commenting on each morsel. He's pouring wine to the brim of the glass. His dolorous eyes look like Jesus' in the mosaic dome. His long fingers have tufts of black curly hair on each digit, and a mat of hair escapes the collar of his shirt. He has the long, four-inch-wide face I associate with newspaper photos of hijackers.

I revive briefly for the spicy *melanzane*—here's a touch of the Arabic, eggplant with cinnamon and pine nuts—but balk at the appearance of the stuffed squid (all those suction cups on the arms) and the sea bream sausage. Is he bringing us everything in the kitchen? Next comes a plate of fried potatoes. *"Signora,"* our waiter says. *"Signora."* He can't believe that I have stopped eating. He pulls up a chair and sits down. "You must."

I smile and shake my head. Impossible. He rolls those dolorous eyes to heaven. *"Ho paura,"* I'm afraid, I try to joke, pointing at the squid. He takes me literally and eats a bite himself to prove there's no cause for alarm. Still, I shake my head no. He takes my fork, gently grabs a handful of my hair, and starts to feed me. I am so astonished I open my mouth and eat. I really hate the texture, like tenderized erasers.

As an afterthought, he brings out *involtini,* veal rolled around a layer of herbs and cheese, but even Ed has stopped by now.

He's thanking the waiter. "The best fish in Palermo," he tells him.

"How do you know?" I ask him on the way out. The waiter bares his teeth in a big grin. No, he looks more like a wolf than Jesus.

"It had to be. That was a down-home place."

~

We're out early. In the Vucciria quarter, the market is stupendous. I've been to markets in France, Spain, Peru, San Francisco, all over Italy. *This* is the market. For the senses, ecstasy and assault. Because Palm Sunday is this weekend, perhaps it is more of an assault than usual. Lines of lambs, gutted and dripping, eyeballs bulging, hang by their feet. Their little hooves and tails look so sad. Their little guts look so horrifying. The rainbows of shining fish on ice, the mounds of shrimp still wiggling their antennae, painted carts of lemons, jewel-colored candied fruits, bins of olives, nuts, seeds—everything is presided over by dealers who shout, sing, cajole, joke, curse, barter, badger. They're loud and raucous. Could it be true, as I've read, that the Mafia runs the heroin trade out of here? A vendor holds out a basket of eels that look like live sterling silver. He gyrates his hips to emphasize their movement. This feels more like a carnival than the decorous Tuscan markets we're used to. I wish for a kitchen so I could gather some of the lustrous eggplants and clumps of field greens. My stomach is growling so loud it sounds like a tiny horse neighing. Cooks here are in paradise. I'll never eat lamb again.

Ed refuses to go to the Catacombe dei Cappuccini, where 8,000 desiccated corpses are on exhibit. I have already bought a postcard of a red-haired girl under glass for decades, her delicate nostrils still stuffed with cotton, a ribbon in her hair. We have visited the same sort of place in Guanajuato, Mexico. I was fascinated; he was revolted. We decide on the Museo Archeologico, and we don't come out until it closes. I find this one of the best museums I've ever visited—so much of what interests me is gathered in this old convent. Phoenician anchors and amphoras dredged from the sea lie around the courtyard. Mysterious stelae painted with portraits were found on ancient grave sites in Marsala. Etruscan treasures, some with traces of paint, from the tombs at Chiusi, near us in Tuscany, somehow have ended up in Sicily. Here we get to see the sixth- and fifth-century B.C. metopes (panels of the temple frieze) removed from the Greek site at Selinunte, one of the most important ruins on the island. We find Demeter, the Cretan bull; Perseus, Hercules, and Athena star in various triumphs. Hera marries Zeus, and Actaeon becomes a stag. Seeing the familiar mythic players as they actually were on temples brings the legends closer to my imagination. These images come from the time when they were real to people, not just characters from the pages of a history of myth—an astounding telescoping of distance. The enormous scale, too, prepares us for the dimensions of the ruins we'll see.

We can't look at all 12,000 of the votive figures also excavated at Selinunte but we look until we can't look anymore. That only leaves rooms and rooms of Roman sculpture, Greek vases, and more and more. We meander through, stopped by painted fragments from Pompei, a fantastic third-century B.C. bronze ram, and a blur of mosaic pavements. Then, out. Onto the plain sidewalk, dazed and dazzled by what we've seen.

All of Palermo is a grand feast. Not an easy city but a challenging one. You keep your wits about you; you're not lulled or allowed to be passive. It's a place to encounter, which makes it memorable. We spend three days among the Palermitani, engrossed in their street life, saturated by their Sicilian Baroque, which out-Baroques Baroque, stiff-necked from looking up into domes. Does the baby in the womb experience light, the way I can see through my hand held to a strong light? If so, to the emerging infant, perhaps the last blurred look back from the birth canal resembles the inside of the bricked Moorish dome at San Cataldo, a concentric expansion of pale light.

The surprise of Palermo was Sicily's fling with Art Nouveau, called "Liberty" in Italy. The metal kiosks around the Quattro Canti, the main intersection at the town center, had all the charm of the famous metro signs in Paris. Our hotel was decorated with extensive paintings by Ernesto Basile, who also finished the decoration of the Teatro Massimo, designed by his father, which recently reopened after over twenty years in restoration. What a father and son duo. Spotting their sources in the Byzantine, Moorish, and Greek motifs around town was an added pleasure. A frustration was how many places were closed. No sign, just closed.

As the freesias begin to wilt in our room, we decide to start our tour of the island tomorrow morning. We have a glass of blood orange juice on our balcony. All we can hear is the rattle of palms below us in the breeze and the jingle of rigging on the sailboats in the bay. "Do you want to come back?" I ask.

"Yes. We haven't seen whole areas of Palermo."

"It's hard to get a sense of the place. So layered, so crude, so complex—a daunting city."

"My core impression is of a chaos everyone here has learned how to survive."

"I don't think I could live here. Besides the horror of the Mafia, I'd never be able to drive anywhere." I don't even like to drive the East Bay freeways.

"Yes, you would. You'd get a used mini-car and if you got a few dents a day you wouldn't care."

"What about dents in my head?" Chaos, I think. Yes, it's here. But I suddenly remember a story a woman I met in Milwaukee   41 told me about someone she knew. "This Midwestern soldier in World War II was on a ship which was bombed by retreating Germans in the harbor of Palermo," I tell Ed. "He survived even though almost everyone else was killed: He swam to shore and was stranded here. I think the Germans were retreating by then. One night he went to the opera—he'd never been before. At the end, he was so moved by the music he began to cry. All the horrors caught up with him. He just stood there during the applause and afterwards, openly crying. The audience started to file out. A man looked at him, paused, and touched him on the head, as though he were bestowing a benediction. As all the people passed him, each one stopped and touched him on the head."

"That's one of the best things I've ever heard. So that's Palermo."

~

Each succeeding conqueror of Sicily—Greeks, Carthaginians, Romans, Arabs, Normans, and all the rest—must have brought pocketfuls of wildflower seeds. The countryside in *primavera* is solidly in flower, rivers of yellow, purple cascading around rocks, roadsides lined with tiny blue-eyed blooms, and almond orchards whose long grasses are overtaken by white daisies. We made an easy exit, considering. We were only lost half an hour. Even though Ed was intimidated by traffic in Palermo, once we were out on the open road, I noticed his new skills, learned from the back seat of the taxis. He's relaxing into the concept that lanes do not exist much; the road is an open field for getting where you're going. The white line is the center of an imaginary lane to be used as needed.

Driving along the coast and meandering inland, the Mar Tirreno seven shades of blue out one window, and rampantly flowering hills out the other, it is easy to see why all those con-

quering hordes wanted this island. The landscape is everywhere
various or dramatic. Anytime the perfume of orange and lemon
groves wafts in the window, the human body has to feel suffused
with a languorous well-being.

Soon we come to the turnoff for Segesta, first of the many
Greek temples we hope to see in Sicily—the number rivals
Greece itself. The Doric temple rises, just off the highway,
where it has loomed on the hillside since the fifth century B.C.,
which is close to forever. Along the climbing path, we see
gigantic fennel growing, ten feet, even more. I always wondered
how Prometheus took fire back to the Greeks in a fennel stalk.
In these you could stash quite a few coals. In the process, maybe
he invented grilled fennel.

The guidebook says of Segesta: "It is peripteral and hexastyle
with 36 unfluted columns (9 m high, 2 m wide at base) on a
stylobate 58 m by 23 m. The high entablature and the pedi-
ments are intact. The bosses used for maneuvering the blocks
of the stylobate into position remain. Refinements include the
curvature of the entablature and the abaci." Well, yes, but it's
beautiful.

So is the equally ancient theater a short hike away. Greece
was the first country I ever wanted to see. My longing was produced by a total immersion in Lord Byron when I was a senior
in high school. In college, my friend Rena and I took a course
in Greek drama. We wrote for brochures from Greek freighters
and decided to drop out and see the world. We wanted to book
passage on the Hellenic Destiny, until our parents said absolutely
not. I've never yet been to Greece. A few years ago I saw the
magnificent temples at Paestum in the south of Italy and the
longing was reawakened. "The mountains look on Marathon /
and Marathon looks on the sea / and musing there an hour
alone, / I dreamed that Greece might still be free." Something
like that—it seems to scan into iambic tetrameter.

Like Paestum, Segesta is stripped down to pure silence, its   43 skeletal purity etched against the sky. No one is here. We're alone with history and swallows swooping from their nests.

~

We check into a country inn with a damp bed where we huddle during siesta. The young spring sun has not yet penetrated these walls. A charming courtyard with luxuriant sage and rosemary, and the room with colorful handmade rugs and iron bed do not compensate. Nor does the view of the sea. It's freezing. A weak square of sunlight reaches halfway across the floor. Bedside lamps with the wattage of Christmas tree bulbs preclude reading. At four, we're back in the car heading for Erice, a craggy medieval town, whose early name was Eryx. Where is everyone? We're alone, as we were at Segesta. Even the well-known pastry shop is empty, except for a languid clerk who seems intent on his cigarette. The almond cake and thick lemon pie topped with roasted almonds sustain Sicily's reputation for sublime pastries. I wish I could take the rest of that lemon pie with me; with the local almonds on top, it's better than my grandmother's Deep South recipe. Even though Erice is small, the village feels disorienting. We look in the few shops, and walk the perimeter. All the churches are closed. We know better than to judge the life of an Italian town by one visit. At a different time on a different day, Erice may be lively. Places have their odd closing days, their individual rhythms.

Finally the restaurants open. This early, we're alone. Ah, chickpea fritters again. We order *cuscus alla Trapanese,* couscous cooked with fish broth in the North African–influenced style of nearby Trapani. The waiter recommends *spigola al sale,* sea bass in a salt crust, a dish I sometimes make at home. Under his arm, he brings a bottle of Còthon, a red wine of Marsala, and holds out the platter with the encased fish on a bed of fennel leaves.

After dinner we emerge and find that we have no idea where

we left the car. We cross, recross the town, enter a dark park, go down- and uphill. The streets shine like polished pewter in the moonlight. No one is out. Where is the restaurant? Eerie Erice.

Back at our room, the sheets are cold again. I open my notebook and write: Erice—radio towers, unusual stone streets. Then I fall asleep.

We're out of that damp *tomba;* this will be an all-Greek day. Selinunte, more ruined than Segesta, spreads from a broad hilltop down to the sea. The name Selinunte, Ed reads, comes from the Greek word for wild celery. Hundreds of colossal broken columns fill one area. Fallen, lying in pieces, they look even more massive. We take a walk downhill toward the ruins on the edge of the sea. This approach shows us the outline of the sixth-century B.C. golden columns against blue water. In soft air, we sit on a rock and stare at surely one of the great classical scenes in the universe. The names "Temples C, G, E" seem ludicrous. Again, we are alone at the site. Having seen the metope in Palermo, it's easy to imagine them positioned around the top but not easy to imagine how the Greeks managed to get them up there.

~

Fancy thoughts of paradisiacal spring don't last long. Soon the scene out the car window changes to fields totally encased in hideous plastic. Growing vegetables under plastic-covered hoops surely extends the growing season and improves farm economy, but it blights the landscape. The growers have been thorough— as far as you can see, the sheen of plastic. No vegetable is as tortured and managed as the tomato. Those grown under plastic look better than they taste. Only direct sun infuses tomatoes with flavor, awakens the full taste. Good Sicilian cooks must wait for summer to make their tomato sauce.

Many of the towns we dip into are hideous. A fifty-year ban

on cement should be imposed. Historic centers are often smothered by postwar concrete, mainly in the form of apartment towers, which form instant slums. The oil and chemical plants don't add to the *bellezza* either. Much of the coast we pass is ruined—everywhere, the phenomenon of buildings started then abandoned halfway along. Plenty of money must be paid for start-up and somehow the project dissolves. Too many payoffs?

Fear in the air probably stops most people from having normal initiative; better to lie low. Having only been here a few days, I feel waves of rage about the Mafia. I can't imagine what it must be like actually to *live* under the pall of their serious evil. I never hear the word "Mafia" from anyone; as a tourist, I wouldn't. Even leading questions are routed around so that answers don't have to involve speculations. Small rocks on Mars can be inspected. Babies can be made in glass dishes. I don't understand why the Mafia can't be stopped.

Imagine Sicily without the Mafia, imagine the spirits of the people lifting. . . .

~

I'm glad I don't have to take a test on Agrigento. For an American used to a comparatively straightforward history, all the Italian past seems hopelessly convoluted. The saga of the Greek ruins multiplies this complexity. Agrigento, since its Greek founding in the sixth century B.C., has been tossed among Carthaginians, Romans, Swabians, Arabians, Bourbons, and Spaniards. Subjected to a name change during Mussolini's zeal to Italianize all things, the old name Akragas became Agrigento. I've seen the same zeal on the plaque outside where John Keats lived in Rome, cut off from his love and dying from tuberculosis. He's called Giovanni Keats, which somehow makes him seem more vulnerable than ever.

Akragas / Agrigento was Luigi Pirandello's birthplace. Travelling in Sicily casts his plays and stories, with their quirky sense of reality, in quite a natural light. The coexistence of the Greek ruins, the contemporary ruins, the tentacles of the Mafia, and the mundane day-to-day would skew my sense of character and place, too. The sun, Pirandello wrote, can break stones. Even in March, we feel the driving force on our heads as we walk in the Valley of the Temples.

All over a valley of almond trees and wildflowers stands a mind-boggling array of remains from an ancient town, from temples to sewer pipes. You could stay for days and not see everything. Unlike other sites, this one is quite populated with visitors. The Temple of Concordia is the best-preserved temple we've seen. Patch up the roof and the populace could commune with Castor and Pollux, to whom it probably was dedicated.

Five days ago I knew almost nothing about these ruins. Now the ancient dust covers my feet through my sandals; I have seen the unlikely survival of these buildings through rolls and rolls of time. The temples, men selling woven palm fronds for Palm Sunday, schoolchildren hiding among the columns, awed travellers like us with dripping *gelato*—all under the intense Sicilian sky. I'm thrilled. Just as I think that, Ed says, "This is the thrill of a lifetime."

Still, at dinner, we find that one temple is beginning to fade into another. Maybe we've seen enough of Agrigento this time.

By the time we're back at the hotel, I've begun to descend into what I've come to call traveller's melancholy, a profound displacement that occasionally seizes me for a few hours when I am in a foreign country. The pleasure of being the observer suddenly flips over into a disembodied anxiety. During its grip, I go silent. I dwell on the fact that most of those I love have no idea where I am and my absence among them is unremarkable; they continue their days indifferent to the lack of my presence. Then an immense longing for home comes over me. I imagine my bed with a stack of books—probably travel books—on the table, the combed afternoon sunlight coming through the curved windows, my cat Sister leaping up with her claws catching the yellow blanket. Why am I here where I don't belong? What is this alien place? I feel I'm in a strange afterlife, a haint blowing with the winds. I suspect the subtext to this displacement is the dread of death. Who and where are you when you are no one?

Downstairs in the hotel courtyard, a wedding dinner is in progress. The shouts, bawdy toasts, and slightly disheveled bride intensify my state. Usually I would savor the position of the almost invisible observer at the window, but tonight I am nothing to them. They belong. I'm a free radical. As the band starts up after a break, two small girls in frilly, silly dresses began to dance together. I could be anywhere on the planet, or not on the planet, and they would dance and dance. *With or without.* The groom would turn over his chair. The grandparents in their stiff country clothes would look as startled. *With or without.* The moon would shed its ancient light on the singular columns scattered over the valley, as it has and will.

Ed already is sleeping. I walk downstairs and watch the party break up. Kisses and embraces. I go in the bar and order a glass of *limoncello,* concentrate hard on the lively citrus taste, conjure to my mind the lovely face of my daughter seven thousand miles from here.

~~~

We drive on in the morning, passing some dire ugliness along the way. Petrochemical—what a hideous word. Poor Gela—I see that it has interesting remains somewhere in this labyrinth but it is so intensely ugly that we speed through. Ed remembers that Aeschylus died here when an eagle flying above him dropped a tortoise on his head. Fate, as in a foretold prediction.

A mythic way to go. I'm sure Pirandello as a child was influenced by this story.

Ragusa—we'll spend the night. This hilltown feels like Sicily as I imagined it—provincial, and so privately itself. Like several other towns in the environs, Ragusa was rebuilt in the Baroque style after the terrible earthquake of 1693. There's an old town and an older town, Ragusa Ibla. By now we just expect to get lost and we do. We hit Ibla at a moment of celebration. How this many cars can squeeze into streets hardly wider than an arm's length, is hilarious. We crawl, turning a dozen times, trying to get out. We glimpse the church of San Giorgio, more fanciful than a wedding cake, which seems to be the focal point of whatever is going on. Is the Saturday before Palm Sunday a special day? Finally, we escape Ibla and find our way to a pleasant hotel in the upper town, which is newer but looks old to us. It's drizzling. We sit in the bar with espresso, looking at books and maps. *Americani* are a novelty here. Two men in suits come up and speak to us, obviously intrigued when we say we're from San Francisco. They want to know if we like Sicily, if we like Ragusa. "*Sì*," we both answer. They insist on buying the coffee.

Walking in the rain, we admire iron balconies and watch the locals dashing into the cathedral for Saturday mass. Surrounding the great carved door are displays of intricately woven palm fronds for sale by boys. Everyone buys one so we do, too. Ed sticks it behind the mirror in our room. Because today is my birthday, we set out for a special restaurant ten or so miles away. Soon we're lost on unmarked roads. The restaurant seems to be an illusion. We turn back and have dinner in a fluorescent-lit pizza place with orange plastic chairs.

Meandering, we stop at a cypress-guarded cemetery near Modica. Extravagant tombs are elaborately carved miniature houses laid along miniature streets. Here's the exuberance of Modica's art of the Baroque in microcosm. Through the grates or gates, little chapels open to linen-draped altars with framed portraits of the dead and potted plants or vases of flowers. At thresholds, a few cats sun themselves on the warmed marble. A woman is scrubbing, as she would her own stoop. With a corner of her apron, she polishes the round photo of a World War I soldier. A girl weeds the hump of earth over a recent grave in the plain old ground. These dead cool off slowly; someone still tends flowers on plots where the inhabitants have lain for fifty years.

Cortona's cemetery, too, reflects the town, although not as grandly. A walled city of the dead situated just below the live city, it glows at night from the votive lights on each grave. Looking down from the Piazza del Duomo, it's hard not to imagine the dead up and about, visiting each other as their relatives still do right up the hill. The dead here probably would want more elaborate theatrical entertainments.

Next on our route, Avola retains some charm. One-room-wide Baroque houses line the streets. Could we take home at least a dozen of the gorgeous children in their white smocks? On the corners men with handheld scales scoop cockles from a mound on the sidewalk. Open trucks selling vegetables attract crowds of women with baskets. We keep turning down tiny roads to the sea. We can't find the beaches we expect—the unspoiled littoral dream of the island's limpid waters—only bleak beach towns, closed and depressing out of season.

It's only in Siracusa that I finally fall in love. In my Greek phase in college, I took Greek and Roman History, Greek and Roman Drama, Greek Etymology. At that point, my grandfather, who was sending me to college, drew a line. "I am not paying for you to stick your head in the clouds. You should get a certificate for teaching so you have something to fall back on." The message being, if your husband—whom you have gone to college to acquire, and no Yankees, please—dies or runs off.

Meanwhile, I was loving Aeschylus, the severe consequences of passion, pure-as-milk marble sculptures, the explorative spirit of the Greeks. Siracusa, therefore, is tremendously exciting to visit. Mighty Siracusa, ancient of ancients. Second to Athens in the classical world. We opt for a super-luxurious hotel on the connecting island of Ortigia, with a room surrounded by views of the water. We're suddenly not tired exactly, but saturated. We spend the afternoon in the huge bed, order coffee sent up, pull back the curtains and watch the fishing boats nosing—isn't that a Greek blue—into the harbor.

After siesta, we find Ortigia in high gear for Easter. Bars display chocolate eggs two feet tall, wrapped in purple cellophane and ribbons. Some are open on one side to reveal a marzipan Christ on the cross. Others have a surprise inside. I'd love to buy marzipan doves, lambs in baskets, chocolate hens. The lambs are like stuffed animals, large, decorated from nose to tail with fanciful marzipan curls. At the Antica Dolceria, they've gone into marzipan frenzy: Noah's ark complete with animals, the Greek temples, olives, pencils. Marzipan—called *pasta reale*—we realize is a serious folk art form. For me, three bites will suffice; maybe you have to have been born in Sicily to be able to eat more.

Ortigia is fantastic. The vague, intuitive sense of oppression I've felt in Sicily entirely lifts. Is the Mafia not in control here? People seem more lighthearted, playful, and swaggering. They look you in the eye, as people do in the rest of Italy. In the late afternoon, we walk all over the small island. It has its own Greek ruins just lying in a grassy plot at an intersection. An inscription carved into steps identifies the site as a temple to Apollo. Dense ficus trees along a walkway bordering the water are home to thousands of birds singing their evening doxology. Views across the water, Baroque iron balconies, Venetian Gothic windows, boarded up *palazzi,* and intricate medieval streets—layers and layers of architecture and time. Suddenly the streets intersect and widen at the Piazza del Duomo. The Baroque facade and entrance of the church in no way prepare you for the stunning surprise inside. Along one wall, the building incorporates a row of twelve majestic columns from the fifth century B.C. Tempio di Atene, Temple of Athena. At evening, spikes of sunlight fall across the *piazza,* lighting the faces of those having an *aperitivo* at outdoor tables. Ordinary people, with the sun, like the sheen of gold mosaics, transforming their faces.

~

Unlike the *Lotophagi*—lotus eaters—Homer wrote about, I have not tasted anything that would make me lose the desire for my native land, not even the tomato sauce, which is the best in the world. The food, everywhere we've eaten, is great, the best. The coffee simply exists in a league by itself. Those who love seafood never will get over Sicilian food. Ed researches restaurants thoroughly before we go somewhere, not wanting to waste a precious night. But tonight we're drawn into a *trattoria* simply because it looks like someone's Sicilian aunt's funky dining room, with painted cupboards, bits of old lace, family photos. We're waved to the last available table. No menu arrives. Carafe wine is plunked down on the table. A woman and her daughter are in animated conversation in the slot of a kitchen. The husband tends the dining room. He's holding a glass of wine aloft as he floats from table to table, taking a few sips as his customers order. Soon a plate of *antipasti* appears— little squid, a vegetable tart, olives. We eat everything then wait. And wait. Ed holds up the small carafe. More wine? The husband is flustered; the wine has not been delivered. He scurries around to other tables and scrounges from half-filled carafes. The diners look somewhat astonished. "Soon it will come," he assures us. Suddenly three men in dark suits arrive and the husband practically bows. They enter the kitchen. The women stand at attention. We can see them from our table, drying their hands on their aprons, rolling their eyes to heaven. Is this a Mafia visit? A demand for payment? But the men open cupboards, bend to the floor, lean over the stove. One takes out a notebook and confers with the others. For a moment they seem to argue. One looks sullen. The wife piles something on plates and hands them around. Everyone goes silent while they eat, then they shake hands with the husband, give him a slip of paper, nod to the women and exit. The dining room is hushed. The husband watches them disappear around the corner then lets out a whoop. A stooped man about four feet tall with a demijohn of wine enters. The husband whoops again, uncorks the bottle and fills the pitchers of all the tables. He lifts his own glass and the women emerge from the kitchen, laughing. The health inspectors have made a surprise visit and everything was O.K. We all toast and more wine is poured. Service after that is chaotic. The vegetables appear ten minutes before the main course. We get someone else's grilled fish but by then we don't care. It's all good anyway.

The next morning when I am out walking alone early, a car whizzes by me and stops. The woman chef from the restaurant jumps out of her car, takes my hand, and tells me how lovely to see me again, that I must come back. She has trailing scarves and stacks of jewelry on her wrists. I definitely would go back.

~

We're ready to put in a full day on foot. In the museum on Ortigia, Caravaggio's painting of the burial of Santa Lucia, a local virgin martyr in 304, who cut out her own eyes when a suitor admired them, occasioned a lecture from the guard worthy of any docent. And where are we from? Ah, he has a cousin in California; we should meet him when we return. Ed loves Annunciation paintings and the peeling one by da Messina enthralls him. Small local museums are my favorite kind. They stay close to the source, usually, and deepen a tourist-level connection with a place.

We walk across the bridge, through a park, then through a honeycomb of streets. The Museo Archeologico in Siracusa proper is world class. Intelligently arranged and exhibited, the art and craft of succeeding waves of life in this area are displayed. Beginning with prehistory, we trace the eras through one stunning room after another. Artifacts, statues, lion faces from the temple in ruins in Ortigia, Greek ex-votos, and an amazing bronze horse—oh, so much.

The amphitheater in Siracusa—what fabulous siting. The stone cup of the hill was chopped out into natural seating, a 300-degree arrangement focusing on a stage. Corridors were carved out for gladiators to enter and exit. In summer, the Greek plays are still performed here. What fun it would be to act in one. The ruins we've seen are the major ones; hundred of other temples, foundations, baths, and unknown stones cover the island. This must be the ideal time to see them because hardly anyone is around. The solitude of these places sharpens the experience of happening upon them, the sense of discovery that for me lies at the heart of travel.

We vaguely hear a thunderstorm in the night but are so thoroughly exhausted from our day that nothing really wakes us until about three o'clock. The room's wraparound glass creaks ominously in its frames and the bed feels as though someone is shaking the headboard. Earthquake. We leap up and look out at the harbor, where quiet boats just seem to be rocking with the water. We wait, as we have other on nights in San Francisco, for whatever comes next. We've experienced so many by now that we can judge the force on the Richter scale, although the 7.5 quake of October 1989 was so far beyond what we'd felt before that we had no idea. I think of what must have existed in Sicily before the earthquake of 1693 knocked down whole areas. But tonight's was only a hard jolt, perhaps 3.4, a reminder that the earth has its own rhythms having nothing to do with us.

～

In the inland Baroque town of Noto, we come upon my fearful fantasy of the Mafia funeral. Maybe it was only a local patriarch laid to rest but we turn the corner and are among mourners with big jewelry and two Mercedes-Benz sedans. A coffin is hauled into the church on the shoulders of men who could play parts in a refilming of *The Godfather*. Three women weep behind veils. I grab Ed's arm and we turn around quickly.

We've backtracked to visit Noto, not only for another taste of the interior of the country but for the taste of ice cream. A gourmet guide to Italy promises the best ice cream in Sicily is here on a back street. I try the tangerine, melon, and jasmine sorbets. Ed chooses almond, coffee, and pistachio *gelato*. In Italy, one always orders several flavors in the same cup. He tastes all of mine and I taste all of his. We're convinced. A cold slanted rain begins. We get our raincoats and umbrella out of the car and walk anyway. Might as well get soaked—who knows when we'll ever get back to Noto.

～

Briefly lost in Catania, we find the airport and fly out. Below us the coast gradually enlarges so that we see a slice of the eastern edge of the island. "What are you writing?" I see Ed is making one of his lists.

"Reasons to come back—we didn't see the mosaics at Piazza Armerina, the Arab baths at Cefalù. I can't believe we didn't make it to Taormina. A week was short. Let's go to the Aeolian islands—for the name if nothing else—and Pantelleria for the *moscato* dessert wines. What else?"

A wisp of lemon scent escapes from my bag under the seat stuffed with lemon soap, a ceramic platter decorated with lemons and leaves, and a small bag of real lemons. "More of the groves along the coast." I remember the hills outside the Baroque towns, criss-crossed with intricate stone boundary walls. "More of the inland part. We never even looked at tile for the bathroom. And we have to go back to Siracusa; the map listed forty-eight points of interest. We didn't see half." I glimpse the slopes of Mount Etna then we bank into clouds, losing Sicily entirely.

A Sicilian Menu

AFTER OUR TRIP TO SICILY, WE'RE INSPIRED TO adapt some of the tastes from that island to our own kitchen. We prepare a dinner for three Cortona friends. Oddly, not one has been to Sicily. We get a glimpse of how they feel about it from Massimo, one of our guests. We use the same plumber he does, and Ed asks him, "You know that man who works for Carlo, the skinny one who talks so fast? Is he Sicilian?"

"Oh no," Massimo answers, "he's Italian."

Ed lugged bottles of Moscato and Passito home in his carry-on bag, along with capers, almonds, and the marzipan fruits we couldn't resist. With dessert, we bring out a plate of them. Everyone admires the verisimilitude but at the end of the evening we still have the adorable peaches, pears, and plums.

For Sicilian recipes from the source, I've enjoyed *La Cucina Siciliana di Gangivecchio* by Wanda and Giovanna Tornabene, which is published in English and adapted to American ingredients.

MENU ⟿

Caponata

I've made *caponata* for years. The Sicilian version was more flavorful than mine. Why? The concentrated tomato *estratto* (tomato paste made from sun-dried tomatoes) available in Sicily, a freer hand with seasoning, the saltiness of anchovies. Spread this on bread or crackers. It's one of those perfect *hors d'oeuvres* to have on hand for guests. At lunch, a couple of tablespoons turns a plain ham or tomato sandwich into something special, and it's also a great pasta sauce—just toss with *penne*.

⟿ *Bake two medium-sized eggplants on a piece of foil in the oven at 350 degrees for half an hour. Coarsely chop ½ cup each of pitted green and black olives. Sauté one large chopped onion and three or four cloves of minced garlic. Cut the eggplants into small cubes, add to the onions and cook to blend. Lacking the intense tomato sauce of Sicily, add five or six minced sun-dried tomatoes to ½ cup of tomato paste and one cup of tomato sauce. Stir into eggplant mixture. Chop three or four anchovy fillets. Add those, 2 T. of capers, a handful of chopped parsley, and the chopped olives to the eggplant. Season with oregano, salt, and pepper. Like many tomato-based recipes, caponata is best if made a day early. It will keep in the fridge for a week. Makes about five cups, depending on the size of the eggplants.*

Olive Piccanti

⟿ *Mince two small hot peppers—one red, one green—and sauté with a small minced onion. Mix with two cups of large green olives, moisten with a little olive oil and lemon juice. Let rest in the fridge overnight.*

Pasta al Limone

If I had to say what one ingredient I must have in the kitchen, it would be the lemon because the flavor, both assertive and enhancing, is like liquid sunshine going into the food. Anselmo brought me two lemon trees in pots. As an essential of the Italian garden, lemons are so valued that most old houses have a *limonaia,* a glass-walled room for storing the pots over the winter. Our *limonaia* functions as a storage room for mowers and tools but this winter reclaimed its function with the two pots taking a sunny spot. In spring we dragged them out in front of the house again, to a place near the kitchen door—very handy for grabbing one for this extremely easy and tasty pasta. When I make this in California, I often add a half pound of crab, but it's a marvelous pasta by itself. With a green salad, it's the lightest dinner imaginable, perfect the day after a crippling feast.

⟶ *Boil pasta—spaghetti or* tagliatelle*—for six. Squeeze enough lemons for ½ cup of juice. Drain pasta, season, and toss with ½ cup of chopped Italian parsley, the lemon juice, and grated* parmigiano *to taste. If you like, sauté a pound of crabmeat in 2 T. of butter or olive oil. Add a big splash of white wine. Bring to a boil for an instant, stir the lemon juice mixture into the crab and toss with the pasta.*

Sea Bass in a Salt Crust

Don't expect a salty fish—the crust seals in the juices but only slightly penetrates. In San Francisco, I go to a fish market on Clement Street for sea bass. They net the fish from a tank, then knock it in the head with a mallet. Not my favorite moment of shopping. Here, we are two hours from both the Mediterranean and the Adriatic. Fishmongers come to the Thursday market in Camucia where the fish are safely dead and on ice.

59

⟶ Ask the fishmonger to clean and prepare for cooking a large sea bass, about 3½ to 4 pounds. Dry the fish well and stuff the inside with slices of lemon, wands of rosemary, and a few sprigs of thyme. Mix the juice of two lemons with 6 T. olive oil and brush the fish all over. Season with pepper and thyme. To the remaining oil and lemon, add some chopped thyme and parsley and reserve this for serving later. For the crust, you'll need about 5 pounds of coarse salt, depending on the size of the fish. Layer the bottom of a baking dish (one that can go to the table as well) with an inch of salt. Place the fish on top then mound the rest of the salt over the fish, completely covering it. Pat in place around the fish. Make a mask of ¾ c. flour and enough water to thin the flour. Brush the salt with this mixture. Bake in a preheated, hot oven, 400 degrees, for 40 minutes, or until the salt looks toasted. Present the fish at the table, cracking or sawing into the hard crust, then take it back to the kitchen and remove the fish to a platter for serving. Heat and pour the reserved lemon and oil over the fish. Serves six generously.

Zucchini with Mint

⟶ Thinly slice or grate eight slender zucchini. If you grate, squeeze out the liquid. Quickly sauté in hot olive oil with some minced garlic. Stir in chopped parsley and mint, season with salt and pepper. Serve warm or at room temperature.

Lemon Pie with Roasted Almonds

I'll never forget the lemon pie of Erice. The crunch of almonds added a wonderful complement to the familiar, luscious textures of lemon meringue pie—the flaky pastry, airy meringue, and the creamy lemon custard. The almonds of Sicily have a perfume and a complex aftertaste. Because fresh nuts make all the difference, at home I order pecans from the South every fall and store the bags in the freezer. I can taste a change in the texture after a couple of months, but still, the nuts keep much better in the freezer. In San Francisco, we have access to fresh walnuts and almonds from California groves through the Saturday farmers' market. Here's my grandmother's lemon pie, enhanced with the Sicilian touch of almonds—and further enhanced when served with the fragrant Moscato of the islands off Sicily. Actually, it's my grandmother's sister Besta's recipe. Besta was otherwise known for her fuming blackberry cordials, which my father refused to drink for fear of going blind.

⁓ *Beat the juice and zest of four lemons with 1½ cups of sugar. Mix 2 T. melted butter with 4 T. flour, ¼ t. of salt. Beat 4 egg yolks. Whip the yolks into the butter and flour and whisk in the juice and sugar. Gently pour in 2 cups of hot water, beating all along, and place on a moderate flame. Cook the custard until very thick, stirring constantly. Keep the flame adjusted so that the mixture cooks but doesn't boil. When thick, add 2 T. cream. Slightly cool. Separately beat 4 egg whites until stiff, whisking in 2 tablespoons of sugar at the end. Toast 1 cup of halved almonds in a 350-degree oven for five to seven minutes, shaking once or twice. Nothing is as easy to burn as nuts! Sprinkle them with a little sugar. Pour the lemon filling into your favorite baked pie shell, arrange nuts on top, then spread the egg whites in a swirling pattern and bake at 350 degrees until the meringue browns.*

Resurrection

BEPPE STOPS DIGGING AND COCKS HIS HEAD. *"Senta,"* listen, he says, *"Il cuculo."* He removes his wool cap and runs his hand over his tight gray curls. "They arrive for Easter." The light two-note call of the cuckoo repeats. "Exactly on time this year."

With forbearance, Beppe is planting lavender along the walk to the lake view, where earlier he and Francesco installed five new cypress trees. Planting cypresses is important work but mere flowering bushes do not interest him. At his place, he and his wife hold to the separation of *campo* and *cortile,* field and court-yard. Flowers—woman's work. He's fast. Is it knowing exactly how to angle the shovel so that three or four movements are all it takes? I shake the plant from the plastic pot, and place it in the hole. Quickly, he pushes the shovel back and forth; it's done. While I seem to have to use my whole body to dig, I see him work with his shoulders, not with his lower body. Sort of the opposite of Latino dancers, who stay so still above the waist but are all action below. He lifts the shovel and shoves hard. No leaping on and off, wiggling it back and forth, no back-wrenching lifting of heavy soil. He raises it as easily as I lift a wooden spoon from cake batter. Whack! Down through the dirt. On to the next one.

Beppe was born in the isolated mountains east of Cortona. He has taken us to his now-abandoned childhood home, an aerie in a tiny *borgo* consisting of a cluster of small, almost windowless stone woodcutters' houses. All his sixty-odd years he has worked the land. Unlike Francesco who is tough (at eighty), wiry, and works with a concentrated vengeance, Beppe's way of working fascinates me. He's upright, and lean. His corduroys and sweater suspend loosely from him as though from a clothes hanger. He works with no wasted motions at a steady pace. I especially like to watch him swing the scythe through long grasses. His rhythm is like a pendulum; he could be marking time in a book of hours rather than cutting weeds.

At ten he pauses and takes a sack from the back of his new green Ape. Time for *spuntino,* a snack. He also takes out a jug covered with woven osier, which he fills with well water. He upends it and takes a long swig, proclaiming it *"Acqua buona,"* as he always does.

While he pauses, I haul water out to the twenty-five lavender plants. *"Un bel secchio d'acqua, signora,"* he calls to me. Idiomatically, he probably means just a good amount, but I hear him literally, a beautiful bucket of water, which makes the carrying easier. Beautiful water, I silently tell the plants, loosen your tight roots, trauma is over, you're home.

The car is full of five-gallon marguerites to be planted in the rose garden. I won't ask him to help me plant the smaller bedding flats or the geraniums for all the pots. The cosmos and hollyhock seeds I've started in the *limonaia* don't get his attention. He wouldn't refuse to help me plant, but he would be in mortal pain. I unload two marguerites. "Would you mind helping me with these big ones?"

To my surprise, he smiles. "Ah, Santa Margherita." She is the loved patron saint of Cortona and still lies in a glass coffin in the church at the top of this hill. We intersperse her white flowers, about to bloom, with the well-established lavender and roses, softening the line of thorny roses just coming into leaf, and hiding their scrawny legs. Contrary to usual practice, which is to grow roses by themselves, I'm going to try filling the beds profusely and see what happens. *"Venerdì sera,"* Friday evening, "at nine, a procession commencing at Santo Spirito goes up to Santa Margherita," Beppe tells me. "A long procession."

Today is Maundy Thursday. The shops in town are filling with life-sized chocolate hens, huge eggs wrapped in bright foil with prizes inside, a mild display compared with Sicily. "What do you eat on Easter?" I want to know. But I'm thinking, what does "maundy" mean?

"Tortellini, a good shoulder of lamb, potatoes, spinach, *insalata,* a little wine." Beppe heads up to the olive terraces to help Ed, relieved to quit the *fiori,* I am sure. I bring more beautiful water to Santa Margherita's namesakes. I open the trunk and take out lobelia, ageratum, snapdragons, dahlias, and the ashen-lavender flowers no one knew the name of. I have a bag of sunflower seeds and packets of creeping thyme, trailing nasturtium, and morning glory. Ed will help me plant them tomorrow. Beside a climbing yellow rose on the main wall (called the Polish Wall because it was restored by Polish workers), I plant the bush with velvety, purse-shaped pink flowers. No one at the nursery knew the name of them either.

Death is coming again to the pinned body on the cross. Strange, I always thought it was important whether or not I believed in the factual truth of "on the third day He rose." My hand around the ball of pale roots, crescents of dirt under my nails, I'm content to believe or not, but to feel a rise in my blood as the sun makes tracks across the equator bringing back my favorite season, the long summer days.

Maybe we were smart enough to make the gods. What better way to explain the darkest moment of the year and how it swings toward light, except by the metaphor of a birth. How to face the incredible rejuvenescence of spring except in a story of a miraculous rising. "Well," I'm quoting myself aloud to the drooping leaves of the nameless pink plant,

> *. . . if there's a God dotting lines along spheres for the sun*
> *to cross, good. And if not, we are more*
> *than we know. I can hold the windflower and*
> *the crucifix nail in mind at once. I wanted truth*
> *and find we form the words we need from flesh.*

I dig a hole for a gray-green santolina, which they used to toss on the cathedral floors in the Middle Ages to keep down the human smells.

I splash water around the roots. "Rise," I command.

~

Hail—banging my tender new plants, hopping off the stone wall like popcorn. This tempestuous weather for Good Friday—where is *primavera* now? The hail stops and wind drives rain sideways against the house so that it seeps in my study window, soaking my notes on Sicilian history into swirls of blue ink that look more like tide pools than facts about the Normans. Several louvers sail into the linden trees, smacking the stone wall. From the bedroom window, I watch columns of rain "walking" across the valley, heading straight for us. When sun breaks through, we dash out the door, trowels in hand, plant flowers until rain starts to pelt again and we're driven back to the front door, where we dry out under the balcony.

By evening the air clears. We're stir-crazy and go into town for a *prosecco*. The streets are packed—everyone from miles around has come in for the procession of the stations of the cross. We try four *trattorie* before we find a table at the cozy Osteria, where opera arias fill the small room, and I can have the *strozzapreti,* priest-strangler, pasta with a cream and hazelnut sauce. The waitress, Cinzia, seems always amused. She gestures with her hands constantly, lights the candle with a large swoop. The owner glides around serenely. Once I asked her if she was local and she said no, she was from Castiglion Fiorentino, five miles away. Ed is about to order a bottle of wine but Cinzia puts her finger to her lips, raises her shoulders almost to her ears, and points with her other hand to a Chianti that is half the price. The other, a 1994—she shakes her head and ticks her finger at him. Ed orders the homey beef braised in red wine, a true *casalinga* dish. We split a chocolate charlotte and think with longing of the peach charlotte they make in summer.

Down the hill to Santo Spirito, a church I've never seen open. The doorway is outlined in lights and as we arrive, eight robed and hooded men are hoisting the crucified figure of Christ onto their shoulders. They look scary to me; I flash on the robes worn by the Ku Klux Klan. As a child, I once saw a Klan meeting around a bonfire. "What is that?" I asked my mother. "A bunch of old fools," she answered. "And there are no fools like old fools." I remember I've seen these odd peaked hoods in Italian paintings, worn by plague doctors along with bird-beak masks. Behind them, eight women are shouldering a figure of grieving Mary, who looks to weigh about a ton. They walk out, accompanied by people carrying torches and we join the procession up Via Guelfa. The town band is playing a tinny dirge. As we go, more people join us.

At each church, we stop. More sacred figures are brought out and blend into the procession through the darkened town. Some people sing with the music and many carry candles, sheltering the flame with a cupped hand. Through roving clouds, the full moon comes and goes. I have the strange feeling of having slipped behind a curtain of time and entered a place and ceremony both alien and familiar to me. The music sounds atonal, shrill, almost something you could imagine hearing after death. The faces of the people stay private, except for the teenagers who are jostling and jabbing each other. We're all bundled in shapeless raincoats and scarves, further erasing connections with present time. Without the signs of haircuts and glasses, we almost could be in the fifteenth century.

For most local people, this service is one of their yearly rituals. I'm short on rituals myself, especially ones involving torches, hoods, and the agonized Christ aloft in the streets. Good Friday, I realize, is major. In the South of my particular childhood, all emphasis was on Easter Sunday, with the main event for me being my carefully chosen new dress and shoes. I remember the thrill of a blue organdy with hand-embroidered daisies around the hem and on the ends of the sash.

When they start to climb through upper Cortona, along the steep way of the stations of the cross made in mosaic by Gino Severini, and on to Santa Margherita, we drop out and go to a bar for coffee. The raw wind has numbed my ears. How can they carry those beams on the shoulders? Quite quickly it seems, we hear the mournful music again and we rush uphill to join at San Marco, then wind back to the *piazza,* where the bishop delivers a long sermon. It's almost midnight by now and we have a mile to walk back to Bramasole in the dark so we leave the throngs of people who have more stamina than we.

Into the spirit of the Easter festivals, we decide to drive over on Easter Saturday to Sansepolcro, Piero della Francesca's hometown, to see his stupendous painting of the resurrection. The countryside between here and there rolls—green valleys and wooded hillsides, a curvy road interrupted by few villages, bucolic Tuscany. Roadsides are flush with dandelions and purple wildflowers, the first poppies are springing out in the grasses, wisteria is climbing over pale stone farmhouses. In this blissful landscape, we are suddenly stunned to see a tall African woman, dressed in tight striped pants and a revealing red shirt, standing on the roadside. Around the next bend we see another, this one equally statuesque and curvaceous. She stares. Every few hundred feet these women are stationed along the road. They stand or sit on wooden crates. One eats from a bag of potato chips. Then we see a parked car, with no woman near her crate. This is surreal. Prostitutes out in rural Italy. Some of the women are regal, with elaborate plaited hair and full red lips. All are wearing red and black.

Who would stop? Surely not local men, who might be seen by their neighbors. And this isn't exactly the autostrada. How many delivery trucks could there be? We must have passed fifteen women just poised on the side of the road, more women than cars. Bizarre and disturbing because this makes no sense in the Arcadian valley of the upper Tiber, which appears in the backgrounds of paintings, this dreamy route known as the Piero della Francesca trail.

———

I like to come to Sansepolcro. On the way we stop either at Anghiari, for its pitched medieval streets, or at Monterchi, an intact and tiny hilltown with a shady *piazza*. Piero della Francesca's mother was from Monterchi so the presence of his painting *Madonna del Parto,* Mary about to give birth, has a personal significance. No longer in the cemetery chapel, the painting is now housed in a building of its own just below the town walls. It has lost some of its former allure because it is now behind glass, and it has lost the tension that came from its location in a place of death. But, still she is staring down, not only

69

remote and austere, as some have described her, but with a quiet inward focus. I don't know of another painting of the Madonna about to give birth. Her hand rests lightly on her stomach. Has she just felt the first mild contraction? It's an unnerving painting—the moment women recognize, when nothing ever will be the same again.

We're so used to hills. The town named for the Holy Sepulchre is flat. It's easy to imagine Piero della Francesca walking diagonally across the *piazza.* His work was here, in Urbino, and in Arezzo. He was a strictly provincial person creating art at the highest level. Walking on Sansepolcro's level streets, feeling the linear perspectives of the *piazza,* and the shadows cutting across upright buildings, I can sense how the town layout influenced his vision.

In the Museo Civico, which we usually find almost empty, some Italian tourists have had the same urge to visit today. It's a typical regional collection, except that the local painter was Piero della Francesca and three of his major works hang in a room of their own, among rooms of prehistoric axes, collections of small boxes, and a couple of dozen other paintings, some of which are quite interesting in themselves but suffer from proximity to Piero. A plump little boy pulls and pulls on his mother's arm, begging to go eat. She's trying to look at the art. He pulls again and she knocks him sharply on the skull with her knuckle and points to a devil in one of the paintings.

Ed and I look first at the *Madonna della Misericordia*—same face as Mary in Monterchi but wearier, tighter. She has gathered many under the protection of her outspread cloak. A standard image in Italian painting, it must have been comforting when the Guelphs and Ghibellines were pouring boiling oil on each other and warring mercenaries ripped around the countryside pillaging and burning. There's still comfort in it.

The plump little boy leans against his mother's leg, pulling her shirt around him. The room empties, except for a man looking earnestly at Piero's San Giuliano, with his puzzled—or is it lost—expression.

Ed and I sit down in front of the famous *Resurrection*. Christ, emerging from the tomb, is draped in a chalky pink shroud, while below him, four guards are sleeping. The second one from the left, the security woman tells me, is a self-portrait of Piero. He looks the soundest asleep of all. "And look," she points at his throat, *"gozzo."* I have no idea what that word is but see immediately: goiter. I've always admired Piero's necks on women. Odd to see that his own had an unnatural bulge. When he lived, the local water lacked iodine. He must have been a man of no vanity not to have edited the disfiguring goiter from his portrait. Behind Christ, we see a landscape, sear on the left, and coming into spring on the right. The composition is simple, the power palpable. "His foot looks as big as yours," I tell Ed. The body is lovingly painted. A muscular man in his physical glory. I wonder if T. S. Eliot had this image in mind when he wrote the line, "In the juvenesence of the year came Christ the tiger." He has raised himself with force from the sepulchre. The pallor of the tomb is not on his flushed cheeks and sensuous lips.

Kenneth Clark's often-cited perception of this painting is close to the heart of its strange emotional magnetism: "This country God, who rises in the grey light while human beings are still asleep, has been worshiped ever since man first knew that the seed is not dead in the winter earth, but will force its way upwards through an iron crust. Later, He will become a god of rejoicing but His first emergence is painful and involuntary. He seems to be part of the dream which lies so heavily on the sleeping soldiers, and has Himself the doomed and distant gaze of the somnambulist."

"He emanates the same mystery as his *Madonna del Parto*," Ed notices. Yes, he's looking at what we can't see.

Driving home, the women along the road are still out, casing cars as they pass. I can read nothing in their eyes. The tragedy, surely there is one, does not show. We turn off to take a short-cut and are relieved not to pass these women again. There are violets, hawthorn, plum trees, and quince to see, spring water-falls slushing over the rocks, and bare deciduous trees glowing red with buds. They don't erase the brutal fact of women for sale along the road nor do they erase the flip-side connection with the stations of the cross.

Ed zips around curves; we don't pass a car for miles. We're rushing back for the opening of our friend Celia's paintings at a gallery in Cortona. The small room is so packed with people that it's hard to see the bright blue and yellow paintings of flow-ers. Trays and trays of food go around, wine is flowing, everyone wishes Celia well. Vittorio, her husband, comes over to us with a plate of slivered truffle *crostini*. Ed asks him about the women on the road. "They're Nigerian. I know you are shocked. They are brought in by the Russian Mafia. They promise them mod-eling jobs, then this happens."

"The Russian Mafia in rural Tuscany? You can't be serious," Ed says. "Why don't the police round up the women, try to send them home?"

Vittorio shrugs. "Prostitution is not illegal. Pimping is but it's hard to catch them in the act. They know when the police are coming and scatter."

"How?"

"Oh, cell phones. Some guy is probably in the village—sees who's heading down the road."

"How do they have that much business on such a road?"

"I don't know but people say there's plenty."

Antonio comes over and the subject shifts. I have questions. On the way into town, I saw a scrawled sign on the door to San Filippo announcing the blessing of the eggs from four to five at San Domenico, and five to six at San Filippo. Vittorio explains that Easter Breakfast is the one time a year when Italians abandon their quick espresso habit and prepare a huge, American-style breakfast. The day before, the eggs, as symbols of rebirth, are taken to the church to be blessed. "Easter week is also when the priest comes by to bless the house. Everyone does a gigantic cleaning for it. He will bless the eggs then, too."

"We did that in Winona," Ed remembers. "After my mother cleaned the house, she sprinkled holy water on the beds to protect us, then the priest came to bless the house."

"Did you have your house blessed, Antonio?" He lives alone and his girlfriend refuses to stay there because of the *"confusione."* He just smiles.

I never knew Ed slept in a blessed bed. Maybe that explains him.

~~~~~

Easter itself is a peaceful day. In my favorite church, San Cristoforo, a red basket of round buns is passed out to the twenty or so worshipers. Bread of life. The priest blesses and shakes a few drops of holy water over them. One woman brings her own basket of bread for her Easter dinner and asks for blessings on it, too.

Many who shouldered those figures through the town must be groaning under heating pads. We take pots of pink hydrangeas to Donatella and to Anselmo, and see to our embarrassment that they already have several, as well as mounds of chocolate.

Families are gathering around long tables and someone—not I—is bringing out the platter of lamb ringed with rosemary. I'm happy not to have cooked all day, happy not to serve forth, happy not to have so many dirty dishes that they must be taken outside and stacked on the wall. Another time, *va bene*. Tonight, we're alone. Because they are so fresh, we have a bowl of peas with plenty of pepper and a hunk of butter melting into them. A lovely first course. A bottle of clean white wine, veal chops, and a salad of wild greens "married," as the Italians say, to our oil and a little fifty-year-old balsamic, so precious that I sprinkle the elixir onto the lettuces with an eye-dropper.

Since Ed is Catholic, I expect him to know everything about the liturgical year. "What does 'Maundy' mean?"

"Um . . . I think mandate comes from the same Latin root."

"What was the mandate on Thursday?"

"To wash the feet of the poor? Seems like that was it. From Mary Magdalene washing Jesus' feet."

"Remember that small, intense Piero della Francesca fresco of her with her hair still wet in the Arezzo cathedral? It's as intimate a look at her as his Jesus just rising. Too bad it doesn't hang near his *Resurrection*."

"Mary Magdalene comes to mind when I think about that music in the procession Friday night."

"Why?" I'm waiting. Having grown up in a very Polish Catholic church where he served as an altar boy for years, Ed isn't as mystified by rituals as I am.

"Well, the word 'maudlin' comes to mind—and 'maudlin' comes from 'Magdalene.'"

"Those cross-bearers from Friday night probably could use some attention to their feet about now." I think of the displaced women on the road to Sansepolcro. "Were there the same number of prostitutes as there are stations of the cross?"

Ed shakes his head. "I'm glad Easter is over. Now it can just be spring."

Following Spring: The Watery Veneto

INFATUATED WITH ITALIAN SPRING, WE FOLLOW it north to the Veneto in April. I am returning to Venice, after an absence of twenty-five years. As we drive into the flat, big-sky landscape, I'm reeling through my earlier visits. Slippery, slippery time—the interim slides away; Venice lives close in memory. I am puzzled by the long interval, equally puzzled by the particular allure of Venice. I've read that bees, their stomachs full of nectar, have magnetic forces in their brains which lead them to the hive—I feel that way toward Venice. Flamboyant and decadent, it is still to me a sacred city. I'm a fool for beauty, and its poise on the edge, facing the exotic east, with its back turned to the rest of Europe, adds to the attraction. I had not meant to stay away so long. There's more to the allure—something I've never been able to articulate for myself, something I've never seen or read, out of all the books and images of Venice. What is it?

Only a few hours northeast of Cortona we are entering a different spring. People with seasonal allergies must go mad here. If we park the car for an hour, we find it covered with yellow, sticky pollen. Whorls of airy white puffs blow across the windshield and tractors spume dust in the fields. Breezes send clouds of gold dust from the pines' white candles and cones. The new green of leaves and crops seems to reflect in the air, giving it a watery tinge; we are driving through an aquarium light.

Near the port of Chioggia, south of Venice, the land turns marshy. Reedy shores wave and blur into water. I always have loved the smell of marshes. My early summers were spent on the Georgia sea islands, still one of my favorite landscapes. Grasses growing out of the sea. Land that is tidal, the slick creatures of both land and water, the thrill of what looked like a log suddenly coming alive and opening hilarious jaws. A salty, iodine, rotting, fresh smell signaled summer and freedom. Packed in the Oldsmobile with my two sisters, Willie Bell, records, toys, clothes, and my mother (my father was driven separately by an employee so as to avoid our chaos), I leaned out the window like a dog, my hair springing into curls, waiting for the first scent. No one seem enchanted in the least when I began to quote the Georgia poet Sidney Lanier's "The Marshes of Glenn," which we were forced to memorize in endless stanzas in the fifth grade. I imitated the declamatory style of my teacher Miss Lake:

As the marsh-hen secretly builds on the watery sod,
Behold I will build me a nest on the greatness of God.
I will fly in the greatness of God as the marsh-hen flies
In the freedom that fills all the space 'twixt the marsh and
      the skies:
By so many roots as the marsh-grass sends in the sod
I will heartily lay me a-hold on the greatness of God:
Oh, like to the greatness of God is the greatness within
The range of the marshes, the liberal marshes of Glenn.

"Can't you make her stop," my sister said. She was turning down page corners in *Mademoiselle,* already planning her clothes for college in the fall. Louder, I shouted:

How still the plains of the waters be!
The tide is in his ecstasy.
The tide is at his highest height:
And it is night.

I loved that chopped-off last line. My other sister remembered that the Marshes of Glenn ran red with blood in some war. My mother began to sing "You Are My Sunshine," which I hated. I rolled down the window again and let the smell wash my face until we entered the sulphur stink of the paper mills.

Marshes, islands, lagoons—the smell of old landscapes where water will have its way. These marshes, too, probably have run red with blood from time to time. Those Doges of Venice did not govern with peace in mind. Chioggia doesn't rate much mention in the guides. We take to it immediately as a racy, working-class version of Venice. Like its elegant cousin, Chioggia stands on low land with canals and medieval rabbit-warren *vicoli,* narrow streets, leading to arching footbridges. Flag-bright colors of fishing boats repeat in the waters. People crowd the wide main street's cafés and shops. The decline of the birth rate currently experienced in Italy must not apply here. Out for afternoon shopping, many young women push strollers, sometimes with two tiny children in tandem. I hope they rotate who's first in the stroller. I would hate for my first world view to be the back of my little brother's head. Fish restaurants cluster near the harbor. How fresh can fish get? We see a man carrying two buckets, fish on top still flapping their tails. Lines of bright laundry string across canals: yellow-striped towels, turquoise blouse, red pants, flowered sheets, quite colossal bras, and a few sad pairs of graying panties. Through a kitchen window I see a woman moistening her hands with olive oil so working with the pasta will be easier.

After cross-checking the Veneto in several Italian guidebooks, Ed has pinpointed a lauded restaurant with rooms upstairs. We're delaying Venice, saving it for last. The restaurant is in the village of Lorregia, our headquarters for a couple of days. En route from Chioggia, the brakes start to grate. Not a good sound. At the hotel we ask about an Alfa dealer but it is late in the day. Unfortunately, tomorrow is Sunday. Ed asks if he could call, just in case someone's still there. If we can't take the car until Monday, we'll be stuck and all we can do is eat in the lauded restaurant. "Bring it over *subito*. I'll take a look at it," the mechanic responds.

The woman at the desk, one of the owners, becomes concerned. "How will you return? That's thirteen kilometers from here." Ed asks if there's a place to rent a car if he needs one. "Closed. They close at five on Saturday. You call me from the mechanic. I'll see."

Where cars are concerned, my participation in the equality of women stops. I want a car to turn on, go. I don't like looking under the hood. All that convoluted metal and the battery that could send you over the moon if you touch the wrong plugs. I trail upstairs and Ed takes off.

The room is severely plain but immaculate. Checking into a hotel, sometimes austere as a monk's cell, sometimes grandly luxurious, I always revel in an anonymous sense of freedom, particularly if I am alone. I take off the bedspread, turn back the sheets, look out the windows, open the drawers and minibar, feel the towels, examine the lotion and shampoo, the glass jar of cotton balls, or whatever amenities are offered. I'm the opposite of my fastidious aunt Hazel, who travelled with her own pillow and a spray can of Lysol disinfectant. She held it over her head, dousing every available surface, backing out of the room for an hour while all the germs died. I like the leather folders of nice writing paper, the pad by the phone with the pencil just sharpened, the slick magazines about the town, the terrycloth robes. This room, however, has few of these checkpoints to explore. It does have a good shower, and I have a good book.

Where is Ed? An hour goes by, then another. Finally, he comes in and tosses keys on the bed. "We now have a Fiat Panda until Tuesday morning. The Alfa's brakes need parts and the mechanic will have to find them in Treviso Monday."

"What was wrong?"

"Nothing drastic. Wear and tear. He can finish early Tuesday morning. You would not believe how nice the *signora* was. I called the hotel and she came and got me, *then* she drove me umpteen miles, at least ten, in the other direction where she arranged for me to rent a car from the Fiat dealer. It was in some industrial zone. We'll probably never find it again."

"How incredible."

"She drives like a real Italian," he said with admiration. He opens the window and the earthy aroma of *funghi porcini* sizzling in hot oil causes him to shower quickly and change into his blue shirt. We descend to the dining room. Because of the adventure, we are treated like old friends. Everyone in the family knows about the *problema* with the Alfa. Glasses of *prosecco* are brought to us and everyone agrees that the Alfa is a fine car, that Italian cars are superior in design to any in the world.

"We're totally in your hands," Ed tells the waiter. "Bring us your favorite local wines, the specialties of the house." This is Ed's favorite way to dine, to give the chef the compliment from the outset of selecting our menu. A more trepid diner, I'm not always thrilled when the sliced *lardo,* basically a buttery fat, or sea urchins are presented. I hope we will not be served the *medaglioni d'asino,* which I spied on the menu. Medallions of donkey I can live without.

The waiter invites us to follow him downstairs. Their wine cellar is an arched brick cave filled with racks of wine. He pokes around and pulls out a bottle of Amarone, one of my favorite wines for its dark taste.

The courses start to roll out. Fortunately, we're served pasta with vegetables, ordinary enough but special because the pasta is made here and the vegetables are perfectly cooked. The waiter comes around with *gnocchetti,* little *gnocchi,* also with vegetables, to give us a taste. The provincial dining room fills with local people dressed out of designer shops. The prosperity in the Veneto, even compared with the high standard of living in Tuscany, is simply astonishing. I've never seen a general population so well-off. A movement has been long simmering to separate this area from the rest of Italy. Economically, it is a country apart, light years from Sicily. I wonder how many of these Gucci- and Escada-clad women have ordered the donkey. Roast rabbit, the next course, is cooked in wine and tomatoes, pine nuts, and currants. The slight raisiny taste just matches the wine. The family makes all the desserts and they look tempting but we order a selection of local cheeses. At the next table, one of the lovely couples is dining with their son, perhaps nine or ten. We'd noticed him examining the menu carefully and asking questions of the waiter. The parents looked bored. He ate with gusto, looking at the plates each time the waiter passed their table. His father poured him a half-inch of wine, then added mineral water to the glass. Now we watch him examine the peach bavarian, the strawberry pie on the dessert cart then plop back in his chair and order the cheeses. We're impressed. A natural gourmand.

Since we're near the source, Ed has a glass of *grappa*. How divine to hoist ourselves upstairs to bed.

⁓

I could move today into the Villa Barbaro, one of Palladio's happiest moments. The garden is bare, mostly just a stretch of lawn, but the house remains felicitous, with its playful Veronese frescoes and intimate rooms. The exterior invites you, unlike some of Palladio's dour houses which seem swamped by architecture with a capital A. This one sings. Scuffing through in the felt slippers provided for visitors, I see that the house is actually still lived in. Two roped-off rooms are filled with family photos and reading lamps beside capacious chairs. Could that be the electric bill on the desk? How odd to vacate on Sunday afternoon, so that we teeming hordes can gaze on their frescoes, admire the view, imagine ourselves penning a note at the gilded secretary.

The Panda seems to know the roads. Somehow we don't get lost. Bassano, Treviso, Castelfranco. We don't encounter any of those mysterious signs we face so frequently in Tuscany that say *tutte le direzioni*—all directions—and point both right and left. We park outside Asolo and walk in because cars aren't allowed to enter this fantasyland, home of one of my favorite writers. No, not Robert Browning, who immortalized the town in his poem, "Asolando," but Freya Stark, who lived here when not on her adventurous travels in Iraq and Persia. What a contrast to her journeys; Asolo makes no demands. I feel that I'm in an older, Italian version of Carmel, California, with many secret gardens, vine-covered gates, and charming houses. A place you could imagine retiring someday, if only you had tons of *lire*. Roses are tumbling in Asolo. Every few steps, new soft fragrances fall in your face from the walls above. I don't look for her house or grave. I am just curious to see where she walked during her many last years after writing her books. Surely she took her tea near the fountain. I'm quite certain she shopped at the paper store in town. I don't emerge until I have bought my next blank book, a yellow one to replace the blue book, where I wrote about our first experiences in Cortona, and a photograph album with a cover of painted wildflowers.

I resist the tiny bottles of lavender, indigo, and green ink sealed with wax, and the rows of expensive pens. The sensuous pleasure of good writing materials is like no other. The attraction links to the excitement of school supplies purchased every year for so long. Few things I've bought exceed the delight of yellow legal pads, spiraled and colored index cards, five-subject notebooks, and leather three-ring binders. And if there's a red satchel with compartments and zippered pockets, so much the better.

The first experience of these joys comes back—the supply cabinet at my father's mill office. He let me take stenographers' pads with a line down the middle, a red pencil that could be sharpened right there in a machine with a dial which rotated to accommodate different pencil sizes. On one of those Saturday mornings when I rode out to the mill with him, I became fascinated with a large gray staple gun. I liked the ka-clink sound it made. My teacher had told our kindergarten class that hair and nails have no feeling, so I put my left thumb in place and pressed hard, sending excruciating bolts of pain through my thin nail. I was stapled. My father said some horrible words and pried out the staple with a screwdriver. The body remembers everything. I still can shudder at the pain. "See this thumbnail?" I hold it up for Ed.

"Yes—what?"

"Can you see the break in the crescent moon?"

He holds it next to the other one. "I guess so." I tell him the story. "Ouch. You make my knees weak. What made you think of that here?"

"Wanting the lavender ink but being afraid it would leak in the suitcase."

"Wait a minute. Is that old clunker of a stapler you use at home the same one from your father's office?"

"Of course."

~

For two easy days we drive about, returning at night to our little outpost of fantastic food. The hallway of the inn is lined with family photographs—men home from war, babies in arms, group portraits. We love this intimate atmosphere and the warmth the family projects as we come and go. Townspeople gather in the bar, banging glasses, watching soccer on TV, exchanging the news about the daughter's first communion and the idiot who backed into the sycamore at the post office. We participate peripherally, briefly, in the ongoing life of this place. Ed tells them we'll be back to try the fall menu someday. As we leave, he looks sorrowfully into the dining room.

———

The *primo* approach to Venice is not Marco Polo airport or the train; having driven around in the Veneto, and stopped in Chioggia, I've absorbed a new sense of this watery location. I'd always thought of Venice as a risen place which not long ago was sinking and might sink again. Wandering in the Veneto, I absorbed the real *geographical* sense, and I'm more awed than ever. The land under Venice is often little more than the sandbars I used to wade to at St. Simon's Island. The feat of establishing an empire on this marshy archipelago shows that the settlers were strong on imagination. They wove willow dikes to keep away the sea. What madness! Foundations were built on wooden poles, driven all the way through the water and silty land to the packed clay substrata. The hundreds of tiny islands were later linked by bridges, giving the impression of canals carved out of a single island. Some waterways were filled in, further changing the reality of the actual topography.

Instinct tells me that by learning to "read" the watery map, I may be able to feel my way toward the source of this place's hold on my imagination. I know already that it's not only Venice's extravagant beauty that pulls me. My clues toward a solution may begin with the realization that Venice's origins are *against all rational thinking*: Build your church—or your insurance company—on a rock.

Ed and I park in a remote garage, leaving most of our luggage in the trunk, and board a boat, which crosses a flat stretch of water and soon enters the Grand Canal. Holy Toledo! Holy of holies! Memory has abstracted the city into watercolor scenes. The reality of the dips of the boat, the working gondolas laden with fruit and cases of *acqua minerale,* the construction barges piled with boards and sacks of concrete, the mind-stopping, stupendous, fairy-tale, solid beauty of the *palazzi* lining the canal and reflecting in the water—I stand at the rail biting hard on the knuckle of my right forefinger, an old habit that returns when I am knocked silent. The beauty does not just pass before your eyes. It ravishes. I begin to feel the elation that a traveller experiences when in the presence of a place supremely itself.

Arriving in Venice seems like the most natural act in the world. Is it this way for everyone? The place is so thoroughly known through film, photographs, calendars, books. Is there another layer to this easy familiarity?

I'm feeling a rush of memories and I want them to end by the time my foot steps out on the *fondamenta.* Venice was "our" city, my former husband's and mine. Although we went only twice, we'd loved the small flower-filled hotel, where we pulled the mattress off the bed when it squeaked. Our gondolier had a piercingly sweet voice and glided through canals, ducking under bridges. Well, yes, he did sing "O Sole Mio," but he also had a good fling with "Nessun Dorma." At the early morning market, a vendor built a ziggurat of ripe white peaches. Every fish in the Adriatic seemed to be lined up glassy-eyed on ice, ready for the women with their baskets, and restaurant owners trailed by minions who balanced crates on their shoulders. Because I am cursed with a bird phobia, I hovered under the arcades of the Piazza San Marco while my husband walked among the thousands of pigeons then came back to describe the *piazza* from the perspective I never will see. We found the paper store with blank books bound in vellum and marbled paper. We tried the pasta with squid in its own ink. I loved the cycle of Saint Ursula paintings by Carpaccio. Ursula, lying there in a tall bed, dreaming, while the angel bringing the palm of her martyrdom steps through her threshold. Four years later we returned with our daughter and had the pleasure of being in her happy company on those canals. She wore a straw gondolier hat, ran to pet cats who wouldn't be petted, left her drawstring pocketbook on a *vaporetto* and cried for the loss of a dozen pieces of broken glass she'd collected on the trip. Odd what fragments of memory stay. I don't remember how she liked the lagoon, the bridges, the *piazza*. She loved the hotel tub's brass swan handles and spout. Strange how memory can reach *around* years and reconnect to the place and time where old loves are still intact. The memory rush subsides.

Many high waters have washed through Venice since then. Now I am back. With Ed. A different life. We'll make our own way here. I look over at Ed and have to laugh. He has the deep-space stare. "Venice," I say and he nods.

He's already tan, and leaning on the rail in his yellow linen shirt, with the pure glory of Venice racing behind him, I think he looks like someone I'd like to run off with, if I already hadn't. The prospect of days with *him* roving around Venice: *bella, bella*. As we enter the widest part of the Grand Canal, it seems to tilt. Soon we're bumping into the dock. "Heaven. Unbelievable."

"Yes, if there's no Venice in the real heaven, I don't want to go there."

⁓

The hotel, a former convent tower, faces a harmonious *piazza* which used to be water but somewhere along the way was filled. Tower means romantic and also narrow. The frou-frou furniture and tiny room seem very Venetian to me. Ed looks somewhat like Gulliver in this Lilliputian space.

We've arrived in time for the shadow rounds. An Italian friend in Cortona told us about the Venetian late afternoon "bar-hopping" custom. Tucked away in the neighborhoods are small bars, often with a counter opening to the street. Neighbors gather for an *ombra,* shadow, a half-glass of wine. The "shadow" comes from the original gathering place in the shadow of San Marco. People visit, sip, then wander on to the next bar. Often those who join don't know each other outside this custom. "He's a friend from the shadow rounds," Venetians say to each other. *Antipasti* are laid out on the counter, savory nibbles somewhat like *tapas*: polenta squares with fish inside, *moleche,* tiny grilled crabs eaten whole, fried anchovies, and various preparations of *baccalà,* dried cod. They visit two or three then go home. The groups keep reconfiguring. We stop at one bar with so many delicious *antipasti* that we decide to stay for dinner in the back room. We try the *sarde in soar,* fresh sardines in a sweet and sour sauce, a dish the old Doges must have enjoyed. Venice has a bad reputation for restaurants but in the neighborhoods, the authentic dishes and the freshest seafood are served in intimate *trattorie.* The classic Venetian repertoire includes calf liver with onions (forget college dining room liver and onions); risotto or pasta with squid in its ink; that great comfort food *risi e bisi,* rice and peas; as well as fish with red radicchio, both grilled; fish soups; various shellfish with pastas; fish, fish, fish. Venice and Sicily, opposite in most ways, share the boon of the sea, and the intricate use of seasoning and spices supplied by the history of domination by many nations.

~

We leave the map in the room. We just walk. Walk and walk. Away from the main sights, the Venetian neighborhoods are endlessly appealing. We happen upon a *squero,* a yard where gondolas are made and repaired. A man brushes on black paint and I remember that once, before plague and sumptuary laws, gondolas were decorated in many colors. I want Ed to see Carpaccio's nine paintings of the Legend of Saint Ursula. She's sweetly asleep in a four-poster bed, a little dog on the floor, potted plants on the windowsills. The other side of the bed is conspicuously empty. She has, I remember, rejected Conan as her groom in favor of virginity. At her door, the hesitant angel will cross the threshold, touch her shoulder and hand her the palm of martyrdom. Irrationally, I say, "She's still sleeping, all these years I've been gone."

In small shops, which make me think of medieval guilds, we see supple cutwork velvet, candied fruit, bracelets of gold chunks, porphyry heads, and colored blown glass. I long to go in the houses, experience from the inside what it's like to have high tide lapping at the lower floor, smell the damp marble, see the rippling shadows of the water on painted ceilings, push back faded brocades to let in the sun.

When we find ourselves at the quay where you catch a boat for the islands, we jump on. The ports of call ten or twenty minutes away are remote from Venice in time and space. Poor little reedy islands barely out of the water—this is what supports the splendors of Venice, too. We pass Murano, don't stop at a farm island, and disembark at Torcello.

From the dock we follow a brackish canal to the remains of a settlement. The deserted town gives me the feeling that all the inhabitants have fled. Malaria did devastate the population but that was centuries ago. The Romanesque-Byzantine church of Santa Fosca was a latecomer to the island in the eleventh century. If I could draw, I would take out my pastel pencils right here and sketch its delicate arched portico. The cathedral, oldest building in the whole Venetian lagoon, was started in 639. From then until the fourteenth century, Torcello thrived. Twenty thousand people lived here, most of them raising sheep and making wool. Not until the early eleventh century were the mosaics laid in the floor of the cathedral. Others later were added to walls, including the standing Madonna holding the Infant, in a field of golden tesserae. Of the thousands and thousands of Madonnas, this is definitely one to see. So is the Last Judgement, with its spooky mosaic skeletons.

After the fourteenth century, Torcello began a long slide into its current decline. I read that sixty people live here but we don't see anyone except at makeshift tents where touristy souvenirs are sold. "What a great place to make a movie." Ed is looking at a wild garden filled with statues, the exotic rounded forms of the cathedral, the blond light.

"What kind?"

"One with nothing of modern time in it. We're in a serious warp. But look, that *casa* is being restored. Maybe some of the workers who commute from Mestre to Venice will move here. Instead of breathing factory fumes they could have land. It would be a great place to live."

"If you had a boat."

"And a garden, and a wine cellar, and a good library."

"Next time I'd like to spend the night at the *locanda*. Even the few tourists would take the last boat back to Venice. Islands at night...." He doesn't finish his sentence.

~

Crowded, lively Burano is the polar opposite of Torcello; it's jarring to arrive after the quiet, and then impossible not to love the bright houses along the canals. I find myself taking pictures of a flowery balcony on a purple house, fishing nets draped to dry over the prow of a yellow boat, a woman in a blue-framed window shaking out a red tea towel. All the colors you'd never paint your house look marvelously festive here. It's as if every resident rushed off to a giant paint sale for bargains on pumpkin and lavender. Many awful paintings must have commenced with a day-trip to Burano. The village feels buoyant and playful. We have a picnic on the grass overlooking the water, then board the boat that plies these islands, passing San Michele, the cemetery, on the way back to the landing.

Standing near the prow, I realize I have my face out for the smell of marshes. Across pale green water, Venice, shimmering in diluted sunlight. Lulled by the slap of waves against the hull, I recall the stunning opening of one of my favorite books, Nabokov's *Speak Memory*: "The cradle rocks above an abyss, and common sense tells us that our existence is but a brief crack of light between two eternities of darkness. Although the two are identical twins, man, as a rule, views the prenatal abyss with more calm than the one he is heading for (at some forty-five hundred heartbeats an hour)." I was rereading him last night and felt the charge of that passage.

Is the passion for seeing what remains of the past a bridge to "the prenatal abyss"? *All this took place before you.* And look, you can touch so much that preceded you. All the clear markers which ultimately led to you, your brief moment in a crack of light. *I'm floating.* Venice is all alluvial light. *Riding the waters.* I'm mesmerized by the nacreous sky and the marshes and the Venice of.... I'm searching. Yes, here, ah, yes, the Venice of the slippery pass, the watery link to the preconscious.

My mind come to rest; this is what I've been trolling these waters to find. The watery city *takes me there* as the cities on land *cannot,* cannot, with their divisible reality of streets under our feet and tires, their exits and entrances so spatially broken.

Venice is simultaneous, like all time before we existed. *Because we are swimmers. The slick creatures of land and water.* And the scent of marsh drifts deeply into the medulla, that old hard-pack.

Now, I finally notice: The gondoliers *stand* as they work the water. They cross from one side to the other side. *Death in Venice,* Thomas Mann wrote; so, of course, of course we recognize that "strange craft . . . with that peculiar blackness which is found elsewhere only in coffins."

But no, the gondoliers don't look like Charons on the River Styx. Instead, they walk the water, miraculously. The shape of the gondola shares more with the treble clef than with a coffin. The death connection is preconditioning, received knowledge, not experienced knowledge. This water is too glorious, a swabbed silver light streaking rose-gold, tesselate and far, far from death. But now I understand why Shelley, Mann, McCarthy, Ruskin, travel articles, films—all the ways I pre-experienced Venice—never got to the Venice I sensed under my skin. *Death* is what they called the mystery of Venice's allure. For me, they had it backwards. For *birth* we cross through the waters.

From a distance, the gondoliers appear as somnambulists, the black silhouettes of the gondolas propelled across the waters of the unconscious by dreams.

~

In the early evening, I'm still reflecting. We're having a glass of wine at a bar right on the Grand Canal. Is it always shimmering and clear? Probably it smells like garbage in August. The waiter is solicitous, friendly. "How can they stay nice when they have to put up with so many tourists?" The American at the next table has banged his glass to get the waiter's attention. His friends are pretending they're going to push each other's chairs into the water. And they're adults.

"Tourists are how they live. They're used to us. Imagine what it's like in July, with crud bobbing in the canals. We'd all be in a mob, sweltering, and oozing garlic sweat."

Since it's April, the throngs have not yet arrived, but enough of the world's masses are here to make me want to avoid the main sights. They're often the unappealing kind of tourists in caps and shorts, trailing McDonald's junk behind them. I cross my arms and look sullenly at my neighbors, who are having a fine time.

When I turn my chair so that I can face the water directly and watch the gondolas pass, I observe the oddest thing: The faces of the tourists who are being ferried by the *palazzi,* the Ca'd'Oro, the lacy Gothic windows, landings lapped with moss, and the umber and old rose facades reflecting and lifting and breaking in the brushed blue water, the faces have gone blank. Their edges soften. Their eyes are full of beauty and the limpid light is on them. They are changed by what is seeing them. They step out of the gondolas like new beings.

All the restaurants we choose are in remote neighborhoods. We get lost and found over and over. After dinner, almost midnight, the *calli* fall silent; our footsteps echo and we find ourselves whispering. Sleeping cats on windowsills and doorsteps don't even look up. Back at the hotel, the desk clerk tells us about Padania, the separatist group dedicated to seceding from Italy. Today they've hijacked a ferry—although they paid the fare!—and loaded a panel truck painted to look like an armored vehicle. They drove across Piazza San Marco, waving guns. They were shortly arrested. "*Carnevale.* They think it's carnival time," he shrugs. Around four, we awake to the sound of "Hut, *uno, due, tre, quattro,*" and rhythmic marching. We look out onto the *campo* and see about twenty Padania men in black, goose-stepping around—surreal flashback to the Fascist thirties. They look well-trained to me but Ed says it doesn't take much talent to goose-step. "I was dreaming," Ed remembers, "of ice skating down the Grand Canal, doing figure eights in Piazza San Marco then I was gliding backwards underneath bridges I had to duck under."

"What do you suppose that means?"

He's falling asleep again. "Venice on ice. Iced Venus. Venus and Venice. Us in Venice."

Now I can't sleep so I read about Lord Byron's wild liaisons with Venetian women, his afternoons of study on the island of San Lazzaro, where Armenian scholars still live, and his swims from the Lido to the end of the Grand Canal. Ed has a talent for sleep. When his head touches the pillow, he's gone. I wonder if Lord Byron's back was as sexy as Ed's, if his luminous skin was as healthy and alive to the adoring wife of some Venetian merchant. Way back *in the prenatal abyss*—Byron's actual body in the cold; he shakes water from his eyes and sees the *palazzi* at sunrise, his lame leg trying to work against the tide. *Almost, I can feel the current rush and the strain in his muscles*. Impossible to read— my eyes are still printed with Venice and the wattage of the bedside lamp rivals a nightlight. Nothing is harder to hold than the reality of the past. My daughter's lost red pocketbook full of treasures. My book slides to the floor but Ed doesn't move. Briefly, I contemplate diving into a canal myself. Although I probably would have to have my stomach pumped, it would be something to add to my résumé.

Deeper into the Country

BATS ARE BACK, SWOOPING ERRATICALLY ABOVE us. They don't seem to fly but to scatter like dark confetti in gusty wind. I used to be afraid one would land in my hair, but after hundreds of dinners under their flight path, I trust their echolocation. I remember seeing an x-ray of a bat in anatomy class. The bones look like a homunculus hidden inside the leathery body. D. H. Lawrence described a bat as "a black glove thrown up at the light, / and falling back," and its wings "like bits of umbrella," but I can imagine only the rudimentary trapped human, fated to eat its weight in bugs. Since they share Bramasole with us, somehow folding themselves into cracks between stucco and stone, they now seem like friendly presences.

They may be excited at the energy emanating from a bowl of fava beans and a board holding a wedge of *pecorino* on the top of the wall, our convenient sideboard. If not, they are the only creatures in the Arezzo province not sharing this Tuscan mania.

To start or to finish dinner each night, we are fated to eat *fave*.

Anselmo's crop, as predicted, overwhelms us. We give bags of the tender young things to neighbors, friends, anyone who will take them. The local ritual of *pecorino* and *fave* is one of the most loved combinations in Tuscan food. Served as lunch in itself, or an *antipasto,* or in place of dessert, this sacred marriage exists for a short, intense season. The *pecorino* of choice is fresh; these two spring arrivals go naturally together.

Tonight's *pecorino* is special, thanks to our friend Vittorio. He grew up in Cortona and works for a vineyard now, after several years of working in Rome, commuting the long distance so he could continue to live the way he wants. He stops by the house after gathering *funghi porcini* in the mountains. When we're in town, we leave a bag of *fave* on his doorknob. He is president of the local chapter of Slow Food, an international organization devoted to preserving traditional cuisines and dedicated to pure methods of growing and preparing food and wine. Slow Food—as opposed to fast food. Naturally, we have joined. Local meetings consist of eight-course dinners with ten or twelve wines from a particular region. A club after my own heart. At the time of our "meetings," other chapters around Italy are meeting, too, and at the end of the evening votes are cast, phoned in, and the best wines are elected.

Late in the afternoon, Vittorio took us far into the hills to meet a friend of his family, a farmer whose name, to our astonishment, is Achille. We waited for him to come in from milking. Outside the farmhouse, a metal bathtub under a cold water faucet was positioned for a perfect view of Cortona in the distance, with orchards sloping down his hills. Half an olive oil can nailed sideways to the wall held soap and a brush. Around the courtyard stood benches made from hollowed-out logs. Achille, around seventy years old, came in carrying a bucket of ewe's milk and a rake, the rake's handle a straight limb smooth from use, the tines strong sticks carved and set into a piece of branch, all finished neatly. He'd *made* his rake. Such a beautiful thing and a symbol of his individuality; rakes don't cost much and he prefers to make his own. Achille is a compact man, grave and slow. His remote tortoise eyes seemed to take the measure of us quickly. Every day he has lived in the sun has added a wrinkle to his face so that now he is completely furrowed and tanned to the color of an old baseball glove. We followed him into a room next to a stall with calves closed inside. His cheeses lined four hanging shelves. Ed noticed jagged tin rounds at intervals along the ropes. Achille smiled quietly and nodded. The *topi,* mice, can't crawl around the tin and eat the cheese.

Grass floated on top of the milk. He took a wad of cotton and covered the mesh of a sieve, then poured the milk through. He took a jug of what must be rennet and splashed in some. I wanted to ask questions but he did not seem cut out for casual conversation. The room smelled like nowhere I've ever been, a powerful, primitive lacteal ripening. Forget European Union rules of pasteurization, this is cheese as it has been made through the eons. He asked us to select a cheese, one with no cracks in the outer layer. He rotated the cheese, looking at me intently (I'm probably as exotic to him as he is to me) and said we should turn it every day. "Why?" I ventured, although I assumed the ingredients were not yet stable and continued to need mixing. No reply, but he almost smiled. The straw-colored two-pound round looked like a little moon. He wrapped it carefully in foil.

Achille's wife came in with another bucket. She wore boots and a housedress, and like her husband, was deeply sunbaked. They are extremely quiet, I think shy, probably from years of isolation. Right away, she started another batch. She has a wood stove in the courtyard for cooking in hot weather. A battered pasta pot on top attests to frequent use. I imagine her in the evening, after all the chores, bathing in that tub, nothing but silence all around her.

Young *fave* do not have to be peeled, just shelled at the table and enjoyed with the *pecorino*. Achille's cheese is smooth and tangy, without the barnyard taste many fresh *pecorini* seem to impart. Ed cuts another piece. I notice he has eaten a quarter of the yellow moon. We walk up on the terraces after dinner, carrying a last glass of wine. The zucchini are starting to bloom. Those audacious flowers deserve a van Gogh or Nolde to capture their melted gold. We linger at the tomatoes, figuring how long until we're coming up with baskets to pull them from the vines. Ed rubs a leaf on his fingers and lets me smell the promise of ripe tomatoes. The chard, more chard than I can imagine for risotto, is ready. We stop at the patch of *fave*. We hardly have made a dent. Something tells me I won't want to see a fava bean for years after this spring.

I'm spending the afternoon with Vittorio, roaming around the countryside in his car with all the windows down. Ed is taking a day for writing. We stop to visit a farmer who lives in a house built in the 1400s and still is owned by a count of the same family, whose villa is down the road. Tommaso is delighted to see Vittorio, who grew up nearby and used to play in the hay barn. He shows us an old painted cart still stored there. These places sequestered from time never become familiar; visiting, we drop behind the years, into a way of life we've imagined but never known.

When I ask about the chapel at the back of the house, Tommaso casually tells us that it has been closed since Napoleon passed by, as though he were saying it's been closed since Wednesday. "Before," he says, "pilgrims used to stop for three days; the count gave them food and lodging." The way he talks, we think it could be the current count, could be his own extra rooms involved.

Tentatively, I ask if we could see the inside of the chapel. He leads us through his house. I glimpse bare rooms where he and his brother live: iron beds, chests, yellowed crochet-edged linen curtains, remnants of a sister or wife, and a few photographs on the wall. No TV, no technology at all, not even a radio in sight. Austere as monk cells and utterly clean. We're winding around medieval corridors with no light. Tommaso's steps are secure. We follow blindly and finally he turns a key with a loud ka-lunk, ka-lunk and pushes open the door. The first thing I see is a copper bathtub, then some farm equipment and barrels. As my eyes adjust to the gray light falling from a single high round window, I make out frescoes of a saint and of the Madonna. A glaring blank space shows where a painting was removed. "It's down at the church now. Stop and the priest will show you San Filippio, who used to live happily here." The chapel is oddly elaborate for a farmhouse of this type. Maybe the count wanted the sweaty pilgrims to stop somewhere well away from his own enclosed park.

Tommaso takes us to the kitchen and pours glasses of *vin santo*, the drink of hospitality in all farms. I've had *vin santo*, which tastes something like sherry, at all hours of the day in various houses. He props himself inside the walk-in fireplace in a chair and he and Vittorio reminisce about telling stories around the fire years ago. Tommaso is the opposite of the solemn Achille. He's lived his life without much of a cruising radius, too, but he's a talker, a storyteller. He stretches out his legs, mimicking how in old times the *contadini* used to toast themselves in winter, while staying close enough to stir the polenta. Looking around the kitchen I see no sign of heat, so I expect they still have this ancestral habit on January nights.

Tommaso shows us his Val di Chiana cows, those white beasts

who turn into the famous Florentine beefsteak, grilled with rosemary. He has four grown ones and three calves, who fix great dark eyes at us and stare. Around their necks he has tied red ribbons to protect them from the evil eye. I always wondered why the steak highlights Tuscan menus yet you never see these creatures in fields. They're raised indoors, babied and petted but cruelly chained to the manger. They are immense, growing to three times the size of a normal cow.

Next to the house an enclosed and overgrown flower garden again attests to a long-lost feminine presence. The old roses trained on iron poles still bloom profusely. The yellow rambler with tiny blooms has spilled from its pole and crawled to a fence where it swoops and spreads recklessly.

I'm following warily because of the roaming ducks and chickens. My old bird phobia is a liability not only in *piazze* full of pigeons. If Tommaso suspects that I'm afraid of a chicken, he will think I am nuts. Two white turkeys peck the ground near the barn. They are the ugliest birds on earth.

We drive past the count's villa, a melancholy shuttered place surrounded by chestnut trees, and stop at the church. Stanislao, the Pole who helped build our long stone wall when we first bought Bramasole, and his wife Renia, live with the priest of this parish, Don Fabio. She cooks and takes care of the house and church. Stanislao works as a mason but does odd jobs for the church property on weekends. Some Saturdays when Stanislao works with Ed at our house, she comes to help me in the garden. Tiny and wiry, she has tremendous energy. The priest is teaching two children their catechism in the garden. Reina takes us in, pausing to show us Don Fabbio's study. It could be the study in the paintings of Saint Jerome. An open window throws dusky light onto a desk stacked with leather books, some open, some turned face down. All we need is Saint Jerome's attribute, the sleeping lion. In a corridor we see the dim painting that used to hang in Tommaso's chapel. On a side wall in the church, snapshots of all parishioners who have died are arranged in rows. Vittorio finds many familiar faces from his childhood. We leave Reina to her ironing of the altar linen, leave Don Fabbio to his two red-haired charges in the garden.

Growing up in a small town, I felt the tight bit in my mouth. I couldn't wait to leave. The pull of cities was strong. I remember, however, a slight pull, too, toward life far in the country.

My boyfriend's grandmother, Mimo, lived near Mystic, a crossroads out in tobacco and cotton country. A porch ran the length of her two-storey house. Her pie safe always was full of lemon and coconut meringue pies. In plain bedrooms her quilts lay folded at the foot of each bed. The porch faced the fields and she sat there in the afternoons shelling butter beans. Occasionally, she picked up a wooden-handled church fan printed with a picture of Jesus and fanned away the flies. I sat in the swing reading *Anna Karenina*. In this memory, I am somehow missing the boyfriend altogether. Through stirred-up field dust, the sunset sky turned lurid and splendid, popsicle orange and grape, with sprays of gold, and cheap-underwear pink. After the wobbling gold blob of sunset, the air over the tobacco turned blue, as though over a lake. We were the solemn witnesses. It could have been Doomsday every afternoon. After that Mimo would go fix herself a tall gin and tonic.

In his book I once loved, *The Mind of the South*, W. J. Cash observed that this air is responsible for Southerners's romanticism—they see through a haze and consequently have a hard time distinguishing reality. Mimo's life appealed to me. She roared in her Buick across rutted roads through crops to check on workers. Long a widow, she ran the farm, put up preserves, birthed calves, quilted and cooked, and always kicked open the screen door when we arrived, throwing open her arms.

Rediscovering deep country life, I wonder now what it would be like to live like Achille and Tommaso. For years I would have thought *What a waste*. I was interested in the dramatic life—maybe someone would throw himself under a train for *me*. I was pretty sure I never would be called on for something that rash.

Now I feel the lure of country dawns, sunsets, the satisfaction of living in a green kingdom of one's own. I feel as well a growing distrust of spending too much of one's life deifying work. Finding that running balance among ambition, solitude, stimulation, adventure—how to do this? I heard Ramsey Clark, then Attorney General, speak when I was in college. All I remember him saying was something like, "When I die, I want to be so exhausted that you can throw me on the scrap heap." He wanted to be totally consumed by his life. I was impressed and adopted that as my philosophy, too. As a writer, I also had an inclination toward meditation and reclusiveness, and so have maintained for most of my life a decent balance. The last few years have pulled me too much in the exterior direction. After devoting five years to chairing my department at the university, I resigned from the hot seat and went back to teaching. I saw how a few months later hardly anyone remembered what I thought of as vast changes, how instantaneously time slid over my absence. I was left with the private satisfaction of a job well done. Considering time, stress, and pure hassle, private satisfaction did not seem like enough. I had wanted to rethink the department from the bottom up and was willing to write endless memos, reports, evaluations, and to straggle home at 8 P.M. What is replenishing? What is depleting? What takes? What gives? What wrings you out and, truly, what rinses you with happiness? What comes from my own labor and creativity, regardless of what anyone else thinks of it, stays close to the natural joy we all were born with and carry always. Mystic, Georgia, was not for me. I would have been hell on wheels by thirty. Oddly, oddly, I probably could live a happy, sensuous life there now. Is the sun still blistering the paint on Mimo's house? Do the fields shimmer in the blue heat? Hey, Tommaso, Achille, do you want to die so exhausted you're just ready to be tossed away? *That American, have you ever known a woman afraid of a chicken?*

~

Anselmo takes his time. Even when he had his office covered with photos of broken-down houses where he hoped someone would invest their souls, he had time to talk. In his transformation to gardener, he lavishes his attention on perfect bamboo tepees for the tomatoes. He brings me roses from his own garden and flats of strawberries. Best of all, he takes us on excursions. When Ed asks him about a cart for hauling the lemon trees into the *limonaia* in winter, he drives us immediately to his neighbor, a blacksmith in Ossaia. The *fabbro* makes a sketch, promises the low cart, which will slide right under the pot, for next week.

Anselmo motions us to follow him. "What is that flower?" I ask, pointing to a compact bush growing out of a stone wall.

"I've seen that all over the town walls. Looks like the flower on a passion vine," Ed notices.

Anselmo looks at us incredulously. *"Capperi."* He pulls off several buds. "I'll plant them in your wall, but they are bad for the wall. You must control them." Capers—wild, everywhere. We'd never known.

In his barn, a royal mess, he leads us far in the back where extensive wine-making equipment is covered with dust: barrels, small casks, bottles, and a grand *torchio,* the slatted vat with iron bands and levers where grapes are pressed. Ed is admiring it the way men admire a new car, nodding his head and walking around it. Anselmo explains the mechanism to us. From a shelf he pulls down two bottles of his own *vin santo*. "Something to drink with *biscotti*."

His *vin santo* looks slightly murky. I wonder how long it has waited for us on the shelf.

Since we are close to his sister and brother-in-law's house, he wants us to meet them. We pile back in his huge Alfa and he shortly takes a rough turn up into their yard. His sister comes out and greets him as though she hasn't seen him in years. His brother-in-law, thinning pears on one of his acre-long lines of espaliered fruit trees, comes running. We are introduced as *"stranieri,"* foreigners. Out comes the *vin santo* for the foreigners. "Is this yours?" Ed asks Anselmo, but no, it is the brother-in-law's own. Ed is looking at the orchard. In the distance I see a corrugated roof on poles has been erected over what looks from here like a swimming pool. "May we look at the fruit trees?" Ed asks.

"Certo." The rows are elegant. The vase-shaped trees are developing vase-shaped pears. They are vigorous, all except for one section, which has a deep hole around it, causing roots to die and leaves to drop. The brother-in-law seems annoyed. He pulls on a nonexistent beard. His mouth curls in scorn.

"What happened here?" Ed asks.

Anselmo shakes one hand slowly in the air, that flinging gesture which means something like Good God Almighty. *"Porca miseria,"* the brother-in-law says, pig misery. He points toward the roofed structure. "They have discovered a Roman villa, the archeologists, and are making an excavation. They have dug here, and have killed this tree." Clearly the sacrifice was not justified in his eyes. In Italy, whatever is underground on your property does not belong to you. "They have killed an olive." He inclines his chin toward an olive now on a raised mound with a ditch around it. We know that to be a cardinal sin.

"A Roman villa?"

"The whole hill is a museum. There was not only a villa, but a whole town. Everyone knows, but now it is a discovery." He shrugs. "If they asked me, I could show them where Hannibal's house is. But they don't ask. Just dig."

Hannibal's defeat of Flaminio was a few miles away. Ossaia means "boneyard" and derived from the stacks of bodies brought here after the battle. He leads us through his vegetable garden and a field to a ruin of a stone house which does look old but not two thousand years old. "*Sì,* Hannibal lived here."

We walk back by the dig. Under a temporary roof, we see a black-and-white mosaic Greek key floor, the geometry of rooms. A large villa stood here, with a view right into the sister and brother-in-law's garden. The dig is inactive at this season.

As we drive away Anselmo tells us they added a room years ago. "They found a mosaic floor right where they poured the foundation."

We stop once more to talk to a widow who wants him to sell her house. Even though Anselmo has closed his office, he still does a little business. "Maybe you would like this house. There is everything to restore." He looks at me in the rearview mirror, almost clipping a bicyclist. He loves his sly little digs.

"Not interested." He pulls inside the gate and stops in the dirt forecourt, scattering chickens. A woman in the old-fashioned black dress comes out, bent as a comma. She is older than Cortona. When we are introduced, she grabs my hand in her dry, hard one and does not let go as we walk around the property. As if anticipating that she soon will enter a silent eternity, she talks nonstop. I can barely look at the adorable bunnies she has scrooched together in a pen. "She sees something different when she looks at them," Ed says. "She sees them roasting in the pan with fennel. She's not focused on their soft ears." She tours the *orto,* where vegetables are thriving, looks in on two cows, flings open the lower doors of the house. Ah, a completely unrestored house, with the mangers and *cantina* still intact. Winemaking equipment crowds every square centimeter, dozens of rotting straw-covered demijohns, oak barrels, and bottles. In a small, immaculate room, she shows me a corner table where she still makes pasta when it's hot up in her kitchen. Jars of tomatoes line the shelves. A straight chair with a cowhide seat stands by the door to catch a breeze and her mending and knitting lie in baskets. Since she is crushing my ring into my fingers in her grip, I wish she would let go, and, at the same time, I am flattered by her instant attachment. "I think she wants us to buy the house," Ed whispers in English.

"Yes, and it's no later than 1750 in here."

Upstairs, she opens the rooms where her parents lived until they died. Their iron bed with a white bedspread dips on either side, conjuring the bodies of the two grim-faced sepia photographs framed on the wall. Bed. Chair. *Armadio.* A commode for the *vaso da notte,* the chamberpot. Her room is the same, with the addition of a lugubrious framed print of Christ, with dead palm branches tucked behind, and a yellowing oval photo of her husband as a young man. Fierce-eyed, tight-lipped, probably in his wedding suit, he stares toward the bed they shared as they grew older and older, older than he could have imagined when the camera caught the hot gleam in his eye. In a water glass floats a set of false teeth with plum-pink gums. His?

Like most Italian kitchens, hers looks and smells recently scrubbed. Even the faucets are polished. Inevitably, she pulls out the *vin santo* and pours, then she brings out *biscotti.* They are stone-hard; perhaps they were made in 1750. She is wonderful to behold. Since she's talking mile-a-minute to Anselmo about going to live with her daughter, and how the place is too much for her, I get a chance to look at her darting eyes full of intelligence, her hair tied under a black scarf. Her thin body is all force.

I feel the indentations in my fingers where she squeezed—at least she had to let go to serve the wine.

She closes the gate behind us and waves until we're gone. Four feet eight inches at most, she's a whirling dervish of energy. I wish I knew her life story. I wish I could watch her make pasta and buttonholes. I wonder what she dreams.

"I hate for her to leave and live in an apartment in Foligno. Who will buy the place?" I ask as we drive away.

"She is asking twice what it's worth. I don't think she wants to sell."

"I loved it. The manger could be a fabulous living room with doors opening onto a terrace."

"I like that upstairs loggia," Ed says.

Anselmo shakes his head. "You never know what foreigners will like. She'll probably sell to some crazy foreigner."

~

"Be prepared for a six-hour feast," our friend Donatella tells us. "Giusi has set up a kitchen in the whole barn so six cooks can work." Her sister, Giusi, helps take care of our house when we are not here. The sisters are opposite. Donatella has an angular, dark beauty, somewhat like the Mona Lisa's, and an ironic humor. You can look way into her black eyes. Giusi in America would be Homecoming Queen. She could captain any pep squad. She's pretty, sociable, and upbeat. They are sisters and best friends. Each time we arrive at Bramasole, they've left flowers in the house, and the kitchen stocked with fruit, coffee, bread, and cheese so that we don't need to dash out if we are tired from the flight. Both are excellent cooks, who learned directly from a mother who still makes her own ravioli.

Giusi's two young sons are taking their first communion. This calls for a feast. We have not seen Giusi for weeks because she has been preparing the *festa*. After the service, around eighty people gather at the house in the mountains Giusi and her husband, Dario, share with his parents. Dario's sister and her family live in another house on the property. They are close to self-sufficient for all their food. The family takes care of a large vegetable garden, raises chickens, rabbits, lambs, and geese. The men hunt, keeping a supply of wild boar at the ready.

Everything they produce, and a lot more, goes into the first communion dinner. When we arrive at noon, the party is in full swing. Giusi gives me a tour of the house. For almost two years she has endured an extensive remodeling. She's kept the warm feel of the ancient farmhouse, but has installed lovely bathrooms, stone stairs, and an up-to-the-minute kitchen, which, of course, includes a wood-burning stove for cooking. Every knob and surface gleams. Every window sparkles. Outside, the *prosecco* already is flowing and women are passing trays of *crostini,* Tuscan *antipasti* of rounds of bread spread with various toppings: *porcini* mushrooms, spicy cheese, and chopped, seasoned chicken liver. Under a white tent, they've set a U-shaped table under balloons and twisted colored-paper streamers. The two boys are seated at the head, flanked by their parents. We've peered in the barn where many hands are at work. A table down the center is crowded with fruit tarts, enormous bowls of salad greens. Each woman has on a flowered dress. The barn whirls with color and motion. They're still chopping and peeling, putting the finishing garnishes together. For each plate, spring leeks, carrots, and asparagus are deftly tied in bundles with a blade of chive. I'm surprised to meet Guisi's mother. Young and red-haired, she looks nothing like her daughters. She has made *cappelli del prete,* pasta called priest's hats, for eighty-odd people.

As we soon find out, there are two pastas. Everyone is served a large helping of *tagliatelle* with a rich sauce of *cinghiale,* the wild boar. Many have seconds of this and I'm wiping the edge of the plate with bread for every drop of the delicious sauce.

Then comes the priest's hats with four cheeses. And seconds of that. The efficient army of women swoops down and replaces our plates after each course. Someone in the barn is washing dishes like mad. Lamb with the vegetable bundles comes next, their own lamb roasted in the outdoor oven. In the distance we can hear sheep and cows, who don't yet know they will not always dwell in the lush pasture below but will be appearing on these same flowered plates. Two spotted puppies are passed around the table, petted and rocked. In earlier years it would have been babies, but with the Italian birthrate the lowest in Europe, babies are in short supply. A four-year-old flirt in a red dress is making the most of her position. She's practically ambushed by admirers. Toasts begin but the two boys, along with several friends, have absconded from the table. One gift to them was a computer with games so they've run inside to strafe the enemy. New carafes of wine replace the empties immediately. I am through. This is a stupendous groaning board. But Ed keeps eating. A little more lamb? I see him look up and smile, *"Sì."* And *patate*? Again, *"Sì."*

Suddenly three men appear, carrying something heavy. People rush forward shouting and snapping pictures. Too large for their ovens, a gigantic thigh of a Val di Chiana cow has been roasted in a hotel oven in town and has just arrived on a tray that could hold a human. Soon platters of beef and more crisp potatoes circulate. I give in and have some. Oh no, it's too good. I can't have more, maybe a taste. Ed is eating like a lord. Two Italian women have asked him if he's in films so he feels particularly expansive. Salad arrives. Then fruit tart, *tiramisù,* and the reemergence of the two boys, galloping out like ponies. They shyly cut a three-tiered cake and offer the first pieces to their parents. The cake has rich layers of lemon filling. Out comes the *grappa* and *vin santo*. I'm astonished. Ed has some of both. He finds himself arm-in-arm with several men, singing a song he's never heard. An accordion starts and the dancing begins. I have

107

never eaten this much at once in my life. Ed has eaten a prodigious amount.

At five, we are the first to leave. Our friends Susan and Cole, who married at our house during the restoration, are arriving in time for dinner. We find out later that most guests stayed until eleven, with the beef making several more appearances.

Our friends have arrived early and are sitting on the terrace. Happy as we are to see them, we barely can walk or speak. Ed describes the meal, ending with, "I just hope we're around when those boys get married. Imagine what that will be like." We collapse for two hours then emerge in the sweet time of day to take them around our garden, gathering lettuces, zucchini, onions, and herbs for a simple salad and frittata. For them. We don't want to eat or drink for three days. We sip tepid water while they enjoy a great Brunello.

In the morning, we awaken to the grinding noise of a truck coming up the drive. Anselmo is directing as it swings backwards up our lane. We get downstairs in time to watch two men unloading the *torchio*, the great wine-press Anselmo showed us in his barn. *"Un omaggio,"* he says briskly. The gift is left in the middle of the front yard. We thank him profusely, wondering where this huge piece of equipment is going to live. He launches into instructions on the mechanism and then moves into the details of *vin santo*. That we are not here in fall, that we do not yet have many grapes does not seem to matter. When we first saw the house, one room was strung with wires overhead and Anselmo at the time had noted, "For drying the grapes for *vin santo*." Susan and Cole, both ardent gardeners, join us and assure us they'd love to come help harvest grapes. Anselmo found this place for us. All along he has helped us with restora-

tion. Now that he is retired, he has transformed two of our terraces into a vegetable paradise. He has taken us on jaunts in his
car, introducing us to country people with their own ways. He
has watched Ed learn about vines from Beppe and Francesco. I
feel a quick shiver in accepting this gift. Now he is passing on
the *torchio,* like passing the torch.

~

Dark never turns black-dark. The stars exert their most powerful kilowatts. Also the moon, glassy in old windows, wavering
and rising from bottom pane to middle to top is a pleasure for
the insomniac to watch. The one nightingale, who must live in
the ilex above the house, pierces the quiet with insistent notes.
Dawn is the sweetest time on earth. In the last moments of dark,
the bird chorale begins. One of us wakes the other. *Listen, they're
starting to sing now.* So many, a rising cloud of birdsong, a lift, an
ushering-in. Then the sky—no rosy finger of dawn but a suffu-
sion of rose out of indigo, the quietest light on the hills and the
rushing songs of the birds still rising over the absolute world
unto itself. Moles, voles, porcupines, snakes, foxes, boar, all the
creatures burrowed for the night return to day with this music, as
we do. The deep freshness of the earth returns to those who sing,
to the fusion of colors. As the sun brightens, colors sharpen and
separate from each other. But where is the cuckoo at this hour?

Our friends wake to the sound of the bird who sings,
"Wheat, wheat." Ed listens every day for the bird he says sings,
"When you're a Jet you're a Jet all the way, from your first cigarette. . . ." from *West Side Story.* We take them on a wildflower
walk around the land. All spring, I've photographed each flower
as I found it. Most amazing have been the wild white and purple orchids. My book with the medieval wildflower cover,
bought in Asolo, now bulges with poppies against stone walls,

ragged robin, purple lupin, cotton lavender, wild carnations, lilies, dog roses, still unidentified spiky blue flowers. The many yellows are hardest to identify with the wildflower book in hand. There simply are too many that look similar.

Susan and I cut off rose leaves with black spots and some with the dreaded rust. These go in a bag to be destroyed. She shows me how to take cuttings from my favorite pink roses in front of the house, which survived thirty years of neglect and still bloom with a clean, violet fragrance especially strong early in the mornings. We spend hours in the garden and on the terraces picking wildflowers, then down to the *orto* to fill a basket with lettuces for lunch.

At home in California we are so busy we have 8 A.M. phone conversations two or three times a week, shorthand exchanges of vital information about our daughters, both of whom are in graduate school, about her bookstore business, and what we're managing to read. A few days to walk, go to a museum, cook dinner, and sit out under the benign lights of fireflies and the Milky Way, reconnects our friendship. "Why don't we have more time at home?" we ask each other, but we don't have an answer.

Like the birdsong, like the droves of butterflies and bees, the volunteer flowers in profusion delight me because they come purely as gifts of the land. Just as I'm waxing about the pleasures of rural life to Susan and Cole, an English friend calls and says they've arrived to find two drowned baby boars in their well and they've fished out the rotting, bloated carcasses with a hoe.

At dinner Cole speculates on why we've taken this place so much to heart. "Is it because it's a return to a simpler time? You get to erase the urban blight from your minds for a few months each year?"

Relaxed and enjoying the evening, with lanterns along the wall, lasagna, and the Vino Nobile they have brought, we agree. By dessert, I retract. "That's not really it. It's the end of the ugly century here, too." I flash on the prostitutes along the Piero della Francesca trail. Trucks on the autostrada polluting like mad. Frustrating strikes, which are so frequent there's a space in the newspaper announcing when public services will not be operating. "The people aren't in a simpler time. Generally, they've just managed the century better than we have in America. Everyday life in Tuscany is good."

"The everyday interactions with people are drastically different—personal and direct," Ed says. "We were too geared toward the long range and the long range is a long shot."

"There's very little violent crime, people have manners, the food is so much better and, we all know the Italians have more fun." I realize I've said "manners," and sounded like my mother. "I love the courtesy of encounters in the streets, purchases in stores, even the mailman seems pleased to hand me a letter. When strangers are leaving a restaurant they say goodnight to the people around them."

We tell them about our recent trips into the countryside and the lives we've glimpsed. Our expat friends talk about how much Cortona has changed. But the changes were rapid—and needed—after the war. Now they have slowed. The life of the town is intact, they've taken the right measures to protect the countryside, the cultural life of this tiny town puts to shame most good-sized American cities. I think of the younger generation—Giusi, Donatella, Vittorio, Edo, Chiara, Marco, Antonio, Amalia, Flavia, Niccolò—bringing along all the good traditions. When our adored Rita retired from her *frutta e verdura* last year, a young man took over. Unlike many rural towns, this one hasn't lost its young to the cities. I've said enough and don't say any more.

A group from town walking by the house is singing together. They walk and sing. In my normal life I cannot imagine doing that on a Wednesday night. We listen to the unfamiliar song.

"Like that—Italian life is still sweet."

"And what's also sweet is this peach parfait," Ed says. "It makes my teeth ache."

⁓

The past few days have added hundreds of images to my mental archives. Finding the taproots of places far in the country counterweighs the noetic life with a powerful reality. Already I return in imagination to Achille's place in the mountains with joy. Right now he may be soaping his wife's back in the cool night air. Could we have a bathtub outside? And Giusi's long, long feast, over in a day, will stick in time for its intense celebratory generosity. Ed probably will dream of the entrance of the beef leg into the tent, adding the blare of a trumpet. The *signora* sleeping near her framed husband with the shining eyes has spanned the century and still grabs my hand, pulling the new into her world. Anselmo has made his last wine in his barn but has his eye on our grapes. We will make the wine someday. His brother-in-law, on intimate terms with the Romans and Hannibal, has a sense of time that irritates the hell out of him; he wants his pears and olives to live right *now*.

The Root of Paradise

ED HEADS FOR THE UPPER TERRACES EARLY. HE wants to cut out a trunk of ivy which is menacing a wall. If he doesn't, tentacles will twist between stones and in two days or twenty years the whole wall will cascade down onto our roses. He pauses to watch our neighbor Placido's fifteen white doves swoop over the valley. Let out twice a day for a few minutes of freedom, they fly in loose formation round and round, then all at once head back to their cage. A movement to his left startles him. From behind the ilex tree, a woman emerges, holding a cloth sack and a stick. The forager!

She is not at all abashed at being caught. *"Buon giorno, signore,"* she greets him. *"Una bella giornata."* Beautiful day. She waves her stick over the valley.

Ever polite, even to someone who may have helped herself to our daffodils, Ed introduces himself. "You're the Swiss professor," she says.

"Not Swiss, *americano.*"

"Ah, *si*? I thought you were Swiss," she says dubiously.

Although the morning is mild, she's wearing two or three layers of sweaters, a scarf knotted at her throat, and rubber boots. She grins, showing gold. "Letizia Gazzini," she says in a loud voice. "I used to live here but many years ago." She opens her bag. "I always come back." She has collected several kinds of greens and a separate plastic bag of snails. She holds up spindly weeds. "You have the wild leeks, naturally." She rummages deeper and pulls out more. *"Prenda, prenda,"* take them, take them, she offers.

Ed is totally disarmed. He likes her tanned, creased face and shiny black eyes. He takes the leeks. "Did you own the house?" He's confused. We'd been told that ancient sisters from Perugia held on to the place, leaving it abandoned for thirty years.

"No, no, *signore,* my husband was the farmer, we lived only in a portion of the house. That part." She points with her stick. Ed knows all too well; that section was walled off when we bought the house and had to be opened on all three floors. "Many years of hard labor. Now my husband is dead and I'm left." She pauses. *"Insomma,"* she concludes, an untranslatable expression, in summary, meaning more closely, what else is there to say.

Ed tells her we'd like to learn more about what's growing on the land. Perhaps she could show us the *mescolanza,* the edible greens. Would she mind?

"Ah, *sì, sì, certo,"* Yes, certainly she will. She waves her stick again and disappears behind the *ginestre.*

~

I yank tender clumps of weeds from the rose bed and dig out evil, thorny ones. The wheelbarrow fills over and over, and the pile way out on the land grows larger than a haystack. When the terrace brush is cut, other haystacks rise. After the next rain, Ed and Beppe will burn them. Dry weeds create a fire hazard so after every rain in early summer, fires start up all over the valley, ruining the just-washed air. The fires always scare me, even though they stand by with buckets of water in case the wind lifts the fire over to dry grass. This spring an experienced farmer burned to death when the blaze suddenly blew back, catching his clothes on fire.

With my stoop-labor fork I loosen the soil. The beds are ready. Time to plant. We loaded the car with flowers at the nurseries yesterday and the day before. Each time we leave, we're given a gift. The *signora* runs out, *"Un omaggio e grazie."* She hands me a campanula, or terrace rose, or a fuchsia. Twice we've been given a burgundy red coleus, a plant I don't fancy. They look like what would survive after a nuclear blast. Naturally, they're thriving in their far corner. Sometimes we're asked to choose something we want. After rampaging through, buying dozens of plants, suddenly it's difficult to select the gift. One of these small pots from two years ago has turned into a bush covered with yellow blooms which last for two months.

Many businesses give customers gifts—a T-shirt to celebrate a store's anniversary, beautiful calendars at the new year, and, once, a box of fifteen different pastas when we spent more than 200,000 *lire,* around $120, at a discount store.

I somehow love the gift plants even more than what I've bought. A scented geranium given last year has tripled in size, a dwarf lavender seems especially fragrant. Maybe the gift aspect makes me care for them more carefully, or maybe something given naturally thrives. I'm even growing fond of the coleus.

After working outside all day, the last task remains. We prime the hand pump and trudge out to douse the lavender and new cypress trees with the icy water. Once established, they won't need watering. The walk toward the lake view, formerly a jungle, then a path, now is a lane. Next year, more grapes on the right side (too late for planting grapes now) and a trail of lavender along the left.

Ed has eggplant *parmigiana* in the oven. While I bathed and fell into reading the poems of Horace in the tub, he picked lettuce and set the table outside. Is there anything more splendid than a man who cooks? I bring my new yellow book, where I have begun to list garden ideas. Before we launch into that all-night topic, I read him something amazing I found in Horace:

> . . . *In spring the swelling earth aches for seeds of new life.*
> *Lovely the earth in labor, under a nervous west wind.*
> *The fields loosen, a mild wetness lies everywhere.*
> *Confident grows the grass, for the young sun will do no harm.*
> *The shoots of the vine do not fear a southerly storm arising*
> *Or icy rain slanting from heaven under a north wind—*
> *No, bravely they bud now and reveal their leaves.*
> *So it was since the beginning of the world,*
> *Here is the brilliant dawning and pitch of these days.*

I love the last two lines. Horace could sit at our table, not having to ask that we keep his glass full of the local wine, while he tells us how little has changed and that we need to thin the fruit in the pear trees.

We assess the current state of the land. Right away, we found the good bones. After bringing back what was already here, although smothered by vines and brush, we are starting our more ambitious phase of gardening with the original structure in place. In Renaissance and later formal gardens, a central axis usually boldly joined the architecture of the house with that of the garden. Walkways were like halls, with glimpses into the interior of the garden from the paths. The perpendicular dimensions of our own front garden approximate the size of the house, with the terraces above and below roughly half the width of the front garden. Vestigial formality remains in the long boxwood hedge with five round topiary trees rising at intervals out of the hedge.

It's time to regard the garden long range, feel my way toward a philosophy of gardening. I visualize how it looks from the third-floor windows, what has lasted these first few years, and, primarily, what truly gives me pleasure, rather than simply what will grow. Ed is interested in what brings bees and butterflies. Because lavender is a magnet, especially for white butterflies, we've seen how they put the garden in motion. Motion and music—the bees' humming forms a sleepy background for the birds' twitters, arpeggios, and caws. I like cut flowers in the house every day. We both love the currents of scents swimming through the garden and how they rise to the house early in the morning. The ripe peach colors of the house rhyme with yellow, rose, and apricot flowers.

Because the land is steeply terraced, our garden has distinct parts:

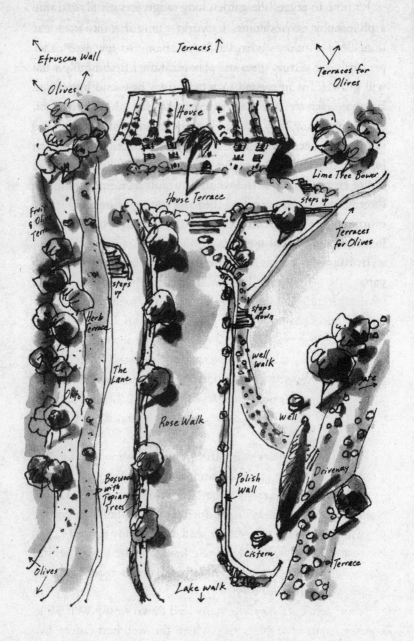

At the side of the house, the shady rectangle we call the Lime Tree Bower stretches maybe sixty feet, then turns into fruit and olive terraces. We've given every area a name, to save each other the bother of saying, "You know, beyond the lilac bushes on the way to the view of the lake," or "On the east side of the house under the *tigli* trees . . ." We've even named each olive tree. All our family members and friends, favorite writers and places are immortalized with a tree. We haven't yet checked to see which ones passed away in the freeze.

Because of the view over the valley and Apennines, the Lime Tree Bower is our noontime outdoor dining room. The front yard, where we live from breakfast to the last firefly count, leads to stone steps then down into a long garden. On this broadest terrace, called the Rose Walk, we have now planted fifty roses on either side of the lawn. I'm confused to see the volunteer, lush lawn, which thrives with a variety of hearty wild grasses. How do you have a lawn without planting a lawn? The top of the immense Polish wall, which we built in the second year, lines one side of this garden. An original stone wall and the inherited boxwood hedge with its ball topiaries line the other. Iron arches mark either end, one covered with jasmine, the other to be planted with two Mermaids, a climbing rose with a flat yellow bloom.

So a slight geometry is in place. While we were clearing jungle growth from the years of abandonment, we followed the cue of the boxwood and reestablished a well-defined rectangle perpendicular to the house. There, during the wall-building era, we unearthed a portion of a former road, with tightly packed stones laid sideways. We hauled away one level, but the next level still lies beneath the grass. I've read that Roman roadbeds were sometimes twelve feet deep.

To the left, curving stone stairs lead down to the Well Walk, another swath of front garden where the well and cistern live and where, previously, we had the well-established hedge of lavender, rosemary, and sage. We didn't know to cut back hard in the winter. At a California vineyard with extensive lavender, we saw the gardener cutting it back beyond belief, almost to the ground. Because we'd never trimmed, the freeze killed all but two.

To the right from the Rose Walk is The Lane, with the box-wood and a tall stone wall on either side. The green underfoot seems to be mostly camomile and wild mint, whose oregano-peppermint smell, I'm sure, attracts the black and white snake who has taken up residence under a rock beneath the faucet. The old well and the spring we discovered during our second summer are on The Lane. It ends with a mass of lilac bushes, then, joining the main garden and the driveway, proceeds to what we call the Lake Walk. From there to the end of the prop-erty, we have planted the cypresses and lavender. We want to reclaim an overgrown track—medieval, Roman?—which leads eventually into town after joining a Roman road. The immense views are from that far end of the property. Most of the land is given over freely to the olive, fruit, almond, and grape, with a few stretches abandoned to wild broom and rock. Two terraces are for herbs and vegetables, the first upper terrace for *le erbe aro-matiche,* and for lettuces, the second for Anselmo's realm, his mega-*orto,* his grand illusion.

I have visions for all these areas. Making a sketch persuades us that we know what we're doing. "Think perennials," Ed says. "We can't reinvent the wheel every year—we plant a carload and it doesn't do zip. We need plants that can take care of them-selves when they grow up. Remember the summer I spent hours hauling buckets to those thirty olives?" We'd planted on various far terraces, not knowing we'd have no rain that year from May through August. With five acres, quantity and size are whole different issues. We've been slow to adjust our sense of scope. Finally we're getting it—our sense of scale needs to cube itself. "Think bushes." He starts a list: hibiscus, forsythia, holly, oleander.

"I don't like oleander. It reminds me of freeways."

"Scratch oleander, then."

"What about more roses? We could build a running arch all along the top of the Polish wall."

When we go inside, an e-mail has arrived from my friend Judy, a rose expert. "Mermaid alert. Beware of Mermaid. It's liable to grow forty feet and it has hideous hooked thorns."

Too late. Two innocent Mermaids are ready to go in the ground tomorrow.

⁓

I'm thinking tonight of Humphrey Repton. He is an ancestor of mine on my father's side. My great-grandmother was Elizabeth Repton Mayes, whose memory is preserved only in my middle name and in a photograph of her cradling my newborn grandfather in her arms. He must have been the ugliest baby born in England at the end of the nineteenth century. He's glaring fiercely at the camera, already full of will. He waves his tight little fists, while she looks lovingly down at him. When he was still a small boy, she died. His father went to America and later sent for his son, who travelled across the Atlantic at nine carrying a small suitcase and a bag of apples. He watched from the railing as his aunt Lily receded on the English shore and finally disappeared. I've remained heartless to this story— impossible that cold, bossy Daddy Jack ever was a vulnerable child travelling alone to a foreign country. Instead, I see him tearing around the deck, terrorizing his fellow-passengers.

Farther back in Elizabeth's line was Humphrey Repton (1752–1818), a garden designer who popularized what we know as the English garden. Since my grandfather was a tyrant, I like knowing earlier men in the lineage loved flowers and trees. Humphrey's father was a tax collector; maybe he had someone to rebel against, too.

Instinctively, my preferences are toward blowsy, abundant, spilling flower beds with everything about to bolt across the grass. I like blue delphinium and foxgloves tall enough to arc and sway in the slightest breeze. There should be plenty of yellow lilies looking back at the sun, and dark gardenia bushes for the evenings, the pure white flowers anticipating the moon. Larkspur, coral bells, love-in-a-mist, strawberry borders, and as many pink roses as possible.

Humphrey wrote five books, plus fifty-seven Red Books, his designs for gardens with transparent overlays showing the after over the before. Even the title of his first book, *Sketches and Hints on Landscape Gardening,* tells me a lot about him. Casual, low-key, inviting. Observations, sketches, and hints, after all, offer a lot of leeway—such a different slant from my grandfather's approach to life, he who went to *the school of hard knocks,* called all my boyfriends "little two-by-fours," and thought my writing *with your head in the clouds* was close to a criminal act. Humphrey's English garden style gradually influenced the more rigidly conceived Italian garden design. I'm searching for a blend at Bramasole, along with our own idiosyncratic preferences.

With only a little over an acre of our five devoted to the frivolity of flowers, I know Humphrey would not devote a Red Book to my garden. But I'll take him along as I plan.

~

During the winter in San Francisco, I began to read about the evolution of the Italian garden. I knew that in ancient times, Pliny wrote about fanciful creatures cut from boxwood, and names spelled out by vines and flowers. His lost garden is thought to be near Città di Castello, just a few miles from Bramasole. During suppers in Pliny's garden, light courses were floated in artificial birds and miniature ships on the surface of a stone pool. As you sat down, a spray of water shot up. His concept of gardens blended sweetly into his version of happiness, a philosophy of *otium,* life spent in elegant, intellectual freedom.

Propped on pillows in bed while wind swirled the trees and scoured the windows with rain and salty mist, I read *Gardens of the Italian Villas* by Marella Agnelli, and *The Italian Renaissance Garden* by Claudia Lazzaro, trying to imagine the decision to build a garden with paths which could be flooded so your guests could drift through the garden in little boats. Some gardens had waterworks which could simulate rain or the wind howling. I was struck with the concept of the garden not only as a setting for the house and a place of pleasure but also a place of surprise and fun—fountains that unexpectedly sprayed you as you passed, and *il giardino segreto,* the secret garden within a garden. Who would not love the idea of a secret garden? I've planted a double circle of tall sunflowers on a high terrace, making a little round room. They're almost knee high. In July, the big flowers and leaves will almost hide the inner circle. I hope someone's children come to visit. As a child, I would have loved that space. *Scherzi d'acqua* or *giochi d'acqua,* water jokes, more than any other aspect of the historical garden, reveal a vast cultural space between us and them. They were a staple of Italian gardens. Rounding a bend, your step on a certain stone would set off a shower, suddenly drenching you. Search the literature; these water jokes were enjoyed and expected. No one went home in a huff over her stained blue silk. I don't know of anyone over ten who would like to be drenched on a tour of my garden. But I'm convinced by water; there must be water in the garden, an element of obvious joy, just as flowers are. Water is music and a place for birds to wash, water is movement and a cool spot for toads.

I take statues for granted in the old Italian gardens. They served ideological purposes, reflecting a philosophical stance or interest, such as theater or music, of the owner. But often, I now realize, they were for pure play, as in the grotto pool at the entrance to the Boboli Gardens in Florence, where three marble children swim and duck each other. As a child I loved the mirrored globe on a pedestal in my grandparents' yard. Looking in it, the oak tree above went wonky and my face distorted crazily. Silver shoots of sunlight reflected so brilliantly that I hoped a fire would start.

Of all the gardens I can think of at home, few are playful. I met a woman in Dayton who has bowling balls scattered around her long sloping garden. Otherwise planted with conventional bushes, the balls certainly surprise. "How did you start collecting bowling balls in the yard?" I asked her.

"I had one. It looked so pretty with the snow on it." She paused, groping for a reason to state; I realized my mistake in urging her to pin down whimsy with some rational explanation. "Anyone can plant flowers," she continued. Long wicked pause. "It takes a real gardener to have balls."

The traditional urge for garden ornaments persists in Tuscany. Olive oil jars, topped with pots of geraniums, decorate country gardens. An iron fence around a house in Camucia is decorated with musical notes. At garden supply departments, statuary is easy to find—David (gross in terra-cotta), Flora, Venus, the four seasons, various nymphs, the Seven Dwarfs. In antique shops, I see sublime travertine fountains with Latin inscriptions and garden ornaments too valuable to be left outside.

The whimsy of the eternal Italian topiary craze, too, seems to come from a great distance. I imagine Ed on a ladder, snipping our ball-shaped topiaries into ships, dragons, the Pope, a deer complete with antlers. One Medici *palazzo* had boxwood in shapes of wolf, dog, ram, hare, elephant, boar, and other creatures. A house in Camucia has topiary squirrels at the entrance.

A neighbor's topiary I finally decided is a peacock. Why not a Ferrari, a glass of wine, the "finger," or a soccer goal?

While reading about the great old Italian gardens, mentally I wandered through the local gardens of my Cortona neighbors, who emulate on a modest scale many of the traditions of the grand historical gardens—paths of river pebbles; little or no lawn; pots, pots, pots for flowers and lemon trees arranged around the garden; aviaries; box or laurel hedges; and shady arbors for dining outdoors. I've never seen roses bloom the way they do in Tuscany. They tend to be planted along a fence or—oddly—just off to themselves in a row. Flower beds and rolling lawns hardly exist; they require what Tuscans instinctively conserve: water. A small garden may have fifty pots of various sizes as well as a *limonaia* for citrus, geraniums, and hydrangeas. Cortona's park starts with a shady area of benches and bordered flower beds around a playful fountain of nymphs entwined with sea creatures. Beyond that area, the park, called the Parterre, stretches a third of a mile along a wall with long views over Lago Trasimeno and the valley. A gesture toward a formal garden remains in the linden-lined walk which is broad enough for two carriages to pass, though now it is only walkers and joggers. While I haven't seen a hilltown park as lovely as Cortona's, many medieval towns have parks just outside the gates, respites for the citizens from the heated stones and cramped streets.

The Italian concept of severe geometric gardens contradicts all my innate preferences. At heart, theirs is an entirely different design aesthetic. Historically, flowers play a minor role compared to statues, patterns of walkways, fountains, hedges, pergolas, and pavilions.

The Italian garden, Ippolito Pindemonte wrote back in 1792, was "ruled more by sun and marble than by grass and shade." Wandering in gardens here, I've felt their austerity, a forlorn quality to the squared-off compartments and the endless box-wood terraces. They seem anti-nature. But by slow osmosis, I've grown to like the architectural and conceptual sense of space, how often garden layout reproduces the proportions of the house, and the statues, stairways, and balustrades create the sense of outdoor rooms. This *is* the Mediterranean, where people live outside as much as in. In the large gardens, these strict arrangements of nature give way to orchards or woods, the last buffers between the house and wild nature, a fine idea that crosses time and architectural styles. The early garden writers refer to gardening as "third nature," first nature being the natural wild, second nature being agricultural cultivation, and third being nature in sync with ideas of beauty and art.

Even though the gardens appear highly artificial to my eyes, trained by Southern lawns of dogwood, azalea, and camellia, and by casual, low-maintenance California gardens, on reflection, they make sense. Italy, until recently, has been utterly fragmented. The castle, walled village, or villa of necessity had an us-against-the-world stance. Gardens, of course, would be enclosed or controlled or designed to make one forget the danger or chaos just beyond the confines.

Over and over, I surrender to the Italian sense of beauty. How to bring the elements I've come to love into my own garden? I want Humphrey's fast and loose arrangements, his rustic sense of comfort and ease. Can I have those along with the Italian geometry and playfulness, those oxymorons that give such a sense of surprise?

Reading about gardens is instructive but frustrating. Photos do not convey depth, and perspective is too limited. Worse, I can't smell the layers of fragrance as my eye follows the paths, can't bend down to rub a furry leaf, or see how a willow in new leaf fractures the light. I was transported only partially by the glossy pages to the grandiose waterworks of the Villa d'Este. The delight and luxury of water spilling from the breasts of women, the mouths of dolphins, the simulated cascades and stepped, downhill courses—the pictures stilled and silenced the gush, splash, and trickle you must bend close to hear.

Two hours in the Roseto Botanico at Cavriglia are worth a whole winter of looking at books. June is an ideal time to see—to smell—the garden of Fondazione Carla Fineschi, the largest private rose garden in the world. I immediately start writing names of roses we like, regardless of the fact that nurseries in our area often don't sell roses with names so we may never find any of these. Every category of rose—Bourbon, Chinese, Damask, Tea, Ramblers, etc.—has its beds and every bush is fully labeled. Ed and I lose each other then meet. Out of the thousands of roses, we hope to identify the two pink ones that belong to the history of our house. We both spot the indecently fragrant Reine des Violettes—similar, but ours are more cupped, like a peony. Maybe the *nonna* who lived at Bramasole never knew the name, or maybe such an old country rose just doesn't make it into the bloodlines. Let's just call it Nonna's Rose. Finally, we wander, watching the gardeners clip the dead, watching other people swooning over the fragrances. Behind the garden a few roses are sold. We buy three called Sally Holmes to sprawl along the driveway, offering white clusters of flat roses among the lavender. I'm not drawn to white roses but why not have a few to catch the moonlight?

~

At Firenze Com'era (Florence as it was), one of my favorite museums for its tranquil convent setting and its lack of other visitors, I'm fascinated by the dozen paintings of Medici villas by the Flemish painter, Justus Utens. These half-moons (painted in 1599 for lunettes in a Medici villa at Artimino) depict bird's-eye views of the houses and gardens as they were originally, a rare glimpse at ideal garden layout of that time. Villa Pratolino shows an elaborate sequence of pools spilling downhill into each other. At Lambrogiana's garden, four grand squares, bordered by pergolas, are subdivided into four others, with square pools at the entrance to each big square. The walled court of all these villas are oddly empty—perhaps a well, but otherwise lacking ornamentation. If I ever win the lottery, I'd like to create a garden on this scale. Ever since the enormous fun I had reading George Sitwell's (papa of the marvelous eccentric writers Osbert, Sacheverell, and Edith) ruminations on his gardens, which involved the creations of hills and lakes, and other ambitious manipulations of the landscape, I've been in awe of gardeners who think on this scale.

The remnant of the Medici Giardino dei Semplici (garden of simples: medicinal plants) is still open to the public in Florence. Since Cosimo the First had the idea for this garden in 1545, botanists have planted specimen ferns, palms, herbs, flowers, and shrubs, as well as studied healing properties of plants. It's a weedy spot behind imposing gates near San Marco. This morning, it's empty, except for a woman wheeling a baby, and a man with a stringy garden hose drowning plants. At his rate, it will take a month to water the garden, which may be why so much of it droops. I take away no ideas from the garden of simples but it is a shady walk out of the heat of Florence, a glimpse back into the awakening of gardening as a subject of study and importance.

The herb garden at San Pietro in Perugia had me taking notes immediately. The San Pietro complex now shares its deserted, pure courtyards, grounds, and austere monks' cells with a university agriculture department. Guidebooks to Umbria don't even mention this peaceful oasis, with its accompanying book (in Italian) explaining the intricate numerology and plant symbolism of the reconstructed medieval meditation garden, which adjoins a clearly laid-out garden of simples. I found that a sticky weed, *la parietaria,* which sprouts from every crannied wall at our house, has a past. In Latin, it is called *elxine,* and possesses the powers to expel stones from the urinary tract, heal wounds, and calm colic. Local people have told me it's a chief cause of spring allergy, as well. As I dig out its tenacious roots, I'll have more respect for its existence. A pink version of what I know as yellow oxalis in California is called *acetosella.* The low, spreading plant Beppe calls *morroncello,* is labeled *pimpinella (sanguisorba* in Latin), good for everything from plague to ulcers. *Santoreggia,* savory, which I thought of as an innocent addition to summer soups and salads, turns out to be a powerful aphrodisiac when mixed with honey and pepper. Even the wild melissa appears in new light: Its leaves produce gold dreams. Since I'm not sure I've ever seen gold light in a dream, I'd like to try this tea. How perfectly blue the flower of borage, a bright spot in a herb garden.

From my reading, I gleaned an unpleasant insight—how unformed and narrow my views of gardening were! In my new yellow book, I'm starting a list of newly realized possibilities for my more mundane-sized garden, beginning with sketches of pergolas. Anyone looking at them might think they're scaffolding or subway tunnels. Almost everyone with a garden in Tuscany has a pergola, not only because they're practical for grapes. Chestnut, stone, willow, iron, they direct a view, provide a focal point, and protect you from the sun, an easy contrast and defining point. Lunching under dangling bunches of grapes imparts a delicious mood of hedonism, while the splashes of sunlight falling over the table make faces beautiful and seduce everyone to enjoy themselves fully. Why have I never built a woven willow pergola in California? I can superimpose one over my memory of the yard of my house in Palo Alto—there behind the house. I should have taken out that ugly juniper hedge and put up a lovely arbor.

~

I have a practice which must release beneficial rushes of body chemicals, purify the blood, and strengthen the heart. When I can't sleep I imagine holding all the animals I've loved; I revisit my happiest moments; I walk through the streets of Cuzco, San Miguel, Deya, recalling views, windows, faces, sounds. I think of everyone I love unstintingly. To this habit I now can add the revision of the gardens of all the houses I've lived in, budgetary considerations of the time notwithstanding. I'm more accustomed to the revisions of interiors, a large topic among the women of my family, any one of whom might say something like, "I never should have papered that dining room, especially with those Chinese cranes coming in to land. I always feel like one will plop down into my soup. I should have lacquered the walls *brilliant* yellow and a mirror should go over that sideboard, not those puny sconces. . . ." I wonder if they, when insomnia strikes, have practices like mine.

~

Formal squares traditionally organize large Italian gardens. I knew that, of course, but did not know that the square was called a quincunx, for its four trees planted at the corners and one at the central point. Ever since Cicero, many gardens are a series of quincunxes linked by paths. Boxwood was the common border but some quincunxes were edged with sage, rosemary, lavender, or myrtle. Within the quincunxes, gardeners planted lilies, roses, and bulbs such as hyacinth, narcissus, and crocus. Pergola walkways worked as boundaries on the sides of the gardens, offering shaded walks.

Reading garden inventories from hundreds of years ago, I see how many of the plants loved then still are—cyclamen, jasmine, honeysuckle, savory, clematis, anise. Others have fallen from favor: hyssop, mugwort, rue, tansy, melissa, black cumin, sweet cicely, balsam apple, black byrony, and woodbine. Herbs often were used interchangeably with flowers. The iris and the orange lily (*giglio selvatico*), both of which grow wild at Bramasole, are mentioned frequently, causing me to wonder how long ago they naturalized.

I'm happy that some plants I've chosen are on the lists of common herbs and flowers in Renaissance gardens. Last summer I planted *issopo,* hyssop, as a border. It rewarded me with long-blooming spiky purple flowers and an ambition to spread into a bush. Francesco recognized it as something good to rub on bruises. Another I planted was melissa, which I then found was the same as the wild mints I'd called lemon balm or citronella. It smelled like the oil my mother used to rub on me in the evenings when mosquitoes swarmed and I played late in the alleys and neighbors' back yards. Now I cut branches and lay them under the table when we eat outside at night. Maybe it helps.

Savory, another mint cousin, I planted by accident. At the market I bought a pot of *santoreggia.* "Use the flowers and the leaves," was all the seller told me.

"In what?"

She raised both arms, "In the kitchen, *signora. Insalata, zuppa,* everywhere." By chance I came upon a mention of *santoreggia* as *satureja hortensis,* the Latin name for savory, and noticed the connection.

Jasmine grows over an arch and along the iron railing on the upstairs terrace. Honeysuckle I also planted early. The scent takes me straight to a white Georgia road in moonlight, when my true love in high school picked a branch and put it in my hair. When we kissed, his mouth was hard and unyielding, then suddenly open and alive. Honeysuckle doesn't dazzle anyone with its flowers, but I can lean out of my study window, look over cypresses and hills and breathe not only the honeyed fragrance but the sand road cooling off behind Bowen's Mill, the wind in long leaf pine, and Royale Lyme aftershave liberally doused on the cheeks of a shy boy years and miles away. I was not shy; I'd been waiting for him to kiss me for weeks.

Southern scents are powerful. I always keep a gardenia pot going in the shade, a connection to the old giant in my mother's yard, a scent I slipped past when coming home late, the green-black leaves and the gardenias so white they seemed to have a nimbus of light around them. I'd pick one and float it in a water glass by my bed. By the time I woke up late the next morning, the scent had invaded every corner of the hot room. My family's garden in Georgia was nothing special, just nice, though by August almost everything looked exhausted. We had camellias, lilies, azaleas, crape myrtle, larkspur, bachelor's buttons, which we called ragged robin, and a back hedge of bridal bouquet. Inside it I had a hideout and would not answer when my mother called from the back door. Through long swoops of white bloom, I could see her fuming. I liked to spy. My other hideout, strategically located near the front door, was under the porch, behind the blue hydrangeas. I could see the postman's hairy leg and black socks, the skirts of my mother's bridge friends, and sometimes hear bits of forbidden conversation about Lyman Carter "running around," or Martha's shock treatments in Asheville.

Here I have pots of pink and white hydrangeas, the blooms as large as a baby's head. Between two of them Ed built a stone bench, an almost hidden vantage point for viewing our garden, though nothing as exciting as who entered and exited my family's home. We have planted both white and lavender lilac, which has the lovely name *lillà* in Italian.

The garden, I begin to see, is a place where I can give memory a location and season in which to remain alive. Ed, too, loves the lilac. They grew all over his hometown in Minnesota and, after the harsh winter, must have been a sweet sight. His neighbor Viola Lapinski, an "old maid" (he now realizes she was in her thirties), used to bring bunches when she came over on Saturday nights to watch "Gunsmoke" with his family.

I'll have to ask my daughter, whose first word was "flava," flower, if she feels a memory imprint from our Somers, New York, back yard of maples, which in autumn dropped knee-deep yellow leaves she and the dog burrowed under. Along the boundary wall, I planted my first herb garden and never since have had one so extensive. Digging beside me one day, she found an amethyst medicine bottle which she kept for years. In the front yard, a peony hedge popped up every year. Ashley thought someone with too much lipstick had kissed the crest of each pink globe. What does she remember? Her room in Palo Alto had one sliding glass wall. She stepped outside every day to mock orange, lemon, kumquat, loquat. The inheritance of those light scents must be floating in the canaliculi of her brain. I wish she had the grape arbor to remember. Perhaps building one here will do.

Scents operate like music and poetry, stirring up wordless feelings that rush through the body, not as cognitive thoughts but as a surge of lymphatic tide. Ed walks by the lilac and simultaneously his mother places the vase of ashen lavender blossoms on the coffee table, his father offers a box of toffee to Viola, whose hair is rolled on orange juice cans in preparation for mass tomorrow, Lawrence Welk starts to bounce, and the room is presided over by the shadowy tones of the framed Jesus over the

TV, pausing to look out at everyone from the garden of Geth-semane. *His eyes follow you everywhere.*

A garden folds memory into the new as well. I have no his-tory with lavender, pots of lemon trees, balconies of tumbling coral geraniums, double hollyhocks shooting up, tree roses, dahlias—but now I see that when (if) I am ninety, a lavender sachet will return to me the day Beppe planted forty lavenders, will bring back summer after summer of white butterflies and bees around the house, dipping in and out of the lavender haze. Probably nothing will stir the memory of the horrid weed that smells like old fish, or the sticky one that makes me rush inside for the allergy tablets.

"If we plant everything you list in your yellow book, we'll live in a botanical garden."

"Or maybe an Eden." Ed has told me the etymological root of the word "paradise" comes from the Greek *paradeisos,* mean-ing garden or park, and farther back, from *dhoigho-,* clay or mud wall, and from the Avestan *pairi-daeza,* meaning circumvallation, walled-around. Paradise: a clay-walled garden. Genesis says nothing about wall-building on any of the seven days, but I can imagine a high perimeter of golden bricks thumb-printed by the hand of God. If He has hands, of course. Was the Eden wall covered with Mermaid, a quick-growth rose? Ours seemed to plunge down roots and surge forth the moment we planted them. Surely the wild magenta rugosas behind our house thrived there, the low branches sheltering the serpent. Maybe a new apple is in order on our land. Since ours are gnarly, they tempt no one.

From much-later historical inventories of gardens, I'm intrigued by black byrony—whatever that may be. It sounds like something entwined over the graves of Catherine and Heathcliff. One writer of the time recommends carnations every three and a half feet, the intervals planted with marjoram, lily of the valley, ranunculus, and cat thyme. Thyme and marjoram would add texture and cover bare dirt. "What about zinnias," Ed says. "Old plain zinnias. What *do* you have in store for me in that yellow book of yours?"

"O.K., I'll skip the plants. We've got a pergola to build. I'd love at least one statue. And a fountain."

"Is that *all*? What about a folly? I like the idea of those ornamental hermits you read about, too. And we could build a fake ruin at the end of the Lake Walk. A broken arch, a piece of a door, a tumbled wall."

"That's a great idea! A place to sit. . . ."

He looks stunned. "No wait, back up. I was kidding. You're not serious, are you?"

Spring Kitchen

ANTIPASTI —

Paolo's Fennel Fritters

Anything Paul Bertolli cooks I will eat. Once he even served me tendons. "Whose tendons are these, anyway?" I asked. He flinched only a little. "Veal. You'll like them." He knows I'm somewhat squeamish and tries to educate me. When he was chef at Chez Panisse, I was allowed to assist him in the kitchen a few times. My first assigned task was to behead a mound of pigeons. Their closed blue eyelids bothered me, but not wanting to be just the lettuce washer, I began to whack their little heads off. Paul has Italian parents and deep affinities with Italian life. His genius is for revealing the essence of whatever he's cooking. His pleasure and integrity are clear to anyone who reads and cooks from his *Chez Panisse Cooking*. Recently he has built an *acetaia,* a barn for the complex process of making balsamic vinegar. He was one of our first guests here and helped us set up our prototype kitchen. When I'm in California, I love to go his restaurant, Oliveto's in Oakland, especially on nights when he celebrates truffles or *porcini* mushrooms. This is his recipe, just as he handed it to me, for fennel fritters. Select young fennel—older plants are too fibrous.

6.5 ounces of wild fennel hearts, cleaned
6.5 ounces of tender fronds and leaves
1 whole head of garlic, peeled
2 ¾ cups of sturdy bread crumbs from a day-old loaf
¾ cup of freshly grated *parmigiano reggiano*
1 whole egg
½ t. sea salt
freshly ground black pepper
¾ cup of olive oil

⟶ *Pare the fennel stalks down to their tender centers and while doing so, separate and retain the leafy fronds. Combine the stalks, fronds, and leaves on a cutting board and chop them coarsely. Place in a bowl, cover with cold water and drain well.*

Place the clean fennel in a steamer along with the peeled garlic cloves. Steam over high heat for 12–15 minutes, or until the fennel and garlic are very tender. Cool and transfer to a cutting board. Chop the mixture finely.

Add 1 ¾ cups of the bread crumbs and the grated parmigiano. *Next add the whole egg, the salt and a little freshly ground black pepper. Stir with a fork until the mixture forms a firm mass.*

Using two soup spoons, portion the fritters evenly. One by one, toss the fritters into a bowl containing the remaining bread crumbs and form them by hand into small uniform patties.

Warm the olive oil in a large skillet. Test the temperature of the oil by tossing in a crumb. It should sizzle and dance in the pan. Fry the fritters over high heat, turning them with the help of a slotted spoon.

Transfer to a platter lined with absorbent paper or towel, then to a service platter. Pass while still warm.

Fried Artichokes

As a Southerner, to me "deep fried" is an enchanting phrase. We never met an artichoke, when I was growing up, except marinated in a jar. Still, this seems like soul food. At the spring markets, vendors sell five sizes. For stuffing with bread, herbs, and tomatoes, I buy the largest ones. For frying or eating raw, the smallest, purple-tinged ones are best. Even with those, trim off any part of the leaf that might be stringy.

⌒ *Select ten small artichokes. Strip any tough outer leaves and trim off the tips quite close to the heart. Quarter and pat dry with paper towels. Heat safflower, peanut, or sunflower oil. Beat three eggs in a bowl with ¾ cup of water, and quickly dip artichoke pieces in the egg then shake them in a bag of seasoned flour. Brush off excess. Fry in hot oil (350 degrees) until golden. When done, remove to brown paper to drain, then pile on a platter and serve with wedges of lemon. Serves eight as an* hors d'oeuvre.

PRIMI PIATTI ⌒

Odori

Usually the greengrocer, whether in a shop or outdoor market, will give you a handful of *odori,* literally "odors, herbs," aromatic flavors for your pot: a handful of parsley and basil, a couple of stalks of celery, and a carrot or two. If I'm not making a stock or stew, sometimes this little gift wilts in the fridge. One night when the cupboard was bare, Ed minced the *odori* and invented this simple mix for pasta. After that, we spread it on *focaccia,* and also pulled apart the petals of steamed artichokes and stuffed it between the leaves, a fresh alternative to lemon butter or vinaigrette.

⟶ *Finely chop—almost mince—2 carrots, 2 stalks of celery, and 3 cloves of garlic. Sauté in 2 T. of olive oil until cooked but still crunchy. Scissor basil and parsley into the mixture, add another 2 T. of olive oil and cook on low flame for 2–3 minutes. Prepare enough spaghetti for two. Drain and mix 2 or 3 T. of the pasta water and a little olive oil into the pasta. Mix 4 T. grated parmigiano into the odori. It should have the texture of pesto. Toss with spaghetti. Serves two.*

Risotto Primavera

"The best meal I've ever had," a friend said, after a simple dinner of *risotto* with spring vegetables. Of course it wasn't, but the effect of a lovely mound of *risotto* in the middle of the plate surrounded by a wreath of colorful and flavorful vegetables inspires effusive declarations. This seems like the heart of spring dining. It could be followed by roast chicken but I like it as a dinner in itself, followed by tossed lettuces with pear slices and gorgonzola. A special local *risotto* is made with nettles. Evil as they are when mature, they're a spring treat when they're very young. Some farmers' markets at home have them occasionally. Chop and quickly blanch them, then stir into the *risotto* at the last minute of cooking.

⟶ *Prepare and season the vegetables separately. Shell 3 pounds of fresh peas, steam briefly. Clean a large bunch of new carrots and cut into pieces about the same size as the asparagus stems. Steam the carrots until barely done. Break 2 pounds of asparagus stalks just where they naturally snap, and steam or roast. Heat to a boil then turn down to simmer 5½ cups of seasoned stock and ½ cup of white wine. In another pot, sauté 2 cups of* arborio *rice and a finely chopped onion in a tablespoon of olive oil for a couple of minutes, then gradually ladle in the stock as the rice absorbs the liquid. Keep stirring and ladling in more until the rice is done. Some prefer it almost soupy, but for this dish it is better moist and al dente. Add the juice of a lemon, stir in ½ cup or so of grated* parmigiano, *and season to taste. Serve the plates with the vegetables surrounding the rice. Serves six.*

Orecchiette with Greens

Orecchiette, pasta shaped like little ears, work well when served *con quattro formaggi*, with four cheeses: *gorgonzola, parmigiano, pecorino*, and *fontina*. In spring, they are popular with greens.

⁓ *Sauté 2 bunches of chopped chard with some chopped spring onions and garlic. Cook enough* orecchiette *for six. Drain and toss with the greens. If you like anchovies, sauté about 6 fillets, then chop and mix with the greens. Season, then stir in ½ cup of grated* parmigiano, *or serve separately.*

Orecchiette with Shrimp

This combination, amusing because of the similar shapes of the pasta and the shrimp, makes a rather substantial course.

⁓ *Shell enough fava beans for 1 cup. Sauté the beans in a little olive oil until almost done, then add a finely chopped small onion, or a couple of fresh spring onions, to the pan. Cook until onion is soft. Season and purée in food processor. Clean and sauté a pound of shrimp or small prawns in olive oil with 4 cloves of garlic, left whole. Add ¼ cup of white wine, turn heat to high very briefly, then turn off. Discard gar-*

lic. Cook pasta for six, drain, toss with almost all the green sauce; stir shrimp into remaining green sauce. Serve pasta on plates, arranging shrimp mixture on top.

SECONDI ⟶

Spring Veal

This completely simple veal, discovered when I suddenly had no tomatoes for the stew I was about to make, has become a favorite. The lovely, pure lemon flavor intensifies the taste of the tender veal.

⟶ *Pat dry 3 pounds of veal cubes. Dredge in flour and quickly brown in a heavy pot. Add 1 cup of white wine. With a zestier, remove the thin top layer of peel from 2 lemons; add to pot with salt and pepper. Cover and bake at 350 degrees for 40 minutes, or until veal can be pulled apart easily with a fork. Stir, add the juice of the 2 lemons. Add the lemon juice at the end, since it would toughen the veal to add it sooner. Put back in the oven for 5 more minutes. Stir in a handful of chopped parsley. Serves six.*

CONTORNI ⟶

Fava Beans with Potatoes and Artichokes

First and most loved of the spring vegetables are the raw *fave*. Fresh *fave* are nothing like the ones I've found in supermarkets, which must be blanched and very tediously peeled, bean by bean. Although they still can be good, basically a bean that must be peeled is past its prime. Easy to grow, they're hard to find at home, although sometimes farmers' markets will have a bin of just-picked tender green ones. In one Tuscan friend's home, a bowl of raw, unshelled *fave* were brought out with a round of *pecorino*, served with a bottle of wine late in the afternoon. At another friend's house, the *fave e pecorino* ritual was observed at the end of a light dinner, a simultaneous salad and cheese course. Any time seems to be a good time for this sacred combination. The following recipe could accompany a veal chop or a pork tenderloin, but is a happy spring main course, too.

⁓ *Quarter and steam 6 small artichokes until just tender. Drain and set aside in acidulated water. Peel and quarter a pound of white potatoes (you can use tiny red new potatoes). Steam these, too, until barely done. Shell 2 pounds of fava beans, as fresh as possible; steam until done. Heat 4 T. olive oil in a big sauté pan. Sauté 2 or 3 chopped young spring onions (or a bunch or two of scallions) and 3 or 4 cloves of minced garlic. Add the vegetables, chopped thyme, salt, and pepper. Squeeze the juice of 1 lemon over the vegetables. Gently toss the mixture until nicely blended and hot. Turn out onto a platter. Serves six generously.*

Roasted Vegetables, Especially Fennel

The larger your oven, the better to roast a variety of the vegetables-of-the-moment. I've come to prefer oven-roasting to grilling vegetables. The individual flavors are accentuated, while grilling imposes its own smoky taste. Oven-roasted fennel is unbelievably good. I find myself stealing a piece as soon as I turn off the oven.

⁓ *Generously oil a non-stick cookie pan with sides, or a large baking pan. Arrange halved peppers, quartered onions, separated pieces* of fennel, halved zucchini and squash, sliced eggplant, whole heads of garlic, and halved tomatoes. Drizzle with olive oil, sprinkle with chopped thyme, salt and pepper. Slide the pan into the oven and roast at 350 degrees. After about 15 minutes, start testing the squash, zucchini, and tomatoes, removing them to a platter as they are done. Turn the eggplant and peppers. Everything should be done before 30 minutes have passed. Arrange on a platter. The garlic requires hands-on attention. Guests pull off the cloves and squeeze them onto bread.

Other Roasted Vegetables

Since my friend Susan Wyler, author of several cookbooks, taught me to roast asparagus in the oven, I've never steamed it again. Even burned and crisp, it's delicious. Little string beans also benefit from a run in the oven. Roasting brings out a hidden taste. With about 200 onions growing like mad in the garden, I've taken to roasting them frequently. Balsamic vinegar adds a sweet surprise. Surround a roast chicken with a ring of these onions.

⟶ *Arrange asparagus spears in a single layer in a pie or cake pan. Trickle olive oil over them and season with salt and pepper. Roast for 5 minutes—or until barely fork-tender—at 400 degrees.*

⟶ *Steam Blue Lake string beans until almost done. Shake them dry and roast with a sprinkling of olive oil for 5 minutes at 400 degrees.*

⟶ *Arrange almost peeled onions—leave a layer or two of the papery skin—in a non-stick baking dish. Cut a large X-shaped gash in the top. Sprinkle liberally with balsamic vinegar and olive oil. Season with salt and pepper. Roast for 40 minutes at 350 degrees. Check a time or two and add more balsamic and oil if they look dry.*

DOLCI ⟶

In *primavera,* fruits aren't ripe yet. Most of the *gelato* stands are still closed for cold weather. As in winter, dessert is often chestnuts roasted at the fireplace, a wedge of *gorgonzola,* or *Baci,* the chocolate kisses of Perugia, along with a glass of *limoncella* or *amaro,* or, for the stalwart among us, *grappa.* One stand at the Thursday market sells dried fruits. Poached in wine, with a few spirals of lemon zest and spices, and served with *biscotti,* the fruits come to life, good to hold us over until the fruits of summer begin to arrive.

Fruits Plumped in Wine

Delicate and light, this homey dessert falls into the comfort food category. Pass *biscotti* for dipping into the sugared wine. Children hate this dessert.

⟶ *Pour boiling water to cover over a pound of dried fruits—apricots, peaches, cherries, and/or figs—and let them rest for an hour. Bring to a boil 2 cups of red wine, ½ cup sugar, a little nutmeg, and spirals of thin lemon peel. Stir in 1 cup of raisins (a mixture of gold and dark), and the drained fruit. Reduce heat immediately to a simmer. Cook for 10 minutes. Remove the fruit. Boil down the remaining liquid until it thickens and pour over the fruit. Better the next day. Sprinkle each serving with toasted pine nuts.*

Frozen Sunset

Just a plain ice, but anything with blood oranges seems exotic and primal. Is it the word "blood" that enters the imagination as a glass of the scarlet juice pours into a glass? Or is it just the jolt of slicing the orange, seeing the two rounds falling open, glistening scarlet, and vinous. The mind is cooled and soothed by the sweet-tart layers of taste in the icy melting of this blood orange sorbet.

⟶ *Make a sugar syrup by boiling together 1 cup of water and 1 cup of sugar, then simmering it for about 5 minutes, stirring constantly. Add 2 cups of blood orange juice, and the juice of a lemon. Cool in the fridge. When well-chilled, process in an ice cream maker according to manufacturer's instructions. Or you can freeze it in ice trays until slushy, break up the icy mixture, then partially freeze again. Garnish with lemon balm or mint.*

Ginger Pound Cake

Baking must be a deeply encoded instinct. When it comes to dessert, I find that I often return to something I know from my mother and Willie Bell's kitchen. Ginger has nothing to do with Italy but it has a great deal to do with fruit. My carry-on luggage would puzzle a customs inspector, if one ever bothered to look inside. She might find a bottle of cane syrup—because how can one have biscuits at breakfast without butter and cane syrup—or a bottle of corn syrup for various desserts such as this old favorite.

⟶ *Sift 3 ⅓ cups of flour, ½ t. salt, 1 t. baking powder, 1 t. baking soda, 1 t. nutmeg, and 1½ T. ginger. Cream 1 cup of butter and 1 cup of sugar. Separate 4 eggs. Stir beaten yolks into sugar mixture. Beat in 1 cup of light corn syrup, then stir in flour alternately with ½ cup of cream. Beat the 4 whites until they form stiff peaks, then fold egg whites into cake mixture. Pour into a non-stick tube pan that has been lightly buttered for good measure. Bake at 325 degrees for 1 hour. Cool briefly then invert on a plate.*

Blood Oranges with Vin Santo

If you do not have *vin santo*, substitute brandy. This is a
vibrant dessert, especially paired with slivers of Ginger Pound
Cake. Later in the season, prepare peaches this way, too, simmering them only five minutes.

⟜ *Boil 2 cups of water, 1 cup of sugar, 4 T. of* vin santo *and 3
or 4 cloves. Add sections of 6 peeled blood oranges, then turn heat down
and simmer for 10 minutes. Drain and cool. Mix 3 cups of mascarpone
with ½ cup of sugar, ½ cup of white wine, and the juice of a lemon.
Serve the mascarpone in 6 bowls, topped with the oranges.*

Circles on My Map

Monte Oliveto Maggiore

A DREAMY DAY TO DRIVE. THE GREEN LANDSCAPE smears across the windshield. Flowering chestnut trees begin to droop under the rain. We cross the valley, skirt the hilltown of Sinalunga, and drive toward Monte Oliveto Maggiore, one of the great monasteries of Italy. The greens! Hills look as though footlights angle across them—neon green, poison green, green velvet, Life Saver green. When I was five, I saw an irresistible green moss and jumped on it. I quickly sank into sludge and my father, in a pale linen suit and shouting "Jesus H. Christ," had to fish me out. I had jumped through a brilliant, thick algae covering the surface of an open septic tank behind the cotton mill. But this green is innocent; I could jump into it and roll like a horse.

We start to glimpse the wild landscape of eroded *crete,* clay, which you see in many Sienese paintings. Dramatic and forbidding in late summer, the crevices are still softened by grasses. The monks who chose this spot definitely wanted to leave the world behind for a place of contemplative seclusion. I try to think of travelling here in the 1500s, when twenty miles was the most you could count on covering in a day and the maps that existed rarely showed roads. A curvy one like this must have been a tortuous track susceptible to washout in storms. Italian roads still depend on a directional sense rather than highway numbers. You see signs to specific places rather than 580 East or 880 North, a custom probably connected with early travel. One traveller in the 1500s wrote, "I have had so little respite that my bottom has been constantly a-fire from the saddle." Obviously a common problem; earlier, the rigors of the road inspired Cato to give a bit of advice, "To prevent chafing: When you set out on a journey, keep a small branch of Pontic wormwood under the anus." The more comfortable Alfa hugs the road nicely and Ed loves the constant downshifting on hills and hairpin loops.

Around a curve, suddenly the red brick complex looms. The moat and stronghold effect of the massive structure remind me that even here in the Middle Ages defense was an issue. Cypresses and chapels and footpaths surround the monastery, which looks like a beautiful prison. At the entrance, a Benedictine monk in an ankle-length white robe that looks unbearably scratchy and hot checks everyone for proper attire. My daughter was turned away last summer by this fashion policeman when she presented herself at the door in a sleeveless Lycra top and a short skirt. The monk wagged his finger in her face and shook his head. Arms may not be exposed. She was furious when she saw men in shorts being admitted but she went back to the car, borrowed her boyfriend's baggy T-shirt and then was allowed to enter. Today, I see him turn away a man in short shorts. If the Benedictines must wear those wooly robes, I suppose flesh has to be a philosophical concept. At least today proves it's not a misogynistic one. He scans my mid-calf–length skirt and yellow sweater and nods me in.

Once inside the fifteenth-century cloister, the impression of a fortress dissolves into the serene quiet of a light-drenched courtyard with pots of geraniums. Somewhere in the complex, monks labor over the restoration of old books, or engage in concocting Flora di Monte Oliveto, a herbal liqueur used as a curative. Their other main product is honey. I would like to see them in their robes, opening the hives, an act unchanged since medieval times.

Behind the bordering carved arcades, the Sodoma and Signorelli (a Cortona boy) frescoes of the life and miracles of San Benedetto—holy inspiration for this order—line the inside walls.

During these years of transforming the house, we become obsessed at different times over aspects of construction. For a while, wherever we were we noticed drainpipes, how they were attached, where they leaked, whether they were copper or tin. When we had a humidity problem on a wall, we found ourselves spotting areas of mildew and rippled paint on cathedral and museum walls, ignoring the art and architecture while trying to pinpoint the source of the problem.

Today, we're riveted by the Signorelli fresco of a falling wall. "Walls fall," in the immortal words of Primo Bianchi when our Lime Tree Bower wall careened into the road below. Falling stone is a particular nightmare of ours. In the background of the fresco, a monk loses his footing when a wall starts to slide, and he tumbles through scaffolding. A little devil hovers above him. Was there a red devil hovering in the linden trees over our wall? In the middle distance, three monks are carrying the lifeless body, and in the foreground the monk is miraculously revived by a blessing from Benedetto. As in other frescoes, this event does not seem to qualify as a major miracle. After all, the monk probably was just knocked out. Benedetto must have been loved and revered, so much so that everything he did seemed miraculous. If I had not bought the guidebook in the monastery shop, I would have no idea of all that is going on in these paintings.

I love the sense of time found in many frescoes: The whole

sequence of a narrative is composed as one painting, with past to present depicted from small to large or left to right; the viewer first perceives the whole simultaneously happening event, then "reads" the progression. Time collapses, as it so often does in memory. The painter, seeking to tell a story, is bound by the Alpha-Omega concept of time, but the structured composition of the whole fresco runs back to an earlier intuition: All time is eternally present.

In the next fresco, four monks cannot move a large stone. Look closer—there's a devil in the stone. The monks have long iron poles exactly like ours and have wedged them under the stone, but the evil force keeps it immovable until Benedetto makes the sign of the cross over it. We have confronted many such stones, without the help of divine intervention. Now I'm understanding his sainthood. The power to lift stones surely qualifies him.

Off to the side in another Signorelli, a woman in blue is three-quarters turned away from the viewer. She's as lovely as the famous Vermeer painting of the woman pouring from a pitcher at a window. Two monks, against the rules of their order, are having a fine meal in a house outside the monastery. They're focused on a laden table, which is served by two women and a boy carefully holding a bowl. The woman in blue pours wine from a pitcher into a glass and you almost can hear it splash. Her hair is caught up in a cap which pushes out her ear. The long line of her neck and the faint indentation of her backbone through her dress give you the muscular sensation of her body in the act of pouring. Everything about her feels intent on what she's doing. The other woman in sea-foam green has rushed over from the fireplace, skirts in motion, carrying aloft what looks suspiciously like a *torta della nonna*. For all her delicate, almond-eyed beauty, she has exceptionally large hands and feet. Perhaps an assistant stepped in and painted them while Signorelli himself went out for a pitcher of cool wine. These women flanking the fresco are two of the most arresting images in the whole cycle. Just out the window, it's later. The two well-fed monks have been found out by Benedetto. They're on their knees begging forgiveness, with the taste of the wine and *torta* still lingering in their mouths.

During the decoration of Monte Oliveto, which he began in 1495, Signorelli left after painting six frescoes, and the Benedetto cycle became Sodoma's project in 1505. Il Sodoma, what a name. He was born Giovanni Antonio Bazzi. The monks called him "Il Mattaccio," which means idiot or madman. On the way over, I pulled Vasari's *Lives of the Artists* out of our travel books in a box on the back seat of the car and read aloud to Ed, "His manner of life was licentious and dishonorable, and he always had boys and beardless youths about him, of whom he was inordinately fond. This earned him the name of Sodoma; but instead of feeling shame he gloried in it, writing stanzas and verses on it, and singing them to the accompaniment of the lute. He loved to fill his house with all manner of curious animals; badgers, squirrels, apes, catamounts, dwarf asses, Barbary race-horses, Elba ponies, jackdaws, bantams, turtle-doves . . . so that his house resembled a veritable Noah's ark."

"Maybe his nickname comes from his love of beasts instead of what we assume—bestial," Ed muses. "I saw somewhere that he also had three wives and fathered thirty children. That seems impossible."

"He thought of nothing but pleasure. . . ." Vasari continues. There's where he's wrong. I've seen his frescoes all over Tuscany. He thought a great deal about working at his art. Oddly, I think of Warhol, who seems decadent and frivolous, tossing off his art. A visit to the Warhol Museum in Pittsburgh cures that impression. He worked like a demon, amassing an immense body of varied, imaginative, playful, and seriously iconographic work.

It's easy to see where Sodoma stepped in because his menagerie starts to appear on the walls—ravens, swans, badgers, an anteater, various dogs, and what I take to be an ermine. His seven dancing women represent the temptations of the flesh, which Benedetto was able to resist. He has a whole fresco devoted to the saint's temptation, in which he restores himself by stripping off his robe and throwing himself onto a bush of thorns—probably more effective than a cold shower. He peers down from a balcony, directing the departure of his monks with a mule; obviously he's orchestrating their escape from the seductive women. This is one of the most beautiful frescoes, with the lovely flowing dresses of the women contrasting with the cumbersome robes of the monks, and the two groups divided by a doorway through which we see a distant curving road leading to a lake. I can't help but think that the rowdy Sodoma took special pleasure in creating gorgeous women for the monks to pass every day. When Sodoma painted them, the viewers experienced even more tension because the lovely women were nude. Someone later dressed them, cutting down on the perpetuation of temptation.

One of Sodoma's great moments is easy to miss. In an archway, Ed happened on his Christ bound to a pillar, with ropeburns swelling on his arms and criss-crossed blood marks of flagellation on his torso. Like Piero della Francesca's Christ in *Resurrection,* Sodoma renders him not as slender and pathetic but as a virile, big guy with powerful muscles. Nearby, Sodoma's own self-portrait appears in the fresco of one of Benedetto's first miracles, the mending of a broken tray, again a homely little act accomplished through prayer. Posed as a courtier, Sodoma looks straight out at the viewer with a direct, bemused gaze. At his feet are two badgers and a bird. He's full of life. I'll bet he was a handful for the Benedictines.

Although no one seems to follow the Sodoma trail, as they do the Piero della Francesca route, we could. In the time-stopped town of Trequanda, in a church with a checkerboard facade, SS. Pietro e Andrea, he's left a fresco. In the Pinacoteca and in Sant'Agostino in Siena, I've come upon paintings and enamels. His San Sebastiano in the Pitti Palace in Florence again shows his luminous talent for the glories of the male body: the delight in shoulder and stomach muscles, the filmy scarf around the genitals looped just so to suggest what is covered. I hardly notice poor Sebastiano's upturned face imploring an angel, or the arrow piercing his neck.

We take a stone stairway up to see the library. On the way, we pass a door marked "Clausura," behind which monks are cloistered, then we pass the door to the monks' dining room, which is open for a deliveryman to wheel in cases of water. The enormous U-arrangement of tables is covered in white cloths. Flowers, water and wine bottles, and a delicious smell drifting from the kitchen tell us that monks don't have to creep outside the walls for a good meal anymore. The room looks inviting and the lectern suggests that they will hear a reading while they eat in silence. I would love to join them.

Despite fellow-tourists here, it's easy to absorb the isolation of this place, the silence that exists in the closed parts and in the courtyard when the last visitor departs. The men are left to commune with time. I leave feeling that I have read a complex biography, and I have. The scenes from the lives of the holy are everywhere in Italian painting. Each panel or fresco is a chapter. "Put the action into scene," my fiction colleagues tell their writing students. Sodoma and Signorelli were particularly good at that.

I collect more images to conjure in nights of insomnia: The pink pate of the monk who nodded to me in the corridor; the fir and spice smell of the frankincense and myrrh in the chapel; an African child staring at the only fresco with a black person in it; a bold intarsia cat on a lectern, a wild-looking thing with eyes fixed on what must be a mouse; a monk singing in the cypress lane. He could be good Benedetto, walking out to help plague victims, or maybe he's just going out to check the hives, to see if the bees have awakened to spring.

Bagno Vignoni and Pienza

Ed is limping from a stone bruise. He leapt when his hoe suddenly disturbed a snake. His foot came down on a jagged rock. "What kind?" I asked.

"A very snaky-looking snake. Scared hell out of me. We were eye-to-eye." He's rubbing his foot with lotion.

"Let's go take the cure. We can be there by four."

"Then we can go on to Pienza for dinner. I'd like to drive up to Montechiello, too. We've never been there."

Bagno Vignoni, the tiny hilltop town near San Quirico d'Orcia, and within sight of the castle on top of Rocca d'Orcia, is built around a large thermal pool where the Medicis used to soak themselves. Where the central *piazza* is located in most towns, the pool (no longer used) reflects tumbling plumbago, tawny stone houses and stone arcades. Not much is going on in Bagno Vignoni. Right behind the village, a hot stream runs downhill, through a travertine ditch. On either side you can sit down and soak your feet, just as Lorenzo il Magnifico did in 1490.

When I first started spending summers here, I read in an Italian newspaper a heated debate over whether or not health insurance should continue to cover yearly sojourns to spas and thermal springs, a practice many Italians take as a birthright. I had been to Chianciano Terme and had seen people clutching their livers while sipping small glasses of water. They otherwise looked tan and fit. I glimpsed tanks where various body parts or the whole *corpo* could be immersed for the absorption of the healing properties of local waters. I've heard workers at our house discuss the merits of various waters as though they were discussing wine. Italians are great connoisseurs of the plainest elixir of all. I see them at various roadside springs filling demijohns. Water is not just water; it has properties.

My grandmother used to take the sulphur waters for a week

at White Springs, Florida, down near the Sewanee River. I was deeply bored and considered her a holdover from Victorian times. I only accompanied her so that I could swim in the cold black springs, emerging from the water smelling something like an old Easter egg. She waved from the third latticed balcony around the spring, a small paper cup of the odorous water in her other hand.

I did not expect to be drawn into this passion. Then I went to Bagno Vignoni. I converted. Ed's stone bruise takes us now but we must go at least once a year.

"Her dogs are barking," my aunt would say when we saw a woman whose feet had swollen over the edges of her pumps. After a few weeks of hauling stone, erecting trellises, and navigating stony streets, my dogs, too, are barking. We like to arrive very early, before anyone has revealed their work-torn, ailing, sometimes frightening feet. We're late today. I take off my sandals, and slowly lower my own miserable feet into the running water. Ed plunges his to the bottom. Then we notice a man with a red, red nose paring his yellow-talon toenails into the water. He must not have cut them for months. We stare as his big toenail, like a curl of wax, falls into the water. We move upstream from him.

At fifty-two degrees Celsius, the shock of hot water on a hot day is intense. Ed's size twelves magnify through the water next to my long rabbit feet. Sometimes the water feels merely warm. Rubbing my heels against the smooth travertine streambed, I concentrate on the invisible but potent minerals which are starting to soothe blisters, relax tendons, muscles, even purify nails and skin. Ed says his purple bruise is fading, fading. The water starts to feel as though it's swirling *through* my feet. When I close my eyes, only my feet seem to exist.

After twenty minutes, I'm back in my sandals, toes glowing lobster-red. Ed slides on his espadrilles under water and squishes out. Cured.

This is the strange part. Walking back into town for a strawberry *gelato,* not only do I feel a surge of euphoria, my feet feel as if they could levitate. Everyday Italian life continues to astound me. What *is* in these Italian waters?

———

We reach Montecchiello by a white road that climbs through fields of purple lupin scattered with the last poppies. The walled town is mysteriously empty. Finally we figure this out: Everyone has simply closed shop and gone home to watch the big soccer match, which we hear blaring from every window. As we wander, we encounter a man peeing outside the closed public W.C. on the edge of town. Much of the castle wall is intact. Inside, the streets are so clean they're like swabbed decks.

"It's tarted up," a friend had warned us. "I've never seen so many geraniums in my life." True, they're on every stoop, step, and sill. The effect is stunning against the immaculate shuttered houses and the pencils of sunlight falling into medieval lanes. It's one of hundreds of such hilltowns but one we'd never visited. We'll have to come back to find the fabric shop I read is here and, since the church is locked, to see the Lorenzetti Madonna. Even the priest probably is riveted to a small ball being kicked around a TV screen.

Down, down from Montecchiello, leaving it to its rioting geraniums, through the wildflower meadows, vineyards, passing abandoned and forlorn farmhouses on hills, through the mellow early evening and pig smells, toward Pienza, the first Renaissance town.

Pienza doesn't look like other towns. A pope with the splendid name of Enea Silvio Piccolomini built it in honor of his own birthplace. He must have knocked down most of the medieval buildings to put up his ultramodern Renaissance town because it's a harmonious whole.

There's a story about Rossellino, the architect, that stakes the heart of anyone involved in restoration or building. The architect overspent outrageously and concealed it from the Pope. When the excess finally was revealed, the Pope told him he was right to have hidden the sums because never would the pontiff have authorized such expenditures and never would he have had as his monument such a glorious town. He rewarded the architect with gold and a fancy cape. Perhaps our first builder had heard that story!

The *piazza,* bordered by the cathedral and several palaces for bishops, canons, and the Pope, is staggeringly, astonishingly beautiful. Pienza is glorious in all its parts, from the felicitous residential street along the ramparts, to the iron flagholders and cunning rings fashioned in animal shapes, where horses used to be secured while their owners did their business in town. Today no horses, and no cars either, which contributes to the silent and unified feeling of the town. We wander the *vicoli,* the narrow streets, with evocative names: Vicolo Cieco (blind), Via della Fortuna, Via delle Serve Smarrite (the lost servants), Via dell'Amore, Via del Balzello (the heavy tax or, in dialect, the man who looks at women), Via del Bacio (the kiss), Via Buia (dark).

The back end of Rossellino's airy cathedral is sinking, the porous limestone soil beneath it giving way a little every year. An ominous crack that looks as if it has been repaired with a staple gun runs down the wall and continues across the floor. I visit my favorite painting here, the martyred virgin Agata, who refused the attentions of Quintino and paid by having her breasts torn off. She comes down through history holding her severed breasts on a platter, which I originally took for a serving of fried eggs. Women who fear for their own breasts invoke her, and she is the patron saint of bell makers, too. Perhaps in a painting somewhere, the dome-shaped breasts were mistaken for little bells.

I once read in a book about the medieval pilgrimage routes

that all the towns along the way were crowded with souvenir shops. So, Pienza's plethora of stores selling ceramics to us on our various pilgrimages has a precedent. This area is famous for its *pecorino*. The street leading into the *centro* is lined with so many tempting shops selling the round cheeses wrapped in leaves or ashes that the pungent smell follows us down the street. We buy an aged *pecorino* (*stagionato*) and taste a semi-aged one (*semi-stagionato*). Honey and herbs also are specialties. Some are homeopathic—we see a honey for the liver and one for the respiratory system. One shop has pots of *ruta,* rue, which I'll add to my herb garden.

I'm drawn by all these food shops and also repelled. Pienza has rather too many; I'd like to see the shoe repair and the grocery store back on the main street. What remains of the ancient craft of *ferro battuto,* wrought iron, is an upscale shop selling lamps and tables and a few antique gates and andirons to the tourists down from Bologna or Milano for the weekend. And to us, of course. We look at their hanging iron lanterns with glass globes that end in a rounded teardrop, reproductions of old ones still on some streets of Siena and Arezzo. We need a light outside by the *limonaia* and one for overhead in a bedroom. They have them. I also buy an old iron that opens up to hold hot coals. The worn wooden handle tells me somebody pushed this five pounder over many a work shirt and apron.

Just outside the main gate we find a *trattoria* with a terrace. I'm thrilled anytime to see fried zucchini blossoms. We fall onto pork tenderloin grilled with rosemary, roasted potatoes with lots of pepper, and a salad of young arugula barely touched with good oil.

Around the cathedral *piazza,* the dignified pale stone buildings have travertine extensions around the bases. They serve as benches and over the years have been polished smooth by the bottoms that rested there while viewing the great well and the Pope's magnificent *piazza.* Over one is inscribed *"canton de'bravi,"* corner of the good. Do we qualify? We're feeling dreamy after dinner, the travertine still warm from the sun. We watch a small girl in a white sailor dress chasing a kitten. The full moon is poised over Piccolomini's perfect *piazza*. "Amazing what a little egomania and a lot of gold can do," Ed says.

"Perhaps he even ordered the full moon to drift overhead every night."

Another soccer match blares from the TV in the bar, so the women and babies are outside, the men inside. In a *piazza* just off the main one, another TV has been set up outdoors beside a Renaissance well and all the neighbors have brought out their chairs into the early evening to cheer and shout for Italy. The blue light of the screen reflects on the semicircle of rapt faces. Arm-in-arm we walk the rampart road. For the second time today, I'm astounded by everyday life in Italy. Ed holds out his foot and says he feels no pain at all.

A Loop Around Lago Trasimeno

With our mad lists of things to do for the house, usually we have a goal, a time limit, a schedule. A sudden "Stop!" or "Let's turn up that road" comes too late. But the landscape around Lago Trasimeno invites you to meander, not to care if the destination you sought turns into another destination. So near, so far from the important towns of Perugia and Assisi and the great Tuscan ones nearby, the lake country is quiet and verdant, with fields of sunflowers and corn around the water. The lake, fifty-four kilometers around, is the largest body of water on the Italian peninsula and its three green islands—Maggiore, Minore, and Polvese—emphasize its size. Little blue and white ferries ply the islands. The lake looks vast. Tumultuous skies cast dramatic moving shadows on water that is dazzling blue on clear middays and often icy silver when the sun rises or sets. Sometimes the lake surface reflects a gaudy, smeared orange and chrome sunset and the surrounding hills go dark purple. I've never seen a more changeable landscape. I've heard that World War II pilots mistook it for a landing field and the lake bottom is littered with crashed planes. The foothills of the Apennines scroll along the horizon, and towers, ruins, and walled towns perch on many hilltops.

I still can't resist the magnetic pull of abandoned farmhouses. Every few miles Ed pulls over, and we step through briars, mentally restoring and moving into the mellow house which often has no roof. In the larger villages, such as Castiglione del Lago, Città della Pieve, and especially in Passignano, which is right on the lake, there are a few other travellers but no one is pouring off buses or steaming through the streets with the kind of determination I often have. Around here, travellers are more inclined to sit on a lakeside patio eating roasted red pepper pizza, or to stroll along a wall under a Renaissance gate, or to drive through the fresh countryside with the windows down, perhaps turning up the tape of Pavarotti singing break-your-heart arias to maximum volume.

The serene villages with panoramas of blue water contradict everything we know about the history of this area. Only the oldest story is romantic: The demigod Trasimeno went to the interior of Italy on a hunting expedition. When he reached the lake, he glimpsed the water nymph Agilla and fell in love. Naturally he dove in after her and naturally, being half mortal, he drowned. The lake was given his name. After that, recorded history lists battle after battle: sackings followed by lootings, castles rebuilt only to be seized, burned, and reoccupied. Mercenaries and warring dukes and foreign kings and the town on the next hill all made constant raids on each settlement, with the castles, so charming today, acting as local bomb shelter equivalents. Their airy positions *were* chosen for the view—but what they looked out for was the next army of marauders. What exactly was at stake? Inland water is a valuable resource, especially in a dry climate. The castles and unwalled towns were therefore of interest in themselves. A glance at the map will make clear the larger significance of this area. Situated right at the heart of Italy, Trasimeno was the crux of many migrations and passages. Commanders of this area determined to a large extent who passed into the north or south. Many of the well-trod pilgrim routes to Rome edged the lake, following ancient routes south.

All that destruction, in a nice irony, left a bucolic legacy.

I love Castiglione del Lago, a walled town almost surrounded by water. On sultry summer days during siesta, we often bring lawn chairs and books to one of the lake beaches. We can cross the prickly grass to a bar for ice cream, walk along the beach, or just sink into midsummer torpor with the lulling sound of Italian sunbathers in the background. I've been in the water once. It was room temperature with a silty bottom. I had to wade forever to get to water deep enough to swim, while little finny creatures brushed my legs.

The local storybook castle, Lion's Castle, has catwalks along the crenelated top and a narrow stone corridor perhaps two blocks long with cut-out windows for defense. Looking forward or backward seems like walking into a mirror. At the tea and coffee store, the owner also stocks local honeys. I've been wanting to try the chestnut honey, very dark, and *tigli* honey from the flowering linden trees. I was curious about the tisanes, homeopathic infusions made from various flowers and herbs, with cures attached to each. She told us that the honey, too, had specific benefits. It didn't sound very homeopathic to me, but she said the sure cure for migraines is acacia honey mixed with *grappa.* I'd always associated *grappa,* that strongest of grape distillations, with *getting* headaches.

After a morning at the lake and a walk, we drive just to the edge of town to the Cantina Sociale, where local farmers sell their grapes. Red wine, produced from these grapes, can be quite good. We could back up our car and lift out a demijohn, which would be filled exactly the way a car is filled with gas. The pump registers the liters and the charge is about a dollar a liter. Bottled wine is more—two to five dollars. Their reds and whites, under the Colli del Trasimeno and Duca di Corgna— one of those old warriors—labels, are DOC (*denominazione di origine controllata*), certifying that the region's wine meets standards that merit this government designation.

We began my favorite topic of discussion—where we will eat lunch. Since most of the towns around the lake are mentioned not at all in guides, we walk around, examining the posted menus, checking out the ambiance of each of the restaurants. Food is robust and traditional in the whole Trasimeno area, nothing vaguely trendy, though pasta sauces made with rabbit or wild boar still seem exotic to us. During cool weather, *ribollita*, a soup so thick your spoon can stand up in the bowl, is my favorite. Most of the special dishes are fish of the lake—carp, shad, perch, *frittura* (a fried mix of tiny lake fish that look like the minnows that swarmed around my legs in the lake), and *tega-maccio*, the local fish soup that varies with the catch. Yellow eels are plentiful here and are often prepared in a sauce for pasta (*spaghetti al ragù d'anguilla*). A highly regarded fish, *lasca* (the European equivalent bears the unappetizing name of *roach*), has disappeared from the lake.

We decide to circumnavigate the lake, turning off on whatever roads lure us, to take the ferry to Isola Maggiore, and to drive to Panicale, Paciano, and Città della Pieve, slightly off the loop. Since distances are very short, it's easy to return home at the end of a day's travelling. It's just as easy, however, to stop for the night along the way. Passignano, the main resort on the lake, looks like a good choice for a night, as does Isola Maggiore. Like the restaurants, hotels in this area are not elaborate but are pleasant and comfortable, with the additional virtue of being inexpensive.

Before setting off, we stop at the *forno* and pick up two kinds of *torte al testo* (crispy, flat bread cooked on a hot iron in a wood oven), one with *pancetta* and the other with *parmigiano*. The cases also display *serpentoni,* almond pastries formed in the shape of a serpent.

Tuoro is our first pause. We want to get a closer look at the marshes along that edge of the lake. And, of course, we know about the famous battle site. A man pulling his fishing nets off his flat-prowed boat points out where Flaminio bivouacked for the night while Hannibal waited for dawn to attack him with his melting pot army of Numidians, Berbers, Libyans, Gascons, Iberians, and other dissidents he picked up along his way. Hannibal was down to one elephant by then, after his famous crossing of the Alps with thirty-nine. He also had lost an eye but still was in complete control of his 40,000 men. He outsmarted Flaminio and on a foggy morning drove the Romans right into the lake. Fifteen thousand Romans died, to fifteen hundred of Hannibal's men. Besides Ossaia (boneyard), where Anselmo lives, Sanguineto (bloodied) also recalls that day. An ugly modern bust of Hannibal at Tuoro commemorates his feat.

When I was a college sophomore, I was amazed that my Modern History course began with the year 1500; 1500 seemed beyond the bend of time. When I started travelling to Italy, finally it began to make sense in a real way, not an abstract way, that 1500 is quite recent. It's still hard to imagine Hannibal duking it out with the Romans, here where the tranquil view looks unchanged from long before that era. Just beyond the marshy edge, poles are stuck in the water, with nets attached, a method that could go back to prehistory.

A four-lane highway runs along the Tuoro/Magione side of the lake. We stick to our good map and stay off the busy *raccordo*;

the small roads are fun to drive. Along the way, we watch for the thin yellow signs, pointing the way to a thirteenth-century church, a *fortezza,* Roman gates, or a tower. It's fun to stop, too, at the *"vendita diretta"* signs posted near the farms or estates that sell their wine or oil or honey directly to you. Out of Tuoro, intriguing roads lead to Vernazzano's leaning tower, to Mariotella, a medieval fortified *casa,* and to Bastia Corgna, a larger abandoned castle from 1300.

Castel Rigone occupies one of the prime positions above the lake. Substantial sections of the old walls of the town still exist. In the early sixteenth century, a fine small church was built because of local miracles associated with a painting of the Virgin Mary. Inside the plain, pure gray stone church remain wonderful frescoes, including an Assumption by Battista Caporali.

We wind downhill to Passignano, a peaceful resort of oleander-lined streets with a medieval section of town and many cafés and hotels along the lake. Two shops spill out onto the grounds with extensive selections of the hand-painted majolica from nearby Deruta; their prices are lower than Deruta's. How can they stand to take all those mugs, pitchers, candlesticks, and platters inside every night? I find the cheerfully designed espresso cups, plates, and pasta bowls irresistible, even if they are a nuisance to lug to San Francisco. Our china at Bramasole is going to be a wild mixture. Butter dishes, *parmigiano* servers, teapots—thank the gods for bubble wrap; I'm well into Christmas. Ed strolls next door for espresso. He can take only so much. I store the bags in the car and see him heading toward a *rosticceria* and pizza shop, headquarters for potato pizza, which is much better than it sounds. The onion pizza is a close second, with onions cooked slowly, almost caramelized.

No need to plan the hour to go to Isola Maggiore and Polvese; ferry service from Passignano, or from Castiglione del Lago or Tuoro, is so frequent that you can jump on often. Twenty minutes over the water and we step out on strange

territory—no cars. Because Maggiore seems so completely severed from time, we decide to spend the night at the island's one
inn. We feel the special isolation of the place after the last ferry
has departed and the island returns to the fishing village it always
has been. A solitary walk down the main street at midnight can
make you feel as though you've been stuck into a time capsule.
About sixty people live here now; the high point of the island's
population was six hundred during the sixteenth century. The
one-street village is lined with golden stone houses, with olive
groves rising behind. Occasionally you see a woman in a doorway catching the light for her lace making. Large, hooped nets,
called *tofi,* dry in the sun. Shaped like cornucopias, the nets are
for catching eels. We walk all the way around the island (about
a mile), passing a spot where San Francesco landed in 1211. San
Francesco was everywhere in Tuscany and Umbria, somewhat
like George Washington–slept-here in the United States. Three
open churches remain on the island. Right on the main street,
Buon Gesù has the feel of many Mexican churches, with naively
executed frescoes. The spontaneity makes you aware of the hand
of the maker. The other two churches are from the twelfth century: San Salvatore and San Michele at the top of the island, a
hot uphill climb through olive groves.

I ask the church caretaker at San Michele about the strange
castle on a tip of the island. We'd skirted it on our walk and had
tried to see inside, but the shutters were so long closed that ivy
has grown over them, splitting the wood and twining into the
stone walls—surely Sleeping Beauty is dreaming in an upstairs
room. Situated on a curve of the island periphery, it has 300-
degree views across the water. The caretaker tells us the castle,
abandoned for years, used to be a monastery. "Any chance of
seeing the inside?" I ask without much hope. But as so often
happens in Italy, yes, her friend is the caretaker and, yes, she will
show it to us. She will be passing the church in an hour, come
back then. We go down to the village again and buy a guide-

book to the island. The castle, we read, was built at the end of the nineteenth century onto a 1328 monastery and church of San Francesco. A marquis built this folly for his wife, Isabella. The family restored the church, built the boat landing, and imported an Irish woman to teach the villagers the art of lace making. By the 1960s, however, this late fiefdom was abandoned, its luxurious furnishings sold.

The caretaker turns an immense iron key and leads us into the castle's church, totally dark except for her flashlight. We make out a blue vaulted interior with gold stars. Chairs, pieces of the altar, and choir screens lie in heaps. Soon we are turning in corridors and following her light through darker and darker rooms. In some she suddenly flings open a window, letting in the stunning blue view, and we see damask walls hanging in strips, opulent painted borders and mouldings. In a courtyard, we glimpse what must have been the monastery cloister with its great stone well. I lose count of the rooms. We see in the circle of her light the ruined game room and theater, with painted scenery and velvet curtains piled on the floor, a castle for generations of mice. It is astonishing how quickly ruin has again overtaken the place. Will anyone awaken the princess? The caretaker says someone from Rome plans to restore it someday. Let's hope he has a boatload of *lire*.

Continuing around the lake, we zigzag among clusters of enchanting stops. I especially like peaceful Monte del Lago, a castle town with impressive walls and gate right above the lake. The hotel there serves an amazing *carpa regina in porchetta,* carp paired with herbs and bits of roast pork, and *zzurlingo al sugo di lago. Zzurlingo* is a dialect word for a thin flat pasta, here served with a rich, fish-based sauce. Their *filetti di persico con salsa della casa,* delicate perch with a herb sauce, is also wonderful with a glass of spritzy white wine. Monte del Lago has wide-angle views of the lake. From the ramparts on cloudy days the gray water near shore stretches to apple green, aqua, lapis blue. No one is about except for a three-legged cat sleeping on a wall.

Equally serene are Antria, a toy walled village, and Montecolognola, with a double-gated entrance. These places rearrange my sense of time. The unchanging places continue to soak in the sun as they always have. The strange gate at Montecolognola accommodates a roaring Moto Guzzi (*why* don't they require mufflers?) as well as a cart pulled by oxen in earlier times.

A larger, less appealing town, Magione sits under a very tall tower encased in what looks like permanent scaffolding. The Knights of Malta also left a marvelous fortification from the time of the Crusades at Magione but it's privately owned now and hard to see because of the trees. Right outside Magione, however, I glimpsed another Cantina Sociale and found their DOC wines as good as their neighbor's across the lake. The cantina stands next door to a large wrought-iron works. *Ferro battuto* is the ancient craft of the area. Cortona, like many towns, has torch and banner holders, rings to tie horses, fanlights, and lanterns. Except for a few masters, the craft is dying. Here, however, is a large-scale operation. They still make traditional iron lanterns with clear globes, fireplace and grilling tools, and andirons, as well as tables, beds, and other large pieces. Their warehouse attests to the fact that they deal in quantity, unlike the scattered one-man forges we've used in our restoration. One of my favorite things about Italy is that even in such a large place, they will do anything to please you. I didn't like the flower on the fire screen. "Is it possible to have it without the flower?" Marco considers. Come with me, he motions. We go into the immense workroom with smouldering fires and pits of paint and stacks of iron parts. With a torch and a touch-up, he has removed the flower in ten minutes. Can we have the andirons without the curve? Yes, next week. I remember the abandoned slab of travertine at the house and ask if they can make a table base. Of course. He takes us into his house and shows us the table he has designed for his family. His wife offers us a Coke, and we sit out on his patio while he sketches a table base he thinks we would like. We do. Expecting him to say six weeks, I ask how soon we can have it. "Would next Tuesday be all right?"

Nearby is Rocca Baglioni, with a double tower, and Zocco, an abandoned castle on a prominent knoll overlooking the lake. In the fishing village of San Feliciano, we find the Fishing Museum, where we learn perhaps more than we want to know about the history of local fishing.

Although it sounds as if we're zooming through Umbria, these are short distances, a few miles between stops. We then drop down to the area just south of the lake, in search of the Santuario di Mongiovino. As we arrive, mass blares from the bell tower and the doors fly open, releasing dozens of children and nuns into a forecourt of tumbling ancient buildings; only the church is intact. Its almost square structure is unique among churches I've seen. When we walk around back to examine the building, we find several mobile units, housing for the Benedictines. Up the hill we come to Mongiovino Vecchio, a military stronghold in ages past and now inhabited by a few families. Not that we see anyone. Many of the castle towns have a day-after-judgement-day stillness. We do see wash flapping on a line and from a high stone window we hear the unmistakable sound of Jimi Hendrix. We sit in the grass by a fallen wall and eat the hot grapes we've left on the back seat of the car.

We are looking for the Torre d'Orlando, a castle with a tower built in 917. The detailed map pinpoints it on a squiggly road between Paciano and Panicale. We drive up slopes of olive trees to Paciano and walk through the medieval gates into a town totally closed down for siesta. A pile of ginger cats sleeping in a doorway does not even look up. At a lookout point over the valley, someone planted a flourishing circle of lavender around two facing benches and we sit down to enjoy the secret garden. Bees and yellow and blue butterflies flash and buzz—the only activity in town. After a light morning rain, the fragrance seems to rise in waves. Paciano, we read, has a museum and two churches built around 1000, as well as several fifteenth-century churches with frescoes and carved doors. All closed, of course.

We can't even find an espresso in the eerie quiet, so we drive on, turning left when we probably should have turned right to find the elusive tower. The road opens up at every curve to another broad valley view of the Umbrian countryside. All the traffic we meet is a flock of sheep in the road, madly munching grass and wild arugula on the shoulder, while a frustrated spaniel tries to herd them up the hill. We turn off the car and listen to their bells.

Soon we come to Panicale, home of Boldrino, a famous mercenary and one of the chief troublemakers of the fourteenth century. Several towns paid him a regular salary just to guarantee he wouldn't turn on them. Despite his pillaging and murders, he is commemorated by a plaque. Could it be that the Mafia is a descendant of these medieval mercenaries? Panicale has much more attractive features than the memory of this bad boy. The impressive gate leads to a fountain in the central *piazza,* which once was a well cleverly designed to catch rainwater in the Middle Ages. Like many towns in Italy, Panicale has a Church of the Virgin of the Snows, commemorating a rare snowfall on August 5, 552. Though Masolino was born here, only one of his paintings is on view, an annunciation in San Michele. The branching streets invite roaming and the distant views of the lake from this high position can't help but remind you of paintings. Perugino's *Martyrdom of Saint Sebastian,* in the church of San Sebastiano, shows, through the arches in the background, the unchanged Umbrian landscape.

Two other Peruginos hang in the same church, his *Madonna and Child* and *The Virgin in Glory.* The artist is buried about two miles away, near Fontignano, where he succumbed to the plague. The Church of the Annunciation there contains his (modern) tomb and a fresco. He lies just down the road from where he was born Pietro Vannucci.

Città della Pieve is one of my favorite towns. This lively and odd little city, the last stop on our tour of the lake country, seems like a wonderful place to live. We sit down at a caffè to take in the daily rhythms of the place. Large groups of men play cards under an arbor, a girl shouts up to a man in the most picturesque jail, monks stride along with shopping baskets, rainbow banners flap above the *piazza*. After all the pale, lovely limestone of Umbrian villages, this one comes as a shock: It's all red brick. With the tile roofs and the human scale of the architecture, Città della Pieve seems especially warm and amiable. The red brick isn't the only quirk. The "narrowest street in Italy," Via Baciadonna, *is* narrow enough for two people to lean out their windows and kiss. The central *piazza*, irregularly shaped, forms a rough triangle with the cathedral as hypotenuse. The cathedral was built over ancient temple foundations; it, too, has its idiosyncrasy. The dark interior is wildly painted with *faux* marble: spiraled columns, bars, panels, circles in all the colors and patterns marble can have and then some. Elaborate painted frames surround the elaborate actual frames of paintings. Of the many paintings here, Perugino's *The Baptism* and *Mary in Glory* are the most arresting. To see them, we dropped *lire* in the *luce* box; the lights then came on briefly.

I knew about the Peruginos in Città della Pieve. I didn't know about the stunning object across the street in the Palazzo della Corgna: a rare, tall Etruscan obelisk from the eighth century B.C. There are Etruscan sarcophagi as well. The town's other local artistic highlight, undoubtably, is Perugino's *Adoration of the Magi* in the Oratorio di Santa Maria dei Bianchi, next to the church of that name. Restored in 1984, the painting is truly splendid. How did he get those colors, dusky lavender, saffron, almond green, sea blues, and that luminous, sourceless light? Because it is the sole painting in the room, and because we are about to leave this idyllic town, I linger over each detail, an angel in the upper right, a shepherd, a white dog in motion, feathery trees, horses, and there in the background, the landscape Perugino knew best—the gentle hills sloping down to the waters of Lago Trasimeno.

From a Yellow Book: Thinking of Travel

I TOOK MY FIRST TRIP ALONE AT AGE SIX. I begged to be allowed to go to Vidalia to visit my favorite aunt and my blind grandmother. My mother drove me twenty miles to Abbeville to catch the train. As we pulled up, the train started to chug away. I don't know why this would have been at night, but in my memory the lighted train is bright. My mother leaps out of the car, calling "Stop, stop!" and somehow the train stops, I am shoved aboard, and we are moving, my mother's blue Oldsmobile scratching off, her arm waving out the window.

The car is empty except for me. I have my round blue overnight bag and a Bobbsey Twins book to read. I would soon be at Aunt Mary's. Tomorrow my grandmother will make biscuits and I'll watch her groping hands do the work of both eyes and hands. She will complain of her liver and sinus headaches without stopping. I will count the diseases to see how many she can have. She's up to seventeen. She'll let me use the green-handled circle to cut the soft dough rounds. I'll play in the damp caves behind their house, make horses and birds with the mucky red clay. The train! Zipping through the dark, all the way—seventy miles—to Vidalia, I am leaving my wicker carriage of dolls, my black cocker spaniel, Tish. Will the conductor tell me when to get off? My mother asked him.

I curl against the window, feeling the clacking metallic noises of the tracks in my shoulder, watching for the lighted windows of farmhouses. *Who lives there?* I wonder about *them,* about the life inside the houses way in the country.

I can almost inhabit the hard little body, almost feel my forehead against the glass. All the mysteries and allures of travel were there at the outset, even the long fascination with the life in a place, that common mystery I recognized years later in one of the last haikus of Basho, written at the end of the seventeenth century:

Deep autumn,
My neighbor, how
Does he live, I wonder?

At the end of his life he was still wondering what I began to wonder at the beginning of mine, and still wonder.

Even earlier, at four or five, I pinched my friend Jane Walker's arm hard and asked her, "How can you *be* and not be me," a preconscious stab at the metaphysical. It's a lifetime quest, finding out who "the other" is, and how life is lived outside your own thin skin.

Setting off to see another country, I set off to see what is more grandly other—whole cultures, geographies, languages. Who am I in the new place? And who are they who live there?

If you settle in, even for two weeks, live in a house not a hotel, and you buy figs and soap at the local places, sit in cafés and restaurants, go to a local concert or church service, you cannot help but open to the resonance of a place and the deeper you go, the stranger the people become because they're like you and they're not. In Pienza, I was struck on that hot night, when I saw the TV dragged out into the *piazza* so the neighborhood could watch the soccer match together. That's not going to happen in Pacific Heights, where I live. Even the smallest things reveal that it's a new world.

I was on a travel-writing panel at the San Francisco Book Fair. One of our topics was "Now that the world is the same everywhere, how do you find a place to write about? And then how do you write about it in a way that distinguishes it from other places?"

There's a short answer to the first: It isn't. To the second, I always think of what Gerard Manley Hopkins advised: Look long enough at an object until it begins to look back at you. It can be dangerous to travel. A strong reflecting light is cast back on "real life," sometimes a disquieting experience. Sometimes you go to the far interior and who knows what you might find there?

I read a lot of travel narratives and newspaper and magazine travel pieces that stop with observation. They tell you where to sleep, where to eat well, and what not to miss. Those articles can become fictions, idylls. An article about a German town that goes on about the colorful characters, the beer and hand-painted toys draws you. Three pages later in the news section there's a huge article on a Neo-Nazi movement shadowing the same town. The *Gemütlichkeit* dissolves. You turn back to the travel article, puzzled. When I've written travel articles, a few times I have been told not to mention poverty or unpleasantness. Well, fair enough. It's a rainy Sunday morning and the reader wants to dream awhile, having waded through the harsh stories of women on death row and starvation in the Sudan.

But the passionate traveller looks for something. What? Something must change you, some ineffable something—or nothing happens. "Change me," Ed writes in a poem. "Change me into something I am." Change—the transforming experience—is part of the quest in travelling.

Often we take America with us. How can we not, being thoroughly products of our culture? We see what we know how to see. Powerful built-in genetic strands that go back to Stone Age territorial instincts make us secretly believe the Danes or Hungarians go home and speak English at night. How much is that in dollars? What are these terrible breakfasts? Where's real coffee? More harrowingly, we are wary everywhere of being robbed and mugged. We fear the violence of America everywhere.

We're not alone in carrying our own country before us. The desire for the familiar is a powerful drive. I've seen the Japanese lined up in Perugia for a table at the Asian restaurant. With all the glories of Italian food right there, they opt for some peculiar version of the food of their homeland and then most likely think it's terrible. It's totally natural, even inevitable, to compare the Via Veneto with Main Street. Unfortunately, if extreme, this acts as a preventative to experience; what we know is simply confirmed. Another Japanese poet wrote: Ride naked on a naked horse. But we are profoundly displaced when we travel and denial of that displacement sets in quickly. If only we could recognize this—suspend the rush to judgement and compartmentalizing. Travel can reinforce the primitive urge to bring the new into the circle of the known.

I went to Pasadena—the word sets me dreaming, Pasadena—and walking around on a perfect day, I saw Starbucks, Banana Republic, the Gap, Williams Sonoma, Il Fornaio—all the high-end chains with identical merchandise in dozens of other cities. Where am I? Nothing happened to me. And yet, surely if I'd stayed longer than a day, there are layers of Pasadena. Pasadena must be unlike everywhere else. In America, with franchises and TV pouring their solvents over us by the second, you have to look longer and harder.

In Italy, it's easier. Each town, city, *borgo,* or *fattoria* is intensely itself. It has its own particular fountain of dolphins entwined with nymphs, its stone chapel with an Annunciation painting, its Etruscan obelisk, its families with names on the pews since 1500.

A writer told me, "Beware of the exotic; it is so easily available." And here across the waters, the exotic is more available. We see but we don't see the gorgeous man in the Armani suit taking his espresso in the bar, glancing at *La Repubblica.* In Italy, there's the concept of *la bella figura,* cutting a beautiful figure. The gorgeous man in Armani might live in a depressing back room of a store. At least he can dress well and go out into the *piazza* in a cloud of divine cologne.

When I first started writing poetry, I kept what I called an Image Bank, a photo album I stuffed with museum postcards of paintings, photos, typed lists of words I liked, anything that struck me as correlative with the writing process. My way shifted over the years. Although I still keep several kinds of notebooks, the images became more internal. Travelling, living in Italy, I'm especially aware of *storing* what I experience and see. If I ever end up rocking on the porch of a dogtrot house in the backwoods of Georgia, I aim to have plenty to visualize. Landscapes, fine meals, solitary walks—yes, I run my mind over those, but it is the lives of people I return to with the most feeling. A hand pulls back a lace curtain. A face appears in the window. Down-turned mouth, gelid eyes naked with disappointment stare out and catch mine. We look at each other for a moment and the curtain drops. *Hello, good-bye.* At 7 A.M., Niccolò, the handsome owner of the tobacco shop, is rinsing the stones around his entrance, sweeping and singing to himself. *Remember him, his hair still wet from the shower, his tune, his sudden smile—who*

179

he is on his own. These glimpses make me understand that hard line of Wallace Stevens: "Beauty is momentary in the mind but in the flesh it is immortal."

It is a miracle to see Pompei, Macchu Picchu, Mont-Saint-Michel. It is also a miracle to wander into Cortona, see the young couple at their fruit and vegetable shop. She arranges a pyramid of lemons in a patch of sunlight. She wipes each leaf with a rag so that it gleams. She's fresh-faced and young in her pink-striped apron, probably trying hard to look like a proprietor. Her long and delicate neck gives her the air of having just landed after flight. He looks like the flute player on the wall of an Etruscan tomb—curly black hair, cherubic face. He sets out the baskets of peas he has picked this morning in his mother's garden, then halves a watermelon and tips it up in the window so anyone can see how ripe and delicious it is. She places her sign above the cash register—all the vegetables for minestrone can be ordered a day in advance and prepared by her at home. Each customer is lavishly greeted. If you want three pears, each one is selected and held out for your inspection. I have entered for a moment daily life in a place I don't know, and the red pear held out to me in a work-hardened hand will come back in memory over and over. *Immortal.*

"THE AREZZO MARKET IS THIS WEEKEND."

Ed is mincing parsley, basil, carrots, and celery for his special version of what to do with *odori*—that bunch of flavors tossed in your bag at the *frutta e verdura*. Do I see him wince? Or is that a reaction to the onions he has chopped? "Do you want to go?" he asks.

"Well, yes, don't you?"

"Sure, if you do." He rolls the blade of the *mezzaluna* over the celery.

"We always find something fantastic." Is he thinking of the time he carried the cherry cabinet over his head through the crowd for half a mile? I glance at the cabinet hanging on the kitchen wall, its glass doors left open and the espresso cups from all over Italy lining the shelves. Many were given to us by our friend Elizabeth when she moved back to America; others we picked up in our own wanderings. Friends who've visited have added a few. Odd, many things we've acquired here have accumulated meaning quickly, as though they were long-treasured heirlooms. This confuses me. I thought objects gathered symbolic value only through time, or, if at the outset, by being significant gifts: my father's gold cuff links, my grandmother's silver syrup pitcher, the lapis ring made from an old earring.

Looking around this house, many "new" things are just as close to me, closer. "Remember, we found the angel painting," I offer. Over our bed this eighteenth-century angel now presides, a lovely blond presence whose face I've come to love. She's wearing boots, and her brocade skirts part to show a triangular panel of lace. Who knew angels wore lace? She's androgynous, with her or his pert face staring off into the mirror on the opposite side of the room. In the reflection, I get to see the face twice.

Ed scrapes the minced *odori* into the sauté pan. The sizzle sends up a quick scent of earth and rain. Carrots add that underground smell, while celery, which does not seem as though it would grow underground, always gives over a misty, crisp essence.

"The last time we went we found those chains. Do you want *bruschette* or just the fresh bread?" he asks.

Those chains, I know, weighed about twenty pounds. Unfortunately, we found them early in the day, before the three gold-leaf angel wings, the Neapolitan *putto*, cherub, with the missing leg, and the yards and yards of silk brocade that once covered an altar. The hand-forged chains, made of lovely iron circles, once held pots of *ribollita* and polenta over the fire. Ours now hang on either side of our fireplace. "They're favorites of ours. *Bruschette*."

The antique market in Arezzo takes place the first weekend of the month. Except in August, when the heat becomes too formidable, I'm there. The market sprawls all over and around the Piazza Grande, and spills up to the Duomo, covers the *piazza* in front of the church of Piero della Francesca's great fresco cycle, then trails out into side streets. On tables, sidewalks, and streets, fabulous furniture, art, and tawdry junk are displayed. With around eighty shops, on any old weekday, Arezzo is a center for antiques. Behind the fair booths, the regular shops line the streets. Some haul their own furniture out onto the sidewalk for the market. You could find anything there—a fancy cradle, a nineteenth-century still life large enough to cover a wall, embroidered postcards from World War I, garden urns, entire choir stalls. Last year, I began to see World War II ribbons, PW shirts, German war memorabilia, and stiffened uniforms. I even saw a yellow star arm badge with JUDE stitched across it for thirteen dollars. I touched the crosshatch threads around the edges. Someone wore it. It seemed immoral to buy it or to leave it there, an object among objects. Garish glassware and Venetian goblets are abundantly displayed, without ever getting smashed by jostling crowds. There is a buyer, it seems, for everything, no matter how fabulous, dinky, or hideous.

~

I collected as a child. Uncle Wilfred saved his Anthony and Cleopatra cigar boxes for me and I left them open in the sun until most of the pungent smell baked away. I kept arrowheads I found in one; buttons, beads, and pretty rocks in others. In shoe boxes, I saved paper dolls with costumes from around the world, postcards, seashells, and tightly folded triangular notes tossed to me in school by Johnny, Jeff, and Monroe. My oddest collection was brochures. I constantly wrote letters to small towns all over America, addressed to The Chamber of Commerce, saying "Please send me information about your town," and letters and brochures arrived, with news of the Pioneer Museum, the Future Farmers of America, the recreational opportunities afforded by an artificial lake, the opening of a tire factory. The longing to *go* seized me early. I no longer remember why, but I wanted to live in Cherry, Nebraska.

Opening a box, spreading out the slipper shells, angel wings, jingles, sand dollars, and scallops, I opened also the memory of a place, a string of moments. When I arranged the shells on the floor, a little beach sand sifted out. As I listened to the conch, the whoosh of my own inner ear brought back the wash of coquina shells against my ankles at Fernandina. I made spirals of the pastel colors and barnacle browns, rubbed the dawn-colored pearly insides with my thumb.

I remember my collections so vividly that I think I should be able to go to my closet and take down a box, spend this rainy afternoon playing with the blond Dutch girl paper doll, with her flowered pinafore and wooden shoes, the Polish twins with their black rick-rack skirts, their ribbons and aprons.

Collecting, like writing, is an *aide-memoire*. An ancient relative bored me wildly with her souvenir silver spoons. "Now, this one I got on a vacation to the Smokies in 1950. . . ." But memory *can* make you live twice. As words fall onto paper, I can again marry the cat to the dog.

Memory, the graduation pearls unstrung, rolling out of reach on the church floor, the choir screeching "Jerusalem."

Memory, they all rise, young again, able to see without looking. They're clamoring for the wishbone, asking what's for dessert. Close the box, close the album, hang the old lace curtain in the south window where it catches the soft billowing breeze, a breeze for a spirit to ride.

As an adult, I have few collections. I started to buy old bells once, but forgot them after a while. I have a number of Mexican ex-votos painted on tin and have accumulated many antique carved or clay hands and feet, and dolls' arms and legs, a collection I never planned and didn't even notice until someone remarked that there were quite a few body parts around my house. My collection must be expanding to other body parts because at the Arezzo market, I've also bought three bisque saints' heads, two bald, one with a golden wig and painted glass eyes. When I find early studio photographs of Italians, I buy them. I'm filling one wall of my study with these portraits, for many of whom I've invented life stories. My real passion at the Arezzo market was never planned, either, but springs from an old source.

I go not only for the chance to find furniture for the many bare spots at Bramasole and to discover treasures, but to see the people, to stop for *gelato,* to wander invisibly at this immense market, which retains the atmosphere of a medieval fair. At 1 P.M., the dealers cover their tables with tarps or newspaper and go off to lunch, or they simply set up lawn chairs and a table, complete with tablecloth, right there for family and friends, and bring out cut-up roast chickens, containers of pasta, and loaves of bread. People jam the bars, ordering little sandwiches, slices of pizza, or, in the upscale *gastronomia,* sausage and asparagus *torte.*

Gilded church candlesticks, olive oil jars, stone cherubs—out of all this, what draws me to the vendors of old linens? "This time," I tell Ed, "I'm not even going to stop. We'll look at iron gates, marble sinks from crumbled monasteries, and crested family silver. I certainly don't need any more pillowcases or . . ."

At first, I succeed. With so much to look at, I can become saturated. Ed is glancing at andirons and a mirror. I spot some painted tin ex-votos. He likes looking at the hand-wrought iron tools, locks, and keys, but after two hours, he gets this set half-smile on his face.

He has an effective way of speeding me along in department stores at home. Other men sit in the comfortable chairs put there for waiting men, but Ed stands, and when I linger at the blouse rack, fingering the silk and examining the buttons, he begins to talk aloud to a mannequin. He gestures and smiles, walks around her. "Love that suit," he marvels. "You look fabulous." People stare, the sales staff looks nervous.

Here, he wanders off for coffee or a paper. He comes back to find me sorting through white piles of linen. I can't tell whether he looks astonished or distressed. I wonder if he thinks to himself, *Oh no, an hour in the rag pile*.

In a heap marked 5,000 *lire*, I turn up a stash of fine hand towels embroidered **AP**.

~

At home in California and here in Italy, slowly I have amassed a collection of old damask, linen, and cotton house linens, some with monograms, some not. "Why would you want someone else's initials?" a friend asked me as she shook out her napkin at dinner. "I find that a bit creepy."

"These are my friend Kate's grandmother Beck's napkins," I answer, aware that nothing has been explained. When Kate had to empty her mother's house, she passed on a stash of linens to me. She wasn't interested in ironing them. They are enormous, with *CBC* scrolled in the center, the hump of thread as thick as a child's little finger. "I have a thing for old linens." Understatement. Spirals and history spinning out from that flip remark.

I do not mention my mother, that I still have in my trunk her monogrammed sheets I slept on as a child. I remember clearly my white spool bed, the sensation of slipping into chilly, fine cotton sheets, with the scalloped pink edge, and right in the center, my mother's curvaceous initials, *FMD*, delicate as bird bones. For her room, she had blue sheets with blue monograms, and every other week, white with blue monograms. I have some of those, too, worn to a softness but still good. When she has a house, I intend to give them to my daughter. Dozens of plain towels, sheets, napkins, and pillowcases have passed through my household without a trace, but the hand towels my mother had monogrammed before my marriage are still in service, though the initial K is gone now from my name. When she gave them to me, I was shocked to see my own initials changed: FKM. I traced the new initial with my finger; K, the letter still carried forward on unused silver napkin rings, silver shot cups, a bread tray, a pepper grinder.

Monograms in my family were not limited to cloth. Baby rattles, silver cups, shoehorns, dresser silver, and the backs of flatware were subjected to this mania. The urge to monogram always seems mysterious to me, and never more mysterious than when I was ten and found my baby dresses. I loved to plunder, as my mother called it. "Plunder and strew! Plunder and strew! You strew faster than I can pick up." Her language was, otherwise, not archaic. I was looking in the hall chest at my father's high school report cards, the deed to the house, a beaded purse with a slippery silver mirror inside, which my mother carried when she was in her belle-hood and did the Charleston, back when a pink feather boa hung in her closet. I was searching for secrets. My hands riffled through the bolts of material that might someday be made into skirts or bathrobes, through the stored-away plastic bags holding my mother's cashmere sweaters, washed and hidden in cedar to protect them from moths. Then I pulled out a flattened stack of blue batiste infant gowns and held one up. There, over where the heart would have been, I saw the monogram: MMF.

A child had died? A secret child? I ran to my mother's room. She was propped in her canopied bed, reading a fashion magazine. "Oh, those were yours, if you had been a boy. M for Uncle Mark, F for Franklin, Big Daddy's name." Her father, the puffy-cheeked man in the photograph, with her pouting in white flounces on his knee, died when I was three. I would have been a Mark and Franklin, not Frances, not Elizabeth. And the inevitable deduction: They had Mark in mind, not me.

"Why did you have them monogrammed before you knew?"

"I don't remember. We thought you would be a boy." Her hair is caught in silver clamps to set the waves. I could almost see this brat. His ears stick out and he has scabs on his stupid bony knees. He looks out with my blue eyes.

Little wheels of logic spin. "Where are the dresses with FEM?"

"There aren't any."

It didn't take long for me to figure that, after two girls, they desperately wanted a boy and that the monogramming was an act of superstition and determination, an attempt to bend the will of fate. Years later, my mother told me that my father disappeared and "went on a tear" for two days when I was born. Odd, my father was wild about me, and when he said, "All my boys are girls," I never picked up any tone of regret.

And is it odd, too, that when I think to myself about a sheet or shirt that is monogrammed, I think of it as a *mark*?

My mother monogrammed AMY on the batiste dress of one of my dolls. Amy, a name I loved from *Little Women,* though the name I secretly desired for myself was Renée. That was the one time I ever saw Mother at needlework. Usually, we took a hatbox full of my father's handkerchiefs and shirts, or pillowcases and my mother's silk slips, to Alice's, a woman who lived in a narrow house with a chinaberry tree out front. I climbed around in the tree, where once I saw a swarm of bees, or sat in the porch swing with her dog, Chap, who had swollen ticks on his ears. Sometimes I waited at Alice's table eating saltines and watching my mother and Alice, who was tall and angular, with enormous hands that looked as though they should be kneading great piles of dough—how did she manage to thread the thinnest of needles? She had bright pink gums that came far down to short teeth. She was brown and lived in "colored town." That she and my mother were friends may not have occurred to either of them. They gossiped and drank coffee, which Alice made in a blue and white speckled tin pot.

My mother pushed out her bottom lip when she concentrated. They carefully cut around printed initials, pinned tissue paper patterns to cloth, and ironed the indigo script indelibly onto the shirt pocket or sheet, leaving behind the outlined initials and the smell of scorched paper. Mother would then leave the imprinted linens for Alice. The preferred thread was silky white, limp figure-eight loops held together in the center with a gold and black label. A few weeks later, Alice walked the mile to our house and she and Mother would spread Alice's handwork across the bed, remarking on how nicely everything came out.

The June market in Arezzo is even larger than the ones in April and May. I find the torso of a saint, lost from the whole carved wood body. I find a gold-leaf wooden cross and a beautiful studio portrait of a young woman, circa 1910. She is poised on the edge of a chair but radiates an inner calm. Several women gather around a stand hung with filmy lace and linen curtains. The woman in charge has starched and ironed for days. She has a heap of my favorite square pillowcases edged in handmade lace and secured by mother-of-pearl buttons on the back. I have these yard-square pillows in all the bedrooms—such pretty substitutes for headboards we don't have, and comfortable for reading, too. Most are too busy with lace inserts to bother with monograms but here's *R N P* in white swirls. At home in California, I have a handkerchief-linen pillowcase with the same initials. It belonged to my friend Josephine's aunt, who lived in a splendid house in Palm Beach. Josephine gave me, too, Aunt Regina's pale, pale pink linen sheets with labyrinthine cutwork above and below her initials. Josephine had them for fifty years, her aunt for thirty or forty; they are perfect. Why do mono-grammed things last, while others are discarded? I have brought the sheets to Italy because in summer heat, nothing is as cool as linen sheets. At the market, I have acquired several more. I also love the heavy white sheets edged in webs of white crochet, and the plain, uneven cotton ones, heavy as a sail. When washed and hung outside to dry, they do not need ironing, just a smoothing with my own flat hand as I fold them.

' Sleeping on linen or the dense cotton spoils me. Occasion-ally, I'll find a bedspread, white cotton, of course, with the raised matelassé design and swags of handwork along the edge. They're short for contemporary beds but I bought one anyway and let my pillowcases show. I fall asleep thinking of the ancient villas and farms in the deep country where these sheets were used for birth, death, love, and ordinary exhausted sleep after a day of digging fields. They have been washed in stone troughs, flapped in spring winds, and have been hurriedly brought in when rain started across the hills. The ornate *DM* or **SLC** were worked by firelight for a bride. Perhaps some were "too good" and were saved (for what?) in the *armadio* shelves with aromatic bay leaves and lavender to keep them fragrant.

All the linen stands at the market have rolls of lace, petticoats, christening dresses, blouses, and nightgowns. I'm not tempted. Once in France I found a long-sleeved gown, buttoned to the neck for modesty or warmth, embroidered in red with my daughter Ashley's initials. That *is* a bit weird, to wear someone else's gown, a French someone with your own monogram. She thanked me but somehow the gown ended up in the trunk with other vintage linens. Maybe the family mania has trailed out in her generation, or has taken another turn. Her art projects have involved damask napkins with her writing on them, and drift-ing rooms made of gauze with poems painted on the hanging panels.

My sister located a place in Florence that still does hand monogramming. They have a book of styles, some plain, some as ornate as a Baroque ceiling. She took them a pile of linen napkins for her new daughter-in-law and three months later they arrived in Atlanta. At markets, I have been accumulating for my daughter beautiful linen towels with circles for monograms woven into the design. My daughter, who does not yet own an iron. I hope she likes them.

When they are almost dry—slightly damp but warm from the sun—I take the six hand towels I bought at the market off the line. Just as I thought, they have come out of the wash white as salt. I hold the monogram to the sun, **AP**. These hand-hemmed linen towels, I notice, have a tab for hanging on a hook. I've never seen that before. Last summer when I travelled to the south of Italy, I saw the grave of one Assunta Primavera in the cemetery near Tricarico. Fresh yellow gladiolus and pink plastic flowers adorned her stone, along with her photo taken in middle age. Rather than an ethereal someone about to be assumed into heaven in spring, as her name suggested to me, she looked hearty and present. She pulled her black hair into a loose bun and her face was lighted by a wide smile. She looked like someone who could take the head off a chicken, no problem, or assist in birthing a breached baby. It seemed impossible that she could be lying under the stone. Surely she was off in some kitchen, the flavorful scent of her *tortellini in brodo* floating up the stairwell.

My hand towels could not have been hers, but her strong face immediately came to me when I saw the initials. And so it is with all these linens. I like to open the lid of my *cassone,* take out a stack, and imagine the dazzling aunt's Palm Beach cocktail parties, jazz on the record player, the champagne, the tiny napkins passed around, the trays of canapés—what did they eat at fancy soireés in the twenties?—the Atlantic Ocean waves spuming over the breakwater. I imagine Assunta's stone house, the walnut sleigh bed where the young husband lay naked, wanting his back rubbed, and later where the old husband snored while she lay awake, wondering if her son would return from the front in Russia, if unweaned lamb would be good for the *festa,* if the cold had killed her fava beans. AP, embroidered by her mother, given on her name day.

I imagine, too, the white nightgowns I did not buy at the market but looked at with amazement. They were as big as tents, all three of them monogrammed with suitably huge letters: *TCC.* A mound of flesh slept in those. *TCC* had to roll out of bed, her pink feet cold on the tiles, twins screaming at once in the night, this swift white messenger flying through the dark hall to comfort them.

The monogram is territorial. This is indubitably *mine,* it says. Under that, the monogram is a fixative of memory. The silver cup always goes back to the moment of the baby's christening. The dozen linen napkins for the bride usher in all the Thanksgiving dinners gathering in the future even now toward her table.

Ubi sunt is carved on ancient stones, short for that most haunting of questions, *Ubi sunt qui ante nos fuerunt,* Where are those who lived before us? Naming is deeply instinctive, a motion against the swallowing up by time of everything that exists. At eighteen, about to go to college, I was given a large supply of green bath towels, hand towels, and washcloths, all duly monogrammed. Green was not a color I liked, but those towels went off to college with me, lasted for years, and, even now, two live in the trunk of my car. Decades later, thanks to Aunt Emmy's graduation gift, I wipe off the car seat where Coca-Cola has spilled, my hand around the balled-up initials of a very distant college freshman who dried her hair with this. *A fleeting touch of wet hair, no, a spilled drink.*

Carolyn, Assunta, Mary, Flavia, Donatella, Altrude, Frankye, Luisa, Barbara, Kate, Almeda, Dorothea, Anne, Rena, Robin, Nancy, Susan, Giusi, Patrizia—we're all having dinner at my house.

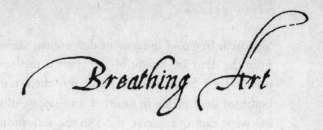

Breathing Art

ACROSS THE *PIAZZA*, THREE BOYS BOUNCE A SOC-
cer ball against the side wall of the Orvieto cathedral.
The sun strikes the great, gilded facade of that stupendous, dazzling, arrogant building. I'm just basking in the
reflected light, sipping a mid-afternoon cappuccino. This month
we're free to roam. Primo restored the fallen wall and even
improved it with two stone pillars for plants. He and his men
"repointed" the stone walls of the cantina, too, closing all the
crevices where dust and mice might come in. The planned projects start in July.

Although Cortona is only an hour away, Orvieto seems far.
My California sense of distance mysteriously expands here.
Sixty or eighty miles usually seem like nothing, but within each
kilometer in Tuscany and beyond, something to discover, study,
eat, or drink is a potential distraction from the goal. California,
at 160,000 square miles, is somehow smaller than Tuscany at
9,000 square miles.

Inside the cathedral, I've already seen the stop-in-your-tracks

Signorelli fresco of judgement day—when skeletons just raised from the dead are caught by the artist as they are about to, and just as they have, melded back into their restored bodies—bodies at their prime of health. I was happy—the reality of seeing what cannot be seen, and also the activation of the phrase, *the resurrection of the body and the life everlasting*: Something known, hoped for, or disbelieved—but unimagined really—suddenly given full verisimilitude.

I looked up until my neck hurt. When I turned away to explore the rest of the cathedral, I passed a woman praying. Her market basket propped beside her was stuffed with vegetables. She'd slipped out of her shoes and was cooling her feet on the tiles. A little girl nearby braided her friend's hair. Their dolls sat upright on a bench. A young priest idly turned the pages of a magazine at a table laden with Catholic family publications.

They are knowing that splendid place through their pores, knowing so intimately and thoroughly that they do not have to know at all.

I, too, recall every inch of the unadorned Central Methodist Church in Fitzgerald, Georgia. I can still see the worn-down claret carpet, a glassy white light, still feel my fascination with the wooden holders for tiny cups of Welch's grape juice, which would magically and creepily turn into the blood of Jesus as it passed through my mouth.

Sitting under the grand Mediterranean sun, poised at the solstice, I say inadequately, "Life would be different if you grew up bouncing your ball against the wall of the Orvieto cathedral." But Ed is trying to parse some *La Repubblica* article on the latest political imbroglio and so I spoon the foamy milk from my cup. What if the resurrection of the flesh had been painted above the heads of our white-robed choir belting out "I come to the garden alone while the dew is still on the roses. . . ." I would be seven, thirty-seven, seventy-seven—all stages of life, staring at that vision. If I turn my mind's eye around the interior of my hometown church, I see no art at all.

~

When I was growing up, a college textbook of my mother's from Georgia State College for Women stood in the living room bookshelf: *Art in Everyday Life*. I remember grainy photos of bowls of fruit on tables. They must have been suggested arrangements for still-life paintings. As a seven-year-old, I had no consciousness that included an act such as painting. I thought the pictures had to do with table settings because I did see my mother endlessly lavishing her attention on tablecloths and polished silver and flower arrangements.

Art meant the English hunting scene over the sofa, the pink ballet dancers in my bedroom, and the oil portrait of me that scared me with its likeness and crude vivacity. There I sat, caught in the hated blue dress with scalloped collar, my thin lips parted to show teeny teeth, the two incisors pointed like an animal's. A woman in town held after-school art classes on her front porch on Wednesday. I dutifully cast plaster-of-Paris shepherdesses and clowns. The next week, after they hardened, and if the teacher's children and dogs had not knocked off the lamb or the big nose, I painted them with brilliant enamel colors that somehow soaked in and mottled disappointingly.

When I went to college in Virginia, many of my classmates were incredibly sophisticated compared to my backwoods upbringing. They chatted knowledgeably about Cubism and Expressionism and the New York School. Soon I was soaking in the pleasures of the National Gallery with them and making further forays to the Museum of Modern Art. I ran up bookstore bills for art books, which enraged my grandfather, who believed in the Public Library, at most. Lautrec, Dufy, Nolde,

Manet—it was exactly like falling in love. My connection with art became intense. So it has stayed.

~

Watching the downshifting of light on the facade at Orvieto, I begin to breath slowly, taking in the shouts of the boys, the man at the next table completing a crossword puzzle, two nuns in long white habits, the angled shadow of the cathedral crossing the *piazza* like the blade of a sundial. I feel a grinding shift occurring in the tectonic plates in my brain. In Italy, it would be curious *not* to be intimate with art. You grow up here surrounded by beauty, thinking beauty is natural.

Art always has been *outside,* something I appreciated, loved, sought, but something not exactly natural. American towns often are void of art and are often actively ugly. In schools, art is usually a luxury which falls with no thud when the budget ax swings. Art, music, poetry—natural pleasures we were born to love—are expendables, fancy extras, so very non-binary. The unnaturalness comes, too, from the hushed atmosphere of museums, where most of us experience art. In Italy, so much art is in churches. Italians are only slightly less sociable in church than they are in the *piazza.* Art and the mass come not from on high, but with a familial attitude.

Cortona has an art gallery with its door opening onto Piazza Signorelli—his bust, perched high, overlooks the scene. The show changes every week, with the work ranging from excellent to ludicrous. But there it is, integral, right along with clothing and tobacco and flower shops. The artist sits with the show, thereby meeting directly with those who stop to look. In summer, the nearby Bar Signorelli serves at outdoor tables, and the artist can take a *caffè* when no one is about. Down the street, changing exhibitions of photographs are shown in a *palazzo,* which is also open to anyone interested who walks in off the street. Caffè degli Artisti's walls provide a casual exhibition place for young artists.

These galleries are light-years from the closed, cool exhibition spaces of Soho, Chelsea, and San Francisco, where just looking often makes you feel like an intruder. Country/city difference, of course, but in small country towns at home I don't ever see a vibrant art gallery as a vigorous part of the main street. A forbidding atmosphere is sad. Such a generalization—and isn't it true?

Cortona's signs say Città d'Arte, city of art, and it always has been. Cortona was one of the twelve original Etruscan cities and, since the seventeenth century, the town has had an active Etruscan museum. Their showpiece was found in a ditch in the nineteenth century—a heavy bronze chandelier intricately molded into shapes of crouching, erotically depicted figures. A few years ago, archeologists discovered important new tombs, and the museum now has a large recumbent animal figure and an ever-expanding exhibit of exquisite gold jewelry, carvings, and pots. A stone worker last year found a bronze tablet incised with Etruscan writing.

I have acquired, not by discovery but by gift, a piece of ancient art, an Etruscan foot. The touch of the maker is solidly in the folded-over slab of clay at the heel. I feel the indentations for the toenails, the long bone of the big toe, the knob of anklebone. Broken off before mid-calf, the ankle is hollow except for some ancient dirt caked inside. The foot reminds me of all the centuries of people who have walked over our land. Many, many people have these bits. In our neighbors' houses I have seen a Roman votive and an Etruscan glass vial, a marble head, a carved medieval door. The Italians take such ancient objects casually. Many a garage is a former house chapel, painted with frescoes which the owner keeps quiet about, not wanting the Belle Arti committee to make them give up their precious garage, home of that most precious macchina.

Even in Italian museums, most guards are dying to talk. I remember the guard in Siracusa giving a spontaneous talk on Caravaggio's *Burial of Santa Lucia*. In dank stone corridors in winter they're usually huddled with other guards around the pitiful space heaters, but, even then, a question will break one of them from the circle of warmth into a conversation about the restorations in progress or a disputed attribution.

~

Cimabue, it is said, discovered the young Giotto drawing a sheep on a stone at Vicchio, where Giotto tended flocks. Surely this is apocryphal but it points to an amazing moment in history when shepherds—and apprentices and clerks and noblemen's boys—took up the brush or the chisel all over Italy. The middle class was on the rise. The Tuscan vernacular began to be used in literary works. The painters' subjects were mainly religious; commissions for churches were pouring like *vino da tavola*. And while the subject might be assigned—the Annunciation, for sure, or the life of a saint—the painters began to bring to their "sermons" in the art of fresco a sweet domestic air and a sense of *campanilismo*, a word that has to do with the sense of community of those who live within the sound of the local parish bell, the *campanile*.

One senses this new feel of the familiar starting in the thirteenth century when Duccio (1278–1318), allowed the flicker of emotion to haunt the face of the Madonna as Christ is removed from the cross, thereby cracking into the static, iconographic, and formalized painting style dominated by the influence of Byzantine mosaics. One probably could trace this new, more expressive, approach month by month. Imagine hanging around those workshops, when new techniques passed from mouth to mouth, village to village. From here, it's hard to gauge the surprise of Duccio's contemporaries. Giotto (1267–1337) codified the new approach in painting and Nicola Pisano (1258?–1284), and later his son, Giovanni (1265–1314) in sculpture. Then the names unroll: Masaccio (1401–1428?), Fra Filippo Lippi (1406–1469), Fra Angelico (14??–1455), Andrea Mantegna (1430–1506), Domenico Ghirlandaio (1449–1494), etc., etc.

When art historians discuss this spreading realism in Italian art, they often speak in terms of the new emotion and perspective, but those are only a part of what happened: When the silly little dog wandered into the foreground of a painting, the imagined wag of its tail caused painting and sculpture to enter the imagination of the viewer at a more direct level. In 1430, when Donatello's David in a jaunty hat jutted out his bronze hip, the fluid sensuality of his pubescent body was lost on no one.

Artists were commissioned to paint churches, chapels, grain markets, banks, cloisters, city halls, lay confraternity halls, bedrooms, cemetery memorials, and standards borne through the streets. Sculptors glorified the rich with statues and local *piazze* with playful and joyous fountains. The people began to breathe the art every day. *Art in Everyday Life*. Not only a superhuman act to worship. Not only a bowl of fruit on the table.

There must be 10,000 Annunciations. The angel is witnessing the laser beam of the Holy Ghost angling toward a startled (who wouldn't be?) Mary. There's no mistaking the message. But the local resident—her basket of vegetables wedged next to her while she prays for her son off at war against the Guelphs— stares at the lake in the background where her husband fishes, the line of hills as familiar to her as the curves of her own hips.

In Crivelli's (1435?–1495) version of the Annunciation, the Virgin herself is the main focus. The impregnating light beam from heaven, so much like an airplane's contrails, illuminates her crossed hands and wide forehead. But our visitor with the basket of vegetables looks for a long time. What is that outside the Virgin's door? An apple and a squash, plain as day. And over her head on a shelf, her six white pasta dishes. A cheese box. A bottle of oil—extra virgin, no doubt—and a candlestick. From her window upstairs, hangs a wooden cage with a songbird. An Oriental rug drapes over a stone railing, with a house plant airing on top of it. We are suddenly at home.

All over Italy, they are kneeling or cooling their feet on the church tiles. In a side panel, a horse has skidded into a ravine, a man falls from a ladder, a stone wall collapses on a monk. The baby Jesus looks just like the neighbor's baby, born with no sign of a father. Ugly little *bambino* with a stranglehold on a bird. Or there, Saint Jerome, major man, in his study with the shadowy figure of his companion, a lion. And there's his bath towel dangling from a nail, a note tacked to his desk, a small cat. *My house is your house.*

A grand Cortona *palazzo* has been divided into thirteen apartments. Behind the Renaissance facade, the medieval house remains. Cutting and pasting those winding corridors and rooms, joined without hallways, into apartments must have been an architect's nightmare. We're having dinner in Celia and Vittorio's kitchen. Formerly, it must have been a sitting room. Vittorio and Celia have found beneath the whitewash a two-hundred-year old garden scene on all four walls. The *tromp l'oeil* iron fence separates the viewer from the flowers and distant hills. We admire the view as we are dipping fennel slices into Vittorio's parents' olive oil. "Oh, all the flats in this building have frescoes in every room," he tells us, "but most people never have bothered to uncover them." He shows us the other rooms, the tantalizing glimpses of melon and aquamarine colors where they have not yet restored the frescoes. How can they bear not to see? I think I'd be up all night, sponging water and rubbing a toothbrush over the powdery whitewash. When we uncovered a fresco in our dining room we thought it was close to a miracle.

A fresco! Since then we've learned that almost anytime you start scrubbing in Cortona, you discover a fresco.

Antonio, who also lives in this *palazzo*, stops in for a glass of wine. He takes us to the mysterious apartment where he grew up. We enter a large room, then another. His dead mother's paintings—portraits and landscapes—cover the walls. Her piano, her furniture, her photographs on the mantel, remain. There is a photo of four-year-old Antonio on Santa's knee. Someone years ago has made a few swipes low on the wall, enough to reveal that something chestnut brown and green lies underneath, but what? I think I see the quick curve of a horse's haunch. This room obviously is unused. We go down a squirrely, low corridor into a vast room under the eaves, with a painterly view of the *piazza* far below. Antonio takes me into a side room stuffed with his paintings. The main room has a long table covered with sketches and squeezed tubes of paint. Two cats fly around the room and then curl together in a mammoth fireplace, where people have warmed themselves since the 1500s. Along the way, who took the brush to these walls and what was painted? And who grew weary of them, decided white was better, and simply wiped them out? Antonio sits by the drafty fireplace with his wild cats, sipping coffee and drawing, walking to the windows to look down at the *piazza*.

He has other rooms we do not see, rooms he has closed. Under paint and smoke, I imagine other garden scenes, Annunciations, mythological trysts, Europas, distant castles, scenes from the lives of saints. But Antonio is showing me the decorative border he has designed for someone's house, a restored house with newly plastered walls, where he will stencil acanthus leaves in gold bounded by lines of Pompeian red. In a hundred years, a woman will wake up one morning, her eye traveling along the top of her bedroom wall, and she will think *no,* she will think *flowers, I would like to see flowers* and Antonio's work will be covered by a border of roses.

I ask Antonio if he and his friend Flavia will paint a border in the bathroom we are about to remodel. I love the stylized, running Etruscan wave. He sketches a few. We decide on milky blue, bordered with two lines in apricot.

The next day, I find myself in the art supply store staring at the pristine watercolor paper, tubes with delicious names, thick sketch pads and trays of colored pencils. When my daughter was small, she and I used to set up a table in the back yard and paint all morning. She had a vigorous sense of color and, even then, thought big. She painted huge purple elephants with backgrounds of wildly splotched colors and princesses in swirling pink. Her boxy houses, with the spoked sun above, always had people in the yard and cats in the windows. And what's that off to the side? A yellow convertible. My watercolors were rolled up and hidden under the bed. The still life of a blue bowl of oranges was born dead. The fragile coral bells against a stone wall conveyed no sense of textural contrast. The immense pleasure of sitting in the sun watching my daughter, thinning carmine to pale pink and dipping in the fine tip, creating something where there was nothing—she had the flow of freedom. I was not spontaneously *good* enough.

In the art shop, I reach for the chalk pastels, the stack of handmade paper. The inkling I began to have in Orvieto slips into consciousness. I'm going to draw the *pleasure* of wild purple orchids springing up every day, the outrageous *upupa,* hoopoe, who lands in my hazelnut tree every morning, and the lines of the hills I can see from my study, how they lap into each other like pleats in a green velvet skirt. I've been breathing these images. And if I could *deeply* breathe art, I would try to paint the *feeling* of all the birds singing every morning splurging all their megahertz on the dawn.

I have always loved that collision point of nature with the desire to create art. For me the form is words. How to pull the scent of wet mock orange through the walls of the house?

Through the ink in the pen, through the keys of the computer? The dark when the birds begin—their songs so tangled together that no one can be separated—so impurely accessible to music, art, words. Song like a *riffle*, a sandbar just under water, sunlight pushed by the tide. How do they know and why do they sing? How to say that although everything is at stake when experiencing or making art, that it is at the same time a birthright joy. How to paint or write the everyday rising green burst of birdsong? The levitation, the silverpoint thread drawn along the black hills, slow melting of rose, opalescent blue, and the pulse of the birds still rising?

I am lying half-awake, wondering if I've died and this is what was promised. The ache in my hind end from digging out stones from the flower beds yesterday reminds me that I am still mortal and that the earth simply has returned to aurous colors; to diffusion, then to the birds scattering from their conjoined song and into their own jactations from tree to tree. I long for the creation.

This is every day, how art slips in and out.

Mad July: The Humming Urn

THIRTY-ONE STRAIGHT DAYS OF HOUSE GUESTS. A seventh set threatens to arrive. When Primo Bianchi stops by and announces that he is ready to begin work, we call these acquaintances, having earlier warned them that we might not be able to put them up because of the restoration project. "We'd love to see the work-in-progress," my former colleague says. "We'll stay out of the way." I rarely see him in San Francisco and can't remember whatever conversation we had at the book signing of a mutual friend, which has now led to him and his girlfriend visiting us.

"I'm afraid it's really not going to work. They're ripping out two bathrooms. I think you'd be more comfortable at a hotel."

Silence from across the Atlantic. Then, "Don't you have three bathrooms?"

"Yes—but you'd have to go through our bedroom to get to the other one." Momentarily nonplussed, he agrees that I can arrange a hotel for them.

When I was in college, I used to imagine a yellow house on a shady street. The indefinite location could have been Princeton, Gainesville, Palo Alto, Evanston, San Luis Obispo, Boulder, Chapel Hill—some college town where bicycles were preferred, tomatoes were grown in the back yard, and one's friends dropped in without calling. My writing desk would face a window upstairs where I could keep watch over the children playing, could run down to check on the roast. I imagined extra rooms with blue toile wallpaper, a dormer room with spool beds for children, and a dining room with a wall of French doors. Friends could stay as long as they liked, their children blending with mine at the great round table. This fantasy alternated with another of living alone in a fabulous city, Paris, San Francisco, or Rome, where I would wear a tight black knit dress, sandals, and sunglasses, smoke thin cigars in a café, while writing poems in a leather book.

Through the years, fragments of those dreams actually came true. But never until now have I had more than one guest room. With three extra bedrooms, my dream of the bounteous table and the open door have become reality.

Revolving door is more like it. Dreams sometimes need revision. During the visits of six sets of house guests, I have needed a conveyer belt from town to send out bread and meat. I strip off the sheets, and the washing machine lunges and churns for hours. I have lapsed into a set menu for lunch: *caprese* (mozzarella, basil, tomato salad), *focaccia,* various kinds of salami and ham, green salad, cheeses, and fruit. "Again?" Ed asks.

"Yes! They don't know we've had it four days running. We are definitely going out tonight."

I'm ready to draw maps to the antique shops of Monte San Savino or the Etruscan tomb near Perugia, but often they say,

"We just want to stay here. Those four days in Rome were exhausting. . . ."

At what point did I flip from *Excited to see you* to *How long, oh lord, how long will you be staying*? It must have been around day ten. For Ed, around day five; he is more solitary than I. He must have his private hours of writing and working on the land. Too much socializing throws the circuit breaker and he comes down with a migraine. By the third onslaught of guests, we were growing tired of the sound of our own voices. By the fourth, we switched to automatic pilot, almost pointing instead of speaking. "Bus is leaving for Siena," I whispered at their door. Feeble humor. We agreed to leave by eight to avoid the heat. Ed filled up the car so we could get an early start. We're showered and ready by 7:30, plates of melon on the table, the Moka hissing on the stove. They're still sleeping at 9:30. If we're out by 10, we'll arrive with an hour or so before the town closes for the afternoon. Our guests will be sorely annoyed at this retro custom. The rhythm of the Italian day seems impossible to grasp. "We're on vacation; we don't want a schedule. Let's play it by ear," he says. "Yes," she agrees, "and besides a lot of places stay open during siesta." No they don't, I think, but don't say anything.

When they left, I couldn't even say hello to the neighbor's gray cat, who sometimes comes by for a bowl of milk.

"Would ten days be too long?"

"The friends we're travelling with have heard so much about you. Would it be all right if the six of us stopped by for lunch?"

"My son's roommate and his cousin will be passing your way and we thought you might enjoy meeting a couple of kids on their first trip to Italy."

My mouth has a hard time forming the word "no" but I'm learning. "I'm working on a project," I say, only to hear, "Well, don't worry about us. We won't disturb you a bit. You just do your writing and we'll go off on day trips." If I say how sorry I am but we have a full house on the dates they propose, the reply often is, "Just tell us when and we'll plan our vacation around you."

⁓

Primo, welcome. You don't know how welcome. We've wanted to remodel the two original bathrooms ever since we first saw them. Because they worked, other more crucial projects came first. We ignored the chipped porcelain sinks and the funky showers that sprayed all over the floor, simply added brass towel racks and antique mirrors from the Arezzo market and turned our energy and cash over to central heating and unraveling electrical wires. Unlike those monster jobs, changing the bathrooms offers instant pleasure.

While our first guests slathered suntan oil on each other's backs, we dashed out to order toilets and lights. During the next guests' stay, we were looking at tile. Time to choose; the order needed to go. Karen and Michael waved from the upstairs terrace, where I left a bowl of fruit and a pitcher of cinnamon iced tea to hold them until we returned.

Selecting tiles in Italy would be daunting even for my two sisters, who can spend entire days examining fabrics or lamps or wallpaper. The attractive showrooms of building suppliers are backed with dusty warehouses. If you don't see what you want up front in the model bathrooms with the space-capsule showers and gadget-laden whirlpool tubs, you're turned loose in the *magazzino* to fend for yourself among racks, stacks, and boxes of pavers in shades of rose-honey, elegant limestone squares, the thousand versions of hand-painted blue and white birds and flowers, slick primary colors, and—oh, no!—the pink and blue butterfly we are about to exorcise from the house. I found immediately that I prefer tiles with the touch of the maker on them, the rougher surface, and the traditional designs. The range of marble and natural stone tiles also is staggering. For the first time ever, I thought I could not choose. When we built the first bath, I knew what I wanted—large marble squares—and, fortunately, didn't even look further.

Finally, we narrowed our choices and decided to come back in a few days. Back at Bramasole, Karen and Michael were glowing and spotless in new linen bought for their trip. Ed and I were grimy from the warehouses and my dust allergy started acting up. But—lunch in a few minutes! And in the afternoon, the Etruscan museum, the churches of upper Cortona, the monastery where St. Francis's narrow bed is still on view.

"La dolce vita," they say, leaning back for a sip of *grappa* in the long evenings, as I'm glancing in the kitchen at the stacks of pots. "Umm, think I'll go up; it's just so relaxing here. You two are *so* lucky—all day with nothing to do but enjoy all this beauty." The lovely guests trail upstairs, forgetting to notice that Ed and I are rolling up our sleeves for a bout with grease and suds. Over our heads, as we scrape and sweep, their bed bangs rhythmically against the wall.

By the time they leave, we've changed our minds about the tile. At last we can just look for a whole morning, without thinking of rushing home to feed ravenous guests. For the original bathroom of the house, called *"il brutto,"* the ugly, by my daughter, we select a rosy natural stone with the same stone in cream for the border. For the nightmare butterfly bath, we decide on a handmade Sicilian tile in a blue and yellow design on white.

The yellow house fantasy is still real. I love having friends and family here. In a foreign country, we see each other in an unfamiliar perspective, which can heighten and enrich the closeness we already have. Good friends jump right in and love walking to the market for strawberries. They come home with ideas for dinner and we have great times frying zucchini blossoms and making watermelon *sorbetto*. They're ready to search for a Roman road we've heard about, to start the coffee, or even to weed the asparagus bed. The bad guest could be anywhere; the good guest seems to know that places are unique unto themselves and gives over to the new heartbeat, letting the place have its way with them.

Now Toni and Shotsy arrive from San Francisco with a list of places they want to see; some are new to us. They're delighted on their first evening when the fireflies crowd the lane. Even a walk into town with them brings new adventures. We're walking past San Francesco, a church perpetually closed for restoration. Shotsy sees a priest at the side door and asks him if we can peep inside. He seems happy that we're interested. A grape-juice birthmark covers half his face. His eyes are direct and he moves his head from side to side as he walks, his black robe catching dust rolls. We spend an hour on a tour inside the vaulted, gloomy church which was re-dressed from its original spare architecture into a Baroque interior. The priest then takes us into a room with closed cupboards. He wants to show us something special, but first he shows us the skulls of several Roman martyrs, eleven or twelve years old. The shelves are full of various hanks of hair and pieces of bone. He reverently takes out a bit of cloth. "The last sash of Santa Margherita, a rare and precious relic." Then he shows us a piece of one of San Francesco's garments. This church, named for him, was built by his friend Brother Elias, about whom little is known except that he was a sometime hermit in the hills above our house. The priest shakes our hands and tells us, "I'll probably go to hell but all of you will go to heaven."

Near Piazza San Cristoforo, a man picking cherries in a tree calls *"Buon giorno,"* and throws down samples for us to try. All this and it's not even ten o'clock yet. They take off for the day and come home with stories to tell. We're sorry when they go.

My two sisters came with me for two weeks early last summer, when Ed was finishing his spring quarter of teaching. Because our mother has been in a nursing home for many, many years, most of our visits revolve around her dips into illness, her emergencies, or just the painful regular visits to her. For the first time in too long, we talked about everything but Mother. We travelled all over Tuscany, cooked pasta, and worked in the garden.

Our aunt Hazel had died recently and left us each a little inheritance. We decided to splurge. After all, we never expected this little windfall. I certainly didn't. Any selfish act when I was a child was corrected with, "You don't want to grow up to be like Hazel do you?" When my grandmother died, Hazel was too upset to go to the funeral. When we filed into my grandparents' house afterwards, we found that she'd loaded her car with all Mother Mayes's best things. Because of another painful memory I wouldn't write about, I had not spoken to Hazel since college.

My sisters and I ate in the best restaurants, ending each meal, with "Thank you, Hazel. We enjoyed that so much." We began to feel rather friendly toward her. We bought shoes and trays and scarves, saying, "Hazel, that was so sweet of you," as we walked out of each shop. As much as I disliked her, I found that her last act toward me stirred up a memory-belief that runs strong in my family, the old impulse, *Blood is thicker than water,* and a late forgiving began to form.

We found ourselves one day in the deep recesses of a medieval building in Florence, being shown rooms of designer bags and jewelry. My sisters were thrilled at the prices and began selecting—gold bracelets, wallets, summer handbags. It suddenly occurred to me that this was stolen merchandise but I couldn't say anything because the *signora* who took us there from her shop understood just enough English. I hoped they'd finish before the *carabinieri* burst in. We left with Gucci and Chanel, the real thing my sisters knew. "We're lucky we weren't arrested," I told them in the taxi. Oddly enough, they paid by personal

check and no one ever cashed them. Just one comment cata-
pulted us back to familiar ground. At breakfast in the hotel
courtyard with a splashing fountain, we were served perfect cantaloupe. Which one of us said, "Mother would have loved this"?
A deep relief to reconnect on a new basis. Now when we send
each other unexpected gifts, we enclose a card, *Love, Hazel.*

⁓

Bathrooms. The Romans loved them. Their bathing pools
with black-and-white mosaic dolphins and stylized sea creatures
never have been improved upon. Their fanciful designs influenced the original designers of bathroom decor at Bramasole
not at all. Early in this adventure, we realized that not only were
the old ones ugly, but our sewage treatment facility—one
cement tank—was inadequate when several people were staying
in the house. Noxious odors and scorpions crept up the drains.
We read books on home water supplies, on waste management
in the country, made photocopies of septic tank diagrams. After
a few hours of digging behind the house, Primo revealed that
the shower emptied right into the tank, an environmental no-
no. More digging revealed that all three showers and sinks
dumped gallons and gallons of clear water right in, forcing the
waste out before the biological action of purification could happen. We are polluting our own land. Or so we think, with our
book knowledge. "That's the way it's done," plumbers assured
us. "Your system is good." We don't think so. We have insisted to
Primo that we want a better plan. We want the showers and
sinks routed out of the septic system. We want long pipes to exit
the septic tank, with rock-filled pits along the way for further
filtering.

⁓

When Primo and the men arrive, we go out and discuss the plan of attack with them. Ed and I have spent ten-hour days decalcifying tile floors, ten-hour days stripping doors, but facing your true love over an open septic tank may be one of those true tests. Primo wants to explain the compartments. How they purify waste and where it exits. "This tank is O.K.," he insists. "I need to make another section on the inside. See, *acqua nera* in," he points to a pipe from the bathroom. He scrapes sand off the septic tank lid and pries it up. I gasp and step back. This is too much. I would like to be anywhere but here. Unfazed, he points, "*acqua chiara* out." Black water in, clear water out. It all looks *nera*. Primo leaps about with the alacrity of a cat on a dining room table. Ed has stepped back, clapped his hand over his nose. "There, then there, then out. All clear." Suddenly Primo makes a little gagging sound as he slides the top back in place and jumps aside. We all start to laugh and run.

Because our steep hill makes the delivery of a huge tank impossible without a crane to hoist it over the wall, Primo suggests two septic tanks, keeping the old one behind the house and installing a new one in the Lime Tree Bower. He shakes his head and shrugs. "Big enough for an apartment building. A hospital. Call the honey wagon; ask him to come today."

He takes off for supplies. The men head upstairs. The minute bath goes first and demolition is fast. Franco and Emilio—how do they both work in there?—cart bucket after bucket of tile. How it didn't crush his Ape, I don't know, but Primo inched up the boxwood lane and across the front terrace with a giant cement septic tank, which must be buried. The old toilet is loaded in the Ape. Zeno, a Pole, starts digging a trench and Ed hauls stones out to our pile, with which by now we could build a small house.

The honey wagon honks in the road below. I look out the window and see a man waving and a tractor pulling a rusty tank. Ed runs out. The driver throws a rope to him and Ed hauls up the hose. Secondo comes up, leaving his tractor heaving in the road. He has cottonball hair and a pouncing step. He greets Ed like an old friend. After my brief view into the bowels, so to speak, of the system, I don't even want to watch. I hear suction and slushing. In a short time, I hear Ed in the shower. He's laughing. "What's funny?"

"That was unbelievable. It's just—you know, I never saw myself that way. Running all over the place helping clean shit out of a tank. The system is empty and rinsed. I really liked Secondo—he wanted to see the olives and told me he'd send his son to plow our terraces."

~

Even though I have trouble writing, studying Italian, or reading when guests are here, I have no problems at all when work is going on. Primo's men work; so do I. Ed, too. He is up two hours before the workers arrive, writing, as he prefers, in the dim light. In the series of poems he's working on, each one begins and ends with an Italian word, often a word that has an English meaning as well, such as *ago*, needle, and *dove*, where. One of his pleasures in learning Italian has been its invasion into his writing. He spends hours poring over etymologies.

I start every day with a walk into town. My ritual is to have my cappuccino in a bar where "Wonder Woman" blares away in dubbed Italian. She's hilarious, and an excellent companion to the news. Yesterday's headline was "Lizard Found in Frozen Spinach." A very short man with a head shaped like a schnauzer's comes in the bar every morning. Instead of asking for a *caffè macchiato*, an espresso "stained" with milk, he always says, *"Macchiame, Maria,"* stain me, Maria. She doesn't blink.

When the men arrive at eight, Ed is through writing for the day. He emerges in shorts and boots, wanting to attack the brush on the top terrace, but he heads instead to the vegetable garden to hack out weeds. Suddenly, the *orto* is ours. Anselmo is in the hospital with pneumonia, odd for July. He calls on his *telefonino* to tell us to water in the mornings, to dig all the potatoes and let them dry for two days in a single layer before we store them in the dark.

When we take him some flowers, we find him in a depressing ward with seven other men in iron beds. He's in a robe, sitting on the side of his bed. Usually full of opinions and jokes, he suddenly looks frail and vulnerable, his bare round belly poking out under the sash. He asks everything about the *orto*. How many melons? Have we picked the zucchini every day? We know he thinks we don't water or cut lettuce properly. We put the yellow begonia we've brought by the bed. As we leave, we hear him on the telephone, "Listen, that apartment on the road to Dogana, I can get you in by next week. . . ."

Primo's men are *muratori,* stonemasons. We're surprised that they actually lay the pipes. We expected that job to fall to the plumbers. For the installation of the wiring and lights, Mario and Ettore, plumber / electricians step in. They're now-you-see-them-now-you-don't men—incredibly efficient and fast. Mario shouts; Ettore is silent. They run, they're sleight-of-hand, they're *bravissimi.*

"*Squilla il telefono,*" Mario calls out the window. He has the loudest voice in the universe. *Squillare*—to ring, and the squeal in the sound of the telephone always grates. Paolo has bad news. "The tile from Sicily—such a beautiful selection, truly the sales representative was pleased that someone had the refinement to select this tile—unfortunately this tile has met with an accident in the form of a wreck of the transport truck and the truck has run into the sea. The driver is not injured but the tile. . . ."

For a minute, I don't take this in. "You mean my tile is in the water?"

"*Sì, mi dispiace; è vero.*" He's sorry but it's true. This is so unbelievable that we both laugh. Little fish nosing the boxes? The truck overturned, lodged in sand. "We must began again. And soon the August holiday arrives. No one will be making tile."

Very close friends are arriving. Inopportune timing, but they're welcome anytime. We hope they won't mind a bit of chaos. We dash to Paolo's and wait while he shouts into the phone about the tile. You'd think he was talking to Mars. He slams it down. "They don't promise but they'll try to get it here on time."

"If it's not here in two weeks, we won't be able to finish the project."

"*Boh,*" Paolo goes through several what-can-you-do gestures. "Sicilians," he explains.

Fortunately, the men have not yet started demolishing the butterfly bath. As compensation, Paolo shows us his truck, which is loaded with the fixtures we ordered for both baths and boxes of faucets. We take off to shop for food. We want to make duck breast ravioli with olive sauce for Sheila and Rob, our friends from Washington.

When we get home, we find them waiting, six bottles of Brunello lined up on the wall as a welcome home for us, and right in the middle of the front yard, two toilets, two sinks, a tub, a shower basin, and a four-foot stack of boxes. The scarred tub from *il brutto* has been brought outside and someone has put a large box turtle inside it. He climbs the slope then slides down again, frantic claws dragging the porcelain. I know just how he feels. From around the corner in the Lime Tree Bower, we hear the unmistakable sound of shovels striking rock and the voices of Franco and Emilio starting their litany of Madonna curses. It looks as if they're digging a grave for a behemoth. They're up to their waists. Zeno's trench has miles to go. Ed places the turtle in the strawberry patch, Sheila and I shell peas, Rob puts on a Righteous Brothers CD and turns up the volume of "Unchained Melody." The men fire up their portable gas to heat the pasta they've brought for lunch. Zeno turns the hose on his filthy legs. I'm completely happy. We're sitting on the stone wall in the sun. Our neighbor Placido calls up from the road, "Edward, Frances, I have a new name for your house. You should change to Villa delle Farfalle [House of the Butterflies] because it is a miracle there are so many all over the lavender. They are like confetti—there's a big party going on every day." Wasps have taken up residence in the old terracotta urn next to me. It's missing a handle, cemented in ages past to the wall so the wind does not blow it over. The busy wasps exit from a small opening like helicopters angling off a pad. Rob pops the cork of a Brunello. I hear the urn humming. Rob pours, telling us about circling Rome twice on the ring road. Ed the poet speaks truly in my ear: *Don't you love it—this urn is like our house.* He cups my hand around the side and I feel the buzz.

~

Cynthia, an English friend who has lived in Tuscany for forty years, has invited us for dinner the night Sheila and Rob, our last house guests of the summer, have departed. Right now, I'm facing the arrival of my former colleague at the hotel next week. Our house is so full of construction dust today that we found it between our toes and on our eyelids. No sign of the tile's arrival, but otherwise the project is going without a hitch.

We find other *stranieri,* all English friends, at the table. When Ed mentions that we haven't had anyone over because we've had nonstop people at the house, the conversation erupts. "Guests come in two sizes: excellent and terrible. Most are the latter. Do you know that expression about house guests, like fish, are good for three days? It exists in every language, the remote Pacific islands, Siberia, everywhere." Max always has guests.

Cynthia happens to be serving a large fish decorated all over with sliced olives arranged like scales. "Do you know my step-brother arrived with two children with colds—and he had car trouble. He hoisted his dirty suitcase onto the white bedspread and began tossing their underwear into a pile. Mind you, I haven't even see him in fifteen years. He stayed ten days—never brought home a flower, a bottle of wine, or a hunk of cheese, and never even wrote a thank-you. He left a hundred thousand *lire* note [about sixty dollars] inside the fridge with a note saying 'for food.' Is that not the limit? No one can top that." Her eyes flash. "And I was afraid I'd misjudged the poor boy all those years." She lops off the fish's head and pushes it aside.

Her friend Quinton, a mystery writer, pours the wine. "I never have guests. Too disrupting."

"Isn't it just?" Peter agrees. "Some friends were arriving by train and I popped down to meet the 1:05 from Florence. They didn't get off. I waited until the 2:14. I gave up. Finally, around 4, quite hot and miffed, they called from the station."

"One guest came bearing all the tiny jam jars, plastic shower caps, and shoeshine cloths from hotels along her way and presented them to me as a gift. Some of the jam jars had been opened and had a touch of butter stuck to the lid," I tell them.

"That's rather sweet," Cynthia says.

"Rubbish," Quinton laughs. "These people never would behave this way at home."

"She kept the nice soaps for herself," I add.

"Something cuts loose when people travel to a foreign country," Ed says. "The words, 'We're going to be in Italy . . . ,' release them. It's as if we're bonded by being miraculously in this alien place at the same time."

Quinton agrees. "We man the campfire and they're the wanderers in the lonely outback who arrive safely."

"The concept that we have work in progress doesn't stick. If you are in Italy, you are on vacation. Period." Peter glances at his watch. "Actually, an old friend is arriving tomorrow."

Our neighbor Placido comes over to ask if we want town water. We could split the cost of bringing a connection from Torreone. His water supply by midsummer is low and he has just put in a new lawn he doesn't want to lose. We'd investigated bringing town water here when we bought the house and found it to be outrageously expensive. Anselmo had a new well dug for us, a 300-foot-deep well he guarantees never will go dry. But Placido has a friend; the cost we were quoted is now quartered. It seems a neighborly thing to do, and if there's a severe drought, we'd be protected. Why not? We can just have the line brought in, cap it, and leave it until we need it. Fortuitous that we have a trench in progress.

The next thing we know, we are in the middle of an immense project adjacent to our other immense project. A gargantuan yellow backhoe digs a ditch from Torreone, a kilometer away, all the way to our house. All day it scrapes and dumps dirt into the road. Shirtless men lay tubing and shout. Heat is on us like the hot breath of a dog who has run all the way home. The men here are hauling rubble, digging, chiseling into rock. We flash on the layers they jimmied out from the living room floor two years ago; but here they're hitting the solid rock of the mountain. The hole for the new tank could accommodate a Fiat 500. They loop the tank with ropes and the four men edge the tank near the hole, then lower it in a controlled fall. After that, the tubes connect quickly. The men all join into Zeno's trench digging. They're at the melting point. Septic and water pipes are laid running out from the house. The electricians connect tubes for wires, in case we ever want electricity farther out. Other tubes are installed for a gas line so we can move the enormous green tank out of the *limonaia* and reclaim space for the lemons.

On the third day of digging along the road, the backhoe reaches us, claws out a path up the hill, and the water line, too, is laid in the trench. We just stand and watch with awe. Did we ever imagine we'd dig a half-mile ditch?

This is Anselmo's first day back. He's pale under his red beret and gingerly climbs the steps to the garden terraces. He surveys the havoc we've caused in his garden. We have not directed the sprawling of the melon vines; they're tangled. We have not removed the proper lateral branches of the tomatoes. Obviously, the carrots have not been watered enough because the ground is hard as bone, stunting their growth. I'm the good student, nodding and asking questions. We've come to see that he's always right. He pokes at the weeds around the artichoke plants, clips the blue thistles of those that went to seed. He agrees with Primo—we're foolish to install another entire septic system, and of course the drainage should have been elsewhere.

Nine men are working here. Our tutor, Amalia, comes out for our Italian lesson because we can't get away to go into Cortona. We're gratified when she leans over the upstairs terrace and listens to the workers talking. "I don't know how you do this. I can't understand half of what they're saying. Do you realize that you've got four dialects going on down there." Meanwhile, plaster is drying in the little bath. Recessed lighting and the tub are in place. Primo's tiler arrives tomorrow.

~

In July, the garden looks glorious. Everything we planted becomes its ideal self. Vita Sackville-West spoke of her garden in "full foison." This one, too, is abundant, outpouring. Only the dahlias languish. Powdery mildew spots the leaves and the flowers rot before they open. Everything else has spread or sprung and blooms outrageously. From the upstairs windows, I look out and think of Humphrey Repton, who might approve of this

Italian marriage to a basic English scheme. Even the spilling pots of geraniums on all the walls have a Humphrey touch. In the corner of each one I planted a morning glory seed. The vines fall down the wall, twine around the outdoor lights or crawl along the stones. They open their pure pink faces to the morning sun. I have found an old stone statue of a woman holding a sheaf of wheat. She stands among hydrangea pots, a nod to the Italian tradition of garden ornaments. Not only has Egisto, master *fabbro* at Ossaia, repaired the house's original gate, he is making iron arches for a pergola of grape vines at the entrance to the Lake Walk. We're still looking for our water inspiration—a small pond, a fountain? At an antique warehouse in Umbria, I sighted a rusted, curvy iron bench shoved up against a fence with some equally rusted iron gates and beds. When we asked the price, the store owner was clearly dumbfounded; he never expected to sell that wreck. We wove back through the mountains with the bench tied to the top of the car. With my arm outside the window, I held on to a leg: at least if it started to slip we could stop.

Anselmo's lemon pots in the garden are purely Italian. He has shaped them to bamboo supporting cages. "Pick them, pick them," he urges. I wait, loving the look of the yellow fruit dangling among the leaves. After their initial spurts, the two Mermaids calmed down and send out a few creamy yellow flat roses. Each Sally Holmes rose we planted among the lavender, cheerleader that she is, gives us white pompom armfuls constantly. They've choked out the decadent lilac-colored rose, a weak sister anyway. Ed comes across a photo of the wild garden taken when we bought the house, and another from a couple of summers later, when it was nothing but a blank stretch of dirt bordered by the boxwood hedge. If I could have had a glimpse then of what we could do, my nights of wide-eyed anxiety would have been fewer. I love the garden transformation as much as the restoration of the house. This green and blooming swath is where the house combines sweetly with nature. Beyond it, the cultivation of olives, grapes, cypresses, and lavender creates a lighter link with nature, before the natural scrub and broom, the wild asparagus and roses. I love the space for these levels of connection, these cruxes between home and the wider world. "Every olive has its own story," Anselmo tells us.

"The roses do, too. They're speaking to me all the time," I joke.

But he does not care about the roses. *"Mah,"* he replies and turns back to the *orto.*

~

The five-inch-square stones look as though they always belonged to *il brutto.* Gone is the floor of black and dun concrete squares. The sink was set into the stone wall. The hollow above it testified to the height of the first owner. Even I, at 5'4" had to stoop a little to see in the mirror. Primo raised and arched the hollow, and I found an old foxed mirror that perfectly fit the space. Just that one change made the cramped sense of cat-inside-a-dollhouse disappear. Antonio arrives with his partner, Flavia. Making frames is the bread and butter of their shop but they love most the decorative finishes and designs. They have made a mock-up of the blue Etruscan wave which will run around the wall. We sit outside drinking tea and experimenting with paints for the exact milky blue, the exact rosy color for the border. Flavia should be painted, with her expressive brown eyes and almond skin. She ties her long hair up and covers it with a scarf, looking more and more like the Madonna about to mount a donkey for the long journey. Still, a strand escapes and trails through the blue paint. Antonio looks nothing like a Joseph. Too full of fun and irony. After a heated discussion about proportion, they make a plastic stencil for the wave. The painting goes quickly. They draw the border lines in pencil then paint them freehand. We've kept the original wooden window with a wide sill where thrushes hatched in June. We've kept the hip-bath–sized tub, although the original had to be replaced. "Who would buy one of those?" Paolo asked dismissively, when we asked if they still were made. "I would," I answered. "It seems to belong in the house."

Antonio comes to get me every few minutes. "Do you like it? Do you completely like it?" He lights a cigarette and Flavia and I both fan smoke from our faces with excessive gestures, which prompts him to rub it out in a paint can.

"Yes, will you paint something in every room in the house?"

Going upstairs, I open the door just to look. "Dear Ashley," I write. "*Il brutto* has become *il carino,* the darling. The tiniest bathroom possible but equipped with mimosa bath salts, the thickest American towels, tuberose soap, and a deserted bird nest on the windowsill. When will you come bathe here?" She is so slender she can slip into the basin half of the tiny tub.

While Antonio is here, I sketch a shelf I would like in the kitchen, one running the width of the room above the brick ledge, where I prop all the serving platters I've collected. A second row, then I can just grab one for whatever I'm about to serve. He takes a measurement; we walk around the house until I identify the exact stain color I'd like. *"Ecco fatto,"* he says, it's done.

~

What's not done, as July comes to a close, is the butterfly bath. The tile is on its way but will not arrive until after Primo's men are on August holiday. Since we must leave at the end of August, we store the fixtures in the *limonaia* and make room for the boxes of tiles. *"Pazienza, signora,"* Primo says, patience. "Next year, another new set of problems." Zeno covers the trench. Tools are cleaned and loaded into the Ape. My colleague does not arrive, explaining he'll come back when he can stay with us. Anselmo hangs braids of onions and garlic in the cantina. Antonio installs the beautiful shelf—some things happen like magic. I lower my tired frame into the new tub, baptizing myself in the cold water that will run out through tubes and rocks and sand, harmlessly, harmlessly, onto the land.

Lost in Translation

AT AN EARLY STAGE IN THE HUMAN EMBRYO, traces of gill slits appear near the throat, faint reminders that once we were finny and swam freely through the streams and seas. Often I feel in myself another vestigial trait—being locked in one language. Multilingual friends assure me that a new personality emerges when one acquires a new language. This is something to look forward to. I would like a personality that includes flowing hair to toss at appropriate syntactical pauses, perhaps those tinted Italian glasses, which manage to look sexy *and* intellectual. I'd like for my natural reserve to fall away when fluency allows me all the gestures and rhythms of Italian. Meanwhile, I can say, "Have you washed yourself well?" and "Sir, you have insulted me! I demand satisfaction"; "Sooner or later I am going to have a nervous breakdown"; "Catherine, have you been to see if the barometer has fallen?"; "Where we come from, we don't have a party when someone dies," and many other useful sentences my textbooks have taught me. These phrases are not the pertinent rejoinders when

Primo Bianchi discusses with us the intricacies of a *fossa biologica,* a biological pit, otherwise known as a septic tank.

Twice a week for two hours, I report to a white room in a *palazzo* in Cortona. I go with anticipation and dread. En route, I pass Caruso, the mynah bird who lives in a cage outside an antique shop. *"Ciao,"* the bird says, and I hear the exact, chomped-on inflection of the local *ciao.* Even the bird has a better ear than I. Amalia is waiting, a pile of photocopied exercises for me to complete in front of her. She plans to make clear to me, finally, the differences among the simple past, the imperfect, and the past definite. I think it goes like this: I shopped; I shopped and continue to shop; and I've shopped until I've dropped. The room's three enormous windows overlook the rooftops of Cortona. We sit at a long table, facing a blackboard. Nothing distracts from the intense study of Italian. We begin with conversation. At half her normal speed, she speaks clearly of a Benigni film, a politician on trial, a local custom. We discuss where we have been, and what we have done since the last lesson.

I am halting, I am corrected frequently, I do not hear the difference in the way she says *oggi,* today, and the way I say it. Because the ceilings are so high, everything we say echoes slightly, amplifying the trauma. With verbs, I hear my own blunders as soon as I make them. Odd—sometimes I understand almost everything she says. We discuss the death penalty, ravioli, or the Mafia. I congratulate myself on a clever question—maybe she can see that I'm not as stupid as I must sound. Other times I feel that my brain is a big potato *gnocco* or a ball of *mozzarella di bufala,* and I'm not hearing half. Worse, I sometimes tune out. She could be speaking double Dutch. I want to cry or run out of the room.

Still, taking on a new language is enormous fun. While waiting for a transaction at the bank or sitting in front of the gas station while the car is washed, I take out my list of past participles. During the afternoon *riposo,* I sometimes close the shutters and listen to conversation tapes. Mine focus on cooking. In the heat, with the cicadas clacking outside, I lie back and hear blow-by-blow instructions on how to make rice fritters and cherry soup. Listening is a thrill because I start to think that I spoke Italian in another life; way inside, I know this language. In his fine World War II novel, *The Gallery,* John Horne Burns was on to something when he said, "Italian can soon be understood because it sounds like what it's saying. Italian is a language as natural as the human breath. . . . It keeps in motion by its own inherent drive. . . . It's full of bubble-like laughter. Yet it's capable of power and bitterness. It has nouns that tick off a personality as neatly as a wisecrack. It's a language in which the voice runs to all levels. You all but sing, and you work off your passion with your hands."

One of those evocative nouns fascinates us. *Galleggiante.* We love the sound—a mixture of "gallant," "gigantic," and "elegant." Ed says, "You're looking so, how shall I say it, so *galleggiante* this evening." I say, "I love Parma. It's *galleggiante.*" We admire the antique iron bench we have bought; truly *galleggiante* in the garden. The real *galleggiante* first entered our vocabularies more practically. When the toilet kept running water, Ed stood on a ladder and looked inside the tank. Lifting the floating ball made the noise stop. There's no way to look up "floating ball inside toilet" in the dictionary so he went to the building supply store for the thingamajig and endured the charade of gestures and sketches. "Ah," the clerk caught on. "You want a *galleggiante.*" Yes, we did.

~

Because I'm learning Italian while living here, I conduct my education in public. In a bar, I once asked for a grenade (*granata*) instead of a lemon slush (*granita*). I have commented on the beauty of a basket of fish (*pesce*) when admiring gloriously ripe peaches (*pesche*). Imagine pointing to a black cabbage (*cavolo nero*) and asking for a black horse (*cavallo nero*). Tiny but huge differences. The worst was at a funeral when I spoke of the deceased not as a *scapolo*, bachelor, as I meant, but as a *sbaglio*, a mistake.

That was early. Now that I have more understanding of Italian, I have greater occasions to make a bigger fool of myself. I know more and am likely to launch into a description of a trip to a balsamic vinegar maker and forget once again that complicated questions will follow, and I'll need to pull out of my head verbs in tenses that I haven't yet faced. Could I pass it all off as a kind of new dialect? Today, I was telling Matteo at the *frutta e verdura* that overnight something has eaten the young melons and corn in the garden. Perhaps a wild boar or a porcupine—I know both of those—and then, uh oh, I finally see it coming; I want to say "gnawed the stalk to topple the corn."

Gnawed—"ate" won't do. The word for "stalk"—no, not a glimmer. Topple—forget it. The closest I can come is "cut" and that's not right. All the synonyms I do know will not convey the sense of something gnawing the stalk to topple the corn. I think for a moment of pantomiming the whole scene with a stalk of celery for the corn and me as the porcupine, but a sense of propriety—thank god—saves me.

But this is good, isn't it? Knowing enough that precision is developing? I'm saved because three other people in the shop have joined the conversation, each with an opinion as to the real culprit's identity. Hedgehogs and nutrias are discussed, but the consensus is porcupine, with one man holding out for wild boar because the tomatoes are untouched. If it were a porcupine, obviously the tomatoes would have been mangled, too. I buy my peaches, never having made *that* mistake again, and leave the shop, realizing I have understood everything, even though I was blocked by my own vocabulary.

At times I am not translating; *arancia* is *arancia* and I'm just listening, the image of an orange flashing in my mind, not the word. This is a mystery to me, those moments when the English melts between the Italian and the meaning. I happily make my way around town, having little conversations in the shops. An Italian tourist asks me, *me!,* for directions and I answer with full confidence. Although I may have sent him to the wrong church, I have faith that he will like it just as well.

Old World–cultured Europeans and the upheaved millions who have migrated in the last half century represent opposite means, but the end is the same—they move among languages— while most of us who were culturally isolated on the great land-mass of North America speak English at best. Already, we are a growing minority. Generations hence, our descendants will say to their children, "Once there were people who spoke only one language," and the children will be amazed. But I have become determined to survive with the fittest.

Having made many blunders and gone home fuming, I've had altogether too much time to analyze my problems. I've come to know why I have made learning Italian more difficult than it had to be, perhaps why all the languages I've studied have been so elusive.

I have the habit of wrenching everything into English. Although we have the same structures—all languages basically have the same parts of speech—there is no way to proceed *ratio-nally* with the obliteration of the Italian pronoun, the fore-grounding of the verb, and the genders of nouns. The idiosyncracies of idioms, just as irrational, are immediate to me because they work with metaphors. I love the graphic figurative image *acqua in bocca* (water in the mouth), which means "I won't tell anyone." Something between us two is something for *quattr'occhi,* four eyes. "I feel oppressed" or "depressed" translates as *sotto una cappa di piombo,* under a hood of lead. Not only is an image conjured, but *piombo,* sounds oppressive, like three low notes plucked on the bass. All the connotations of the English "rolling in money" are not at all the same as the Italian "swimming in gold."

Sound unwittingly often translates meaning where it shouldn't. *Stinco,* a savory cut of meat, and also a thin loaf of bread, sounds unappetizing even when you know *stinco* means shin-bone. And how *foreign* the saying, *"Non è uno stinco di santo,"* He's not the shin-bone of a saint; he's no saint. *Bar* conjures solitary figures hunched over mixed drinks, or more sophisticated scenes, not the Italian version, which is centered on coffee and quick bites. Most certainly, an Italian "bar" is not a "pub."

The common word *più,* more, is hard for an English-speaking person to say without suspecting a bad smell. So I purse my lips and say we're eating tonight at Amico Più, a *trattoria* on the edge of the valley, where to the satisfaction of my inner ear, the odor of pigs sometimes wafts from farms across the grassy outdoor dining area from nearby farms.

"Your friend certainly is handsome but he's so cruel to his dog," my friend Deb said about stop-traffic good-looking Silvano. "He kept telling the poor thing to die." Silvano was trying to talk to her, and his playful *pastore tedesco,* German shepherd, pestered him to throw a stick over and over. *"Dai, Ugo, dai,"* he told the dog as he threw the stick yet again. *Dai* sounds like "die," but he simply meant "give"—*basta,* enough, give it up, Hugo.

I know well from French, that if one is hungry or thirsty, that you have hunger, you have thirst. This is imprinted on my mind from my first trip to France. I went to a restaurant alone and was seated by a door where blasts of cold air blew in my face. I asked the waiter for another table, explaining that I was cold. Back in the hotel, I realized I had not said *j'ai froid* but instead had said *je suis fraise,* I am strawberry. The waiter graciously had directed me to a cozy table near the fireplace.

Strange that a cat purrs differently in Italian; a cat "makes the purrs." *Ha sonno?,* You have sleepy?, now comes naturally. Some things may never. If I forget and take to the literal, I'm often left with "Now I must to go myself of it," for "Now I must leave." Or "I myself was forgotten of this," for "I had forgotten this." Translation is approximation; the original doesn't say that at all.

Mark Twain, who obviously had an ear for language, had fun with a literal translation of his own speech, given to the Press Club in Vienna:

> *I am indeed the truest friend of the German language—and not only now, but from long since—yes, before twenty years already. . . . I would only some changes effect. I would only the language method—the luxurious, elaborate construction compress, the eternal parenthesis suppress, do away with, annihilate; the introduction of more than thirteen subjects in one sentence forbid; the verb so far to the front pull that one it without a telescope discover can. With one word, my gentlemen, I would your beloved language simplify so that, my gentlemen, when you her for prayer need, One her yonder-up understands. . . .*
>
> *I might gladly the separable verb also a little bit reform. I might none do let what Schiller did: he has the whole history of the Thirty Years' War between the two members of a separate verb in-pushed. That has even Germany itself aroused, and one has Schiller the permission refused the History of the Hundred Years' War to compose—God be it thanked! After all these reforms established be will, will the German language the noblest and the prettiest on the world be.*

I've had the late realization that English is a spoken language, whereas Italian is sung. An opera teacher at Spoleto told me she has her American students listen in class to someone speaking ordinary Italian while following the tones with their own voices la, la, la-ing. Then she has them perform the same exercise with someone speaking English. The English voice-graph modulates gently and regularly up and down while the Italian zips dramatically around. I knew this instinctively. When people are walking toward me, long before I can hear words, I can tell if they are speaking English, German, or Italian. I know it, too, from my own very plain buon giorno and the exuberant response from the Italians, with several lifts and slides of sound. Italian spoken by a native English speaker is much easier for me to understand—the pacing is still in English even when the words in Italian are grammatically perfect. Catching the rhythm—that's the hardest part. The lucky few who have a natural grasp of ritmo are understood by Italians even if their grammar isn't so hot.

Too bad you can't take a language in a series of injections labeled "indirect pronouns," "the pronunciation of *glielo*," and "tile installation terminology." But I tell myself, *Roma non fu fatta in un giorno*. Dante, the five-year-old son of an American mother and Italian father, moves easily, thoughtlessly, back and forth between English and Italian. I can't fool him on the phone into thinking that I'm Italian. I say *"Posso parlare con la tua mamma,"* May I speak with your mother, and he says, "Sure, she's right here."

I recently read in the paper that those who acquire multiple languages when they're young learn them in the same thimble-sized spot in the brain. Those of us who try to learn later must locate the new language in an entirely different territory. The new area must be something like frozen tundra. As I study Italian, I can feel that journey. The new words buzz to the real language spot—top center—for translation, then slide back to the new one, which is being chopped out somewhere in the obdurate back right corner. On the way, many new words fall off into lost canals and abysses. Some do make it all the way back to the new quarry. They become natural. *Gioia* is no longer joy, it's the buoyant feeling of *gioia*. Hundreds of other words are now themselves. Still, I pick up a novel by Pavese and I'm sunk by the third paragraph. *Piano*, slowly, *piano*, I tell myself, there's no exam coming. As if there will be a final, I compulsively concentrate on what I don't understand. I make lists of *all* the cases when the imperfect is used, spending hours writing examples for each of the cases I don't understand and neglecting to reinforce examples of what I do.

~

Besides the luxury—and necessity—of being able to converse easily, I am desirous of another literature. My long habit of browsing in bookstores and leaving with a nice sack of books has been stymied in Italy. I have become a great appreciator of cover designs.

Travelling or living here as a foreigner, I experience the life force of Italians acted out every day on the streets, in the cafés, and on the roads. As I walk by open windows, I'm transfixed by the aroma of *ragù* and the cascades of concurrent voices. So often I'm bearing witness to the rich *outer* life of Italians, knowing that the direct route to the inner life always is literature. Novels, essays, books of place, the philosophical treatises, poetry—here's the big news of the place, the territory most hidden from me in my friendships and brief sojourns in this *bel paese*.

Gradually, my summer reading has shifted to native Italian writers: Eugenio Montale, Umberto Eco, Italo Calvino, Natalia Ginzburg, Primo Levi—all the heavy-hitters whose work appears in English. Sometimes I've bought a difficult book in Italian, as one might buy a skirt a size too tight, hoping to lose the ten pounds by summer.

First, their guidebooks. All the Slow Food Arcigola Editore books, especially the yearly guide *Vini d'Italia*, quickly convinced Ed that the Italians' own perspective on food and wine was the one we wanted. The Gambero Rosso guides to restaurants and hotels led us to uncrowded places of intrinsic character. They're easy to follow because of clear ranking symbols.

Then we began to pick up poetry, simply for the pleasure of reading it aloud, even if we mispronounced the author's name, as we did with Quasimodo for too long. Cesare Pavese revealed all the dark and melancholy layers of the countryside that I missed in my own elation over the landscapes straight out of Piero della Francesca and Perugino. Leonardo Sciascia's stories gave me the heart of Sicily, which I otherwise would have encountered with a raft of fears and assumptions. "Once there was a special room in old Sicilian houses that was called 'the *scirocco* room.' It had no windows, or any other communication with the outside other than a narrow door opening onto an inside corridor, and this is where the family would take refuge against the wind." That is the way I want into Sicily—an island where weather rules and the isolation of geography is reflected in the microcosm of the family. Thank you, Leonardo; I did not focus overly on the Mafia when I was there but on the wind in the thousands and thousands of palms.

The lavish Italian sense of design extends to books as easily as it does to shoes and cars. I found the art books irresistible, the crisp, fresh colors in both the cheap booklets on individual artists and in the grand tomes of the Uffizi Gallery and the Vatican collections. Paperback novels attracted me most. I took them down one by one, staring at the cobalt covers, each with a small reproduction of a painting tipped onto the cover. These books lead me farther into the language. To sit in a café with a cappuccino, a book, and a dictionary is not a bad way to spend an hour or two in the morning. Of course, I bought Dante. How can you not buy Dante in Italy? I had a dark secret—I'd never read Dante, except in snatches. Translating a few stanzas provides an instant cure from the textbook tedium of: The tide was ebbing. She dreaded snakes and spiders. The servicemen are on furlough. The fair was rained out. Their behavior will improve. She was looking very coy. I was a fool from the beginning. Precisely so!

Since I have been coming to Italy for so many summers, my friends assume that my Italian is completely fluent. "Oh, you pick up Italian," they say flippantly. "It's so close to Spanish." Well, I never picked up Spanish that easily. From a summer of studying in San Miguel de Allende, most of what I remember is going off-road in a taxi with my instructor whose passionate interest was Chichimeca pottery. He responded to my interest in the culture more than to my need to translate the story of the little mouse. We searched through middens for bits of black-painted pottery and I came home with more shards than words.

But my friends are right; you travel to Italy, you pick up a few phrases. Italians are so courteous and responsive that you're lulled into thinking, *This is a cinch.* I have long since spoken restaurant-Italian, travel-Italian, shopping-Italian, and a lot of house-restoration Italian. But I never have "picked up" the imperfect subjunctive or the past remote. I have not learned to understand the various dialects spoken around Tuscany, not to mention the rest of Italy. I read in *Italian Cultural Studies* that dialects are used by sixty percent of Italians, and are spoken exclusively by fourteen percent. Since we've learned on the fly, our vocabularies are unholy mixes of dialect words and the Italian we've learned in classes. The local dialect often changes the "ah" sound to "eh," producing a harsher sound. We don't always hear the difference. Our store of curses is rather vast, since hauling out stone and digging trenches and wells elicits those from workers. *Madonna cane, Madonna diavola*, Madonna-dog, Madonna-devil, are two drastic curses. The use of some expressions we've picked up still escapes us. *Non mi importa una sega*, Don't bring me a saw, accompanied by a sawing motion, has something to do with masturbation.

Some aspects of this amazing language confound me. I admitted to myself recently that I am going to give up on the idiomatic and incomprehensible use of the invariable pronoun *"ne"*; whatever Italian I speak will have to be without this protean word. I have not admitted this to Amalia.

❧

American friends say with modesty, "I did quite well in Spain," or "It's amazing how it all comes back." Comes back from where? I've travelled with some of those same friends, have seen them point at the menu, have seen them meekly hold out their hands for the clerk to take the cost of a purchase from their palms because they get dizzy when *duemilaquattrocentosettanta lire* (2470 *lire*) spirals out of the clerk's mouth. One friend belongs to the speak-loud-and-clear-and-they'll-understand-English school. Another, who visited me in Italy, was annoyed that local shopkeepers had made "no attempt to learn basic English phrases that would help them in business," not noticing that we are in *their* country, and in a rural area at that.

Even though I "took" years of French in high school and college, it never really took to me. I never met anyone from France, and my high school teacher believed in the method of a verb workbook, with tiny spaces to write all the conjugations. Even if we had no idea what those conjugations meant, we still had to write the *passé composé* for hundreds of verbs. For the last half-hour of class she turned on scratchy records of Paris street sounds and stood clasping her hands and looking out the window. We filed out to "Under the Bridges of Paris," Carl Twiggs slapping

Mary Keith Duffy's girdled bottom and shouting "Monobut-tock," by far the most inventive linguistic moment of the hour.

In college, the class focused on "lab"—tapes about *mon moulin*, letters in a crabbed French, which I had to listen to in a cubicle in the gym at seven in the morning. News from a faraway French mill was accompanied by a basketball pounding the gym floor and a wafting odor of pine oil–scented disinfectant. When I was called on to read in class from *Les Misérables*, our endless text, the professor would say with a smirk, "Miss Mayes speaks French with a Southern accent." I slammed the book shut and sat down. His Midwestern accent wasn't *magnifique* either.

Later, I took classes in Spanish and German. They all seemed somehow so *fake*. Surely these people went home at night and spoke English. A friend who has had similar experiences says she would like "I studied languages" carved on her tombstone. I endured German even through a bout of explosive flatulence from the instructor. *"Pflaumenkuchen,"* plumcake, he explained and continued with *Es war einmal ein junger Bauer*, There was once a young farmer. The day I dropped out of German was when I came across the word for nipple: *Brustwarze*. A glance, and even I translated "breast wart."

⟳

Several local people speak many languages. Isabella, a neigh-bor, speaks eight; her son, a journalist, also speaks eight, but not exactly the same eight. She is in her seventies. "I tried to learn Greek a couple of years ago," she tells me, "but it's getting hard. I used to learn a language in three weeks. If you know Russian, Polish is easy. English and French I spoke as a child. . . ." I walk home sulking after this conversation. I still am having trouble learning the uses of the simple word *"ci,"* a chameleon of a word that shifts meaning shamelessly, while she picked up French like a warm croissant. She arrives at dinner and surveys the other guests. "What language are we speaking tonight?" she asks brightly. At one party she and her Danish, Dutch, and Hungarian friends began to recite French poetry. They all knew the same poems by heart. Then they moved on to Latin poems.

In a dream, I am sitting by a window, writing on pale blue paper. Reading the wet ink as I write, I see that I am writing a poem in Italian. But maybe I am not this person. Could I be? The blue-black ink fluidly moves into words, phrases, lines—even my handwriting is better in this dream—and the woman I am or am not has on a wool sweater, a dark dress. Her hair is twisted up, like Maria's, like Anna's, like Isabella's, like the older women I know here, all of whom are at home in wider worlds than I have known. This is a poem to be sung, I can tell, the shiny ink, the wind lifting the edge of the paper, my hand moving rapidly, yes, my hand.

Bergson says the present does not exist; it is always disappearing as the past gnaws into the future. With my own language and now with the vast voyage into Italian, this feels true as well. *The past gnaws at the future.* What to say always disappears into the saying, leaving me wanting to say more. *Gnaws*, there's that word again. To gnaw the stalk to topple the corn. To gnaw: *rosicchiare*. Language: the house that Jack built.

Since language always has been crux and core for me, I was pleased to discover that we could make friends when we knew very little. My mother always thought that attraction was based on smell. Those good flashes of energy between people can supersede words. At the *frutta e verdura*, Rita was welcoming me with a hug before I could talk to her. At the same time, our neighbor invited us to dinner. We wanted to refuse. We imagined three hours of halting words and awkward silences. *"Grazie, mille grazie, ma non parliamo bene italiano."* Thank you, but we don't speak Italian well, we apologized. "Later, when we speak better. . . ."

He looked incredulous. His eyebrows shot up. "You eat, don't you?"

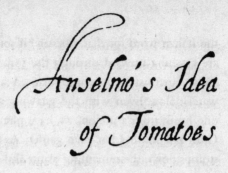

Anselmo's Idea of Tomatoes

"DO YOU HAVE THE BEANS OF SANT'ANNA?"

"No, they were in season *last* week." Matteo points to the fresh *cannellini*. "These are ready now. From all over—Roma, Milano—they come to Tuscany for these beans." I know the *cannellini*. Simply dressed with oil, sage, salt, and pepper, they have restorative powers beyond all other beans. I've seen Ed eat them for breakfast. They are Tuscan comfort food.

When I walk out of the *frutta e verdura,* I'm struck. He said the Sant'Annas were *in season last week.* I had these skinny string beans once. Now they're gone for a year. With Anselmo's garden burgeoning, I've hardly been shopping. The cookbook watchword "seasonal" has taken on an immediacy I've never dreamed possible. Ed and I take the baskets up on the terraces late in the day and pick dinner. Anselmo has sown waves of lettuces all summer, providing tender salads constantly. We can't eat enough; when it bolts, Beppe wields his sickle and bundles the greens for his rabbits. When we cut the *bietole,* chard, it comes back. I like the Italian word for that, *ricrescere;* it sounds as though the stalks are crashing upward through the soil. We give sacks and sacks away. Fortunately, Anselmo planted a lot of cantaloupe and watermelon. Even with the gnawing animal raiders, who take one hunk from a melon, we have plenty. I try to give them to Giusi but she has her own garden. As a crop finishes, Anselmo stomps down the remaining plants and stalks, letting them decay into the ground. I'm delighted to pick eggplant and zucchini while they are small. His one flop is celery; the stalks never developed.

In the spring, we were convinced he was planting too much, and we were right. It's divine. We never have eaten so well in our lives. Or as simply. As it turns out, Anselmo's idea of tomatoes is my idea of tomatoes. I am up to my knickers in tomatoes and I love it. Every day, a heaping basket of perfect, absolutely perfect, red, red tomatoes. I look on these brimming baskets with more pleasure than I felt when I saw my new car last year. Not a bug or a blemish. He planted three kinds. A plain round tomato he calls *locale.* This local favorite is the kind to bite into while picking—a sweet, dripping, crisp, paradigm tomato. For sauce, he planted the ovoid San Marzano, with a meatier texture and less juice. For salads, we have cherry tomatoes, tight little balls that explode with flavor.

Once upon a time, Italy had no tomatoes. Imagine the poor Etruscans and Romans, the centuries of people who lived before the New World was explored. Their garlic and basil went unpaired with tomatoes. Now, so many people grow up thinking those pallid blobs arriving in supermarkets all year are tomatoes. They should have another name. Or perhaps a number. I'd hoped to pair our Italian tomatoes with American sweet corn. What could be better? Since the animals discovered this new-on-the-mountain crop, our yield from the two packets of seeds I sowed was only three scrawny ears. Anselmo had disregarded my corn plot. "Pig food," he pronounced.

The giant sunflowers I planted along the edges of several terraces are in bloom. I'm cutting a bunch early, before they have a chance to droop from heat. Suddenly, from behind my circular "room" of sunflowers, a small woman emerges. I recognize her immediately from Ed's description as the forager of daffodils and asparagus. *"Buon giorno, signora,"* I greet her and introduce myself. Even in summer, she is wearing a dark cardigan.

"Venga," she invites me. Her basket is heaped with the yellow flowers of wild fennel. She leads me up one terrace to a spot behind some broom. A dozen or so tall fennel plants are untouched. She has come prepared with scissors. She clips off the flowers and tells me to spread them under the sun to dry, then to rub them between my hands to remove the flowers from the stems. She pulls a plastic sack from her pocket and begins to snip some for me. She points up to the ridge of locust and oak trees. "In autumn, you find the *porcini* there."

"And truffles?"

"Never. But you find other mushrooms, too. I will show you after the rains."

"We'll be gone, unfortunately."

"Peccato," too bad. "You will go back to Switzerland?"

"No, the United States. We live in California." I remember she seemed not to believe Ed when he told her he was not a Swiss professor.

She shakes her head. *"ArrividerLa, signora.* The fennel you will use with all the meats, with rabbit it is very good and always with roast potatoes." She starts to head down the terrace path, then turns back. "I like the house now."

I've reverted to another old love. I could have fried tomatoes for breakfast, lunch, and dinner. Cream, an almost forbidden ingredient now, is so good with them that I risk a blip in the next cholesterol count. Heresy to some Southern cooks, I prefer fried red tomatoes over green ones. I like them sliced about $1/2$-inch thick. I pour some flour on a piece of waxed paper and turn the tomato slices to coat them lightly then fry them on both sides in a hot skillet with 3–4 T. of peanut or sunflower oil. Then, as my mother before me and hers before her, I turn the heat to low, pour on heavy cream to cover the bottom of the pan. Shake to blend, grind a lot of black pepper over the tomatoes, salt to taste, and add a little thyme or oregano. I find them best eaten alone. Willie Bell would sometimes coat the slices in cornmeal and fry them in hot, hot oil so that they're crisper. With a plate of fried tomatoes in front of me, I feel a longing for Willie Bell's fried chicken, especially for her cream gravy over mashed potatoes, and her creamed corn. Why were we not huge from all the pints of cream that went into most meals? She always cut the kernels off the cob and cooked them with onion and chopped peppers, then stirred in cream. Longing for these brings the memory of her yellow squash casserole, too. Southern summer food rivals Italian food in my affections. Willie Bell and my mother would sit all morning shelling the delectable tiny lady finger peas, which I've never seen outside the state of Georgia.

When Ed grills, he tosses on thick slices of tomato just before we eat, just for a little smoky taste. Nothing surpasses a plain tomato sandwich if the *focaccia* is made in heaven, as it is here in Cortona. The chewy flat bread with crackly sage and sea salt on top lifts the sliced tomato into the realm of gastronomic highs. How long would it take for us to tire of fresh tomatoes? Simple stuffed tomatoes, what's better? Only one thing—the addition of chopped hazelnuts. Anselmo alerted us that ours are ready to pick. We cracked and roasted about a cup, mixed them in equal part with bread crumbs, chopped some parsley and stuffed four big tomatoes. On top, a pat of butter and a square piece of cheese such as *tallegio,* which melts in the oven. Supper is a zucchini *frittata* and these tomatoes, along with a Southern touch, a pitcher of iced tea sweetened with a little peach juice.

—⁀

On a Tuesday after siesta, the dazzling heat of the morning abates. I decide we should go to Deruta, majolica *paradiso.* An English guidebook to Umbria dismisses Deruta, "You will probably not wish to linger in Deruta, the center of Umbria's majolica industry, whose approach roads are lined with shops selling all manner of hideous ceramics." Is the writer crazy? My new kitchen shelf was built especially to display all the platters I've found irresistible. Some Deruta majolica is hideous, but much of it is based on traditional regional designs and is delightful. I wonder what the English writer's breakfast dishes look like. Mine from Deruta have hand-painted Tuscan fruits and a yellow border, something that certainly could cheer up a drear English morning.

In Italy, I've learned the art of serving on platters. Along the stone wall I place one for roasted vegetables, one for cheeses, one for breads, another for the main course. Every night during this season, we have a platter of plain sliced tomatoes. They can be passed family-style or guests can get up from the table under the trees and help themselves—again and again. Pitchers, too, pitchers for iced tea, wine, water. The hand-painted majolica suits the casual and abundant Tuscan style of dining. I love the colors. Some bright, others slightly muted and soft, like fresco colors. Setting the yellow table outside, or my round dining room table in San Francisco, the table comes to life instantly. True or not, it appears that a great meal will arrive.

I bought cups with pink flowers for cappuccino at Christmas, and hope now to find breakfast plates to match. Deruta must have a hundred shops selling handmade majolica gaily painted in traditional designs.

"Which shop was it?" Ed asks. "How can you remember? There are so many." His enthusiasm for Deruta is limited.

"The one on the corner, right where the street ends." No other town looks like Deruta. Church, fountain, facades are decorated with tiles. This has been a hub of this ancient craft for centuries.

"*Ah, sì signora,*" of course. The shop owner calls a friend who will bring the plates I want from the studio. While we wait, we wander to three other shops on the main street and in one we find a lamp for Ed's desk. There must be other stores in Deruta: hardware, grocery, shoes—but somehow I've never noticed them. We stop and watch a woman painting geometric designs on small saucers. At the bar, a very old man in wide suspenders, which hold his pants almost up to his armpits, asks where we're from. San Francisco sets him into a frenzy—he was there on a ship in 1950. He remembers the *strada del mercato*. Market Street. He insists on buying our coffee. Yes! The water was right at the end of the street. When his friend comes in, he introduces us as though we were visiting relatives. The instant bond of San Francisco, a place Italians love.

Many of the ceramic shops are just outside town on Via Tiberina. My sister and I have shipped home whole dinner sets for ourselves and for my daughter, Ashley. Only one cup was broken. They pack not in plastic bubble wrap but in wet straw. Shipping is expensive but not nearly as expensive as buying Italian ceramics at home, even if you could find the variety that is available here. Choices are staggering. Most popular is the sunny yellow and blue Raphael design, a stylized dragon in the center of each piece. I don't fancy seeing a dragon as I eat, even a benign one like Raphael's.

Bisected by the Apennines, many areas of Italy developed their own designs, as well as their own dialects and habits. In

Deruta they make the rooster of Orvieto, the bluebird of Amalfi, the black Siena pattern taken from the cathedral floor mosaics. There's an effort toward contemporary designs as well. Some are garish; others are playful and bold, pleasing to hold, hang on a wall, or punctuate a glass coffee table. You even can design your own dinner service, with your monogram or flowers you like. My sister chose a pattern with a blue and yellow border and Ashley loved the white set with a grape-and-vine embossed border. When I chose mine, with a pomegranate, cherries, or blueberries painted in the middle of each dish, I asked, "What is the name of the pattern?"

He lifted his shoulders, *"Frutta."* Glad I asked. Three months later—my order was individually made and painted—the dishes arrived in San Francisco. They translated perfectly into my American kitchen.

Today I am looking for a wedding present for a friend's son. Espresso cups? A teapot? A wonderful salad bowl? Ed looks rather wild-eyed after three or four of these majolica stops. "Everyone likes a teapot," he insists. "Let's just get one."

"Which one do you like?" I like one that is all tiny flowers and green leaves. Also a white one scattered with sprigs of spring flowers.

He picks up the white one. "Let's go."

I look longingly at my other favorite shops on the way to the highway but Ed has his foot firmly on the accelerator. "We might run over to look at ceramics in Gubbio and Gualdo Tadino one day soon. We could go to both places on the same day." Is he just being nice?

On the way home, we stop in Assisi in spite of the tidal waves of tourists. My favorite paper store is on the main *piazza,* across from that mysterious church which began as a temple to Minerva. I need a new gift supply of hand-printed stationary, beautiful pads, note cards, and blank books to take home. In San Francisco, I almost never have time to go shopping. These forays for *things* are a treat. Ed wants to pick up a few bottles of Sagrantino, his favorite Umbrian wine, which we usually can't buy in Cortona.

We walk past the delicate roseate church of Santa Chiara, the houses of amber and pearl stone with faded blue shutters. As usual, two dogs are sleeping on either side of the door to the paper store. After I stock up, we walk, as we always do, to the Chiesa di San Rufino—the opposite direction from the undertow of tourists headed toward the famous Giotto (or according to many, school of Giotto) frescoes at San Francesco—to look at its almost primitive Romanesque facade of gargoyles and animals of the imagination. It faces a blessedly empty *piazza* with a fountain. No number of tourists totally can destroy the enchantment of Assisi. We've lingered until seven-thirty, might as well have dinner at a favorite resturant where the roasted rabbit is superb.

~

I forget the heat that comes every August. As I finish cleaning a room, I close the windows and inside shutters three-quarters of the way. Air still comes in, if any is moving, but the direct hit of the sun is closed out. My coolest white linen dress touches me only at the shoulders. It hangs like a nightgown. Emily Dickinson wore only white. I can see her point. Sometimes even that is too hot and I unbutton it all the way down, then when the heat seems to bank against me late in the afternoons, I throw it off and read in my underwear with the fan blowing straight on me.

The day we make tomato sauce must be the hottest of the summer. After several trips to the *orto*, we've filled the sink and a laundry basket with ripe tomatoes. Ed cores, I seed. We don't peel because the skin is thin, unlike commercial tomatoes which often seem to be encased in rubber. When I splash juice on my blouse, I take it off and throw it in the washing machine. Ed already is down to shorts. Soon juice is running over the chopping boards, onto the floor. We're chopping heads of garlic, a whole braid of onions, stripping leaves off the thyme, snipping basil, and tossing a handful of salt into the cauldron. The kitchen sweats with the aroma of cooking onions; we sweat with the aroma of cooking onions. In go the gallons of chopped tomatoes. Ed empties a bottle of local red wine. Everything is from right here. All year we, and our guests when we're in California, will feel the July sun in every spoonful. We put the cauldron on to simmer and start to mop.

"I have a taste in my mouth, a wonderful taste."

"What is it? Do you smell the tomato sauce? Maybe it's that." But I don't smell anything. We're out in the Lime Tree Bower recovering, reading after lunch, and trying to catch a breeze.

"It's a taste I can't describe. It's like the song you can't get out of your head. I've had it for two days."

"Is it like mint or honey or iron or salt?"

He shakes his head. He's watching an ant carrying a rose petal, a coverlet for his worker-comrade. The ant falters and struggles on. "The taste, I think it's happiness."

We walk up two terraces to the tree laden with Golden Delicious apples. No crunch. Delicious they are not, except in their mellow color. "Next year, let's plant more apples." I throw mine in the bushes. "They would make decent apple butter." After the tomato frenzy, I don't think I'll be making apple butter. "I can imagine a whole row along this terrace, companions for this poor stunted Golden Delicious."

"It's not stunted; it's a dwarf tree." Ed is filling his shirt front with apples. "Maybe a small batch of apple butter." He adores apples. A favorite memory of his is of an apple-picking job he had in Iowa one fall. "I read about a man near Rimini who grows the *limoncella,* a small apple with the flavor of lemon, and one called *pum sunaja.* The seeds inside are loose and rattle like maracas. This man has 300 kinds of apples, lost varieties he's bringing back." From his tone, I know that we will be journeying to meet this fascinating person.

My original desire to live here came partly from a belief that Italy is endless and could never be exhausted—art, landscape, food, language, history. Changing the direction of my life by buying and restoring this forsaken house, committing a portion of every year to life in a foreign country, seemed like acts of high risk if not madness. At that time, I wanted to accomplish something I did not know how to do. I thought—and now know—that Italians claim more time for their lives. After a long marriage and a horrid divorce, I thought Italy certainly would be a more than adequate replacement for just one man. I wanted a big change.

I had no concept of just how lucky my primary instinct was. At home in California, time often feels like a hula-hoop, a ceaseless whirl on a body fixed but rocking in place. I could kiss the ground here, not to feel myself in that tight space where the past gnaws the future but in the luxuriant freedom of a long day to walk out for a basket of plums under the great wheel of the Mediterranean sun. At the tail end of the century, continual splashes of newness: Eight summers here and still we're babes. What luck.

I stuff two shopping bags with potatoes, onions, chard, melon, tomatoes and drive them down to Donatella in the valley. Earlier this summer, the boars destroyed her garden in one full-moon orgy. She's not home so I leave the bags under her arbor of Virginia creeper, just on the edge of a carefully tended olive orchard. Crossing the valley floor as I leave her place, I look up and catch a glimpse of Bramasole. I stop, amazed to see the house as a peach-colored smudge against the steep hillside, with the Etruscan and Medici walls above it. Far away, it stands totally within its own green landscape of terraces and trees, clouds and sky. No sign at all that we have been there or will be there. As I drive on, a spur of hillside suddenly cuts away the view.

Cold

ON AN EARLY OCTOBER MORNING IN SAN FRAN-
cisco, Ed puts aside a stack of student papers and begins
to look through an Italian guidebook. I am busy, super-
busy, in my study—eleven graduate theses, memos, letters of recommendation, and a pile of overdue correspondence.
Tomorrow, meetings of the laborious sort and appointments in
three corners of the city. These madhouse weeks seem both to
stretch endlessly and to fly. Ed turns on the espresso machine,
still reading. My study is across the hall from the kitchen, which
is why I don't get as much done as I could. Anyone cooking or
wandering in for a snack naturally visits with me. Kitchens
develop powerful magnetic fields around them and pull all
humans and animals within the four walls their way. My theory
is proven by my black cat, Sister, who perpetually lies on the
black-and-white kitchen tiles right in the center of the floor.

"Don't you think it would be a perfect gift to go back to
Venice for Christmas?" For several years, since we bought Bramasole, we've endured the twenty-hour trip from California

across the waters for the brief winter season at Bramasole, when we harvest our olives, feast with our friends, and escape the frenetic pace of our usual holidays.

"Um, oh, yes," I answer. Soon I hear him dial a long telephone number, then request a room with a balcony on the Grand Canal for December 23, 24, and 25. The heaps of paper start to look less and less formidable.

~

We arrived in Cortona early this morning from Rome. We are spending a week here, just enough time for our favorite December activities, then we'll drive to Venice. Arrival at Bramasole is easy now. What a marvel, everything works (for now); heat, hot water—what luxury. We even have neatly stacked firewood—one of the bonuses of pruning olive trees.

While I unpack, Ed starts right in picking olives, a wicker basket strapped around his red wool sweater. After the sun drops behind the hill around 4 P.M., a chilly wind comes up. He drags a sack into the *cantina* then runs hot water over his hands a long time to warm them. "Two more days," he says, "with both of us working. There are a lot of olives." We make a quick supper of *tagliatelle con funghi porcini,* thin pasta with mushrooms sautéed in our oil. Ed builds a fire and we sit in front of it, eating on trays. Tomorrow we will pick all day then go up the mountain to a favorite *trattoria* for pasta with wild boar sauce. The day we take the olives to the mill for pressing, we'll celebrate the new oil with a feast for friends. We feel compelled to drive over to Assisi to find out how the violent earthquake has changed that place of peace. Then it will be time to get ready for Venice, where it may be colder. We have coats, boots, gloves, and I bought a delicious cut-velvet scarf in dark, dark green, as green as a Venetian lagoon. I hope for snow in Piazza San Marco. Ed has a special wine to take. I have ginger-lily soap, and lilac-scented candles to burn in our room. We promised to buy only one gift for each other since the main gift will be Venice. I have a sumptuous yellow cashmere sweater for Ed, with a volume of W. S. Merwin's poems tucked under the sleeve. His box for me, glimpsed in his luggage, looks intriguingly small.

Around eleven the phone rings. Since we've bought this house I've hated the sound of the telephone. It reminds me of workers calling to say a pump did not arrive or the sandblaster is extending his vacation at the beach. In bed, cozy in flannel sheets, with jet lag just about to pull me under, I'm finishing the novel I started on the plane. I hear Ed answer "Hey, how are you?" enthusiastically, then his voice drops. "When? No. No. How long?"

He sits down on the end of the bed, frowning, his shoulders hunched. His mother has been taken to the hospital and is in grave condition. "I don't get it. Two weeks ago she was baking bread. She's strong. My sister said myo-something, a blood disease. I got the doctor's number."

In the morning, we repack and take the train back to Rome. Beppe and Francesco will pick the olives for us and take them to the mill. The doctor was more definite than Ed's sister. "Come at once," he said when Ed called him. "It could be anytime. Today, a week, could be a month." Reboarding and flying, practically meeting ourselves coming over, seems surreal. Sometimes the weather has a way of reflecting emotional states. When the skies neatly express emotions in my students' poems I always write, *Beware of the pathetic fallacy; it's a weak gesture,* but here we are tossing across the Atlantic, seatbelt sign blazing. The storm finally grounds us in Philadelphia. All connecting flights into Minnesota are canceled. We load our luggage onto a cart and walk through malls to an airport hotel. We spend a long night watching the storm worsen on the TV weather station. Why do people die at Christmas? A strange call to pull the family home again? My father died on a December 23, when I was fourteen. The pink net dress I was to have worn to the dance that night hung on the back of the closet door until it looked limp. The Christmas tree was taken down.

During a break in the storm, we fly out and are greeted in Minneapolis by the coldest temperature on record for that day. At the rental car desk we run into Ed's sister Sharon and her husband and daughter, just in from southern California. They're heading straight for the hospital, too. His brother, Robert, and other two sisters, Anne and Mary Jo, already are there. We step out of the airport into crusty snow and ferocious wind chill, a cut-glass air. My thin boots seem like no more than socks. Ed has to chip the car out of a block of ice. We take off for Winona, two hours south, on plowed roads through snowy fields which look to my new eyes like the absence of everything. I do not know Ed's mother well, only through one visit and through telephone chats on Sundays. I know that she raised Ed to be the person he is and therefore I feel immensely grateful to her.

~

She has rallied with the excitement of all her children return-ing at once. Mary Jo has put lipstick on her and she's sitting in a chair. Seeing her is easy; unbelievable that she is in danger. But she tires and, back in bed, her long frame looks gaunt, her breathing sounds scary. The children set up a rotation so that someone always is with her. His sisters are staying at his mother's house so we go to a generic motel. Ed keeps flashing on the unreality of Venice—how we had expected, at this moment, to be reading aloud from Shelley or Mann in a great bed above the immortal waters. Now his mother, whom he loves easily and unequivocally, is sliding by the moment away from him.

Days are long. Back and forth to the hospital. Visitors tiptoe-ing in, the I.V. tubes, the imperial visits of the doctor, the little errands. The sisters are busy with the house, trying to give away, sort, and deal with the contents so the work won't be left to Mary Jo and Robert who live there. Not that there is much. Opening drawers and cupboards, I see how clearly his mother's life was not about acquiring things. Her name is Altrude, one I've never heard. The connotations of altruism fit well; she is a woman given to her five children. In the afternoons, we take long drives. Ed knows the weather intimately, having grown up loving winter camping, cross-country skiing, and snowshoeing, and all those foreign—to me—activities of a cold climate. With absolute wonder, I keep asking him, "Why would anyone choose to live here? It hurts."

"No, you just have to get into the rhythm of it. Watch—if it ever gets above freezing, there's a Minnesotan obligation to put on a pair of shorts and a T-shirt and pretend it's warm."

Ed is driving, the mid-sized heater blaring. I'm looking out the window. *In Venice, the aroma of fried calamari drifting from a win-dow, a dusting of snow on the lions of San Marco, a thick hot chocolate at Florian's where they're playing schmaltzy music.* But no, here's the purity of an emptier landscape. A rust-red barn etched against a faint sky, a forest of iced birch trees glittering fantastically, a deer running across a frozen lake, his hooves sending up puffs of snow. We pass small huddled towns, the farms where his parents grew up. *His family's place, the place that formed him. He saw fish swimming under clear ice. His life before he knew who he is. A place of overwhelm-ing winter, a death-grip that releases a poignant, intense spring.*

"What will you do for Christmas?" his mother asks. "You're all together." She does not say *probably for the last time* but every-one knows that. Mary Jo, a nun for thirty years, gives her com-munion every day and they talk bluntly about death. Seeing Ed at her bedside gives me new glimpses of the sweetness of his character. He is simply there. He feeds her, washes her face, talks about her graham cracker pie, her ritual of putting up beets, about the neighbors' ugly garage, and about his father, who died two years ago.

~

In the closet of Ed's old room, the sisters pull out a box of his books and Anne holds out a dusty copy of Mann's *Death in Venice*. "What's it like?" she asks. Italy has become interesting to them by osmosis. And they've learned, from reading what I wrote about our lives there, things about us they never knew. Living in scattered places with vastly different lives, these five have grown apart, after a childhood intensely close together in this small house. Now the walls come alive; synapses reconnect; everyone tells their stories. Mary Jo's reinvention of a life outside the order, Sharon's complex family, Anne's relocation to Stillwater and her juggling of job and mother to two boys dressed in grunge with earphones perpetually beating into their ears, Robert's unconventional life of refusal "to work for The Man." The whispers, *She was prom queen, he tiled his bathroom with rejects of all colors, she wants the sofa but he doesn't want her to have it, look at how dignified Mom looked in her wedding dress, we only got one game at Christmas, how could you have married that creep, I don't remember it that way at all.*

Ed goes to the hospital at six-thirty every morning, cherishing quiet hours with his mother. And "What will you do for Christmas?" she had worried. When in doubt, cook. On Christmas Eve morning, Ed and I scour the grocery stores of Winona, buying olive oil and wine, garlic, a mounded cart we push through the frozen ruts of the parking lot. His mother is remote today, far into her dying. We visit the lawyer; the family puts the house on the market. We rush into the florist's, stunned by the humid warmth and the perfume of roses and lilies. Candles and flowers for her room. There is so little to *do*. The temperature falls; how low can it go? Another new record. We take a two-block walk and I am afraid we won't get back without lost fingers and toes.

The one luxury in the plain motel is the Jacuzzi tub. *Ya-coot-see*, the Italians say. Back in the room, after a last late visit to the hospital, we empty the complimentary vial of bubble bath into the water, light a candle and lie in the swirling hot water, finally warm.

On Christmas morning, Ed's mother feels well enough to be wheeled to the lobby to watch the thumb-sized yellow birds in the aviary. I wonder what it is like for her to see gathered around her bed the five children she raised, all now forty to fifty years old, living their lives, health all over each of them, and strong good looks and bodies.

Too cold to go anywhere. Most of us are at the house all afternoon. Going through kitchen drawers, the sisters find the famous family recipe for graham cracker pie and the three—all self-proclaimed non-cooks—launch into baking, consulting with each other over the consistency of the custard and when to stop beating the egg whites. Meanwhile, Ed and I make little pasta rolls with spinach and cheese, a grand beef stew with carrots, potatoes, and red wine. We make broccoli (one of the few fresh vegetables we could find) purée, and, for an Italian note, we'll serve *bruschette,* grilled slices of bread rubbed with garlic.

At dark, we take Ed's mother's dinner on a tray to the hospital. She eats most of the slice of graham cracker pie, giving it high praise, even though we all know the custard could have been a little firmer. As we drive back, snow starts again, bringing down its dazzling silence.

At dinner Ed puts on a tape of Puccini arias. Everyone gathers around Altrude's table. I look out the window at the lights of the house falling in gold squares on the snow, a scene repeated all over the white town. We pour the wine. "Cheers." "To Mother." *"Salute."* The parents are absent and the house is poised to roll under into memory. Dinner is ready. We are hungry and we eat. 259

Graham Cracker Pie

This favorite pie in Ed's family is a mid-century classic. In my family the same pie was flavored with lemon.

⟶ *Crush 12 graham crackers into fine crumbs with a rolling pin. Mix with 1 t. of flour, 1 t. of cinnamon, and ⅓ c. of sugar. Melt ⅓ c. of butter and mix with the crumbs. Press into pie plate.*

⟶ *For the custard, blend ½ c. of sugar with 2 T. of cornstarch. To 2 c. of milk, add 3 beaten egg yolks. Mix with sugar and cook on moderate heat, stirring constantly, until the mixture thickens. Whisk in 2 t. vanilla. Beat 3 egg whites until stiff. Whisk in 1 T. sugar. Pour custard into the pie shell, top with meringue and bake at 350 degrees until meringue has toasted.*

Ritmo: Rhythm

IN THE MIDST OF THE TORRENTIAL EL NIÑO
winter in San Francisco, we decided to move. I was
reading the paper one Sunday and saw a small drawing
of a Spanish/Mediterranean house with two balconies
and what looked like a tall palm in front. "Look at this house—
doesn't it remind you of Bramasole?"

Ed stared. "I like it. Where is it?"

"It doesn't say. Isn't the balcony nice? You could line it with
those yellow orchids that seem to grow everywhere in San Francisco." Ed called the listing agent and found out the house was
sold.

Living at Bramasole makes us want to import into our American lives as many Italian elements as we can. More urgently, the
death of Ed's mother in January heightened our sense of *carpe
diem*. Our flat, which I bought as my former marriage slowly
dissolved, is the third floor of a large Victorian house. I loved the
coved ceilings and moulding and all the light flooding through
skylights and thirty windows. The dining room looks out into

trees and then onto a city view, with a slice of the bay in the distance. After years there, every room reflected the way we live. The kitchen I'd remodeled the year we bought Bramasole. Black and white tile, mirror between the glass-fronted cabinets and counters, and a six-burner restaurant stove with an oven where I easily could roast two geese and a turkey. What we began to miss was living outdoors. Stepping outside as though it were inside, stepping inside as though it were outside. Suddenly, I needed herbs in the ground and a table under a tree. Besides, it's good to move. I throw away all the accumulated junk—jars, papers, shoes in the back of the closet, black-splotched cookie sheets, tired towels. Remembering every move, I see that a new period of my life began with each change of house. Is the irrational instinct to move now (the flat is large and pretty and in a great location) also a pre-knowledge of change, or a readiness for the new?

We began to circle ads for houses in the paper, to drive around on Sunday afternoons to open houses, to look at neighborhoods we hardly knew, since our own Pacific Heights neighborhood was not remotely affordable, given what we wanted. The real estate market was wild: Asking price turned out to be a base in what quickly became an auction. Houses were selling for up to a hundred thousand dollars over the list price. Confusing. John, our agent, agreed. And we weren't finding anything we especially liked. I wanted the *this is it* feeling I experienced when I first saw Bramasole.

We'd give up for a couple of weeks, then John would call and say we might drive by a certain address, we might like this ranch house with a large garden with redwoods and a greenhouse. As we were driving toward the peninsula one day to see a Carmel-type cottage, we followed an open house sign and turned into a wooded area of San Francisco originally landscaped by the Olmstead firm, designers of Central Park. The houses live among trees and lawns. The Tudor house for sale was in "original" condition, meaning every plank and pane needed attention. We started talking to the agent, and told him we were about to give up for a year or so, until things calmed down. "I have a house I think you might like. Meet me at four and I'll show you." We drove on to see the overly charming cottage, where multiple offers were being made during the first hour.

When we pulled up at the address the agent had given us, I recognized the house I'd seen in the paper, the one that had set me dreaming about moving. "We saw this house advertised and called about it. We thought it was sold."

"It was, but the deal fell through. It's not yet back on the market." Steps curve up to a tile veranda with a large arched door from the dining room opening to it. Three upstairs balconies and a sunroom with eleven windows—the house is speaking my language. I can see Sister moving from one sunny patch to another in this light-flooded house.

We bought it. Even though we'd not even listed our own flat, we had to act quickly. I started sorting through letters and sweaters. My daughter became engaged. We were getting to know Stuart, her fiancé. Ashley and I began to plan their wedding. Visits to photographers and florists were fitted between trips to the hardware store to find hooks and doorknobs. She was studying for her PhD qualifying exam, then her orals. High panic set in. Several of her classmates had failed the year before. We listed the flat and it sold within three days. We closed on the new house and ripped out miles of thick white carpet, blotched with spills. Underneath, the seventy-five-year-old herringbone hardwood floors were intact. Dirty but intact. We found a brick stairway spattered with paint, which had to be stripped. We began having the floors refinished, new wiring and alarm system installed, the interior painted. We had to have a new tile roof put on. While I was out, the wrong room was painted yellow. Ashley and I looked at wedding dresses—she quickly decided that she wanted the floating-cloud variety—and invitations and bridesmaids' dresses. We met with caterers. Ed went to Italy to prune during his spring break. I was running between the flat and the house, dealing with workmen who spoke no English. The people we hired to work spoke English but when the actual labor began, they sent workers newly arrived from Cambodia, Malaysia, Korea, and all parts of South America. Often, they couldn't even talk to each other. Restoring Bramasole was so much easier! One Honduran painter locked a bedroom door from the inside and closed it as he came out. When I showed him that the door wouldn't open, he looked at me with great brown eyes and sadly uttered his only two American words, "Fook sheet." I looked at him for a moment before those popular expletives registered.

Blithely, I'd said I loved to move. It would be fun. When the truck loaded our furniture and boxes for an entire day, I wondered how we ever would unpack. Sister yowled all the way from our flat, which she'd lived in always, to the new house. The bookshelves we bought—and painted three coats—did not begin to accommodate all our books. Sixty boxes were stored in the new basement. In the large living room, our sofa and chairs looked like dollhouse furniture. The men set about unpacking but I didn't know where vases and platters and paintings should go. They were left in stacks and heaps on the gorgeous new floors. We were happy with the house every step of the way. Our bedroom has a fireplace and floor-to-ceiling windows opening onto a balcony, tropical trees, and then, in the distance, the Pacific Ocean. I had the walls painted a color called "Sicily," a faint shade of peach. Studies for both of us, extensive storage, a little walled garden, and a bougainvillea that must have been planted when the house was new—we were too thrilled to be overwhelmed by our dawn-to-midnight days. Ed came back from two weeks of solid work at Bramasole. Re-entry was rude. A pipe burst and the basement started to flood. He was up to his ankles in water, telephone in one hand, a box of books under the other arm. Two plumbers worked for eleven hours and finally found the leak. I travelled three times to southern California to give talks. Locally, I spoke at several events. We had a new window made for the stair landing, replacing with clear glass a pair of staring, stained-glass owls on a limb. We had a gardener hacking ivy, a reminder of buying Bramasole. The entire garage door had to be replaced. Oh, and I was teaching full time. I had ten MFA theses, classes, and meetings.

We decided to get married. We told no one. I recalled my primitive instinct that moving is a signal that one is ready for change. I ordered two cakes from Dominique, my favorite pastry maker, we sent invitations for a housewarming to about thirty of our closest friends. Then I told Ashley and two friends. We dashed downtown for the license, which was shockingly easy to obtain. Twelve dollars, sign on the line.

All the years after my divorce, I had avoided the subject of marriage. Even when it was clear that Ed and I would be permanently together, I'd say, "Why bother?" Or, "I'm not in the important business of raising children anymore. We're adults." I feared my friend who said, "Marriage is the first step toward divorce." To myself I'd say, *I don't want to put my hand down on the hot burner twice.* Also, I never wanted to be financially dependent ever again. My former years of writing poetry while my husband worked, I'd paid for dearly. I knew I'd never marry without stepping into it with full financial freedom. Miraculously, and thanks to my own writing hand, I felt secure.

A carload of flowers, a big board of cheeses, strawberries, the cakes, *gelato,* champagne—no wedding ever was easier. Our friends arrived bearing soaps, plants, bowls, and books to warm the house. Our close friend Josephine, a licensed minister, called everyone together in the living room for a blessing of the house. We stood beside her in front of the fireplace. Ashley and Stuart stood with us. And then Josephine said, "Dearly beloved, we are gathered . . ." Our friends gasped and clapped. She talked about happiness. Ed and I read poems to each other. That was it.

The next day we were back into unpacking boxes and changing locks and arranging insurance. But we were breaking into big smiles at the mailman, and now and then dancing in the hallway.

Most of the arrangements for Ashley's August wedding were finished. She did well on both exams and had a paper accepted for a conference. Stuart broke away from his company and started a new business. They moved his office and hired people. He talked on the phone as we drove to restaurants. Who could cook? We were all so far beyond the beyond that we seemed calm. They brought us a grill and one night we managed to burn both steak and vegetables. Changes, changes, changes. The house looked spare but settled. We lived there two weeks. I never knew where the forks were or how the new washer worked. We'd compressed a half-year of house restoration into six weeks, thanks to our Italian training. Sister looked at us accusingly and wouldn't budge from the top of Ed's suitcase. We were searching for tax papers, having filed extensions during all the confusion. We filled in final grade sheets and cleared up our school offices. It was June. The house sitter arrived. Time to move to Italy.

On Italian time I wake up by the sun, not by my alarm clock. In shock from the chaotic spring, I look blankly out the window. Ed has risen in the dark, only to fall asleep on the sofa. We have come back to Bramasole for summer. I wonder if we could stare into the trees without speaking to anyone for at least a week. I would like a nurse in the hallway, a silent white-uniformed presence who would bring in crescents of melon on thin plates, her pale hand soothing my forehead. The first week of June—odd, the garden is at prime bloom. Even the yellow lilies are open. The linden trees Ed and Beppe pruned in March have spread umbrellas of fresh leaves. Some roses already are waning from their first flush of flowers.

Beppe arrives and Ed steps out barefooted and shirtless to say hello. Beppe hands him a sack. *"Un coniglio per la signora, genuino."* In its seventy days on earth, the rabbit has eaten nothing but greens, salad, and bread. I look in the bag and see the head. "Put the head in sauce," he tells me. "The meat of the face is . . ." He makes the corkscrew gesture of rotating his forefinger against his cheek, signaling a fine taste. Beppe says rain fell every day in spring and all the plants are two weeks early. The air feels heavy with moisture and it seems that I'm looking through a green lens at the wet light over the valley. He tells us he has planted the *orto* because Anselmo is sick again. When we call Anselmo later, he sounds weak but says he'll be well in a couple of weeks. Ed makes coffee and we lower ourselves into chairs outside in the sun, ready to let the rays restore us. We're discussing symptoms of post-traumatic stress disorder and whether we have them.

Primo Bianchi drives up in his battered blue Ape. As we walk down to meet him, we see him limping badly. He's dressed in pressed gray pants and loafers, not in his usual work clothes. Immediately he sits on the wall and slips off his shoes. Even through his socks, his ankles look swollen. He grimaces every time his foot touches the ground or moves. "Gout, perhaps gout. I have not been able to work for a month. And the pills they give me are bad for my liver."

We are poised to finish the bathroom project we started last summer, which had to be aborted when the Sicilian tile ended up in the sea. We also plan to build a stone terrace and grill in front of the *limonaia* and to make a pergola of grapes, a continuation of our garden master plan. He tells us he spent the entire rainy spring reconstructing a stairwell in a *palazzo*. On his knees on damp brick, pouring cement and hauling—no wonder his feet rebelled. Maybe we should find someone else, he suggests. "No, no, we'll wait until you are ready," Ed tells him. "We like your work and your men." We're crazy about him, too. He knows how to do anything. He looks at a problem, moving his head from side to side, pondering. Then he looks at us with a smile and explains what we will do. When he works he sings tuneless songs like those I've heard on a tape of traditional Tuscan and Umbrian farm music. The songs don't seem to venture far from three or four notes endlessly repeated in a humming drone. His blue eyes have a far sadness in them which totally contrasts with his immediate smile. He hoists himself up and promises to call when he can begin.

Although we are worried about his feet, we are ecstatic over the delay. Now a few weeks of *dolce far niente,* the sweet to do nothing, which we love most. It seems accidental that we keep falling into enormous projects. The sweetness of the early summer is intense. The double-time, triple-time rhythm of the past few months suddenly starts to fade and the long, long Tuscan days present themselves like gifts. Even the Mad Spring was motivated by our desire to bring a piece of our lives here to San Francisco, although at this moment that seems like bomb-the-village-to-save-the-village thinking.

Reliving the spring, we ask each other what we could have done differently. And what *can* we take back to our lives in the new house? What accounts for the dramatic shift in our minds and bodies when we live here? And, in California, aren't we frequently out of control? When over-commitment kicks in, I feel my concentration start to flit. After a few days here, my scattered consciousness gradually melds, mends. Even that seems a level of happiness: the absence of anxiety. Clearly, factor one is not working at our jobs in summer. But we like teaching and must continue, so, given that, what else?

Here, almost all media are subtracted from daily life. I notice the enormous difference immediately. The habit I have, of turning on the radio news as I drive to work, comes to mind as a destroyer of the natural rhythm of the day. Subtle, because flicking on the radio *seems* almost an automatic gesture, a neutral gesture. But in the half hour from my flat to the parking lot at school, drug lords are shot, children are abused by those who are supposed to protect them, car bombs go off, houses are carried off by floods, and my waking psyche has absorbed a load of the world's hurt. The bombardment of frightening, disturbing images assaults any well-being that might have accrued from a lovely night's sleep. TV probably would be worse; I rarely watch TV news except for reports of earthquakes and dire events. At school, I get out of the car already tense and not knowing why. The constant overload of recurrent horror on the news and in the papers we assume is normal until we live without it. Has any study focused on the correlation of anxiety and level of exposure to news? I read the paper here two or three times a week, enough to more than keep up with crucial events. "I'll start the day without that negative drone," I tell Ed. "On my own terms."

"I do like the traffic report, though. All the words rush together; it sounds like a Dylan Thomas poem. Instead of the news, try the Bach cello suites." He is normally not as pushed as I am because the teaching load at my university is double that at his. "Taking buckets of time back is the main thing."

"In the new house let's get up early and walk, the way I do here. Another way of starting out on our own terms. We could walk to the ocean."

"If only we could take back the siesta—free hours in the middle of the day."

"Wouldn't you like to call one friend and say 'How are you?' and not hear the answer, 'I'm so busy'?"

"Well, 'I'm busy' means several things—partly it means 'I'm important.' But maybe living life is so important that we shouldn't be busy. At least not busy, busy, with that buzz-buzz sound." Ed tells his students to figure out how many weekends they have left, given the good fortune of normal life expectancy. Even to the young it's a shock to see that there are only 2800 more. That's it. Done for. *Carpe diem, sì, sì,* grab the days.

~

We decide on hedonism. After two days of stocking the house with essentials, planting the last annuals we can grab before the nurseries are emptied, and just breathing in the life we know so well here, we start taking long walks. The wild-flowers must be at the peak of the century. All that spring rain coaxed every latent seed, and from the fire roads around the hills we see meadows knee-deep in bloom and hillsides golden with *ginestre,* the broom sending its scent down the breezes in rivulets. We gather strawberries the size of two-carat rubies and sit in long grass eating them. We drive around in Umbria, look-ing at antiques, hoping to find a desk. One shop owner tells us, "I can find anything you want; just tell me what you want." I flash on the grandiose promises of my father when I was a child. "You can have anything in this world. Just tell me what you want." I could never think of anything except a swimming pool, to which he'd say, "You don't want that; you just think you want that." We travel to San Casciano dei Bagni, where the Romans bathed, and eat pigeon ravioli at the restaurant on the main street, then on to Sarteano and Cetona, with meandering drives around the blissful countryside.

When the exhaustion we brought over finally disappears, we go up to Florence and spend the night. I must find a dress to wear to Ashley's wedding in August. Already the browns, plums, and grays of fall are on view. Ed slips easily into a fall mood and finds two soft-style sport coats. When we have shopped in Florence before, I never bought anything except shoes and handbags. Especially when Jess (Ashley's former boyfriend and now our friend) visits, Ed loves a day in the men's stores. He and Jess incite each other and I'm the spectator. Now Ed visits shop after shop with me. I'm getting used to the Italian mode of shopping. You say what you are looking for and they show you. It's a mistake just to browse through what's out, since many shops only have one size on display. The salespeople are there to be of service. The self-service we are used to is still unusual here. As soon as I say I want a dress for my daughter's wedding, everything in the shop comes forth. They understand totally that the occasion is *molto importante*. Most brides' mothers, I think, do not want a mother-of-the-bride dress. All the lavender lace and beige crêpe dresses designed with that in mind must go unsold. The suit I finally choose at a small shop, which makes everything especially for the customer, is orange. I never have had an orange dress in my life. It's a frosty silk orange, which requires two fittings. My sister will loan me her coral and pearl necklace. I find beautiful dull gold shoes with high heels that could kill. The wedding will be wonderful. The hitch being that I will see my former husband for the first time in years.

⟋

Vittorio calls to invite us to a dinner on a boat. The Lago Trasimeno wine consortium has arranged for a ferry to take a group on what we used to call a "progressive dinner," a different course in four places around the lake. We meet at Castiglione del Lago on Sunday at noon. When we arrive, glasses of *prosecco* and plates of *bruschette* with tomatoes and basil are being passed. We're given a wine glass and a pouch to wear around our necks where we can store the glass when we're not drinking. The crowd is larger than we expected. We find Vittorio and Celia, their children, and several friends of theirs. Maybe two hundred people are piling onto the ferry, with a bar set up at the entrance. People are drinking more *prosecco* as we pull away from the dock. I love boats and islands and the sky shifting as we ride the rises and falls of the water. We disembark on Isola Maggiore, and the hotel staff serves us pasta with the roe of carp and baskets of excellent bread. The workers of the wine consortium of the lake area generously pour all their whites. After the pasta, there's time for a hot walk along the beach. Back on the ferry, we move farther into the lake toward Isola Polvese.

The red wines are open. Various *crostini* are passed. The lake silvers under the flaring white sun. The children start to tire but a band begins to play and some people are dancing. I'm ready to go home but there is no exit. We've been gone four hours. An empty island for birds and small wildlife, Polvese has grassy beaches full of people over for the Sunday afternoon in the sun. One man spread out on a towel has turned so red he looks like an *écorché*, a body without skin. We troop across the island to long outdoor tables. We're served carp cooked in the style of *porchetta,* grilled and stuffed with herbs and salt, and also wrapped in *pancetta*. It's rich, meaty.

On the boat again, I realize that the Italians have had long training for this kind of day. All the first communions, baptisms, weddings, and other *feste* totally prepare them for the long celebrations. We've had steady wine poured into our glasses all afternoon. Faces are glazed with sweat. The bar is popping cork after cork. The band cranks up its speakers and the singer in a slinky dress starts in on "Hey, Jude," then speeds up to Italian rock. Suddenly everyone is dancing. The boat is swaying. Could we tip? A retarded man is dancing with his mother, grannies are swinging their hips, a man twirls his three-year-old daughter. The drummer announces a soccer score into the microphone and everyone jumps up and shouts so loud I think the boat will sink. We disembark again at Passignano for dessert. Children turn cranky. But back on board the wine keeps pouring, spinach and cheese crêpes are passed around, and we enter our eighth straight hour of eating and drinking.

Finally, the ferry heads back toward Castiglione del Lago. We see the other two Americans on board; he looks stony and she looks as if she could cry. The sun falls low and the sherbert colors of the sky reflect on the water. We lean over the rail, watching the wake while all the Italians join with the band singing *like a bridge over muddy waterrrr, I will lay me down* in English, and then Italian songs everyone knows. As we gather our sunscreen and camera, we hear several groups talking about where they will go for dinner. They have a secret gene that we don't have.

⌒

Beppe's *fagiolini,* the green beans we call Blue Lake at home, are ready. Tender and small, they don't even need topping and tailing but I do it anyway. Steamed just to the right point, their full flavor emerges. Underdone, they squeak when you bite them and taste slightly bitter. We eat them alone, with just a little oil and salt and pepper. They're not hurt by toasted chopped hazelnuts, or a little sautéed onion, or by my old favorite, sliced fennel and black olives. My mother liked green beans with tarragon, oil and vinegar, and crumbled bacon. I remember what a fine thing we thought that was, since beans usually were cooked to pieces with a hunk of fatback. In memory of that ultra-sophisticated recipe, I clip branches from my tarragon, which has turned into a towering bush. I'm searching my books for ways to use it, other than plunging the wands into vinegar. Medieval pilgrims to the Holy Land put sprigs inside their shoes to give energy and spring to their feet. I'd like to try that.

Green beans are the one vegetable Anselmo did not plant last year when he established our garden. Beppe's garden thrives, though he has narrowed Anselmo's scope. We have onions, potatoes, green beans, lettuces, garlic, zucchini, and tomatoes. Anselmo's artichokes and asparagus gave us several treats just after we arrived. Beppe plans to plant fennel, and to reseed the lettuces every few weeks. We miss Anselmo—his ironic humor and bossy control of the garden, as well as his adventuring spirit which landed us in new situations constantly. When we call to check on him, we're told that he has been taken to the hospital.

We pick a bunch of lavender and tie it to a jar of honey. How strange to be going back to the hospital. He's a vigorous man, full of opinions and laughter. He'll have his swollen leg propped up, saying *"Senta, senta,"* listen, listen, into his *telefonino*. Ed parks and goes to the machine to get a parking receipt. I walk on toward the hospital, pausing to wait for him.

I glance up at the black-bordered *manifesti funebri*, funeral notices, posted on the wall. Anselmo's name. I scan it, unbelieving. I force myself to focus. Read. *Yesterday, with all the religious comforts . . . funeral tomorrow . . . no flowers but good works . . . Anselmo Pietro Martini Pisciacani. . . .* Unlike the other plain notices, his pictures a sappy pastel Christ in a crown of thorns, upturned eyes, surrounded by roses. Because he would have mocked it, I think there must be a mistake. He was not a churchgoer. He could not be dead. But then no one else could have that name. As Ed approaches, I shake my head and point. "No. How can this be?"

We walk on up to the hospital. At the front desk Ed says, "We have a friend who was a patient and we're afraid he has died. Is he still here? Anselmo Martini."

He finds no record—maybe there's a mistake but then I remember "Pisciacani," the name he hated and dropped after his mother died, was on the death notice. Pisciacani means dog piss in dialect. "Pisciacani," I say.

"Yes, I am sorry, he is in the chapel. If you die in hospital, you must remain for twenty-four hours." He leads us downstairs. Ed waits at the door and I walk in. There lies Anselmo on a stone slab, dressed in his brown suit, his feet splayed and a little dust on his shoes. Four women in black pray around him. I put down the honey and lavender at the door and flee.

At home the land feels charged with Anselmo's presence. He rebuilt that stone wall, he cleared two terraces for the *orto*, he planted the grass in the Lime Tree Bower. The potted lemons and the three roses the color of dried blood and the wine press—he gave us these with few words but I could tell with immense pleasure. On the third terrace he planted two apricots, and near the road, two pears. For all the years we will have here, we still will be enjoying the literal fruits of his labors. In the *limonaia,* his red beret hangs on a nail.

We feel we've lost a good uncle. Ed is still reeling from his mother's death. Anselmo's brings a double rush of grief. The hurt of loss is too hard, then there's the incomprehensible fact that the loved person simply is erased from the planet. The basic facts of birth and death I've never remotely been able to fathom. *The prenatal abyss, out of it you came, into the tumult of life, light, and on to the other void. . . .* I hope to be dazzled by the news of an afterlife, when the last plug is pulled on me. *I can't take non-life.* Anselmo stood at the Thursday market with fifty or sixty men every week for decades, talking weather, business, jingling change in his pocket. In his office on Sacco e Vanzetti, he always dropped everything when we walked in. I quizzed him about the farms for sale in photos on the wall, and if one looked wonderful, he'd say "Let's go look," and grab his hat. He had all the time in the world. Now, none. *"There's no one hundred years guaranteed or life cheerfully refunded, young lady," my grandfather warned.*

People are crammed into the church. We stand in the doorway. Out on the porch, thirty or so men smoke and talk during the funeral mass, just as though they were at the market. I recognize many of them. Their sunbaked faces attest to work in the fields. The older ones are short, dressed in suits too thick for the brutal July sun, the younger ones are taller, beneficiaries of postwar nutrition, and wear pressed short-sleeved shirts. Inside, heat and incense swirl. Who will faint? Family members support each other as they walk by the casket for communion. It's hard to grasp that Anselmo lies inside that box. The wailing Catholic hymns drag on forever. The casket is loaded into the hearse. We have seen these processions before. Now we join the crowd walking behind the hearse up to the cemetery. I hope he is not going into one of those thirty-year slots that look like dresser drawers in a wall. No, there's the raw hole. He is going into the earth, this man of the earth. No ceremony, he's just lowered by ropes into the ground. Not even a thud. When my father was buried, the ground was so saturated that the coffin floated for a moment before whooshing down into water. *"That's not true at all," my sister says. "They didn't even lower the coffin when we were there."* She's wrong. I see the red rose blanket slide off into the arms of the undertakers and the bronze box start to sink. *"You were dreaming," she insists.* His family steps forward and everyone throws on a handful of dirt. No denying that he will be in the ground. We talk to the family. Everyone leaves quickly. There's no dinner or visiting. Monday, back to work.

At home, Beppe is tying grape vines to wires. We tell him about Anselmo, how quickly he was gone, and he stands up slowly, saying nothing. He takes off his hat and his eyes fill with tears. He shakes his head and goes back to the vines.

~~

When the excitement of death is over, the shock and disbelief subside quickly and we're left with the fact of absence. A funeral cools emotion because it leaves not a doubt. It's over—the traditional sacraments are wise ways to instantly internalize the major events of life. Now we begin to say, *His first night in the ground, the men at the market are gathering around a space that was his, look, Anselmo's pears.* The last work of his life was here on this land. He had the oldest knowledge of what grows where and when. Did we ever thank him enough for finding Bramasole for us?

"Hearse is a strange word," Ed says. We are walking home from town over the Roman road. "In Middle English it's *herse*—I know this because it came up in a poem I wrote when my father died. *Herse* comes from Latin *hirpex,* meaning 'harrow.' You know how the harrow has all those prongs—in Italian they call them *quarante dente,* forty teeth. Well, *hirpex* reaches way back to the Oscan *hircus,* which means wolf, a connection to teeth. It felt strange to follow that hearse."

"Show me the poem again."

SCORPIONS

The heaving, sweating, cento per cento *heat broke today,*
as if it can break as unexpectedly as a car breaks,
or as the large glass demijohn that shattered on the tiles
when I bumped into it while carrying an armload of books
from one bookcase in one room to another bookcase
in another room: the heavy inhale of heat into my own lungs,
my bare feet surrounded by sharp glass. Which brought me
to "booklungs" (what the dark hollow lungs of scorpions
are called), lined up in their own bodies like blank books.

All week, an inch-and-a-half long black scorpion
has stayed in the shower, not because of the heat but because
it has eaten a slightly smaller scorpion, who had come in earlier,
perhaps looking for water. The one ate all of the other,
except for three of its eight legs, still scattered on the porcelain.
I remembered hearing the woman at the restaurant,
her overly large white teeth crunching through a plateful
of chitinous shrimp. The scorpion carries its carapace, too.
It too proved it could continue to eat, to chew through shell,
to decisively end its quarrel with the other, which was surely
over nothing important enough to die for. The one has the other
completely inside itself, is running on two histories.
I was reminded of Kronos eating his own children, lungs and all,
crunching through skull, into brains, and then Zeus tricking him
into vomiting them all whole and alive. But the proof is
in the eating—better to eat than not to. Which brings me
to my father, who ate his last on August 8th, and felt his lungs,
sacks of cheap cloth, let all the air out. Now the coffin is his new
carapace, shiny steel—we could see our faces distorted in it.
Here I hear pears drop in late August, skins pierced
by sharp wasps and armored iridescent beetles, and
there's a heavy sweetness under the tree when I rake up
the bruised fruit: Rake, *as in* harrow, *as in* hearse *(the one*
I followed August 12th) from the Oscan for wolf—
because of its teeth, strong enough even to break through bone.

We have had not a drop of rain all summer. The flamboyant flower garden I had last year has limped through the hottest summer on record. "I can eat only watermelon and *gelato*," la signora Molesini in the grocery store tells us. No matter how much we water, the grass burns. The voluptuous roses of early June gradually have shed their leaves. The tiny buds they send out refuse to open.

The year we bought the house it was the same. Clouds would gather over the house and thunder practically shook the fillings out of our teeth—but no rain. Our well went dry and I remember thinking in the middle of the night, *I must be certifiably insane. I have no idea what I'm doing.* The singed oaks and locusts defrocked early, leaving dead-looking trees all over the hills. The next summer was soft, with wildflowers spilling over every terrace. We slept under a light blanket until July. We love living close to the pulse of the seasons, even the searing dry heat, which has sent foxes and wild boar into our yard for the first time. I hear the *cinghiale* snorting across the lawn at night, making their way to the faucet where they lap water from the stone basin. They scuffle with, what—squirrels and porcupines? Then they thunder off with their strange "ha-ha" cries. They have not managed to get through Beppe's fence around the vegetables but they find plenty to love in the fallen plums.

At the beginning of August, we return to foggy, cold San Francisco for Ashley's wedding. All my Southern relatives are arriving—the clan is stomping. My college roommates and their husbands are coming, Ashley's New York friends from her artist life, Stuart's friends, family. Ashley and her bridesmaids arrive at the house with the wedding dress and hang it in front of one of the many still-bare windows, where it drifts on its own, bringing home the reality of the wedding. Ashley suddenly is struck with the magnitude of what's coming. She comes into my room while I'm unpacking and throws herself on the bed. "Any advice for me?"

I remember asking my mother the same question. She thought a minute then said, "Don't ever wear old underwear." I tell Ashley I'll try to come up with something better but I'm not sure I can. She's very grown, as is Stuart, and they seem to be entering this marriage not only with love and excitement but with enormous relief to have found each other after a lot of false starts. Ashley is one of the most decisive people I've ever known; when she makes up her mind there's an iron will behind her.

We're having all the out-of-town people over for drinks, and my family will stay afterwards for dinner. At this party, one of the strangest things of my life happens. Ashley looks glorious in a short red dress. Two waiters are passing champagne and Ed is going over the toast he's about to give. My sisters, brothers-in-law, nieces, and nephews are in full reunion mode. Ashley is in the foyer greeting guests. I'm talking to friends in the living room when I see my nephew arrive in the crowded foyer. As I walk toward him, I introduce myself to the man talking to Ashley. "Hello, I'm Frances, Ashley's mother." I shake his hand and see the startled look on his face. "And I'm Frank," he answers with a laugh. My former husband. Ashley's father. We were married for a lifetime. I do not recognize him. He thinks I am surely joking. Of course, I am distracted with all the arrivals, trying to circulate among the guests—still, I look straight at him and do not know him. Once he said to me, *I'd know your hand in a bucket of hands,* one of the strangest intimacies I have heard. I step outside and take big breaths of air and try to adjust to the jolt—the snap of that imagined entwined umbilical of the past. He doesn't even look that different. I've seen him in my mind and in dreams many times over the years. I'd expected a flash-flood of memories, a by-pass connection to the now historical past. Looking at him, I used to feel I was looking in a mirror, my equal-opposite. For a long time, I will be feeling my hand go out to shake that of a stranger.

The garden wedding is at an inn in the wine country, a dreamy dream of a wedding, with pink and apricot roses everywhere, a golden light over the vineyard hills, a bride descending as though from a cloud, a groom with the heart to cry as she walks toward him, and the tenor sealing us all together with *"Con te partirò,"* With you I will go. Her veil catches on a rose thorn and tears, her father frees her, takes the torn piece of veil into his pocket, and they walk. A moment, and of such moments myths are made.

For dinner, candles all over the garden, and a Tuscan feast. As we sit down a snowy egret flies over and lands on the feathery top of a tree. "A great omen," someone says. "No, the stork," someone else answers. For my toast, I remember a line from Rilke, "Love consists of this, that two solitudes protect and touch and greet each other." Her father gives an eloquent toast about the enormous support the presence of all the guests will give to Ashley and Stuart. Soon Ashley is dancing, floating under the full moon, then everyone is dancing. Ed is smoking a big cigar. I wish everyone would stay all night.

The newlyweds take off for hot tropical islands. My sisters and their families leave over the next few days, we see friends, adjust to the decrescendo, pack, pack, pack again, and board the plane for the long haul back to Bramasole, taking a duffle of books, fall clothes, and a handful of moments to last a lifetime.

The end of August and still no rain. In earlier times, farmers prayed to saints. If no rain came, the statue of the saint might be flogged, thrown into a river, dragged out, and stuffed in the mouth with salty sardines to make him thirsty. Whatever rituals occur now, they're private.

For nine summers I've lived on this hillside in Tuscany. I've spent scattered winter and spring holidays here, and last year had the great boon of a whole spring. I am about to spend my first fall. The *feste* of August—beefsteak and *funghi porcini*—are over; the streets are emptying by the day as tourists head home. The sun has been tamed, softening the evening light to rose-gold. An early fall; truffles and mushrooms and sausages will be coming. Already we're peeling the green Sicilian tangerines, exactly the color of a parrot, and buying apples that taste like our earliest memories of apples. Primo has left a load of cement and sand; in a week he will begin the project. Beppe today has planted *cavolo nero,* the black winter cabbage, and has set out fennel for next year. He picked the last little bunch of beans and another basket of tomatoes. All summer we eat outside in the long twilight, now the days are short enough that we set out lanterns for dinner.

Vittorio, always with his taste buds anticipating the season, calls to invite us to a goose dinner, the last feast of the summer. His voice is the siren's call. Our Slow Food group has just celebrated the foods and wines of the Verona area at an eight-course dinner. "I think of goose as a Christmas treat," Ed says.

"No, you do not eat the white geese after summer. They are too old, too fat. The flavor is best now." So we wind far into the mountains to a *trattoria* where we gather at two long tables near the fireplace. Vittorio is pouring the wine, his treat, the Avignonesi reds we love. We see Paolo, the winemaker of that noble vineyard, at the other table and toast him. The *antipasti* begin, the usual *crostini,* served with the special stuffed goose neck. The pasta with rich *ragù d'oca,* goose sauce, is followed by roast goose, easily the best I've ever tasted. The noise level rises until it's impossible to hear what anyone is saying. That's O.K. We just eat. The baby in the stroller at the end of the table sleeps through everything.

⌇

Margherita, daughter of signora Gazzini, forager *par excellence,* stops by to introduce herself. Driving by, she happens to witness the felling of the dead palm. We waited all summer while it shed dry fronds one by one. We hate to cut it, especially since its thirty-foot mate on the other side of the house still thrives, but the completely bare trunk, like a giant elephant leg, looked bizarre. She watches from below as I watch from the window. Heavier and denser than they thought, Ed and Beppe both yell as the palm starts to fall off-course, crashing into a pot of geraniums.

Margherita lived at Bramasole as a child, when the palm was small. I am stirred to hear that she still dreams of the rooms and land she knew at four years old. From my first glance, Bramasole always has been a house of dreams. Coming upon it now, I see that it belongs to the Etruscan Bramasole wall, to Torreone, to Cortona, to Tuscany. Beyond my possession, still it is mine—the contraries meet—and transitory as my tenure may be, it is a fierce and primitive tenure. "Don't give up the house, no matter what happens," I recall a friend advising another friend, who was divorcing. "You're discovering the irrational power of a woman's domesticity," my friend Josephine tells me. "Possession always has a secret root."

I don't say any of this to Margherita. Since I've just met her I don't want her to think I'm some sibyl of the mountain. While Ed and Beppe cart away the carcass, she tells me that her mother stays out for six or eight hours some days. Not only does she gather lettuces, asparagus, snails, and mushrooms, she cuts greens for her rabbits. "She's a person who likes to live outside," she explains. "We don't know where she goes—sometimes she's just roaming the hills. She's been roaming this mountain for a lifetime."

~~~~

I understand the impulse. Walking the ridge road toward the Porta Montanina gate to town, I'm reading Keats's ode "To Autumn" and feeling how closely his words anneal to the subject. Of all the poems about the season, his brings me the closest to the unsayable sensation I experience as summer circles toward the autumnal equinox. The internal clock turns, too, a visceral knowledge of change. Earlier, the pale dog-roses bloomed along the road; today the branches are studded with bright orange rose hips. The air seems to hold a calming sense of peace as the landscape turns toast, amber, wheat, and the grasses dry to—what? The shade of lion's fur, the tawny crust of bread, the gold of a worn wedding ring. A moment ago the grasses were a fervent green. "Season of mists and yellow fruit-fulness," Keats writes, and I see the valley mists and laden branches of pear blotched and gnawed and bumbled by birds, bees, and worms. I like the idea of the season conspiring with the sun to "load and bless" the fruit and vines. I taste his phrases: "hair soft-lifted by the winnowing wind," the furrows "drowsed with the fume of poppies," "fill all fruit with ripeness to the core." And yes, we do think "warm days will never cease," that first moment in the poem when the innocence of the perspective gently darkens. The resonant hint of change and cold trip easily along the tongue. And that's his skill, to tinge the mind with knowledge, while simultaneously reveling in the season when gold ingots of light fall across the road. Entering the Etruscan gate into upper Cortona's immaculate streets, I see a woman setting out small cyclamen plants in a pot by her front door. Pink, white, magenta, she's mixed all the colors into a little blaze to warm her during the cold months. Beautiful, I tell her, and she points to dark green spikes and a tight yellow bud pushing through the ground. "This kind of crocus comes back in autumn, but only briefly, only a few." *We're riding the earth, she and I.* Sitting on the front steps of San Francesco, listening to the bells early Sunday morning, I don't want anything more than this poem rolled in my hand, 5000 *lire* in my shirt pocket for coffee and pastry, my new red loafers which navigate the stony streets so well.

I wander at night, too. Ed and I have walked into town for a *gelato* and he starts a long conversation with Edo about installing lawn irrigation. Our wild-herb lawn has not survived the summer drought, though fall rains will bring back the green hills. Out of chat, I start back, walking over the Roman road with a flashlight, then down onto the cypress-lined road toward home. Before it was paved, the white pebble *strada bianca* used to reflect the moonlight. Now with the asphalt and the *luna nera*, black moon, the road is dark, the cypress trees seeming to gather into their massive shapes all the light from the stars. I have the ambition to see every cypress tree in Tuscany. Like the California oaks in the Bay Area countryside, the cypresses seem to speak for the landscape. The bare oaks of California interact with light, giving their skeletal shadows to the hills and their silhouettes to the sky.

But the cypresses play no games with light. If they were in the sky they would be the black holes and if I were in America, I would be petrified to be alone on a deserted road at night. Because each of these trees was planted for a local boy who died in World War I, they are huge presences, not only in form but in a silence stopped inside their fixed curves, something of the unlived life of each boy. The tips, pointed like sable paintbrushes, wave back and forth against the stars.

Hot from the climb over the hill, I unbutton my blue linen dress all the way down and let it lift behind me. *Oh, for a life of sensation,* our friend Keats also told us. The cypress trees are grand companions. If anyone were coming, I would hear them because sound carries along the mountain, like the last sigh of the gladiator in the amphitheater heard on the last row. Around the curve, the house rises above the road, a rough translation of my body into a mute language of windows, doors, and stone.

Ed, I think, is translated by the olive trees and vines, which now droop with dusty purple grapes.

From the yard above the road, I see the cypresses graph a rise and fall against a sky blown clean of clouds by this afternoon's wind. Stars are shooting over the valley, stars that fell even before the Etruscans watched from this hillside. I recognize the cadence of Ed's step below in the road. "Are you home?" he calls up to me. Five, six, stars streak across the sky. I hold out my hand to catch one.